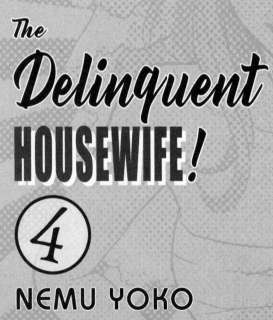

The
Delinquent
HOUSEWIFE!
④

NEMU YOKO

GN
Nemu

CONTENTS

Chapter 31: **BUSINESS KISS** ⋯⋯⋯⋯⋯⋯⋯⋯⋯3

Chapter 32: **FAMILY MEETING: BIKER JACKET EDITION** ⋯21

Chapter 33: **THE KOMUKAI FAMILY SPECIAL** ⋯⋯⋯⋯39

Chapter 34: **I TOTALLY HATE YOU, DAI** ⋯⋯⋯⋯⋯57

Chapter 35: **SEASIDE AT NIGHT, TOGETHER** ⋯⋯⋯75

Chapter 36: **ONLY THE MOON SAW** ⋯⋯⋯⋯⋯93

Chapter 37: **THE DAY AFTER: TWO VERSIONS** ⋯⋯⋯113

Chapter 38: **NO USE CRYING OVER SPILT MILK** ⋯⋯⋯131

Chapter 39: **A TERRIBLE HOUSEWIFE** ⋯⋯⋯⋯149

Chapter 40: **THE RETURN OF THE HAMMER GAME** ⋯⋯⋯167

Final Chapter   **PROMISE ME** ⋯⋯⋯⋯⋯⋯⋯⋯185

31 BUSINESS KISS

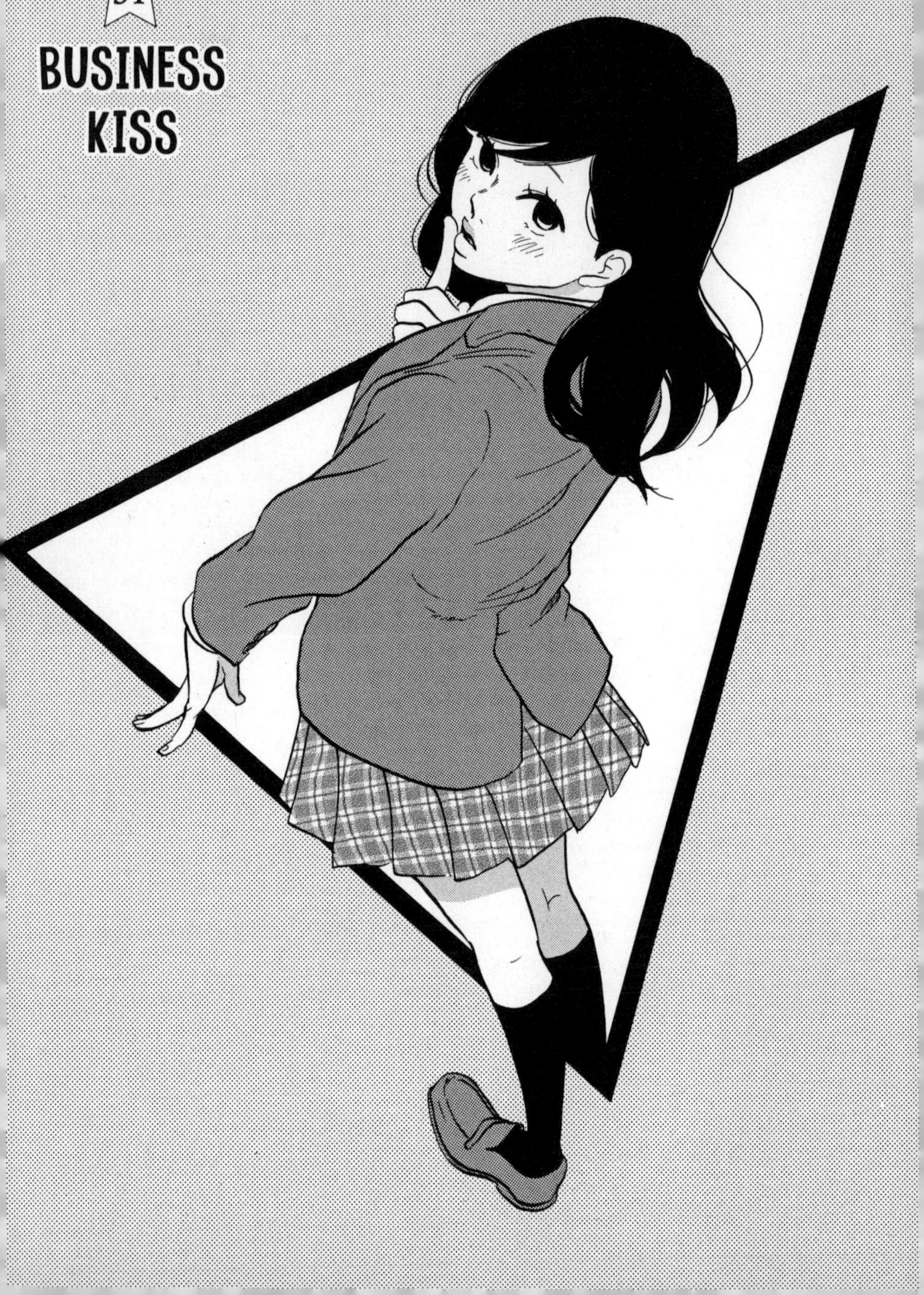

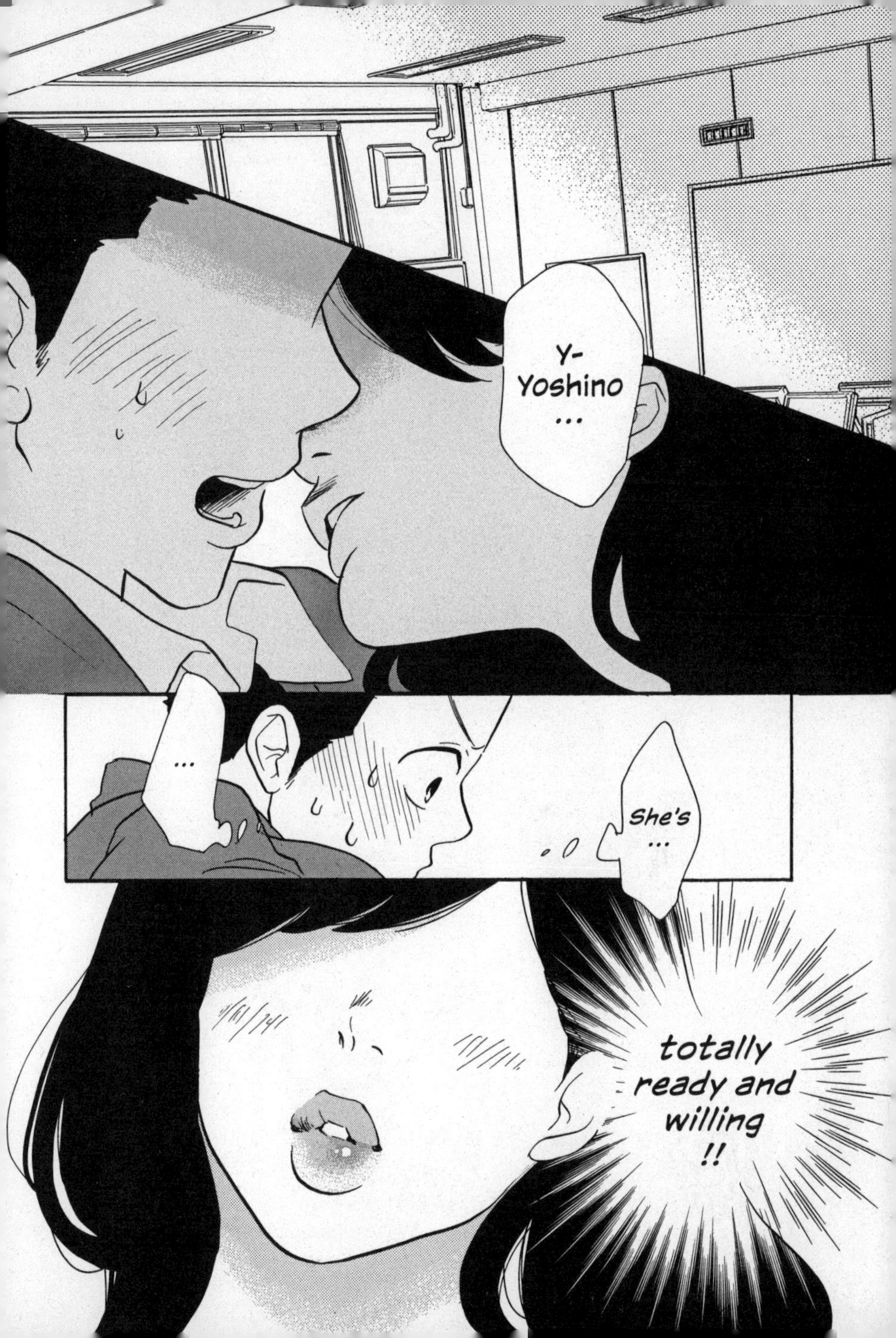
Y-Yoshino...
...
She's...
totally ready and willing!!

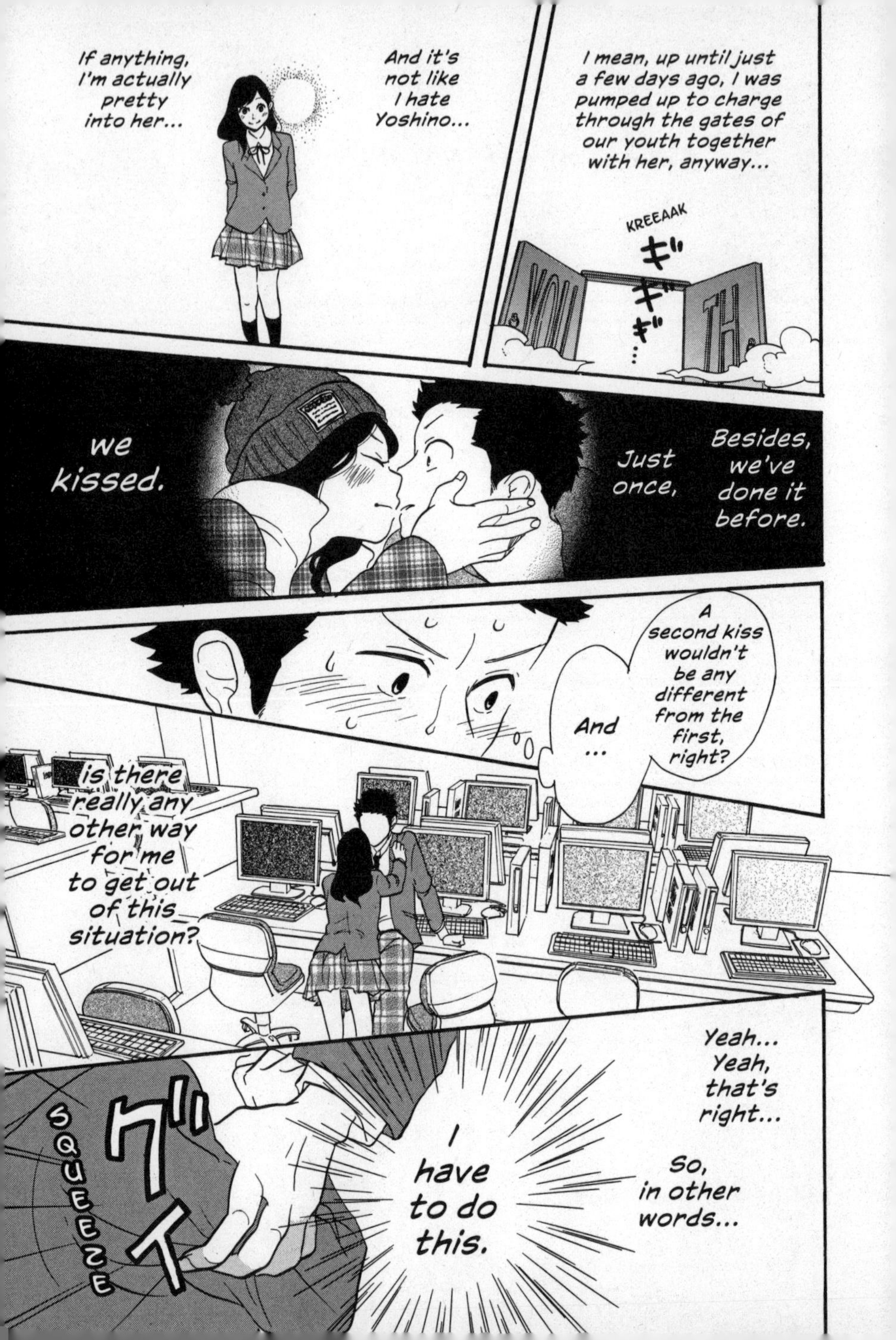
I mean, up until just a few days ago, I was pumped up to charge through the gates of our youth together with her, anyway...
KREEAAK
ギギギ…
And it's not like I hate Yoshino...
If anything, I'm actually pretty into her...
Besides, we've done it before.
Just once,
we kissed.
A second kiss wouldn't be any different from the first, right?
And...
is there really any other way for me to get out of this situation?
Yeah... Yeah, that's right...
So, in other words...
I have to do this.
グイ
SQUEEZE

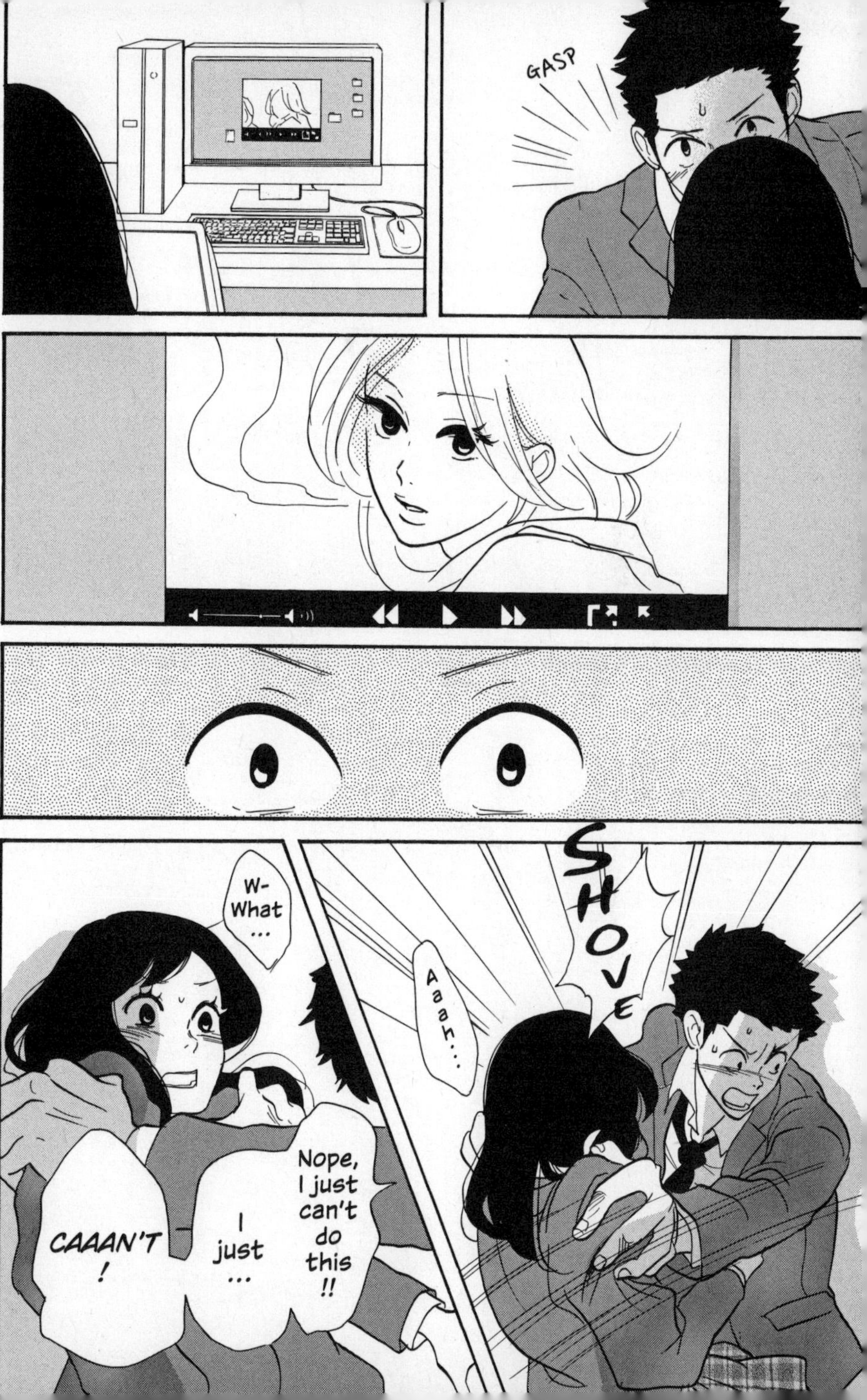
GASP
SHOVE
Aaah...
W-What ...
Nope, I just can't do this !!
I just ...
CAAAN'T !

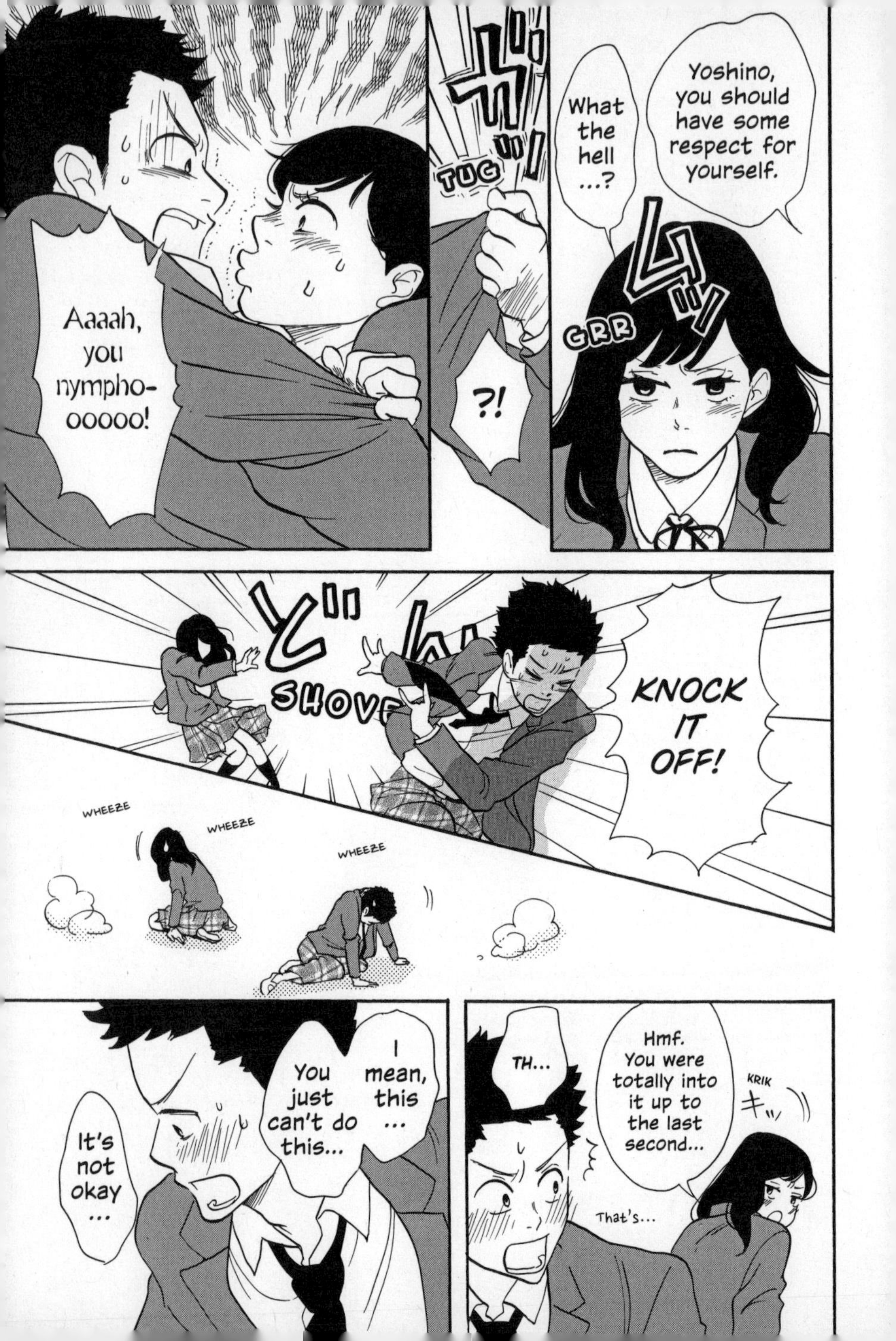
Yoshino, you should have some respect for yourself.
What the hell ...?
GRR
TUG
?!
Aaaah, you nympho-ooooo!
KNOCK IT OFF!
SHOVE
WHEEZE
WHEEZE
WHEEZE
Hmf. You were totally into it up to the last second...
KRIK
キッ
TH...
That's...
I mean, this ...
You just can't do this...
It's not okay ...

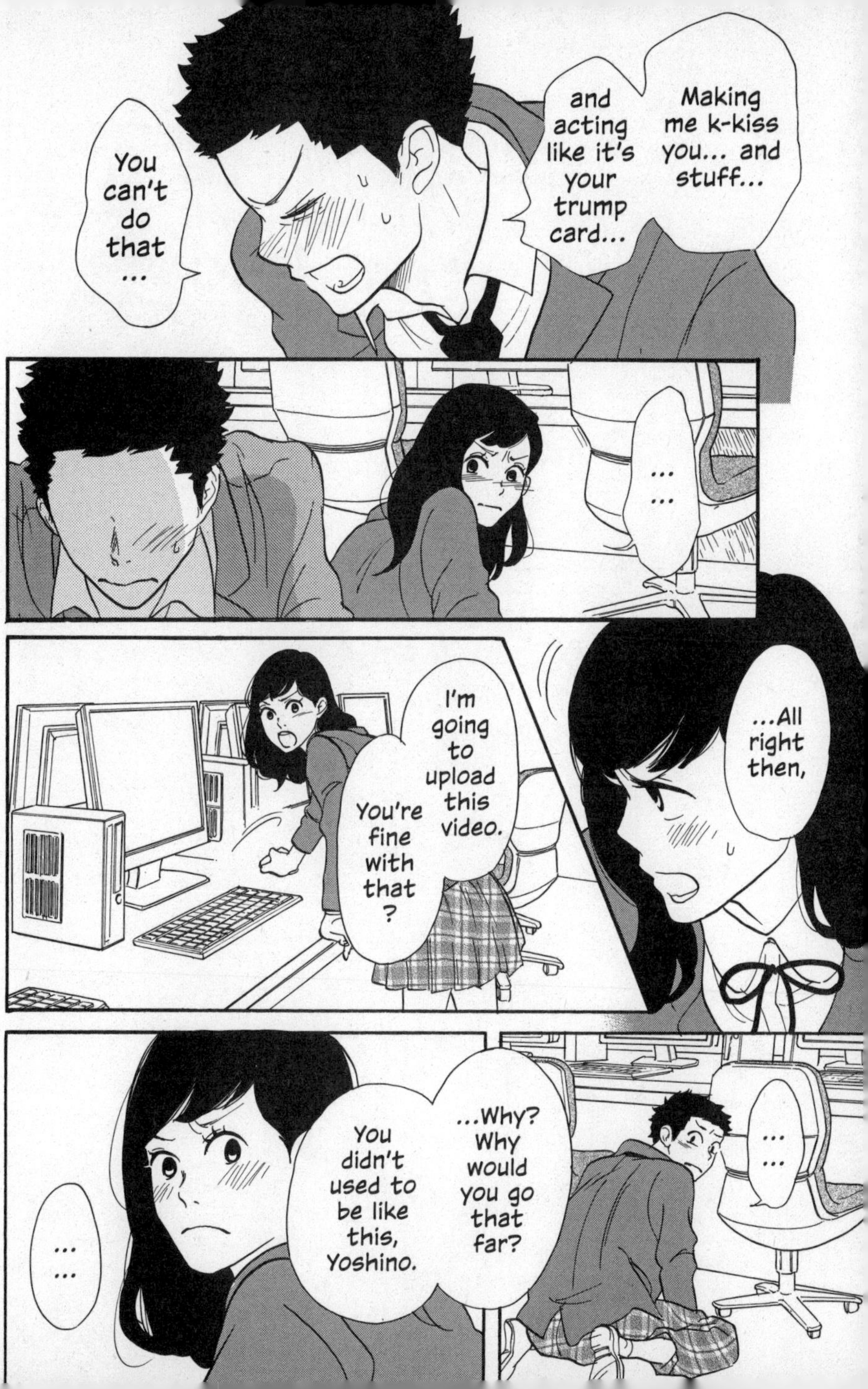
Making me k-kiss you... and stuff...
and acting like it's your trump card...
You can't do that ...
... ...
...All right then,
I'm going to upload this video.
You're fine with that ?
... ...
...Why? Why would you go that far?
You didn't used to be like this, Yoshino.
... ...

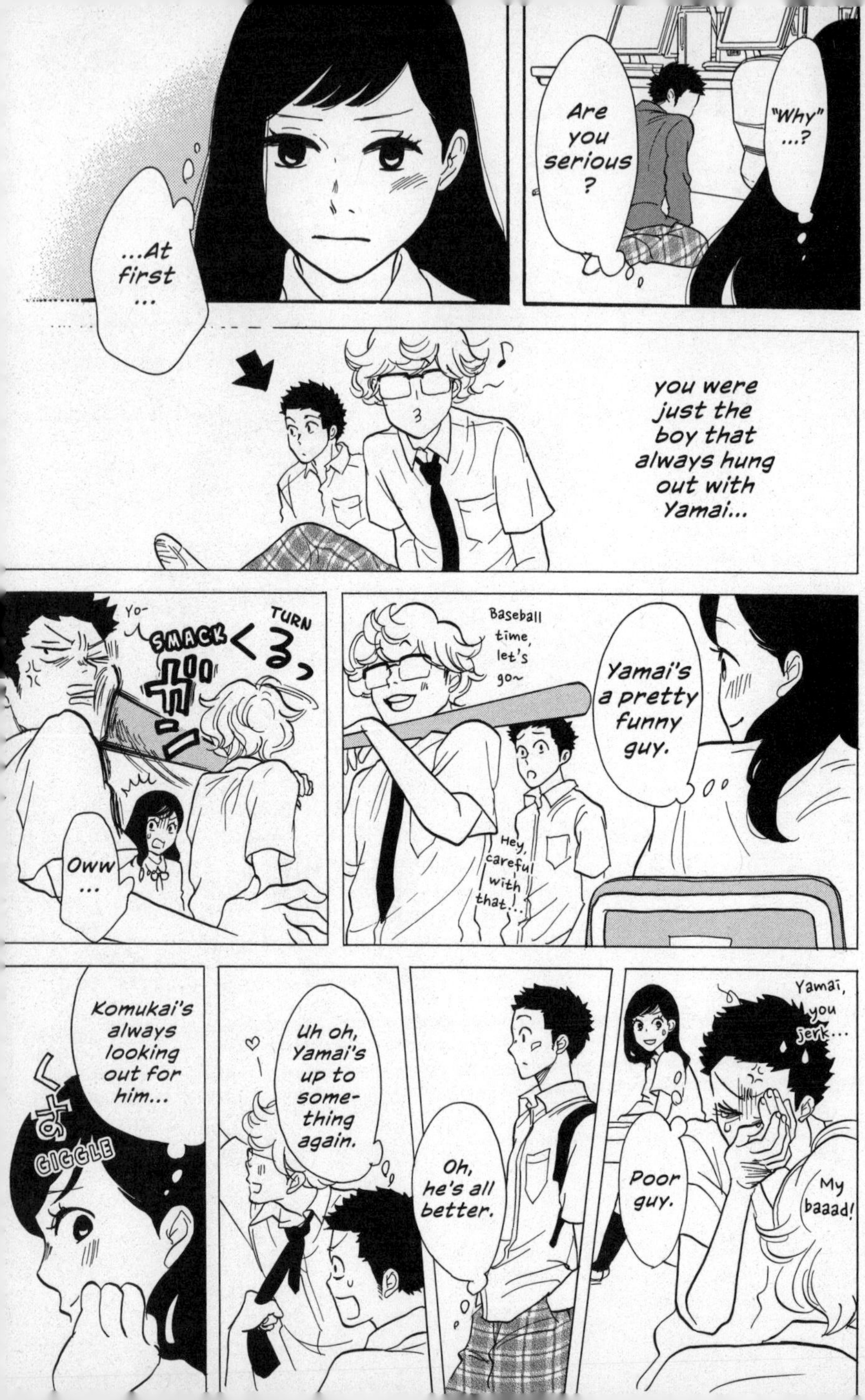
"Why"...?
Are you serious?
...At first...
you were just the boy that always hung out with Yamai...
Yamai's a pretty funny guy.
Baseball time, let's go~
Hey, careful with that...
Yo-
TURN
SMACK
Oww...
Yamai, you jerk...
My baaad!
Poor guy.
Oh, he's all better.
Uh oh, Yamai's up to some-thing again.
Komukai's always looking out for him...
GIGGLE

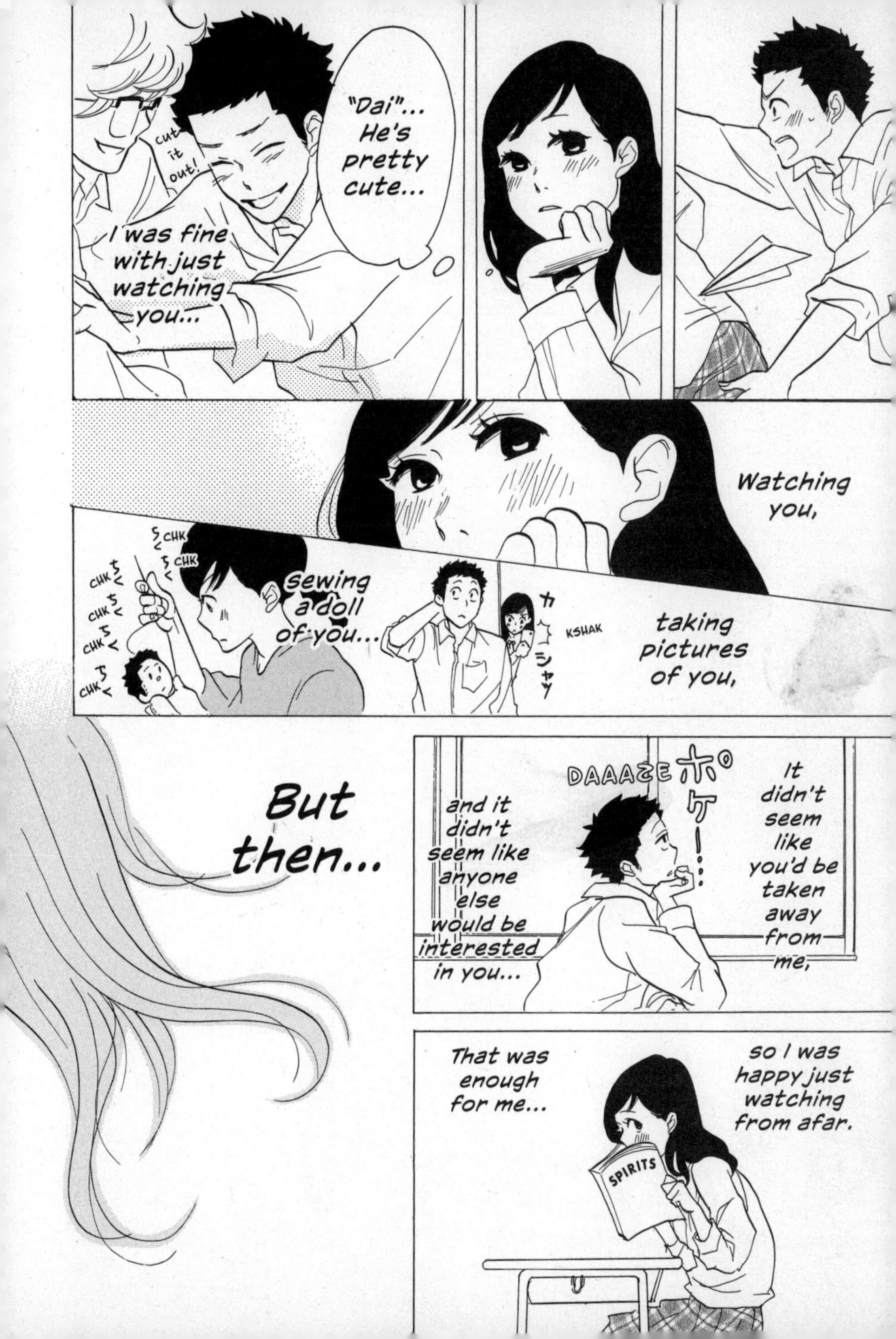
"Dai"... He's pretty cute...
cut it out!
I was fine with just watching you...
Watching you,
taking pictures of you,
KSHAK
カシャ
sewing a doll of you...
CHK
ちく
It didn't seem like you'd be taken away from me,
DAAAZE
ホケー!..
and it didn't seem like anyone else would be interested in you...
so I was happy just watching from afar.
That was enough for me...
SPIRITS
But then...

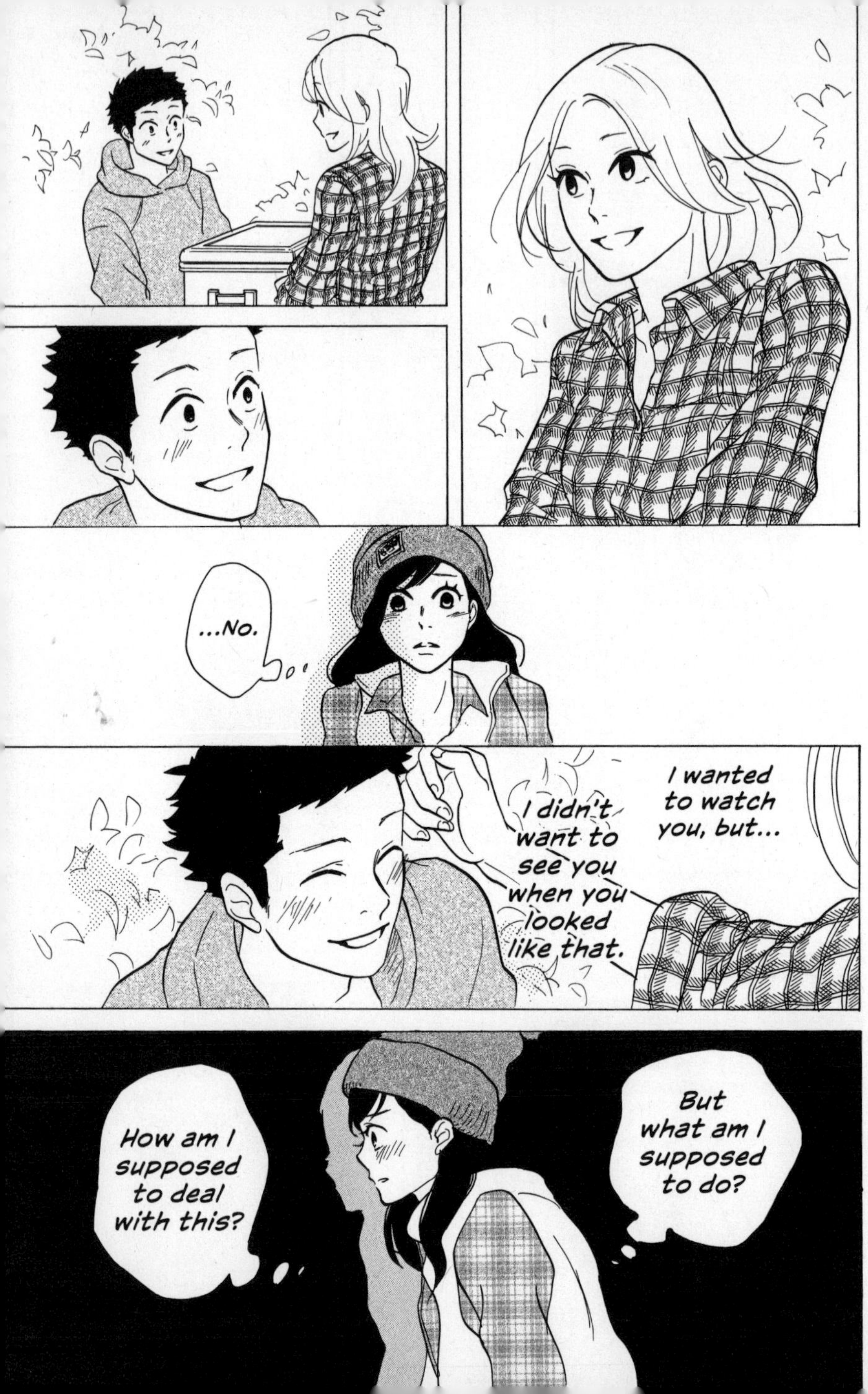
...No.
I wanted to watch you, but...
I didn't want to see you when you looked like that.
But what am I supposed to do?
How am I supposed to deal with this?

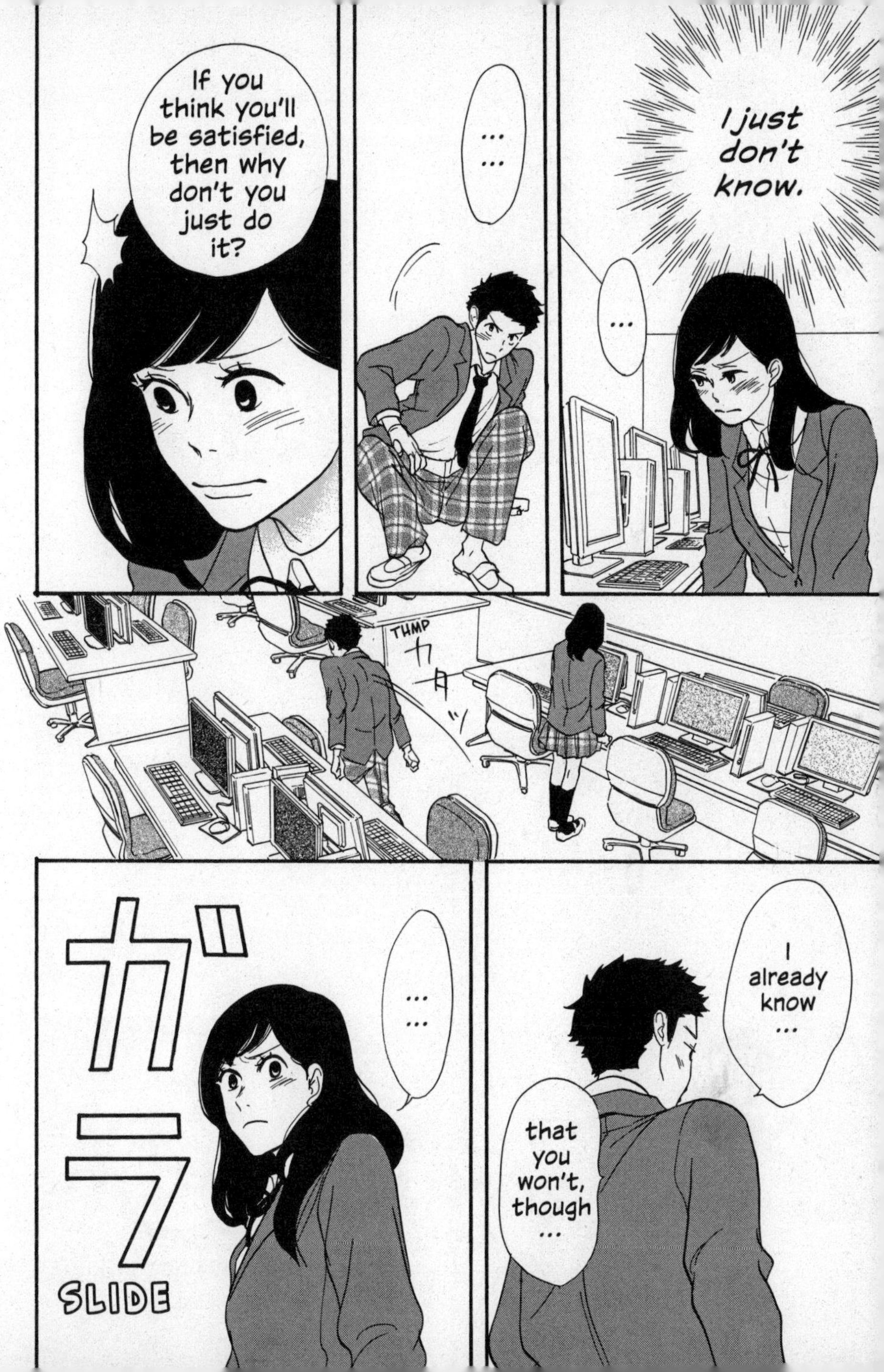
I just don't know.
...
... ...
If you think you'll be satisfied, then why don't you just do it?
THMP
カタッ
I already know ...
that you won't, though ...
... ...
ガラ
SLIDE

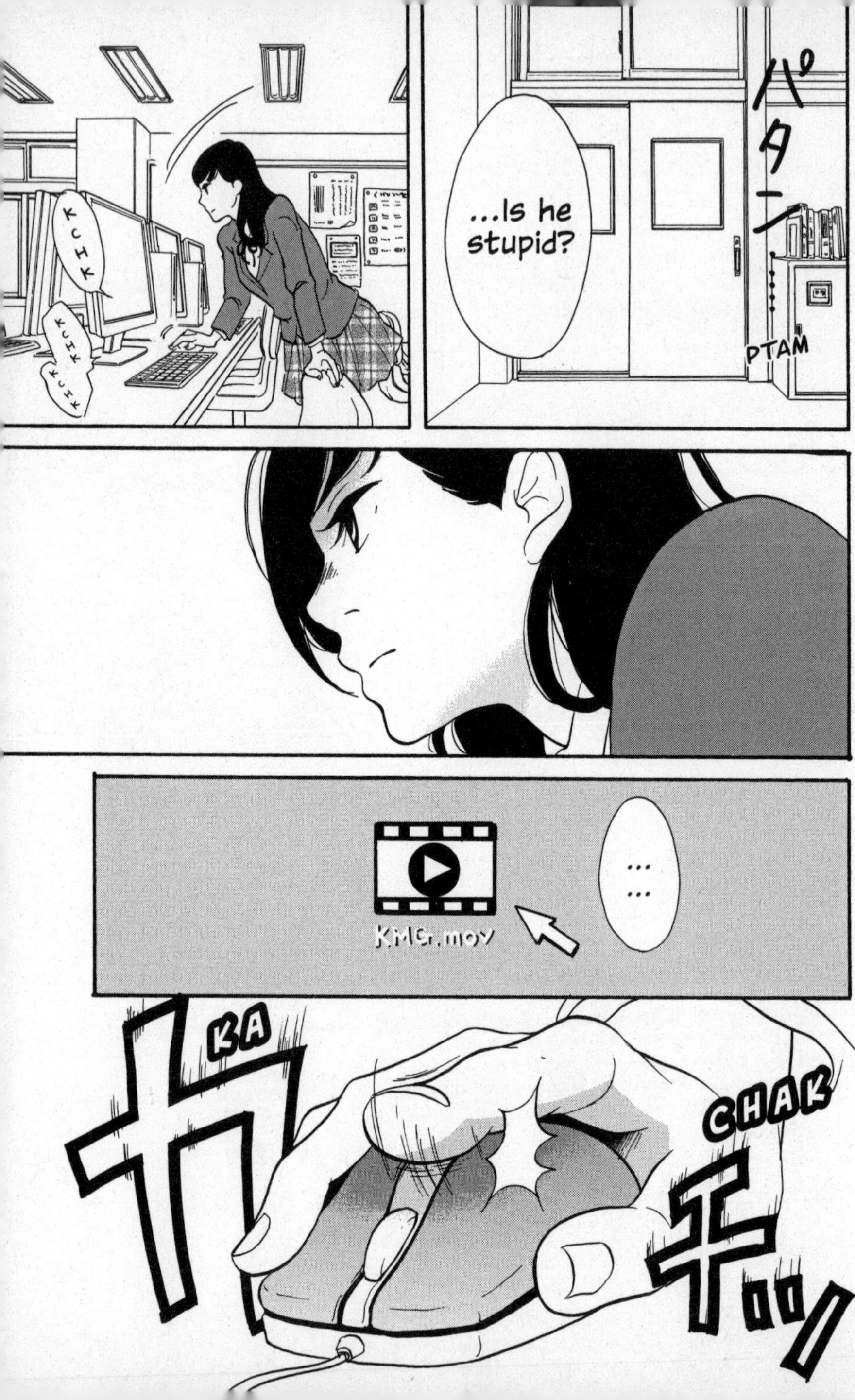

...Is he stupid?
パタン
PTAM
KCHK
KCHK KCHK
KMG.mov
......
カ
KA
チッ
CHAK

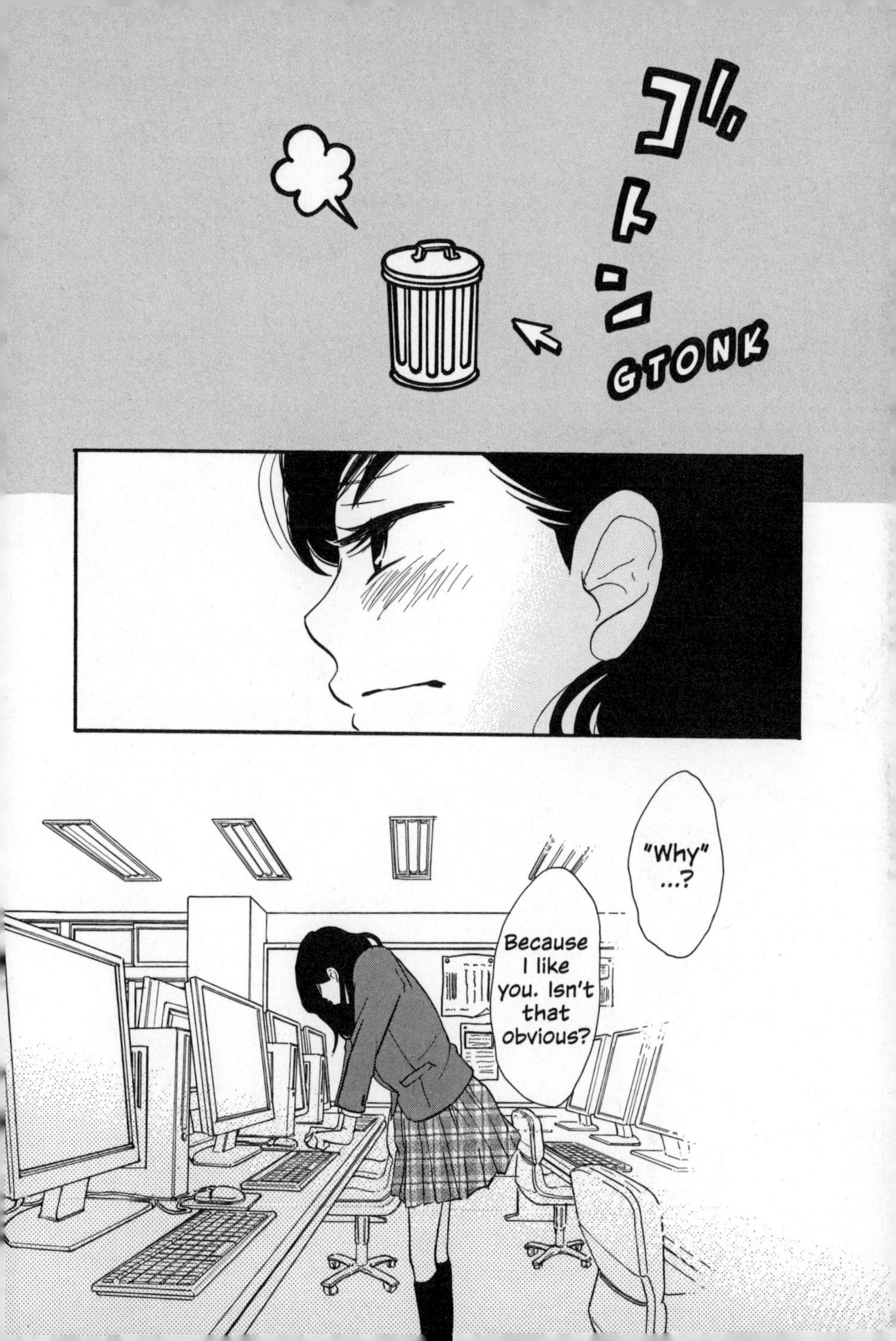
GTONK
"Why" ...?
Because I like you. Isn't that obvious?

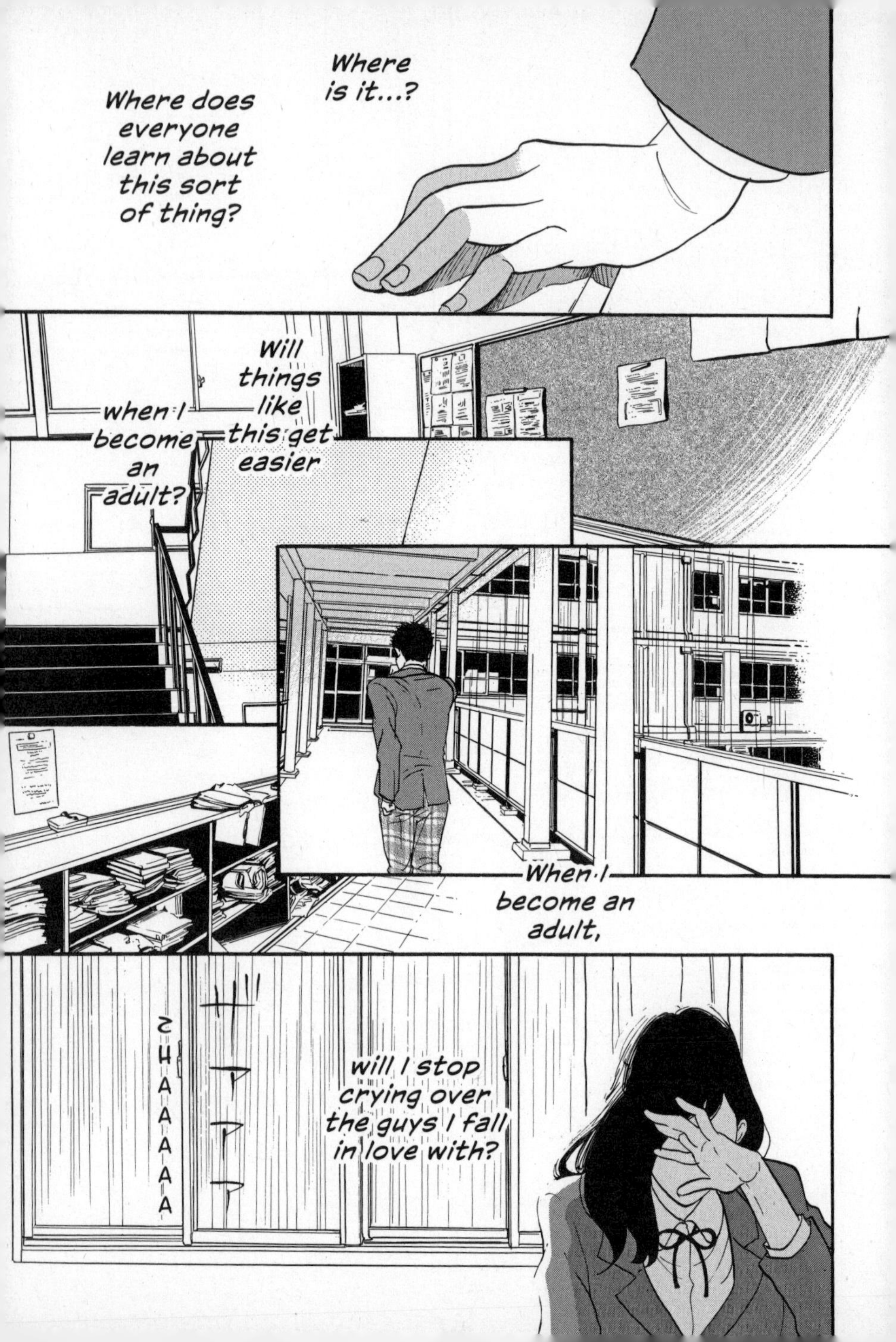
Where is it...?
Where does everyone learn about this sort of thing?
Will things like this get easier
when I become an adult?
When I become an adult,
ザァァァ
ZHAAAAAA
will I stop crying over the guys I fall in love with?

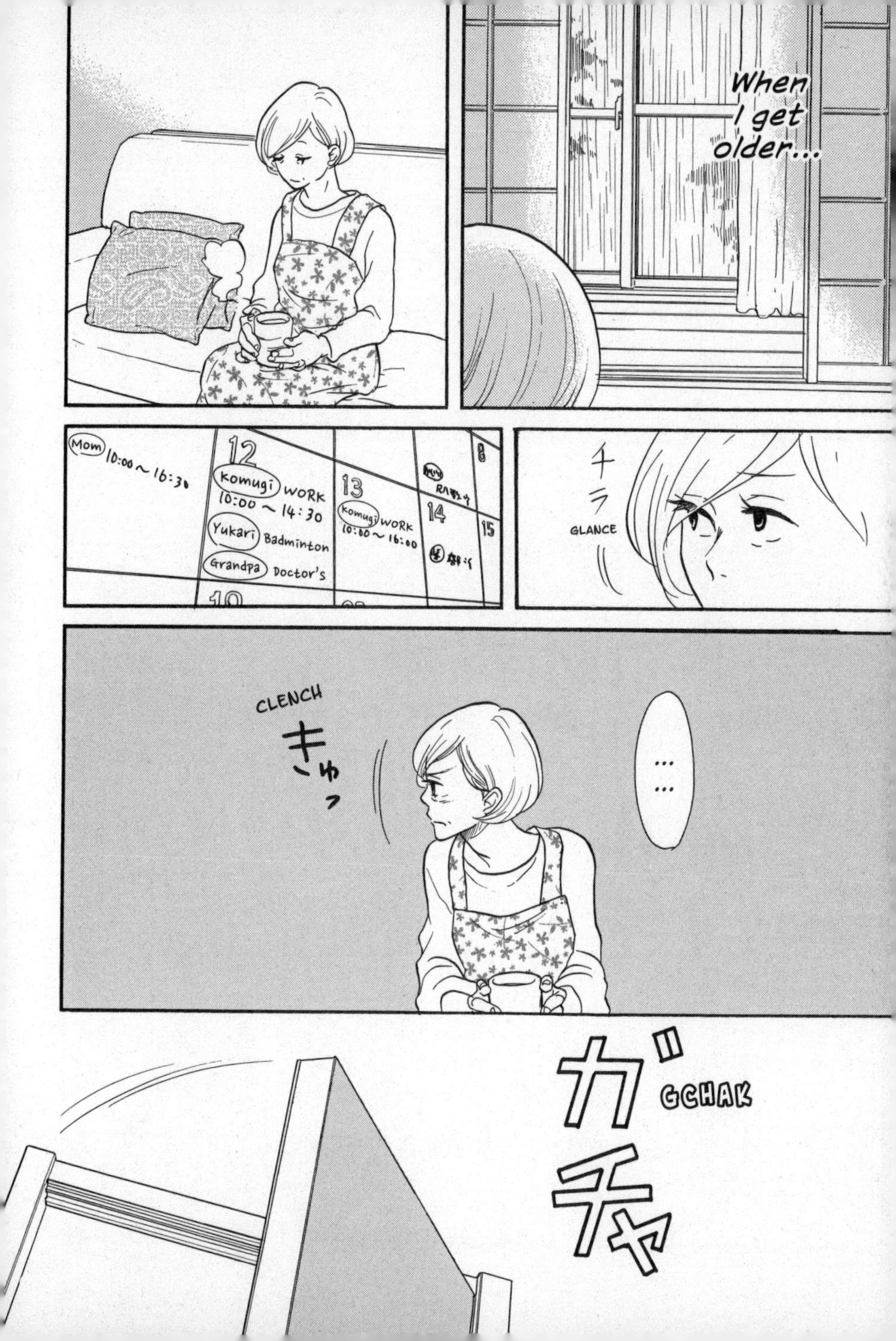

When I get older...
チラ
GLANCE
Mom 10:00~16:30
12
Komugi WORK 10:00~14:30
Yukari Badminton
Grandpa Doctor's
13
Komugi WORK 10:00~16:00
14
15
CLENCH
きゅっ
……
ガチャ
GCHAK

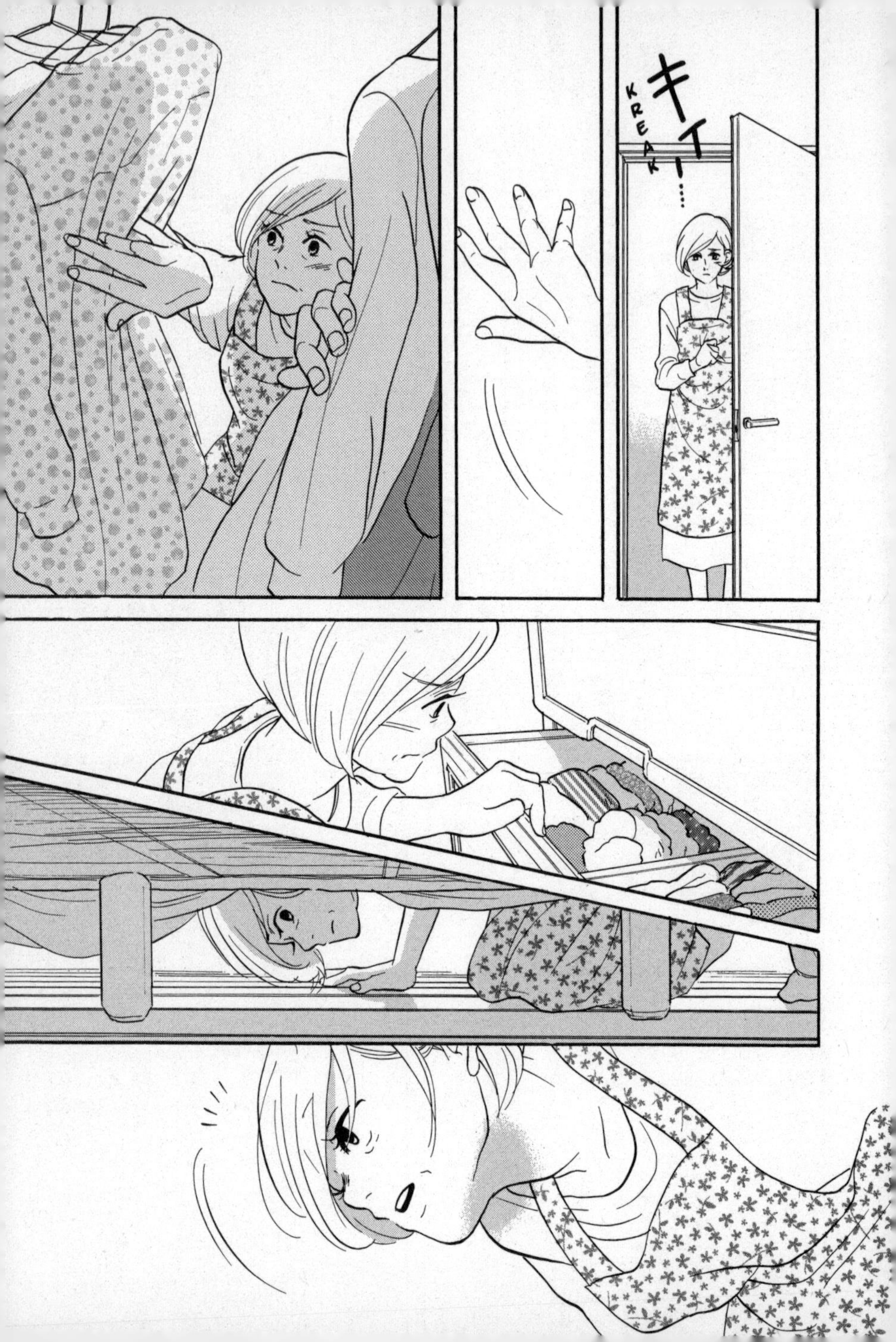
キイー....
KREAK

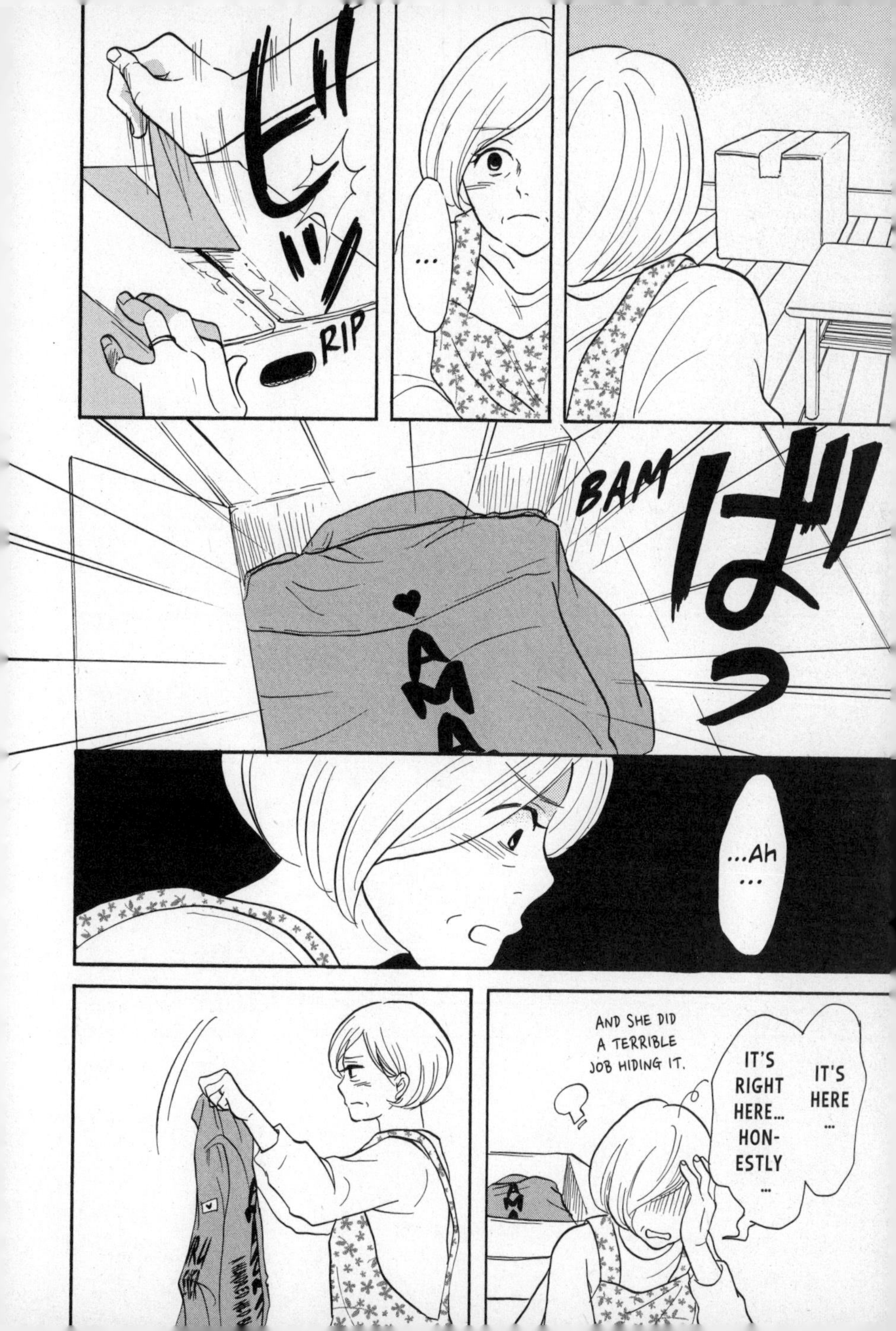

...
ビリッ
RIP
BAM
ぱっ
...Ah ...
IT'S HERE ...
IT'S RIGHT HERE... HONESTLY ...
AND SHE DID A TERRIBLE JOB HIDING IT.

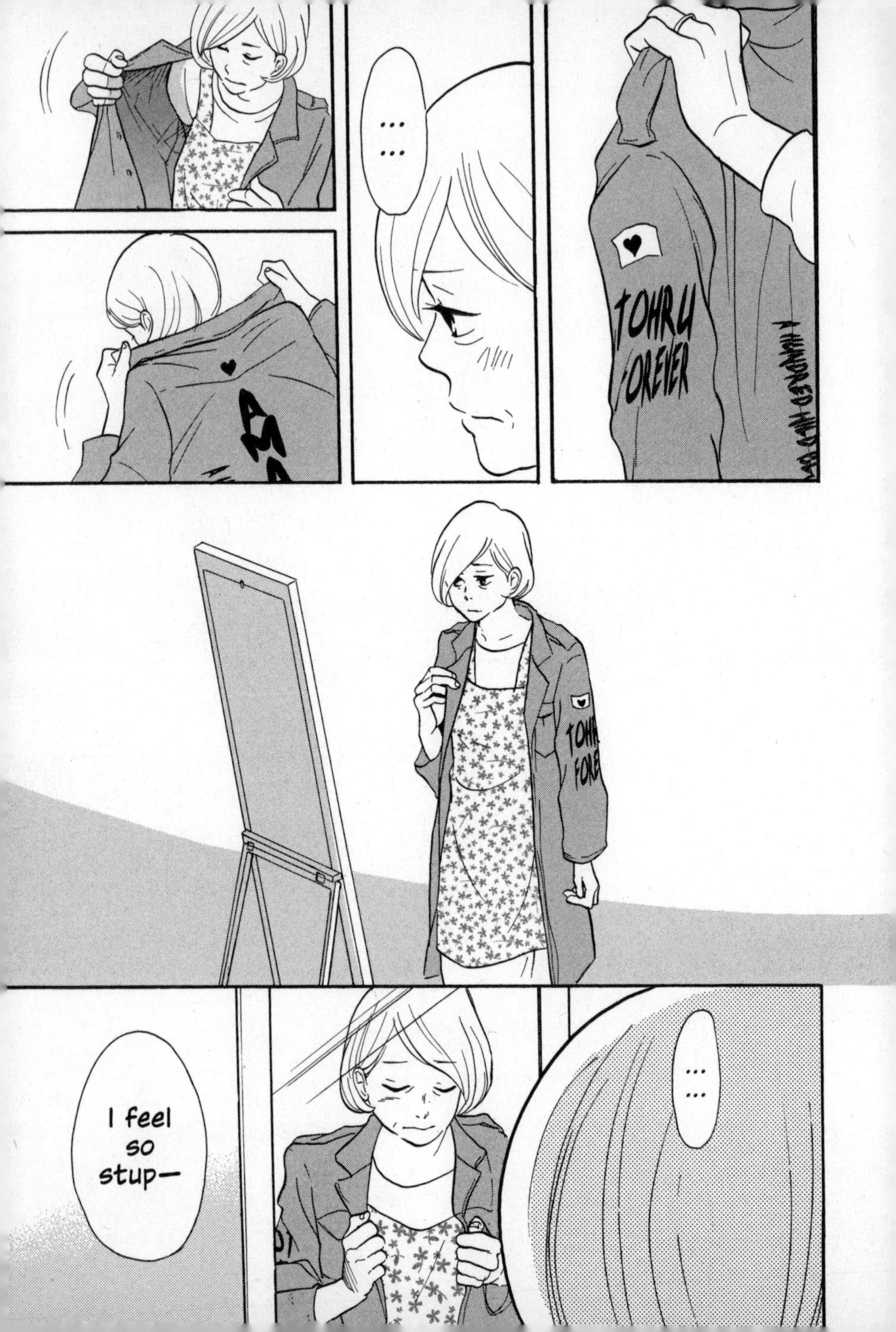

TOHRU FOREVER
......
......
I feel so stup—

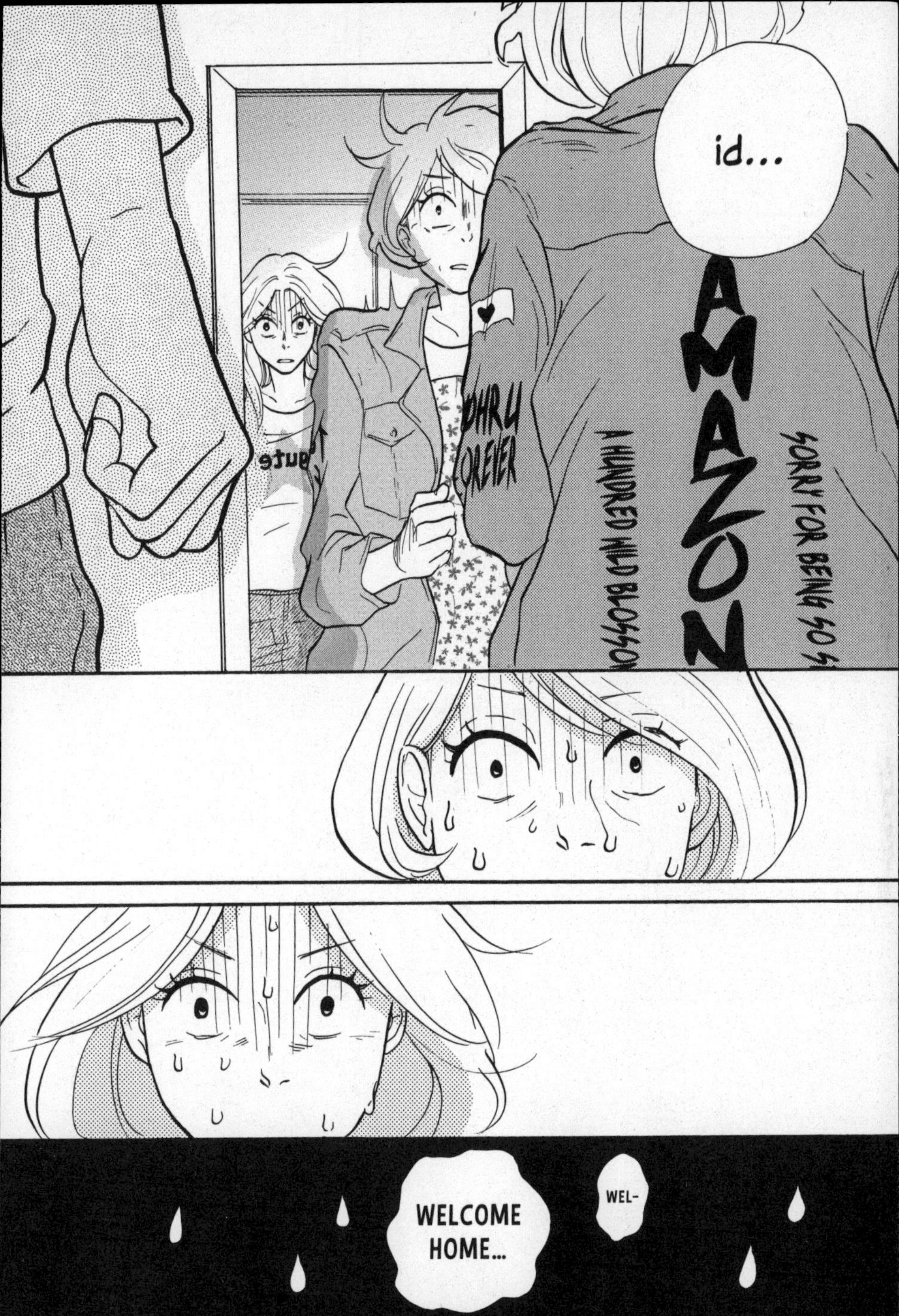
id...
AMAZON
SORRY FOR BEING SO S
A HUNDRED WILD BLOSSOM
WEL-
WELCOME HOME...

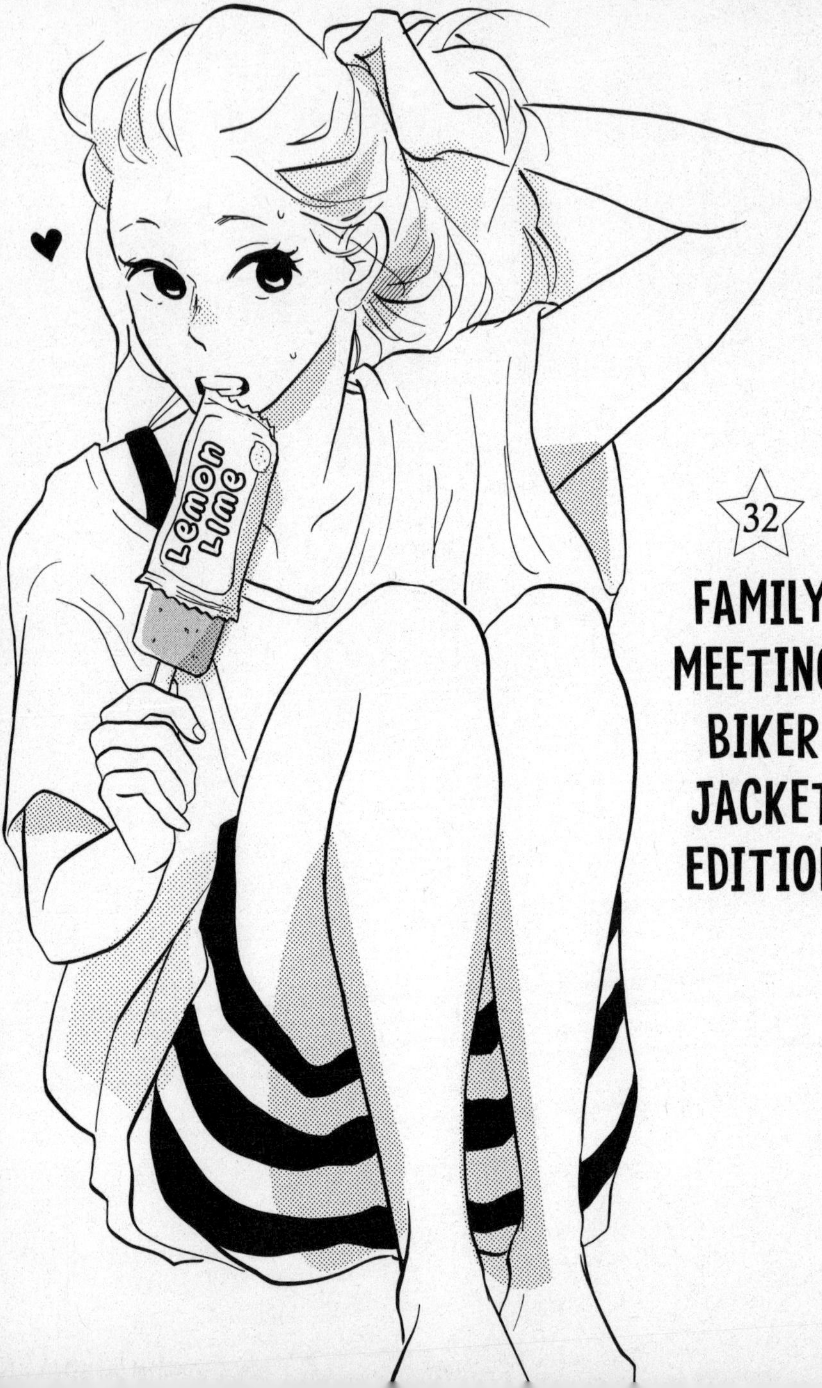
Lemon Lime

32

FAMILY MEETING: BIKER JACKET EDITION

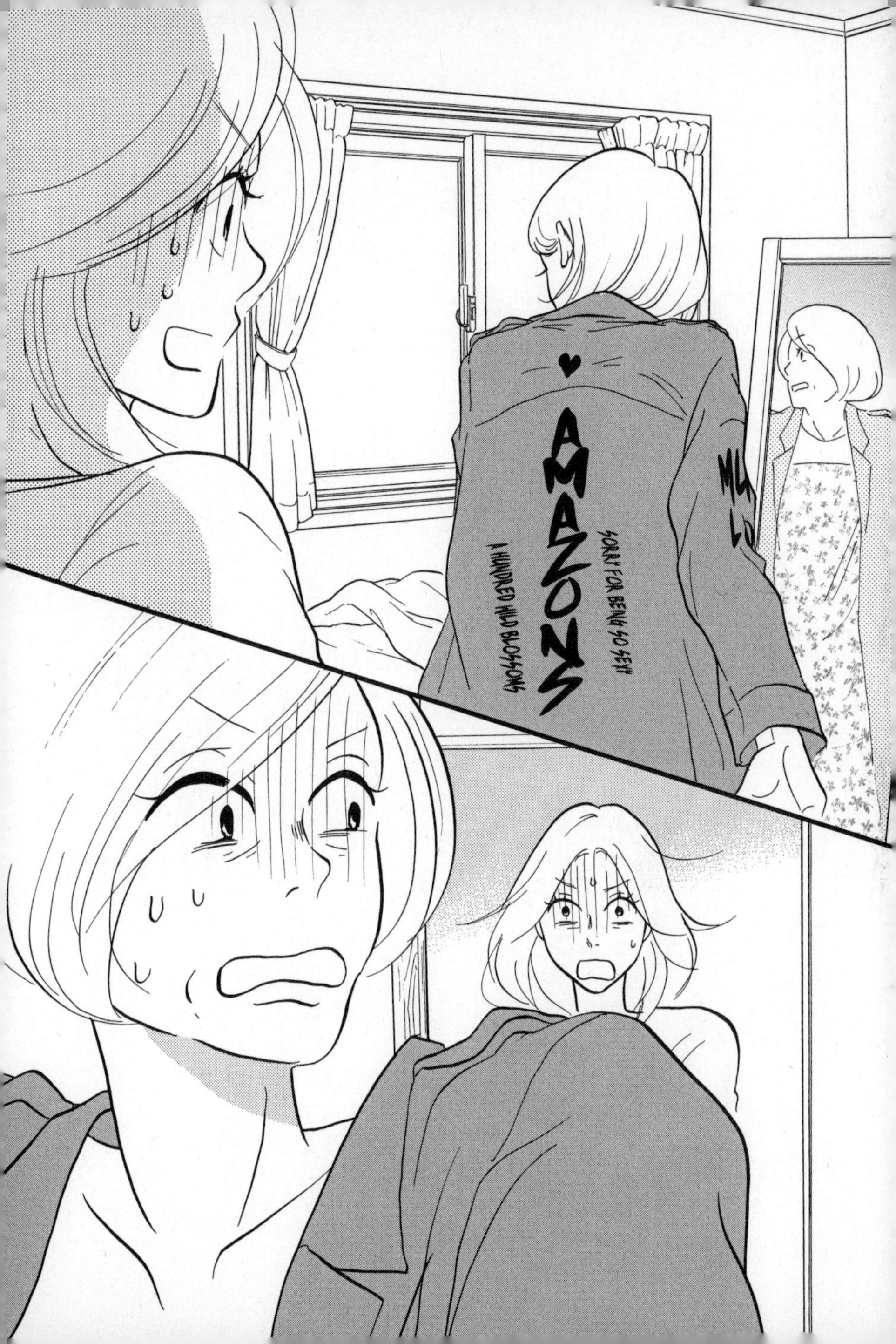
AMAZONS
SORRY FOR BEING SO SEXY
A HUNDRED WILD BLOSSOMS

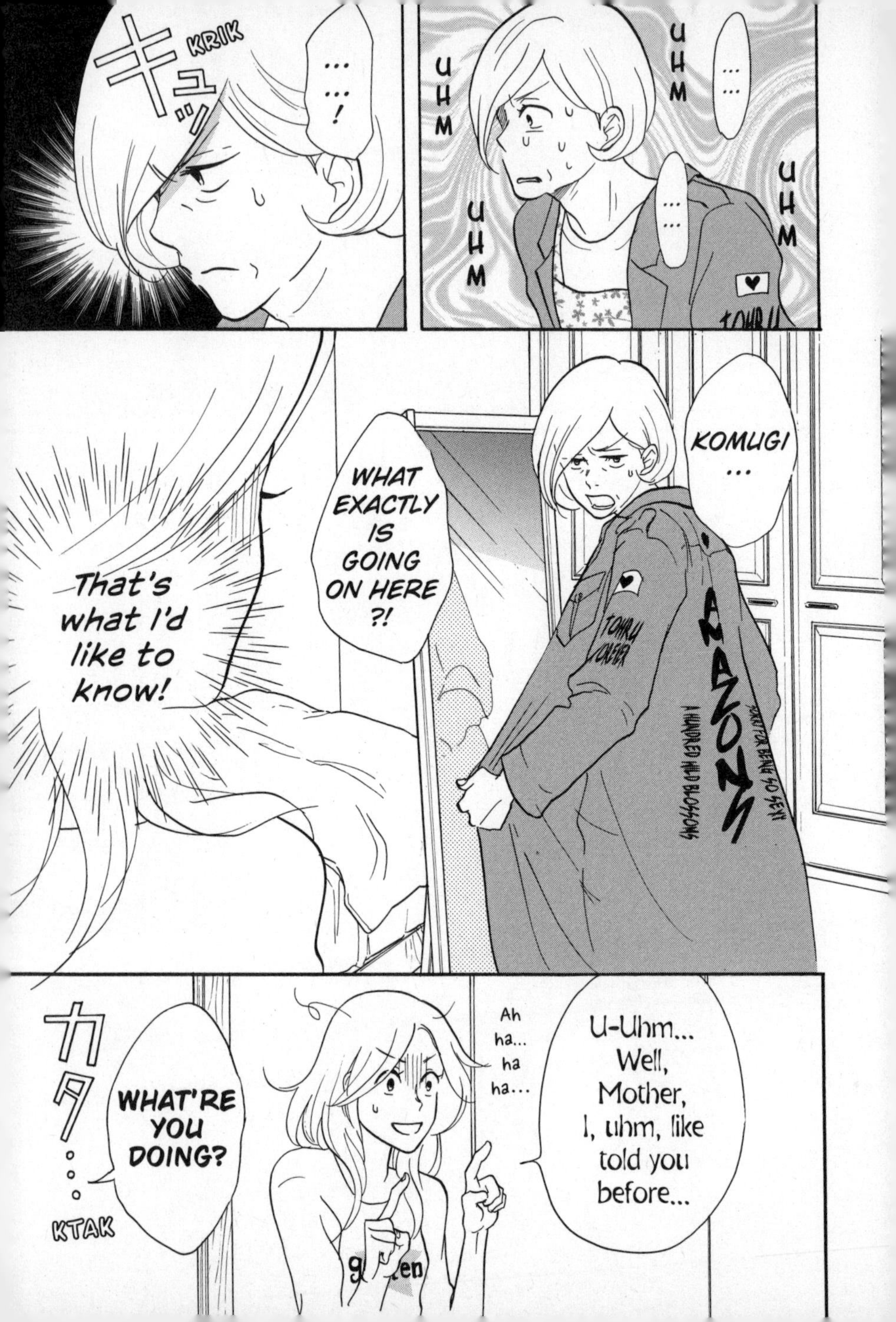
UHM
UHM
... ...
... ...
UHM
UHM
KRIK
キュッ
... ...!
KOMUGI ...
WHAT EXACTLY IS GOING ON HERE ?!
That's what I'd like to know!
TOHRU
AMAZONS
A HUNDRED WILD BLOSSOMS
U-Uhm... Well, Mother, I, uhm, like told you before...
Ah ha... ha ha...
WHAT'RE YOU DOING?
カタ。。。
KTAK

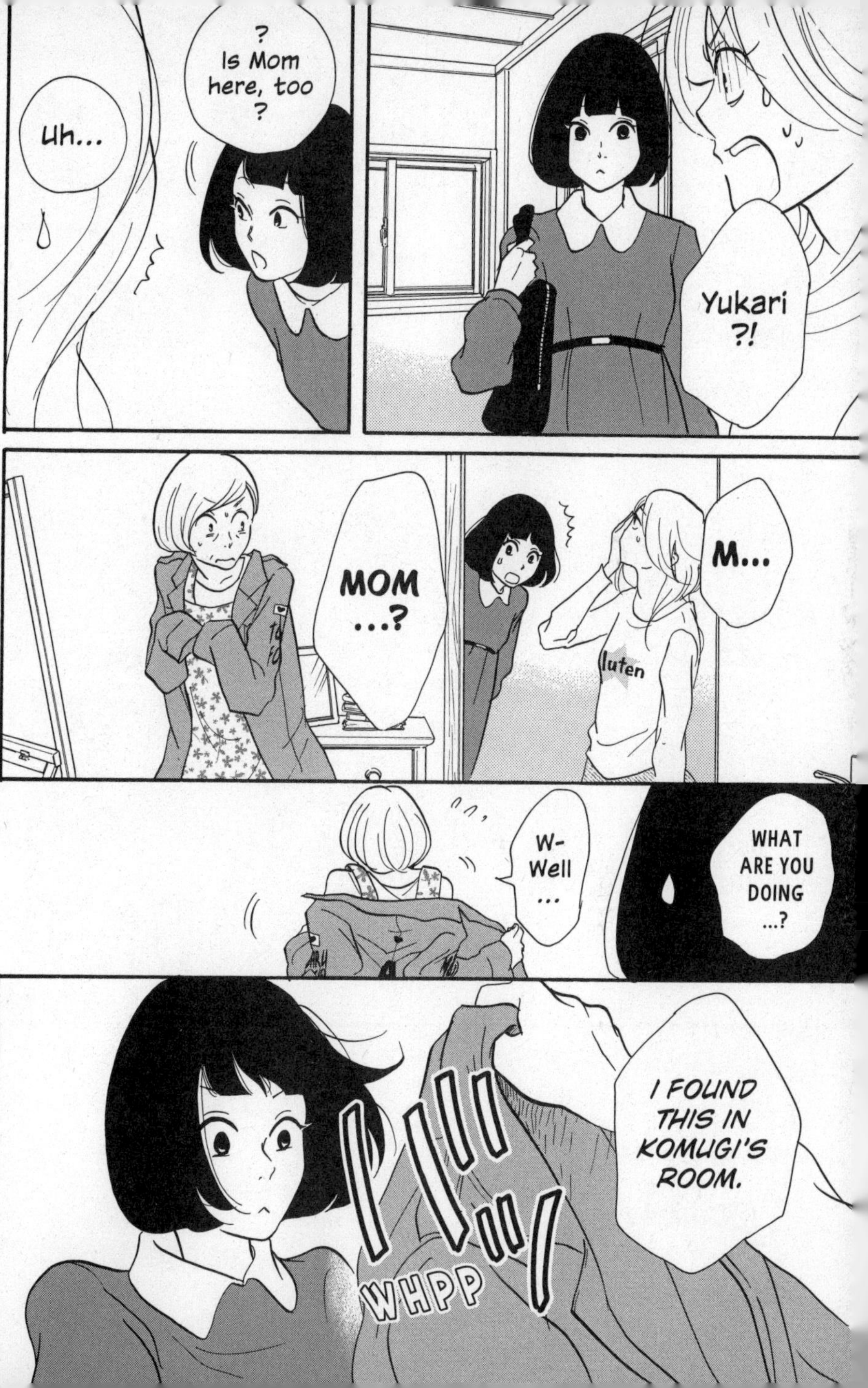
Yukari ?!
? Is Mom here, too ?
Uh...
M...
luten
MOM ...?
WHAT ARE YOU DOING ...?
W- Well ...
I FOUND THIS IN KOMUGI'S ROOM.
WHPP

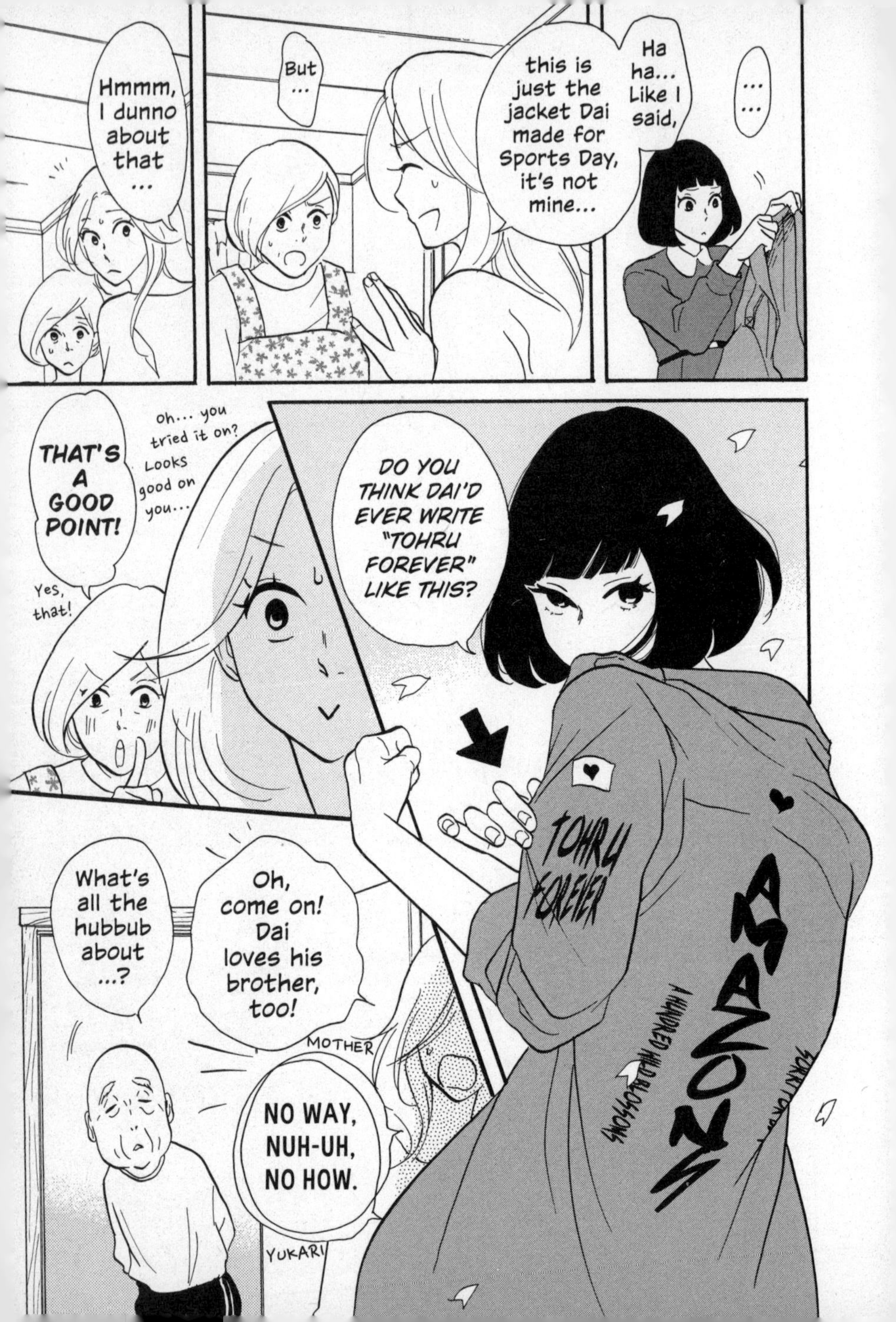

... ...
Ha ha... Like I said,
this is just the jacket Dai made for Sports Day, it's not mine...
But ...
Hmmm, I dunno about that ...
DO YOU THINK DAI'D EVER WRITE "TOHRU FOREVER" LIKE THIS?
TOHRU FOREVER
THAT'S A GOOD POINT!
Oh... you tried it on? Looks good on you...
Yes, that!
Oh, come on! Dai loves his brother, too!
What's all the hubbub about ...?
MOTHER
NO WAY, NUH-UH, NO HOW.
YUKARI

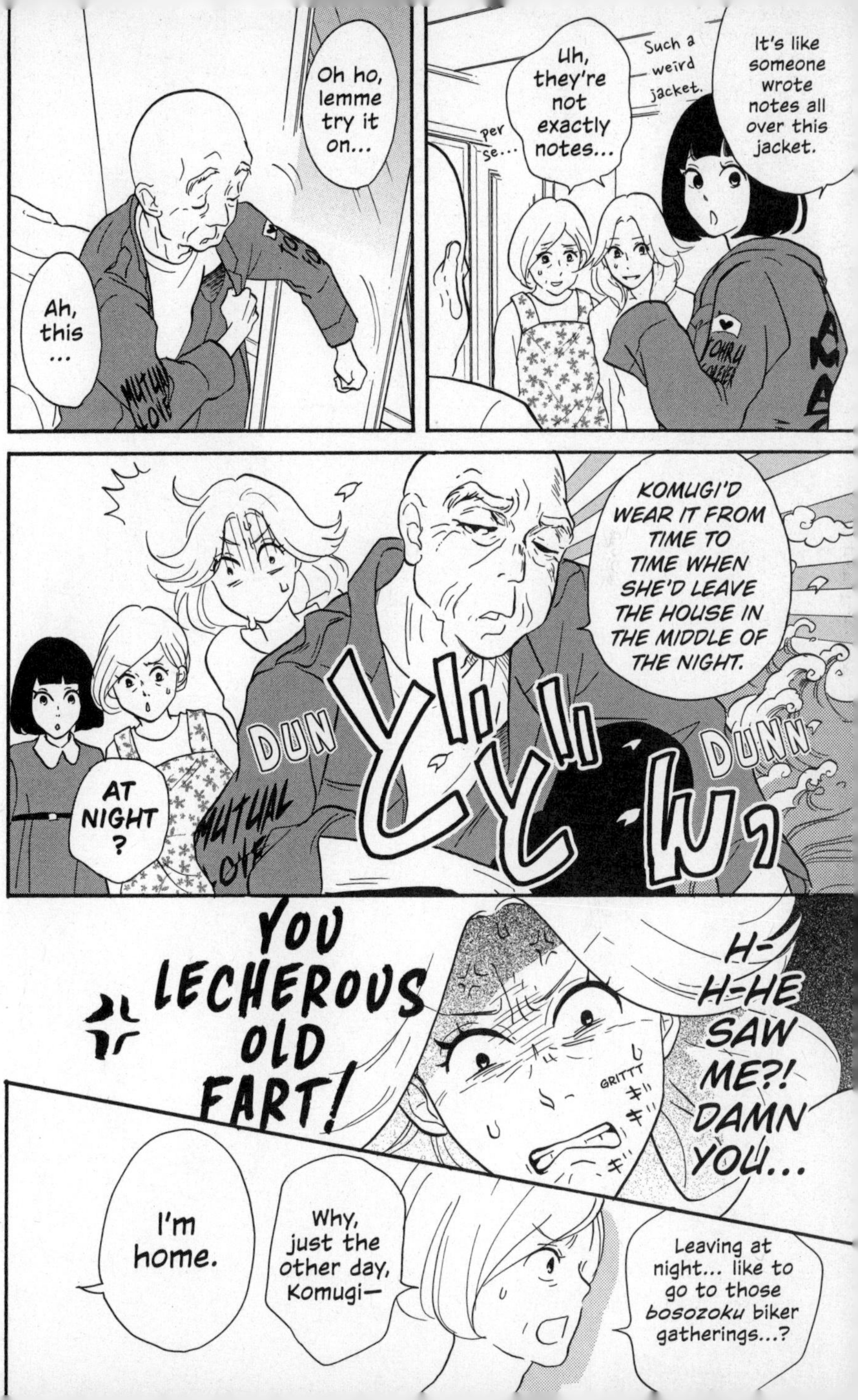
It's like someone wrote notes all over this jacket.
Such a weird jacket.
Uh, they're not exactly notes...
per se...
Oh ho, lemme try it on...
Ah, this ...
KOMUGI'D WEAR IT FROM TIME TO TIME WHEN SHE'D LEAVE THE HOUSE IN THE MIDDLE OF THE NIGHT.
DUNN
どどん
DUN
AT NIGHT?
H-H-HE SAW ME?! DAMN YOU...
GRITTT
YOU LECHEROUS OLD FART!
Leaving at night... like to go to those *bosozoku* biker gatherings...?
Why, just the other day, Komugi—
I'm home.

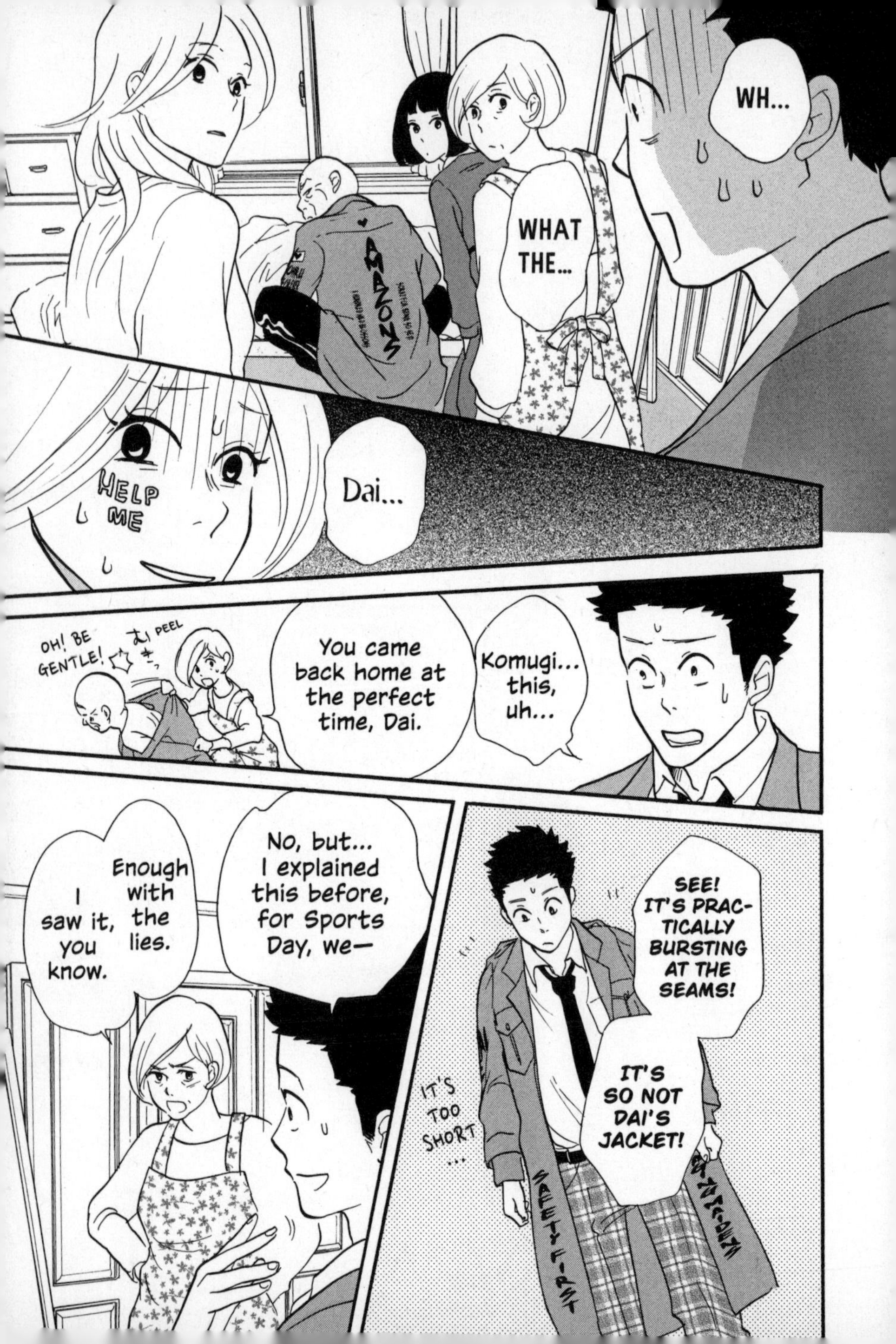
WH...
WHAT THE...
AMAZONS
Dai...
HELP ME
Komugi... this, uh...
You came back home at the perfect time, Dai.
OH! BE GENTLE!
PEEL
SEE! IT'S PRAC-TICALLY BURSTING AT THE SEAMS!
IT'S SO NOT DAI'S JACKET!
IT'S TOO SHORT...
SAFETY FIRST
No, but... I explained this before, for Sports Day, we—
Enough with the lies.
I saw it, you know.

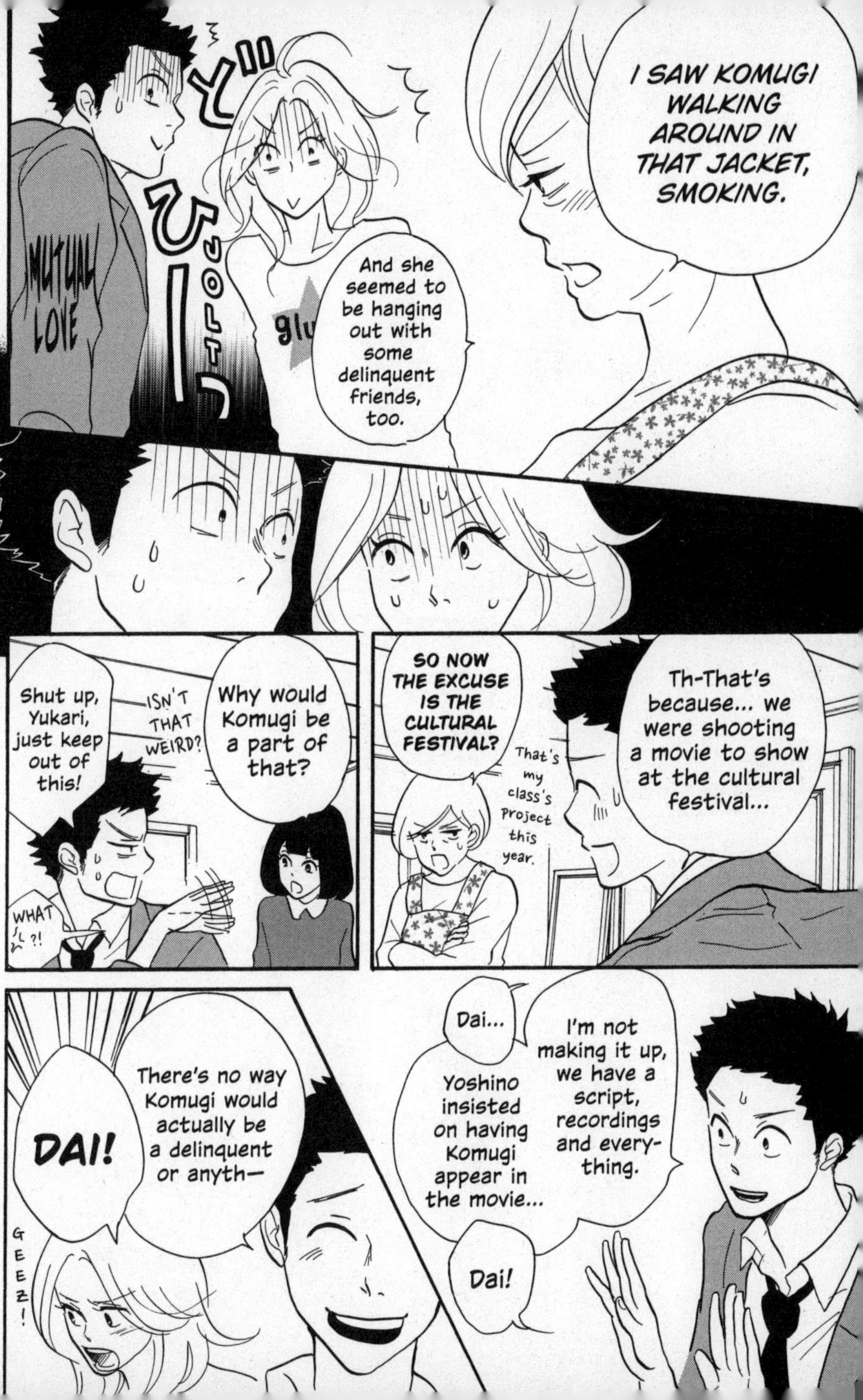
I SAW KOMUGI WALKING AROUND IN THAT JACKET, SMOKING.
And she seemed to be hanging out with some delinquent friends, too.
JOLT
MUTUAL LOVE
Th-That's because... we were shooting a movie to show at the cultural festival...
SO NOW THE EXCUSE IS THE CULTURAL FESTIVAL?
That's my class's project this year.
Why would Komugi be a part of that?
ISN'T THAT WEIRD?
Shut up, Yukari, just keep out of this!
WHAT ?!
I'm not making it up, we have a script, recordings and every-thing.
Dai...
Yoshino insisted on having Komugi appear in the movie...
Dai!
There's no way Komugi would actually be a delinquent or anyth—
DAI!
GEEZ!

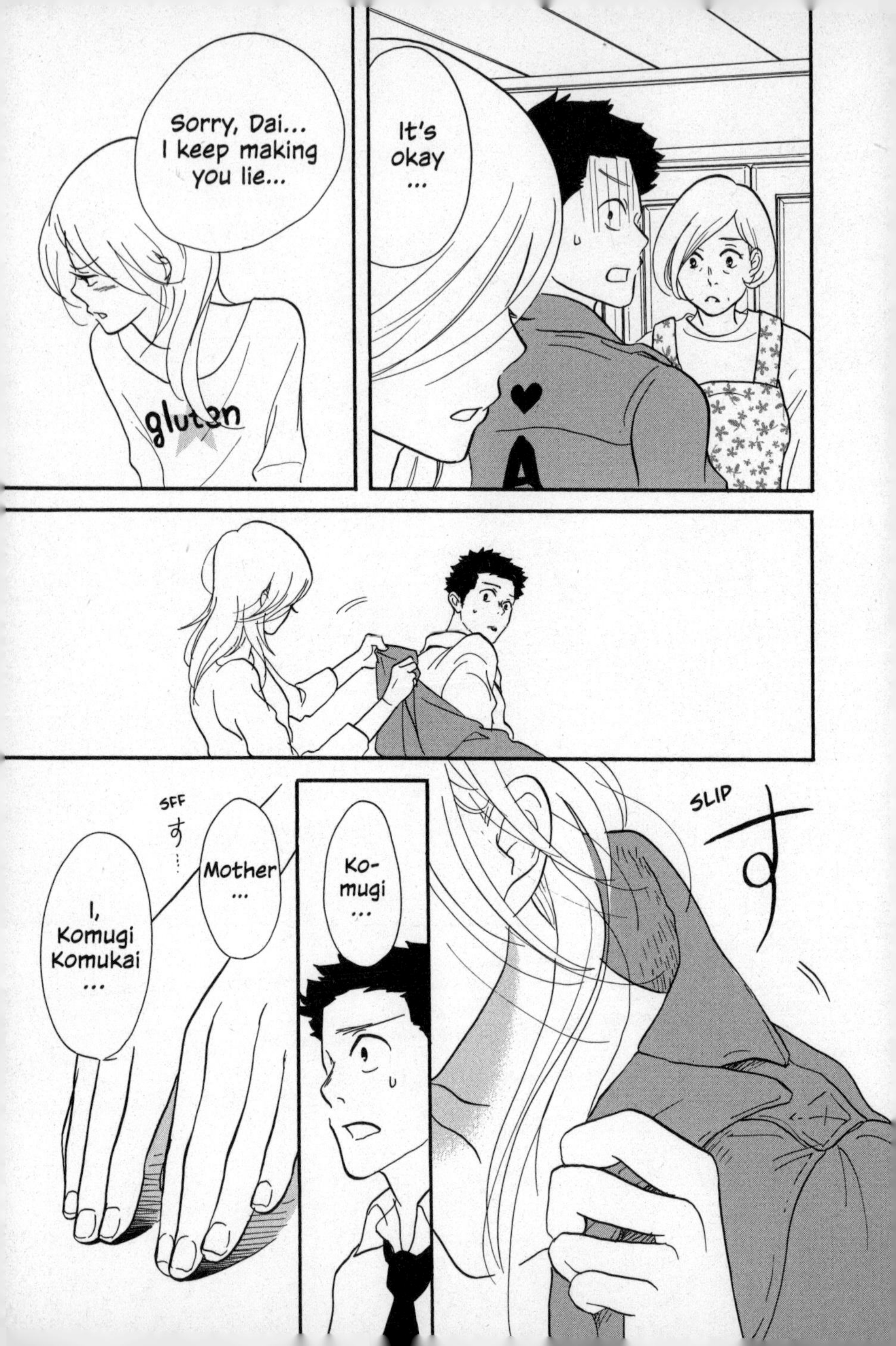
It's okay ...
Sorry, Dai... I keep making you lie...
SLIP
す
Ko-mugi ...
SFF
す...
Mother ...
I, Komugi Komukai ...

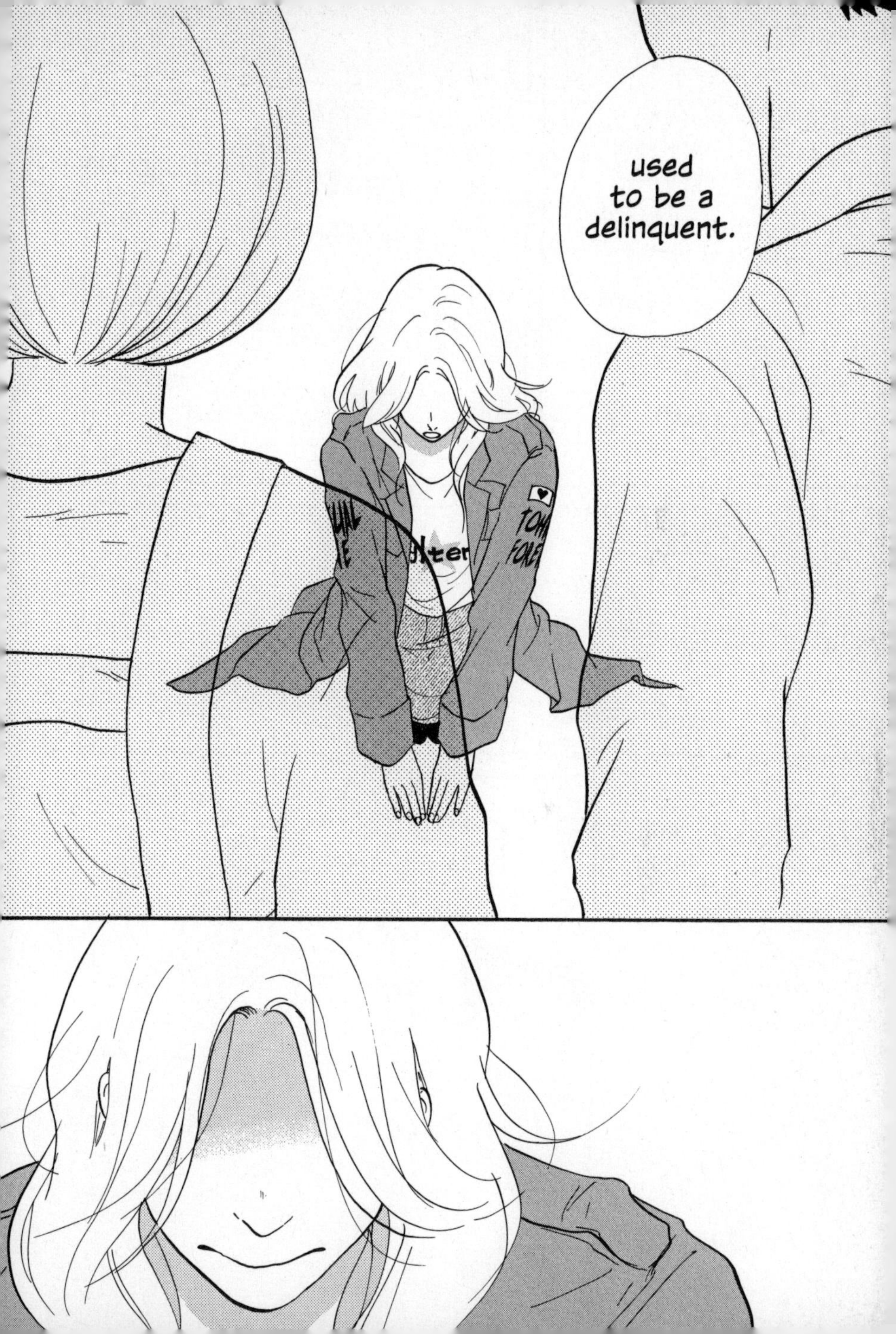
used to be a delinquent.

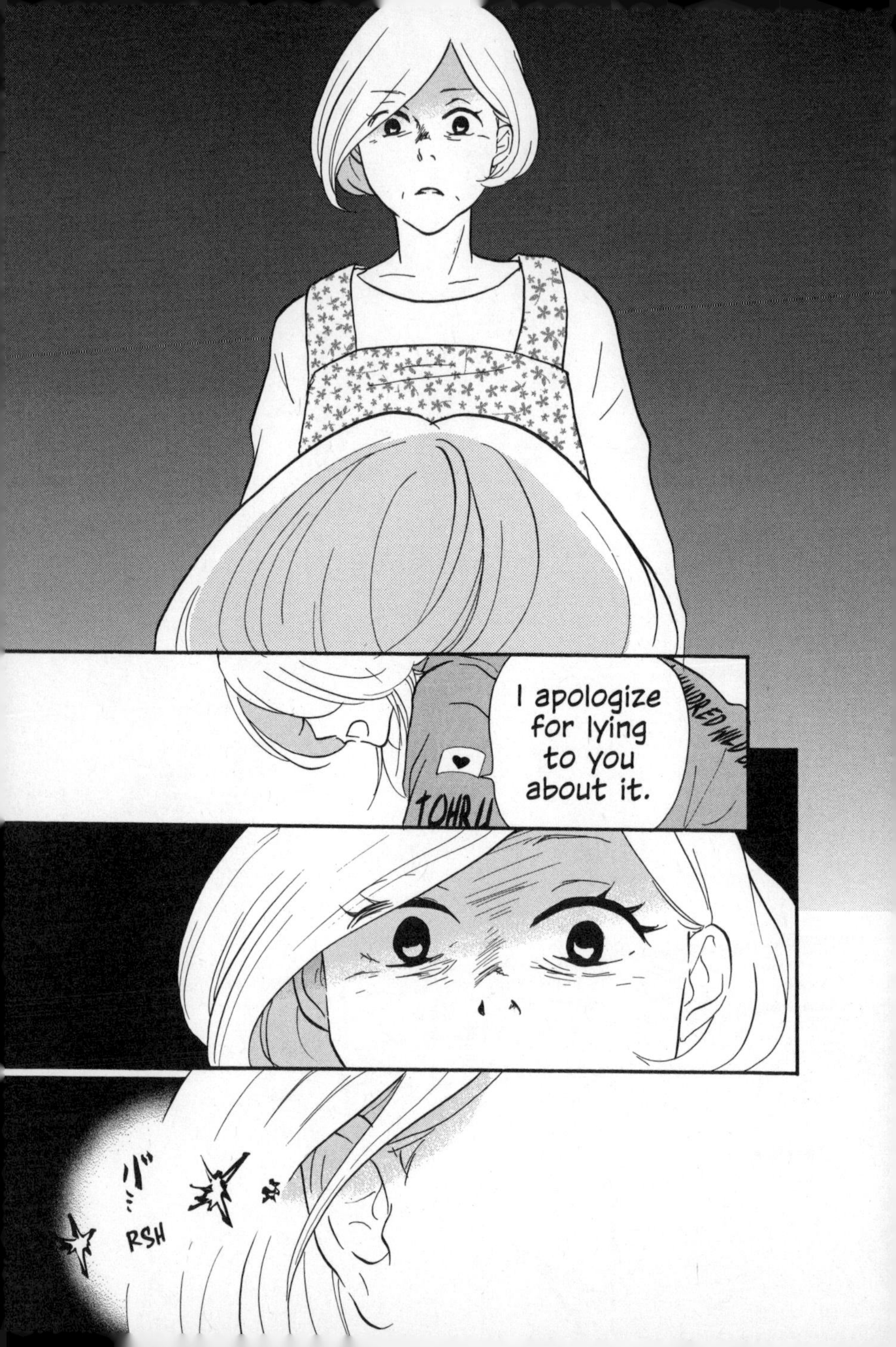
I apologize for lying to you about it.
RSH

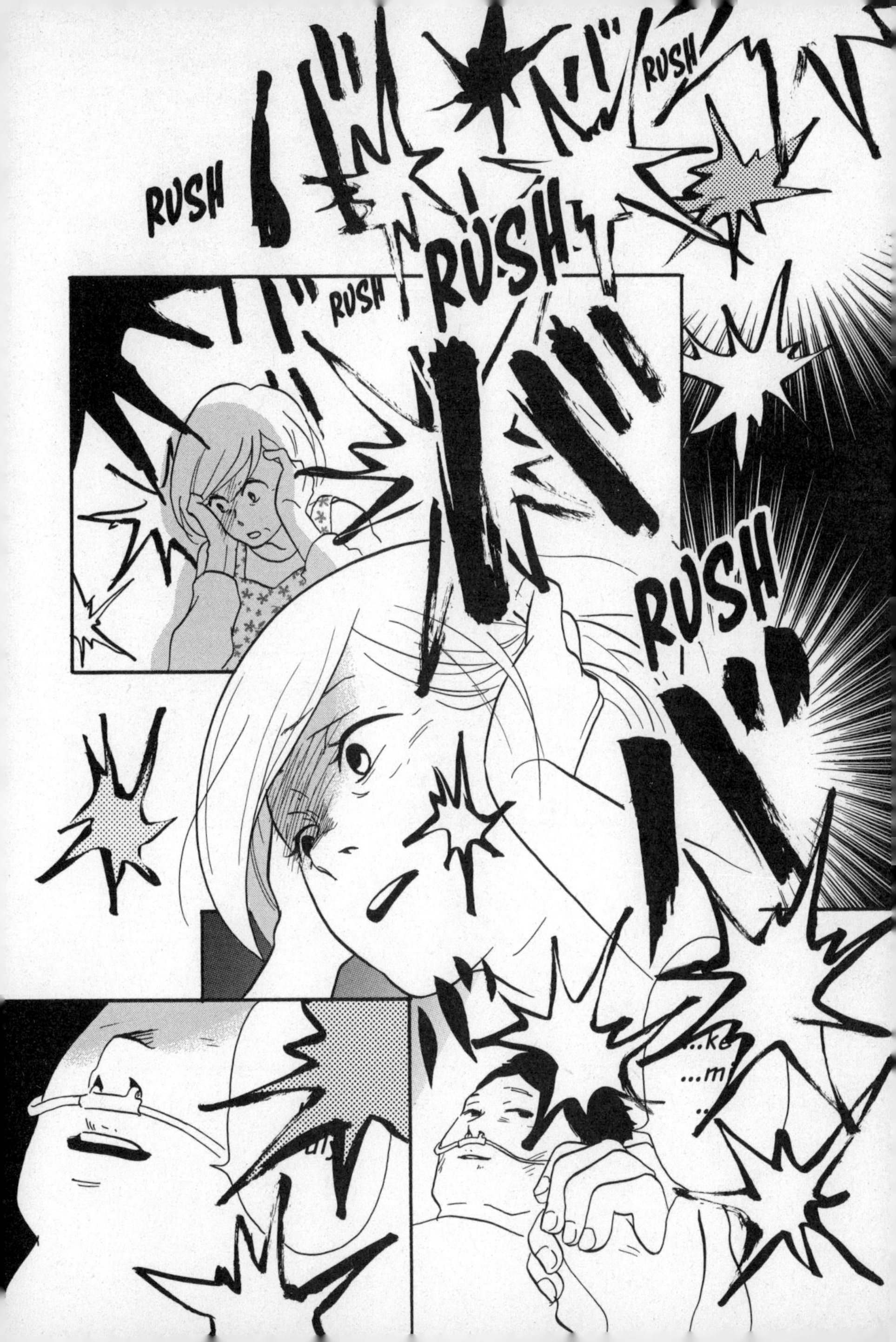
RUSH
RUSH
RUSH
RUSH
RUSH
...ke
...m
..

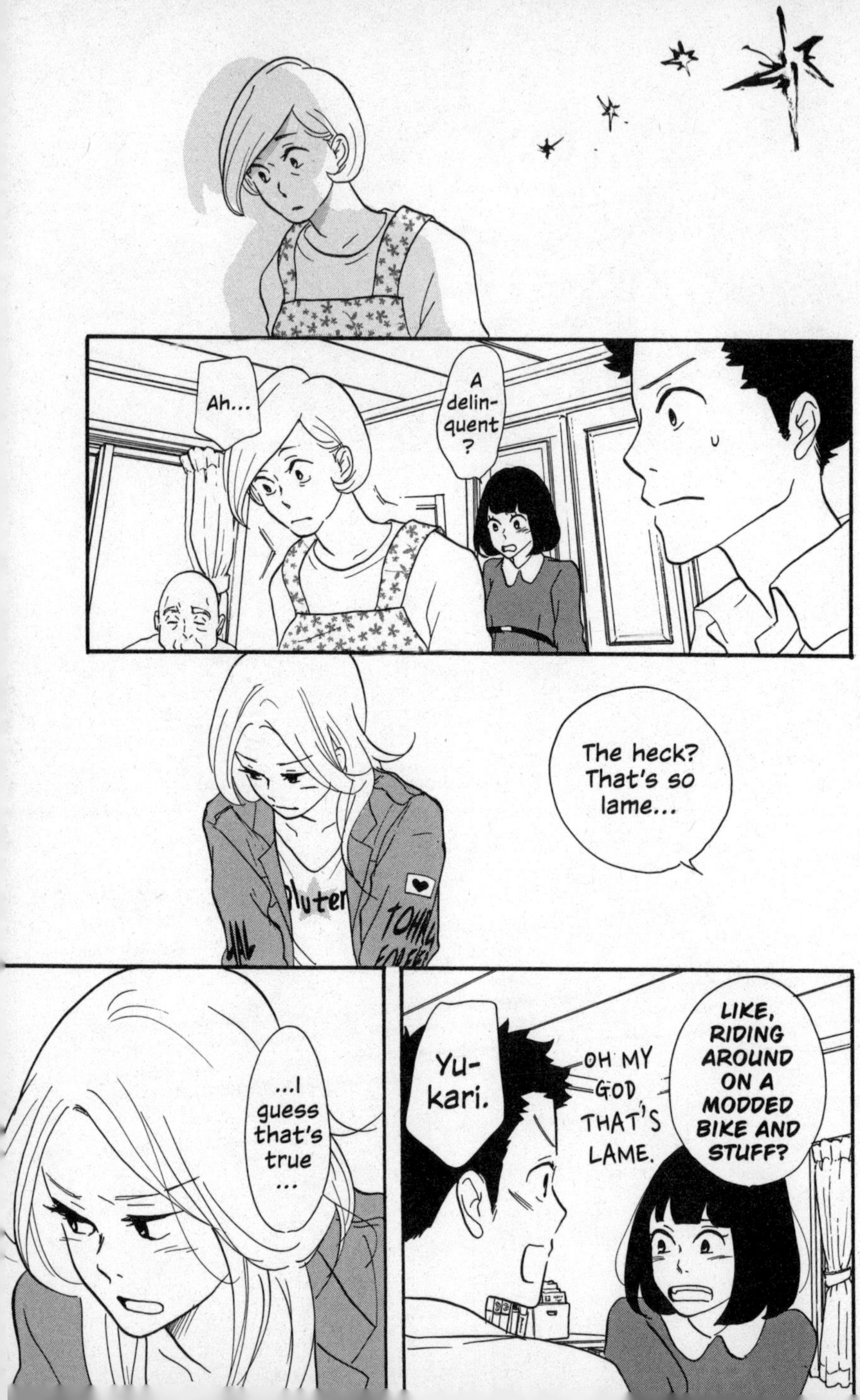
A delinquent?
Ah...
The heck? That's so lame...
LIKE, RIDING AROUND ON A MODDED BIKE AND STUFF?
OH MY GOD THAT'S LAME.
Yukari.
...I guess that's true...

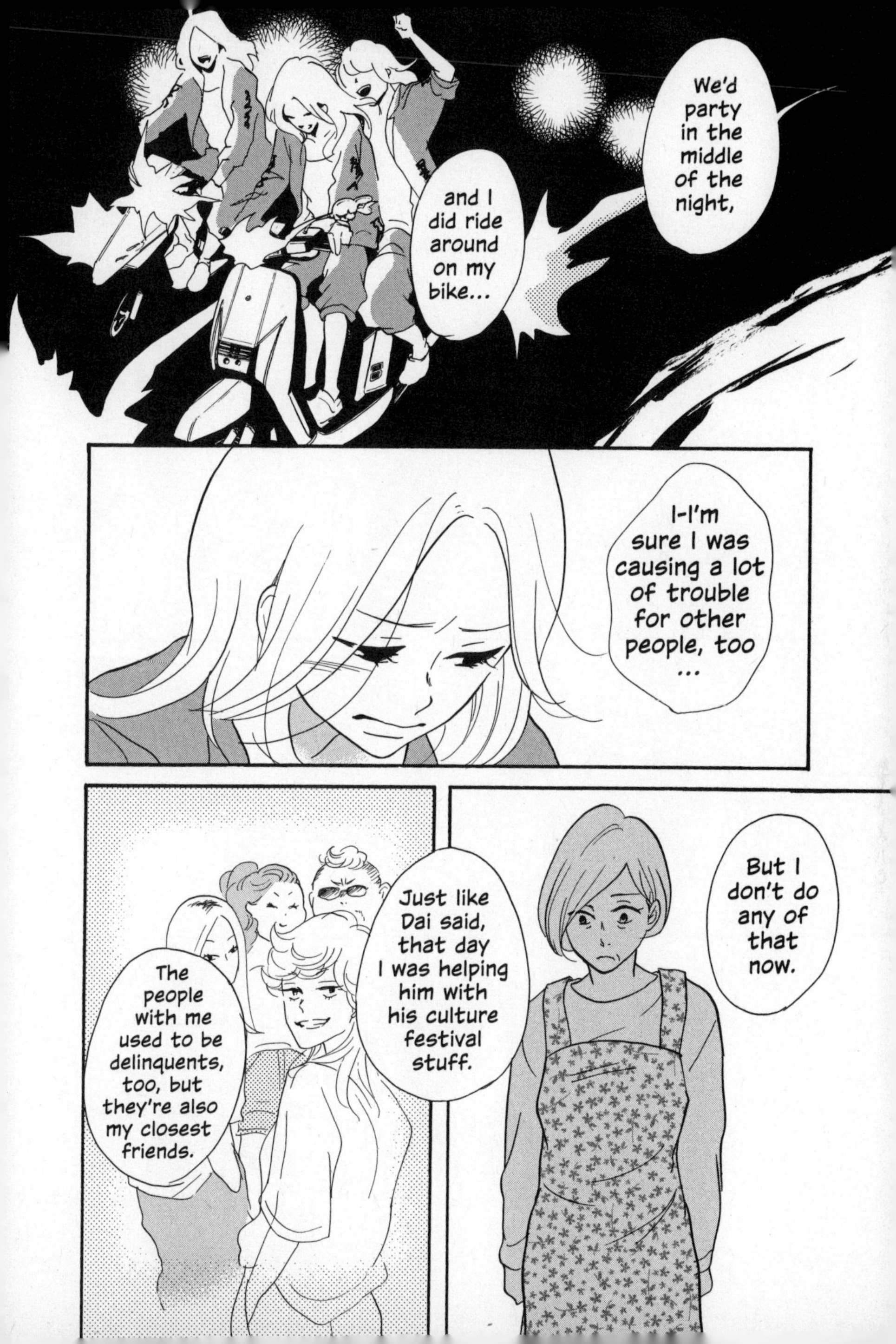
We'd party in the middle of the night,
and I did ride around on my bike...
I-I'm sure I was causing a lot of trouble for other people, too ...
But I don't do any of that now.
Just like Dai said, that day I was helping him with his culture festival stuff.
The people with me used to be delinquents, too, but they're also my closest friends.

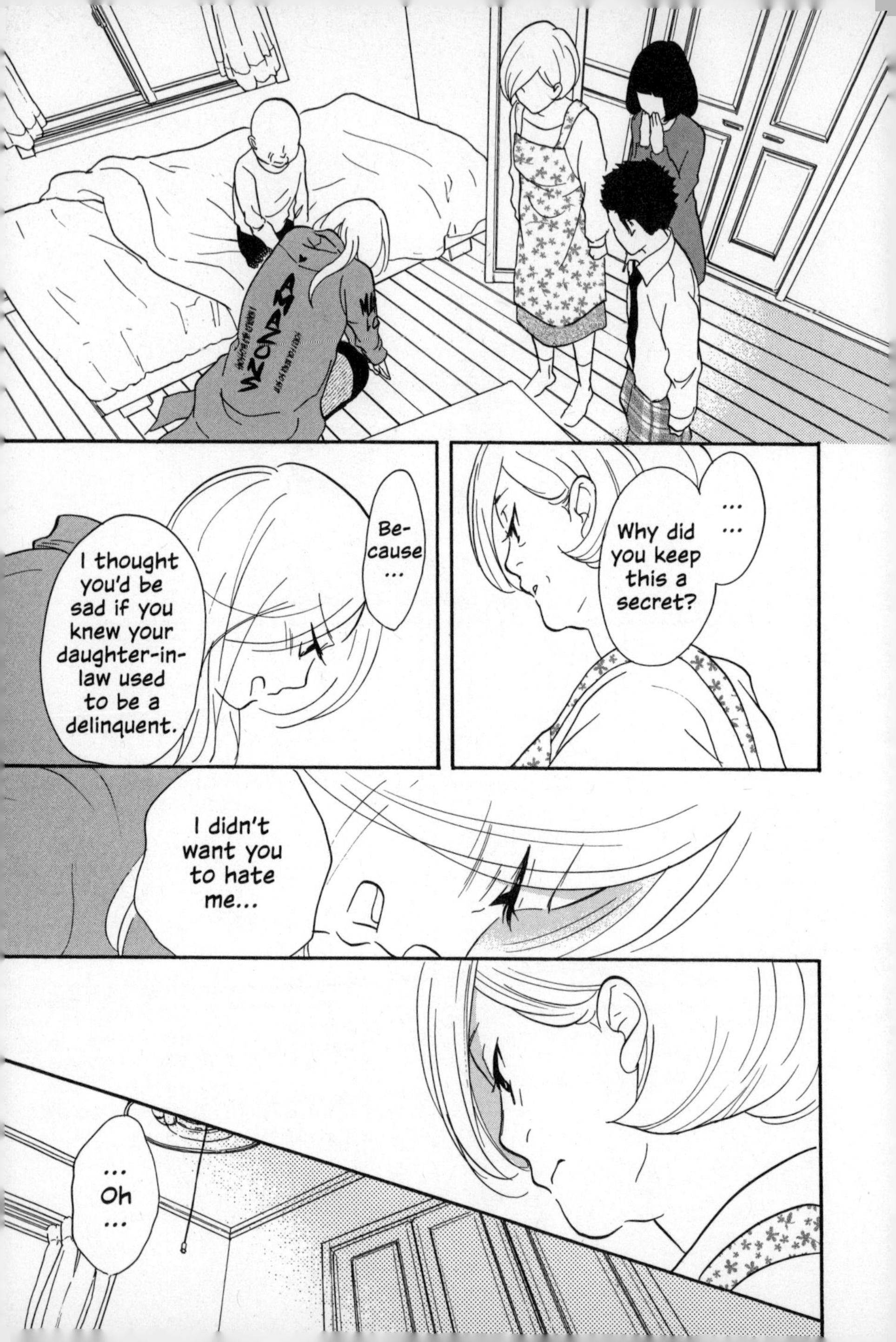
......
Why did you keep this a secret?
Be-cause...
I thought you'd be sad if you knew your daughter-in-law used to be a delinquent.
I didn't want you to hate me...
... Oh ...

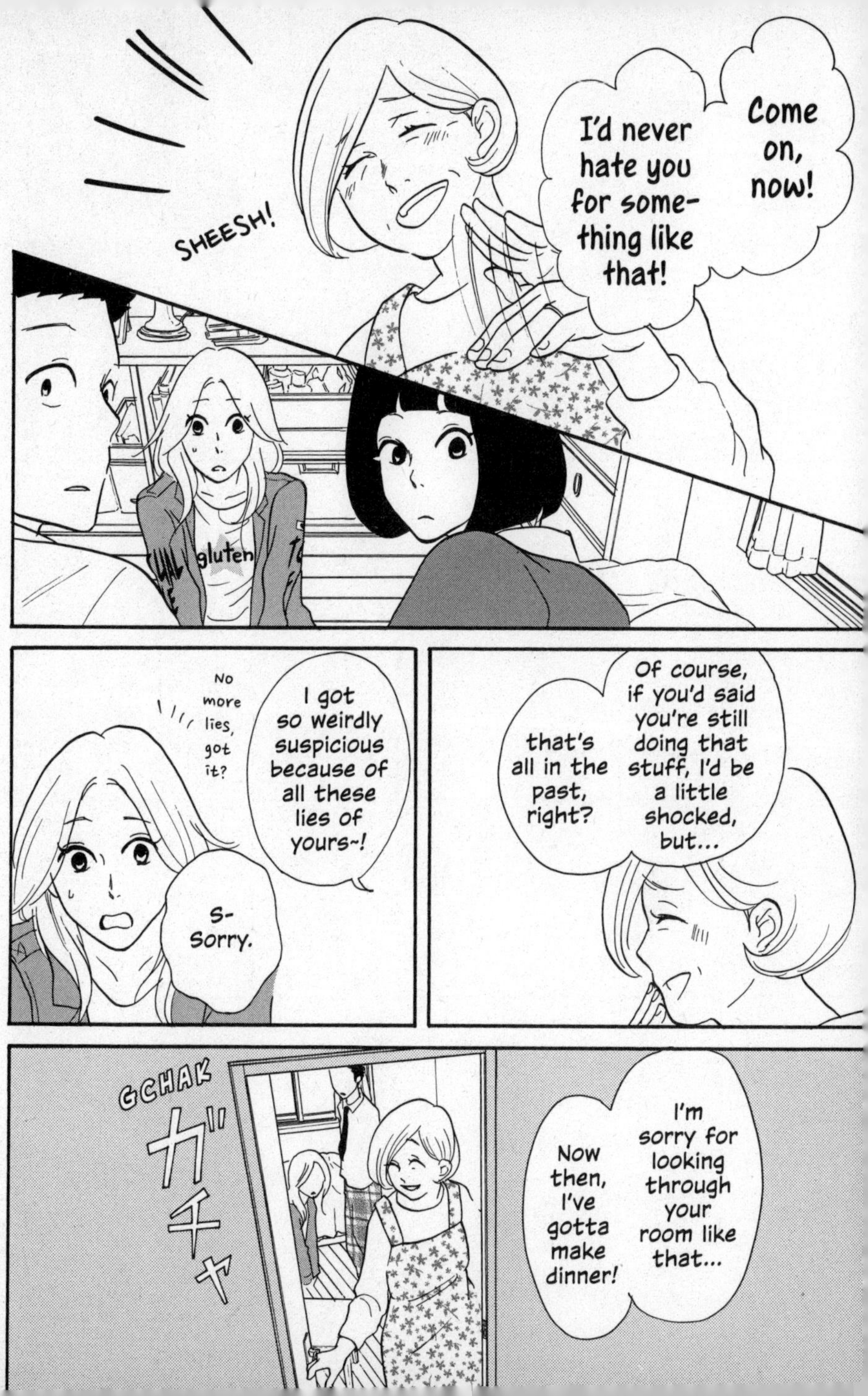
Come on, now!
I'd never hate you for some-thing like that!
SHEESH!
gluten
Of course, if you'd said you're still doing that stuff, I'd be a little shocked, but...
that's all in the past, right?
I got so weirdly suspicious because of all these lies of yours~!
No more lies, got it?
S-Sorry.
I'm sorry for looking through your room like that...
Now then, I've gotta make dinner!
GCHAK
ガチャ

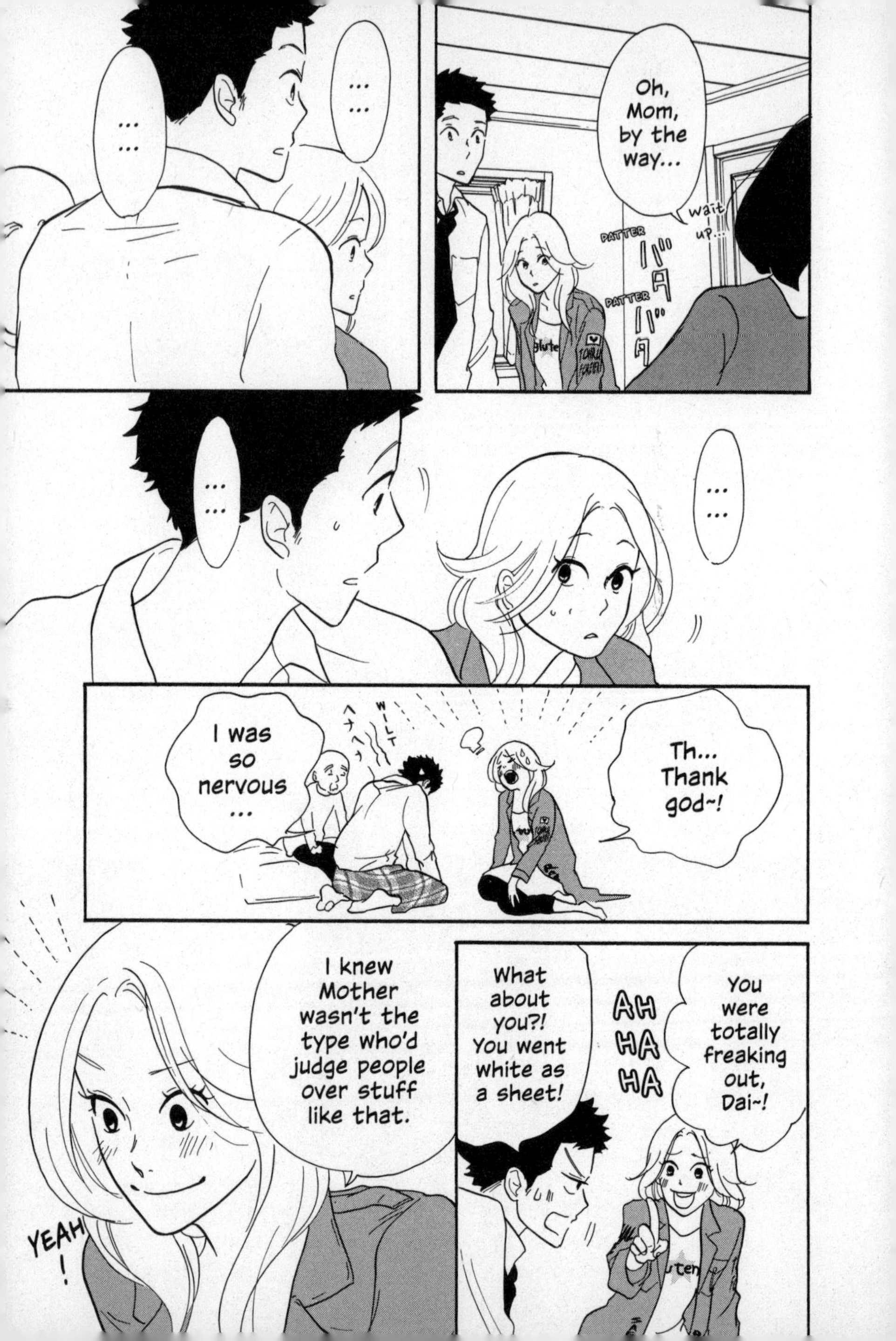
Oh, Mom, by the way...
wait up...
PATTER
バタ
PATTER
バタ
... ...
... ...
... ...
... ...
Th... Thank god~!
WILT
I was so nervous ...
You were totally freaking out, Dai~!
AH HA HA
What about you?! You went white as a sheet!
I knew Mother wasn't the type who'd judge people over stuff like that.
YEAH!

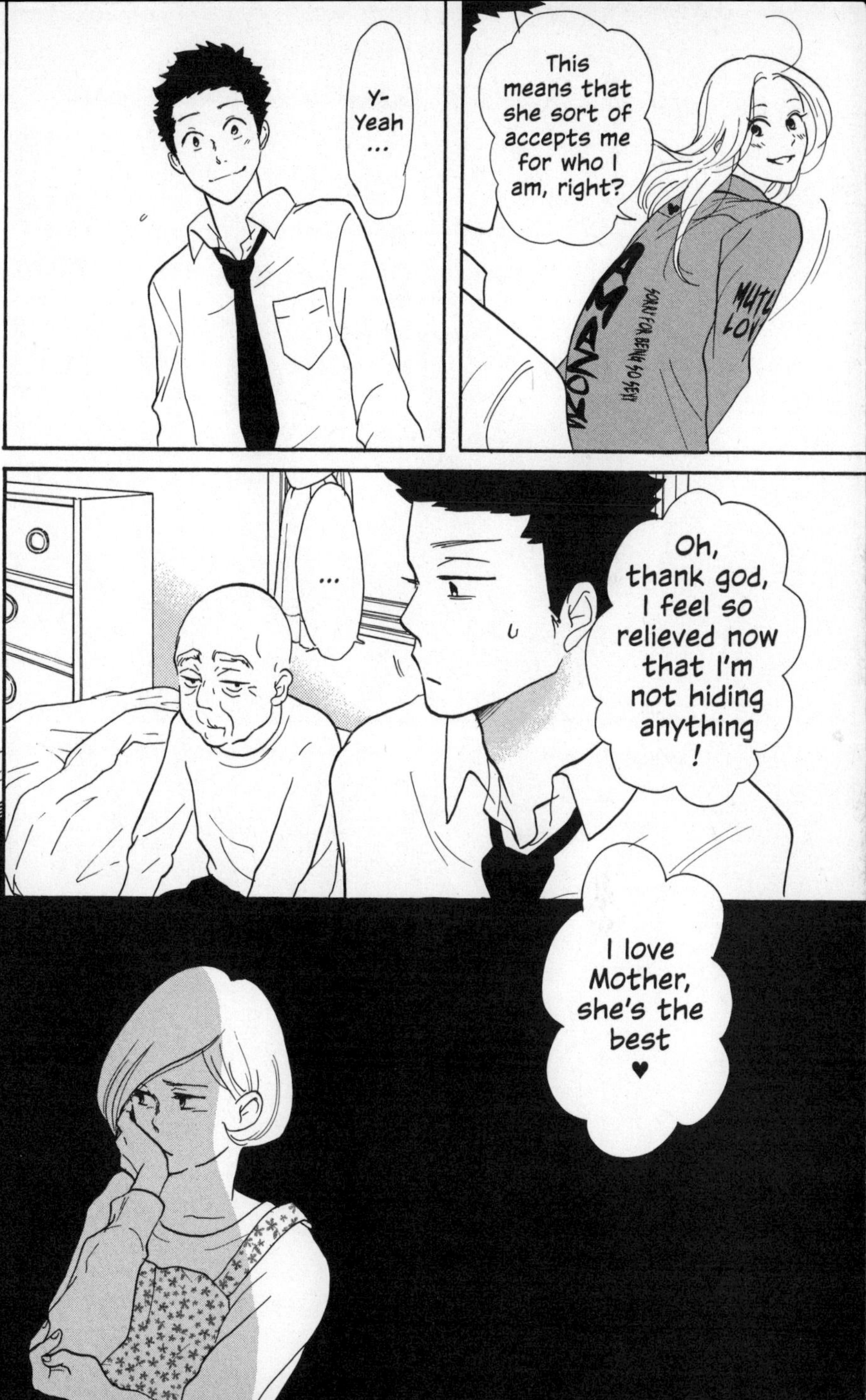
This means that she sort of accepts me for who I am, right?
Y-Yeah ...
Oh, thank god, I feel so relieved now that I'm not hiding anything!
...
I love Mother, she's the best ♥

33 THE KOMUKAI FAMILY SPECIAL

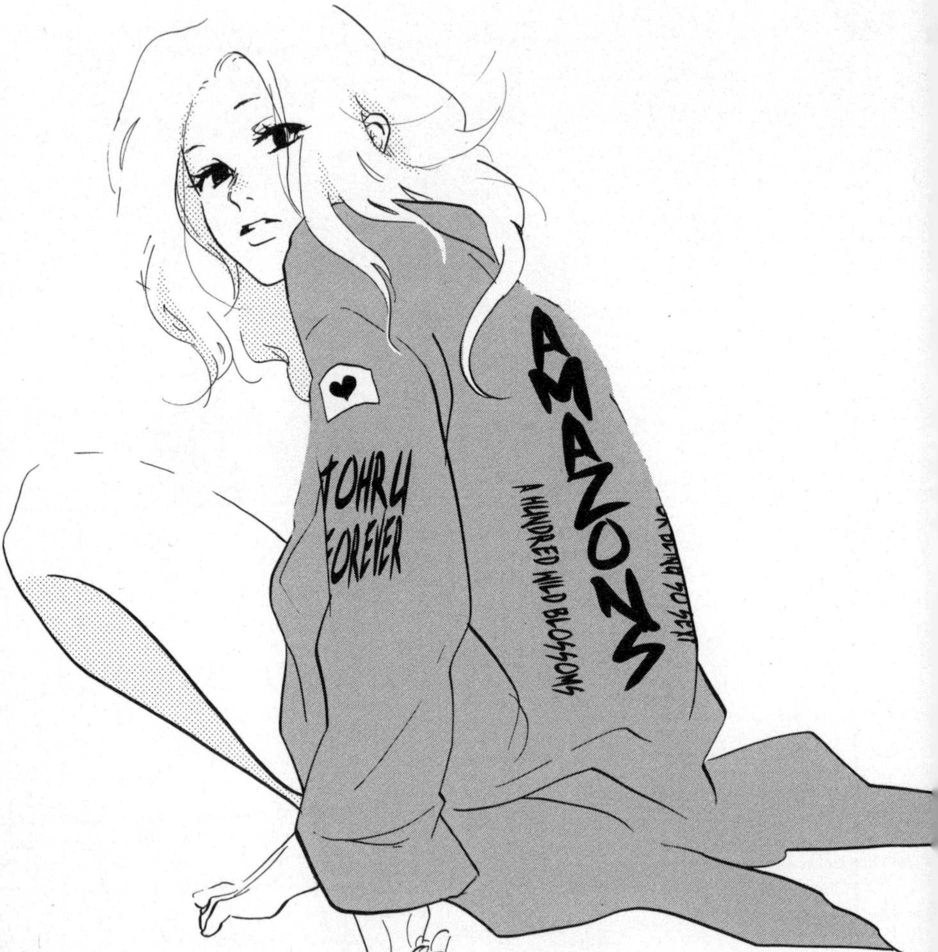
AMAZONS
A HUNDRED WILD BLOSSOMS
TOHRU FOREVER

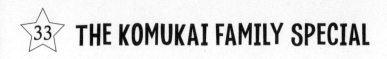

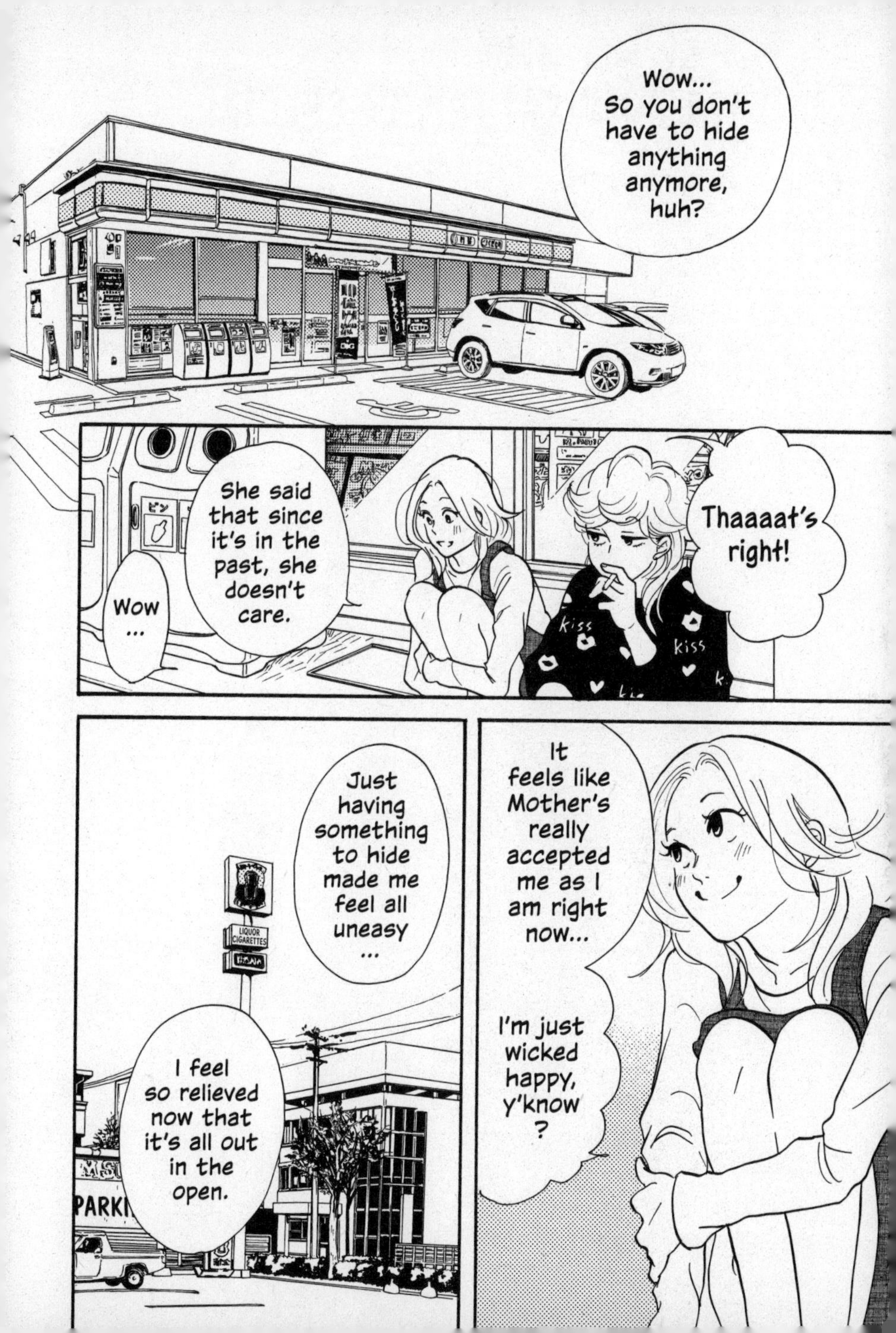
Wow... So you don't have to hide anything anymore, huh?
Thaaaat's right!
She said that since it's in the past, she doesn't care.
Wow ...
It feels like Mother's really accepted me as I am right now...
I'm just wicked happy, y'know ?
Just having something to hide made me feel all uneasy ...
LIQUOR CIGARETTES
I feel so relieved now that it's all out in the open.

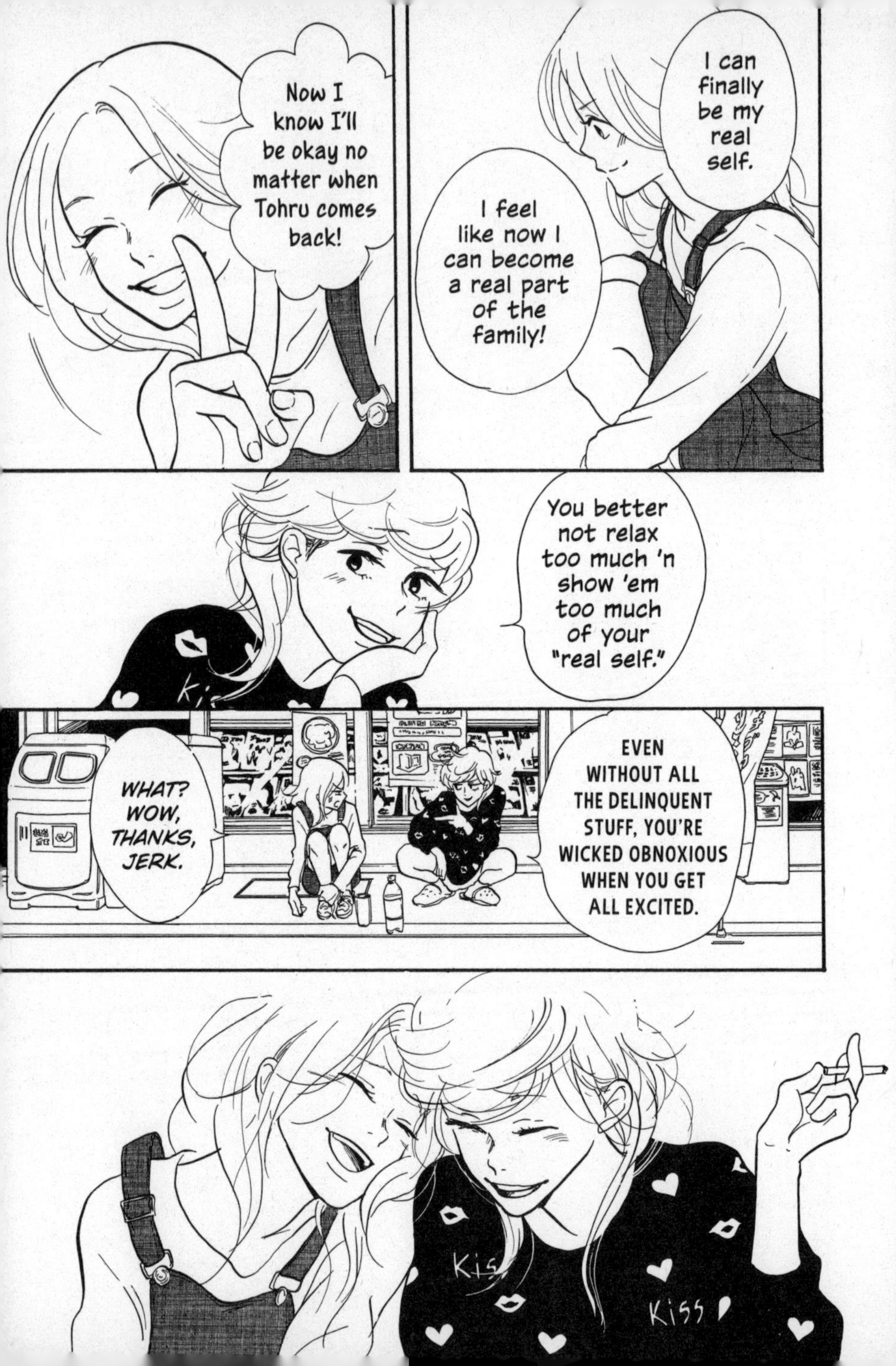
I can finally be my real self.
I feel like now I can become a real part of the family!
Now I know I'll be okay no matter when Tohru comes back!
You better not relax too much 'n show 'em too much of your "real self."
EVEN WITHOUT ALL THE DELINQUENT STUFF, YOU'RE WICKED OBNOXIOUS WHEN YOU GET ALL EXCITED.
WHAT? WOW, THANKS, JERK.

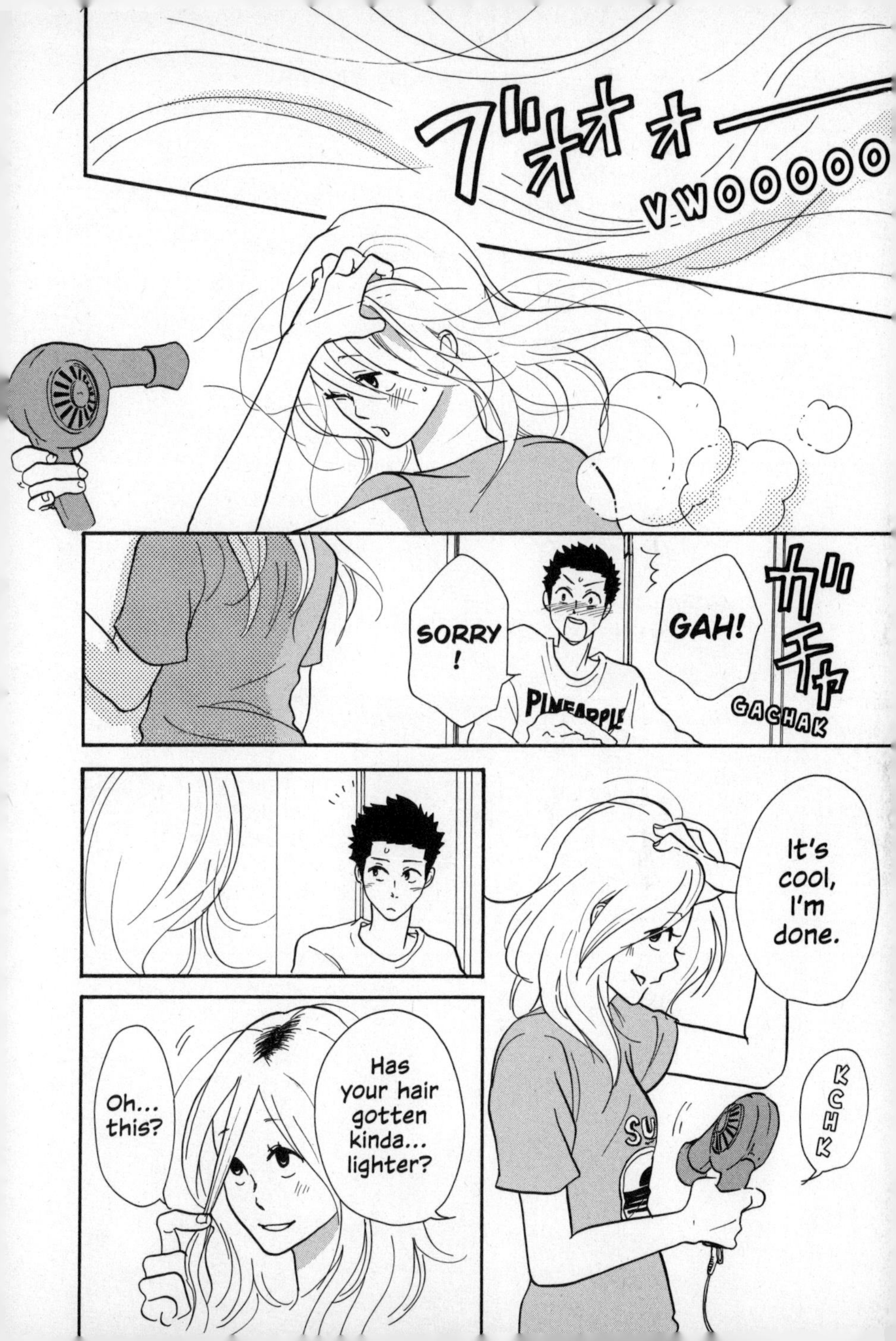
ブオオォー
VWOOOOO
ガチャ
GACHAK
GAH!
SORRY!
PINEAPPLE
It's cool, I'm done.
KCHK
Has your hair gotten kinda... lighter?
Oh... this?

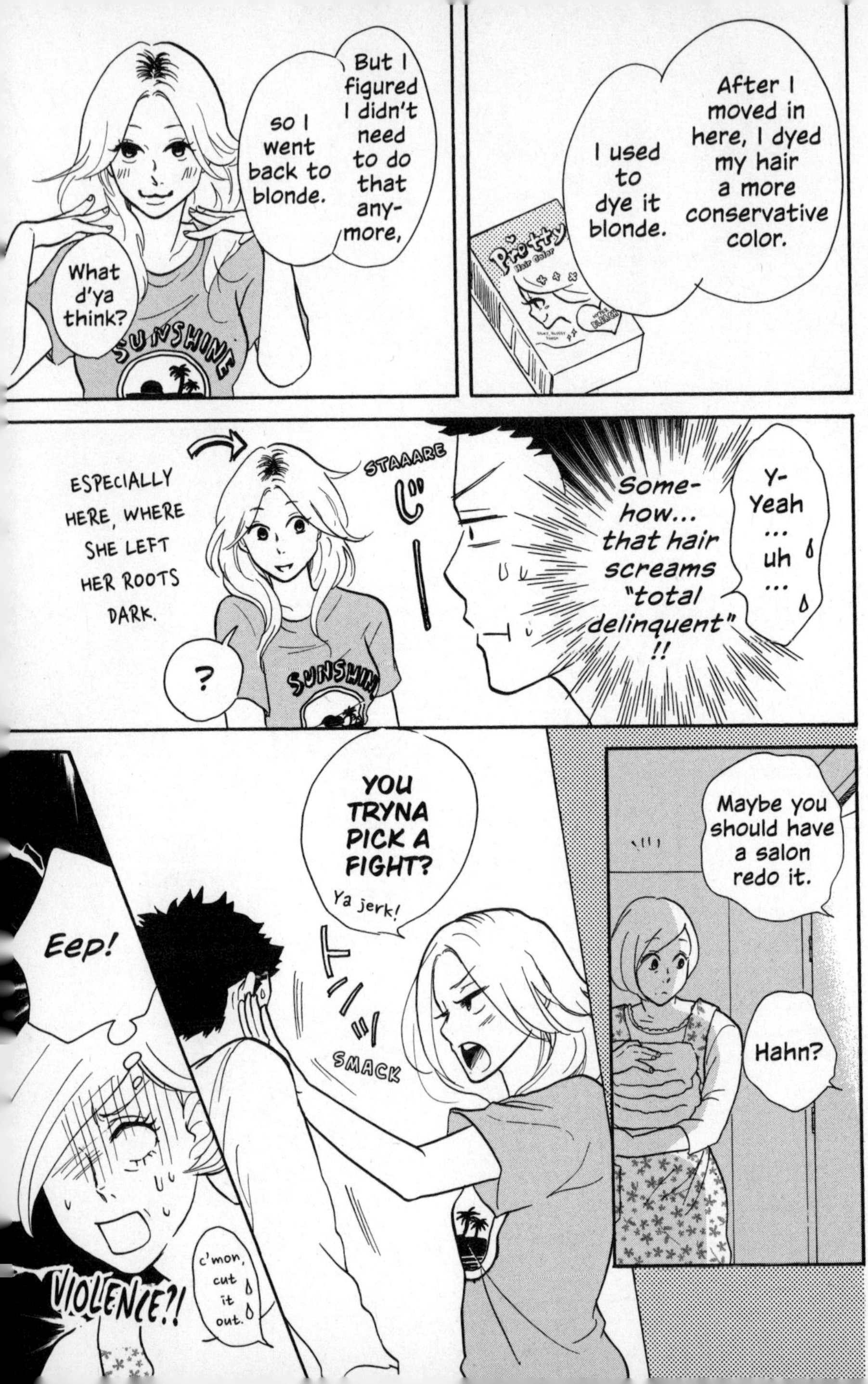
After I moved in here, I dyed my hair a more conservative color.
I used to dye it blonde.
Pretty Hair Color
But I figured I didn't need to do that anymore,
so I went back to blonde.
What d'ya think?
SUNSHINE
Y-Yeah ... uh ...
Somehow... that hair screams "total delinquent"!!
STAAARE
ESPECIALLY HERE, WHERE SHE LEFT HER ROOTS DARK.
?
SUNSHINE
Maybe you should have a salon redo it.
Hahn?
YOU TRYNA PICK A FIGHT?
Ya jerk!
SMACK
Eep!
VIOLENCE?!
c'mon, cut it out.

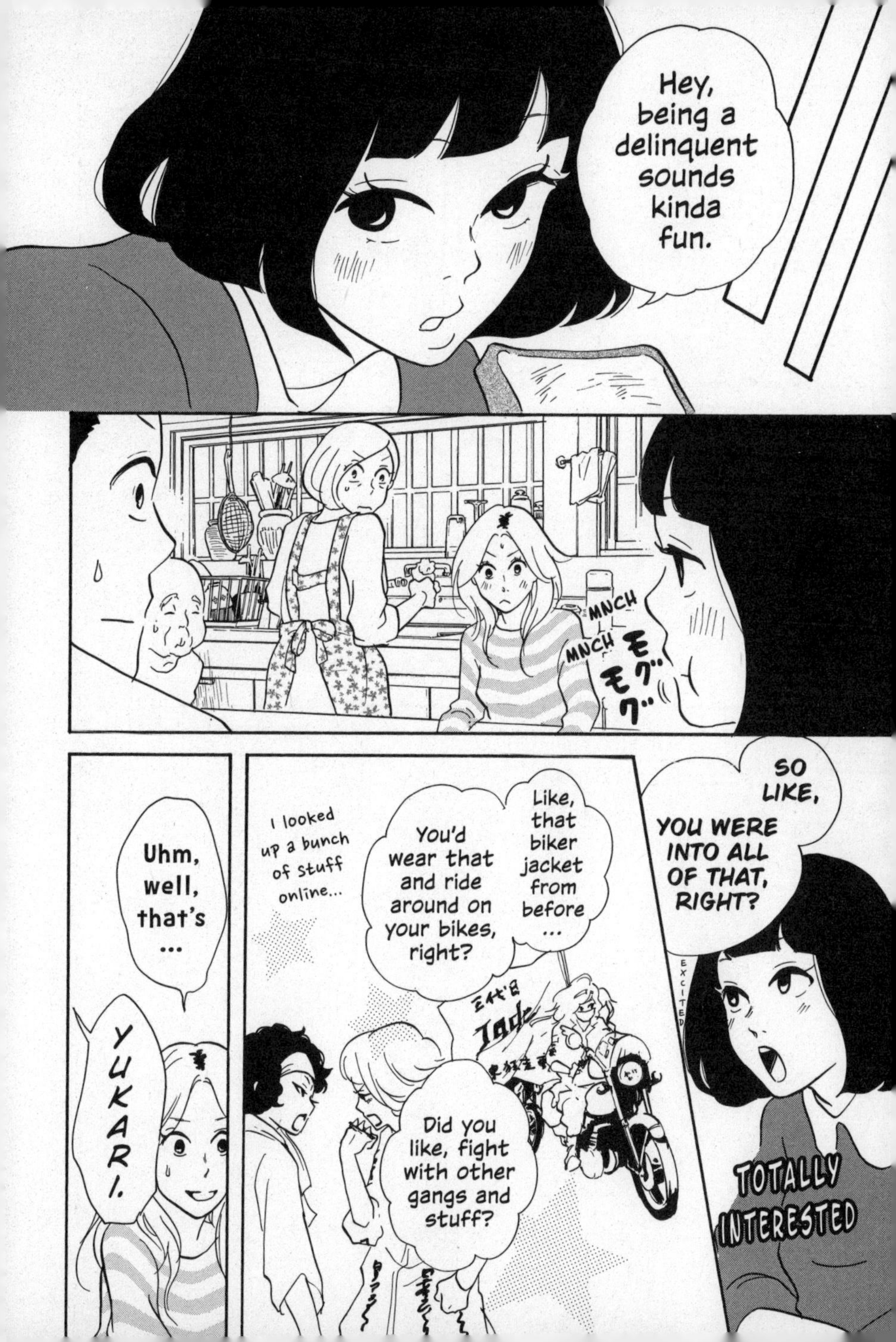
Hey, being a delinquent sounds kinda fun.
MNCH MNCH
モグモグ
SO LIKE, YOU WERE INTO ALL OF THAT, RIGHT?
EXCITED
TOTALLY INTERESTED
Like, that biker jacket from before ...
You'd wear that and ride around on your bikes, right?
I looked up a bunch of stuff online...
Did you like, fight with other gangs and stuff?
Uhm, well, that's ...
YUKARI.

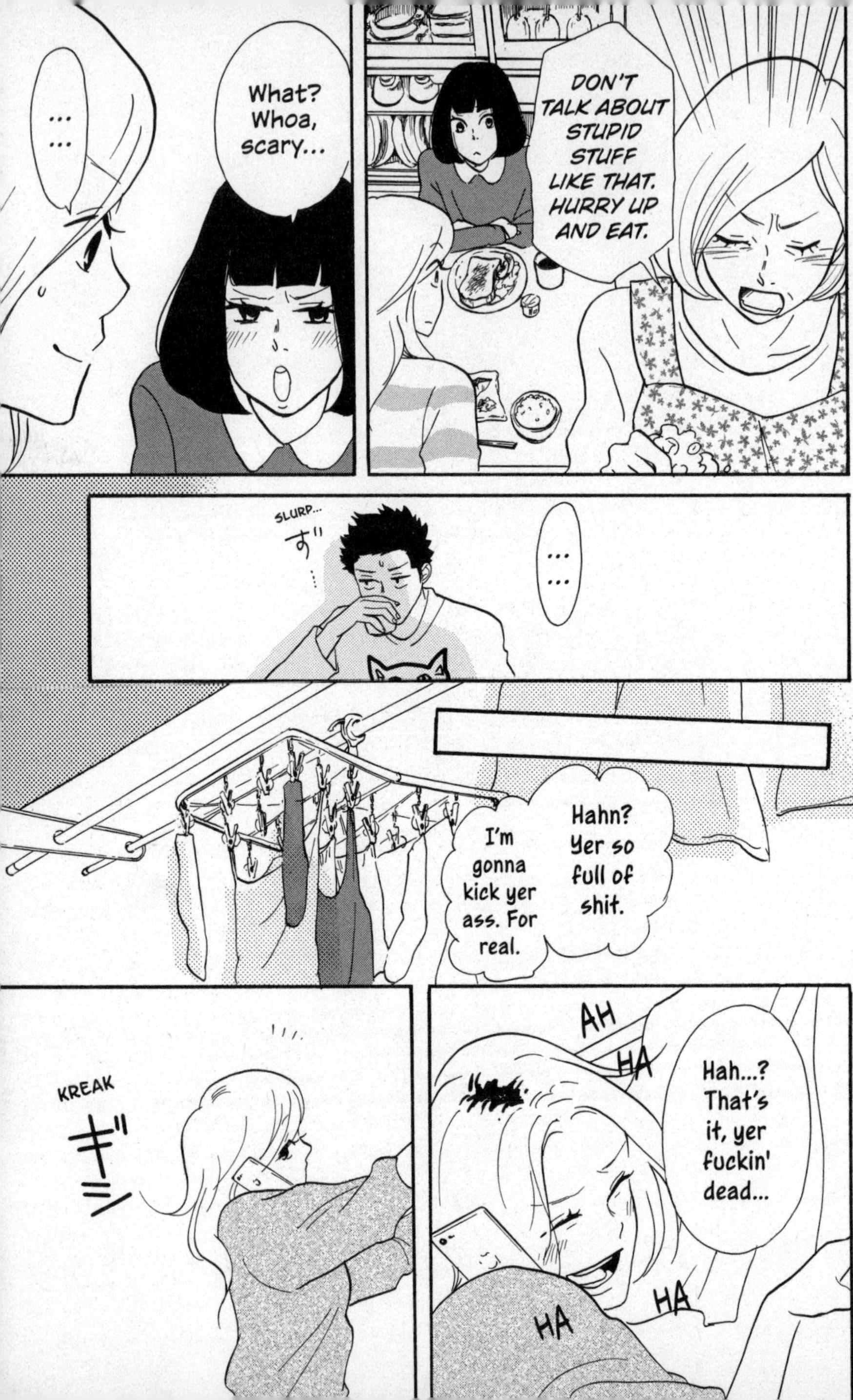
DON'T TALK ABOUT STUPID STUFF LIKE THAT. HURRY UP AND EAT.
What? Whoa, scary...
... ...
... ...
SLURP...
ず
I'm gonna kick yer ass. For real.
Hahn? Yer so full of shit.
AH HA
Hah...? That's it, yer fuckin' dead...
HA HA
KREAK
ギー

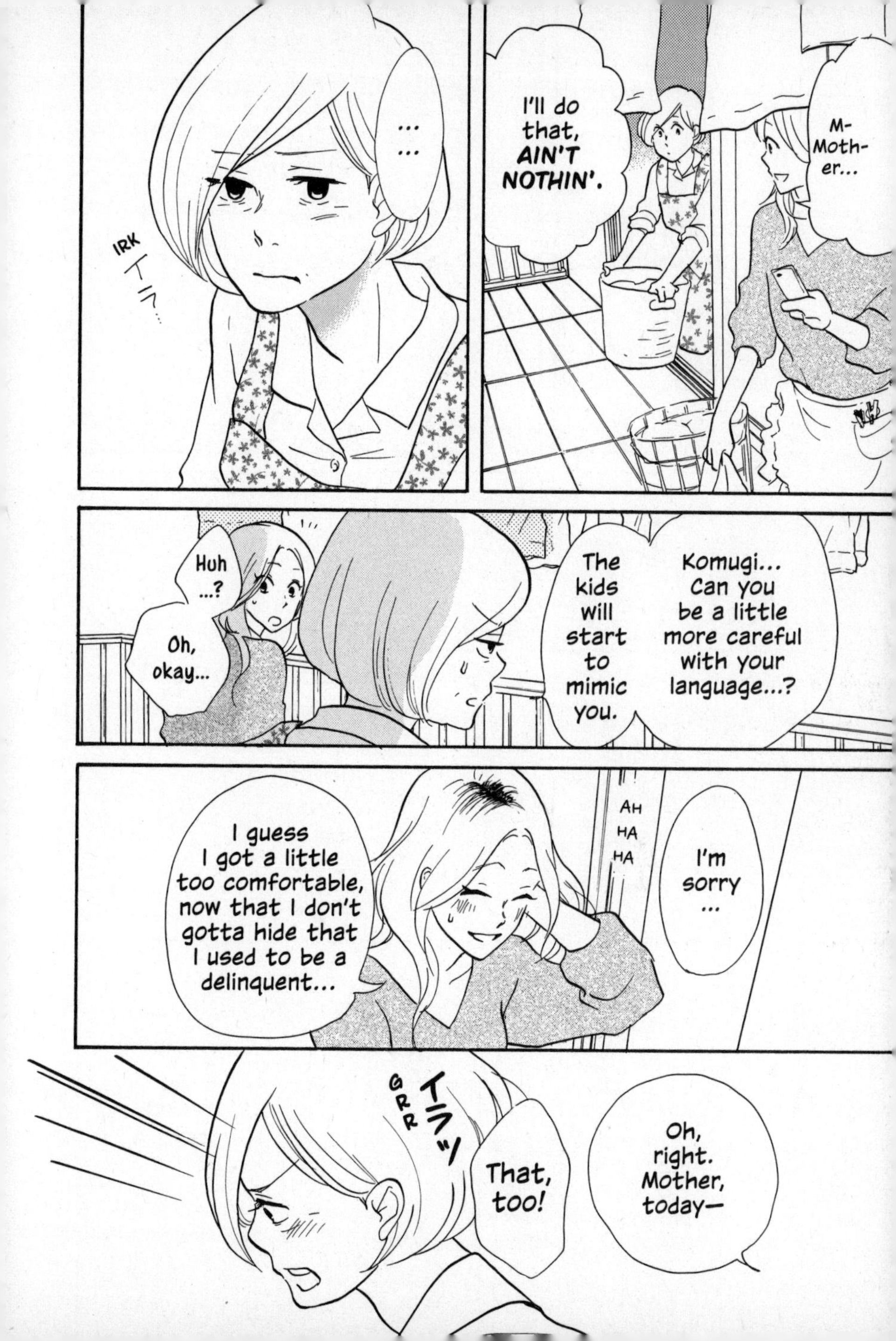
M-Mother...
I'll do that, **AIN'T NOTHIN'.**
... ...
IRK
イラ...
Komugi... Can you be a little more careful with your language...?
The kids will start to mimic you.
Huh ...?
Oh, okay...
I'm sorry ...
AH HA HA
I guess I got a little too comfortable, now that I don't gotta hide that I used to be a delinquent...
Oh, right. Mother, today—
That, too!
GRR
イラッ

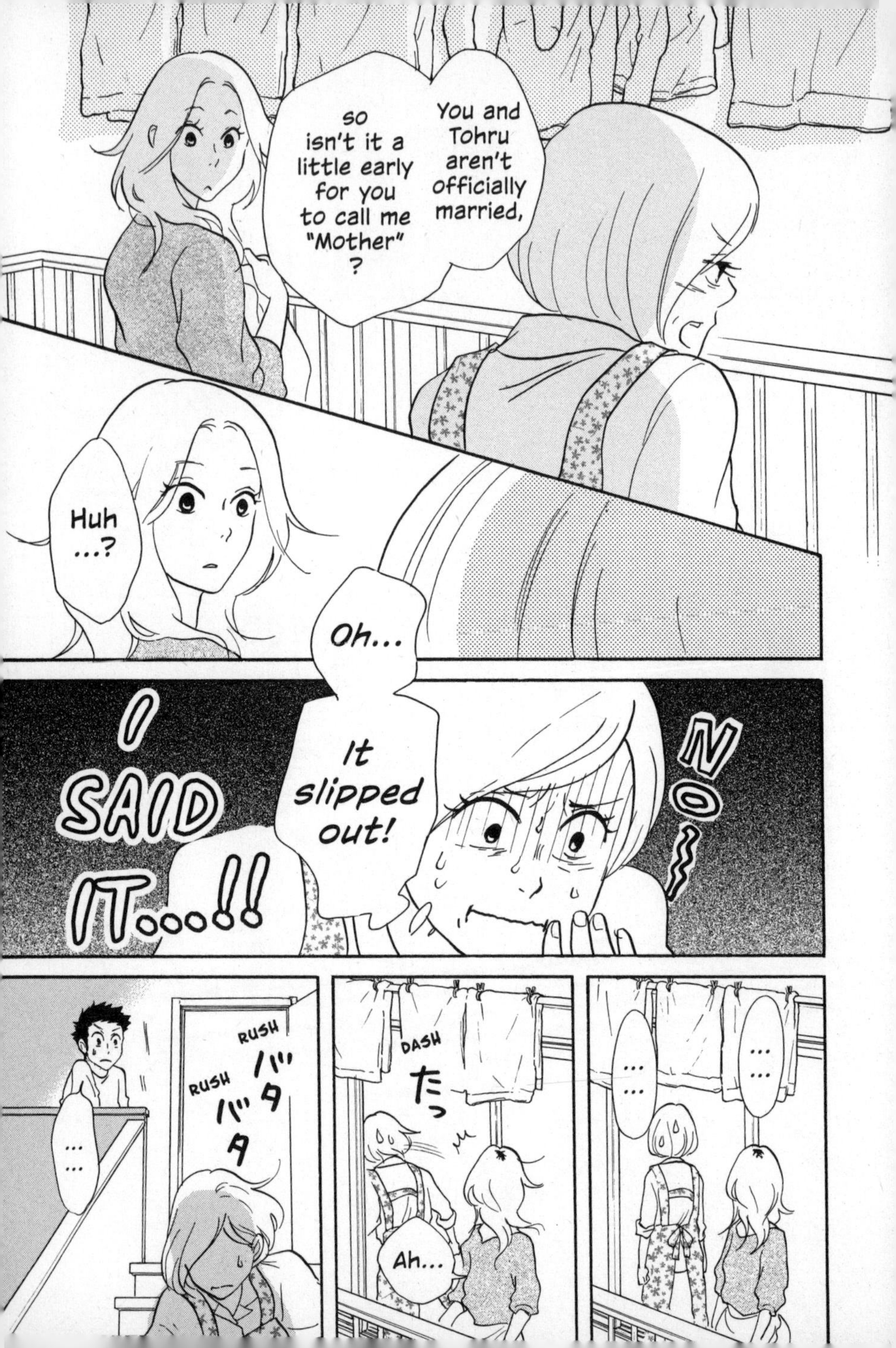
You and Tohru aren't officially married,
so isn't it a little early for you to call me "Mother"?
Huh ...?
Oh...
NO~
It slipped out!
I SAID IT...!!
... ...
... ...
DASH
たっ
Ah...
RUSH
バタ
RUSH
バタ
... ...

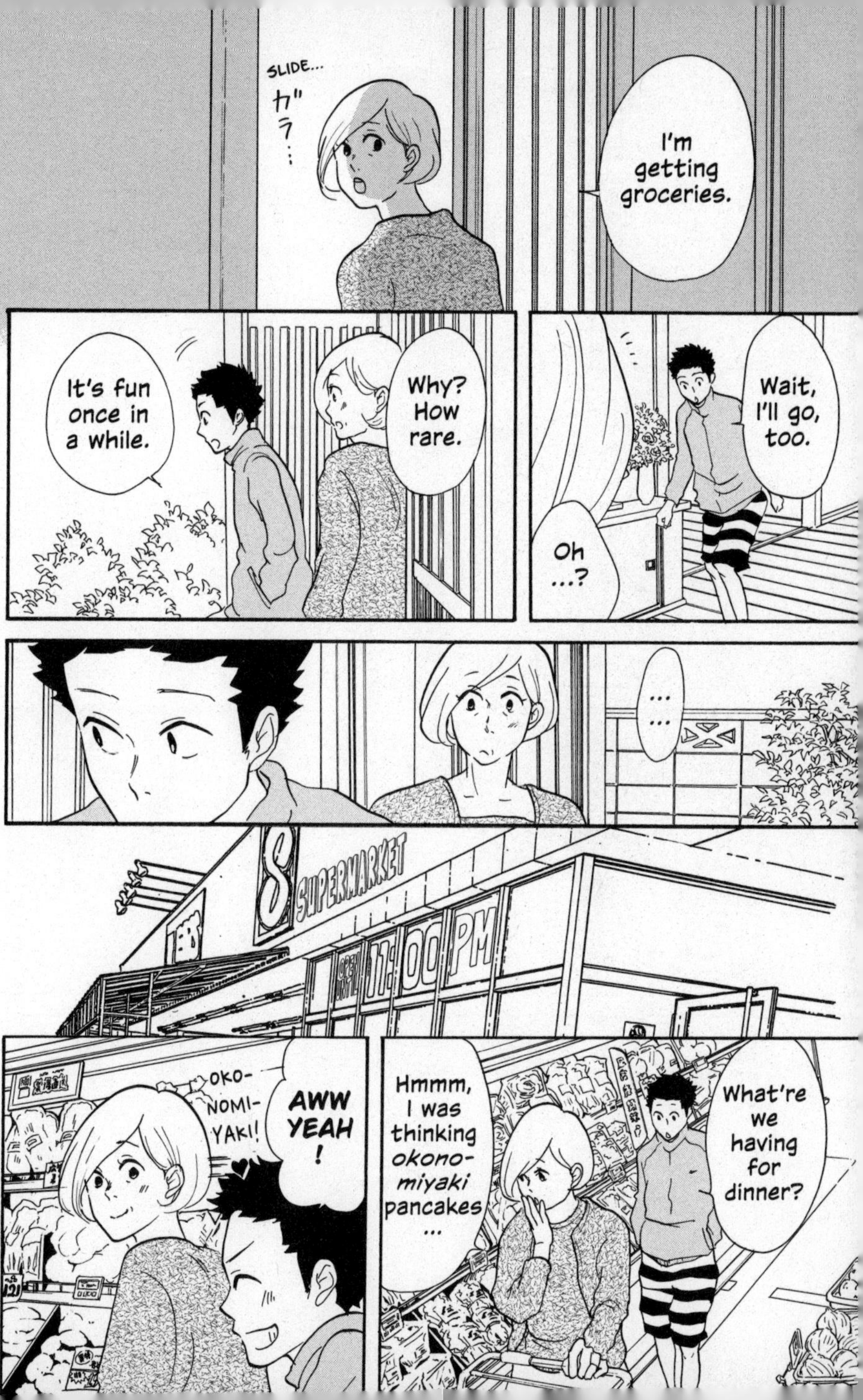
I'm getting groceries.
SLIDE...
ガラ…
Wait, I'll go, too.
...
Oh ...?
Why? How rare.
It's fun once in a while.
... ...
S
SUPERMARKET
OPEN 11:00 PM
What're we having for dinner?
Hmmm, I was thinking *okonomiyaki* pancakes ...
AWW YEAH!
OKO-NOMI-YAKI!

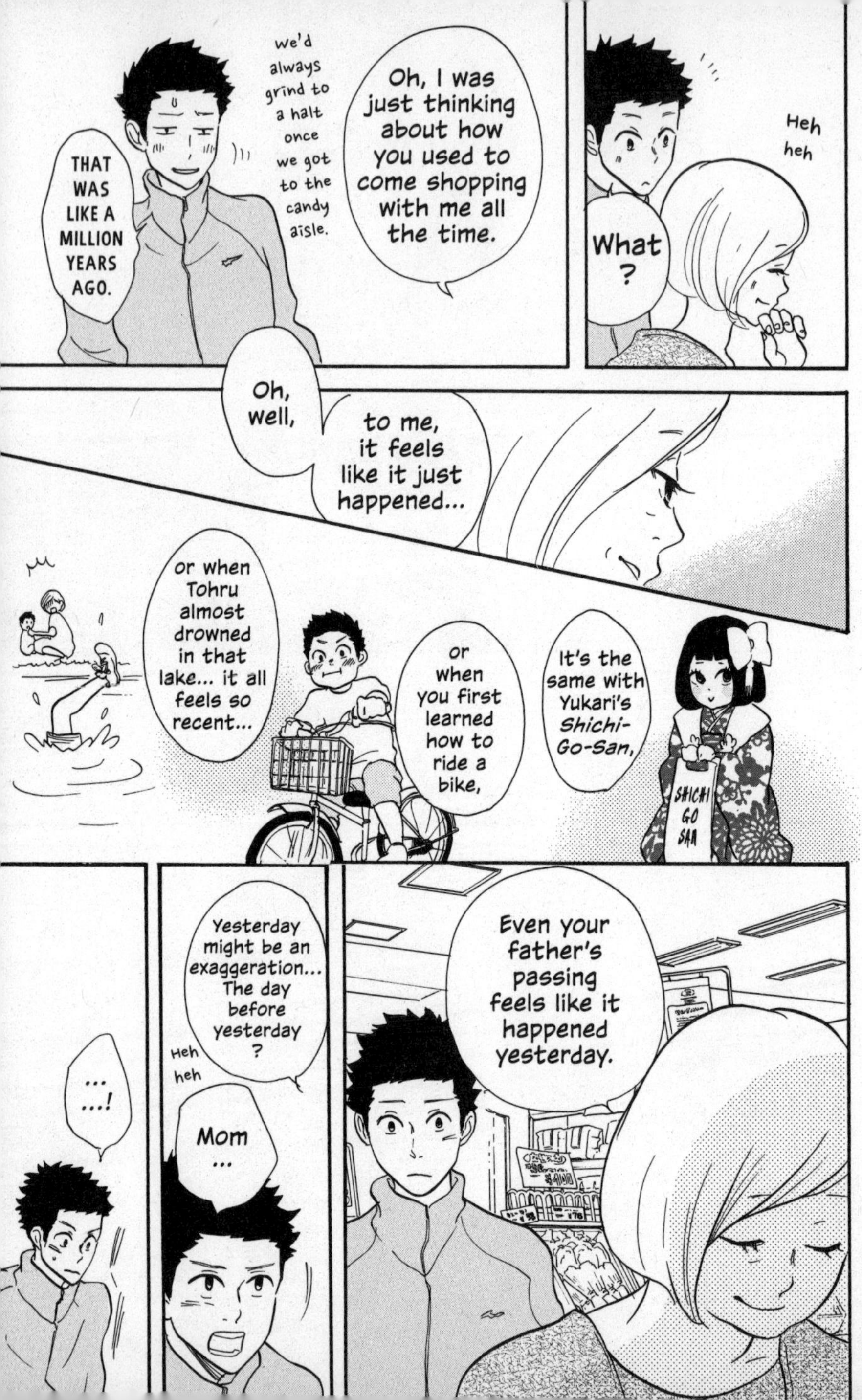
Heh heh
What ?
Oh, I was just thinking about how you used to come shopping with me all the time.
we'd always grind to a halt once we got to the candy aisle.
THAT WAS LIKE A MILLION YEARS AGO.
Oh, well,
to me, it feels like it just happened...
It's the same with Yukari's Shichi-Go-San,
SHICHI GO SAN
or when you first learned how to ride a bike,
or when Tohru almost drowned in that lake... it all feels so recent...
Even your father's passing feels like it happened yesterday.
Yesterday might be an exaggeration... The day before yesterday?
Heh heh
Mom ...
... ...!

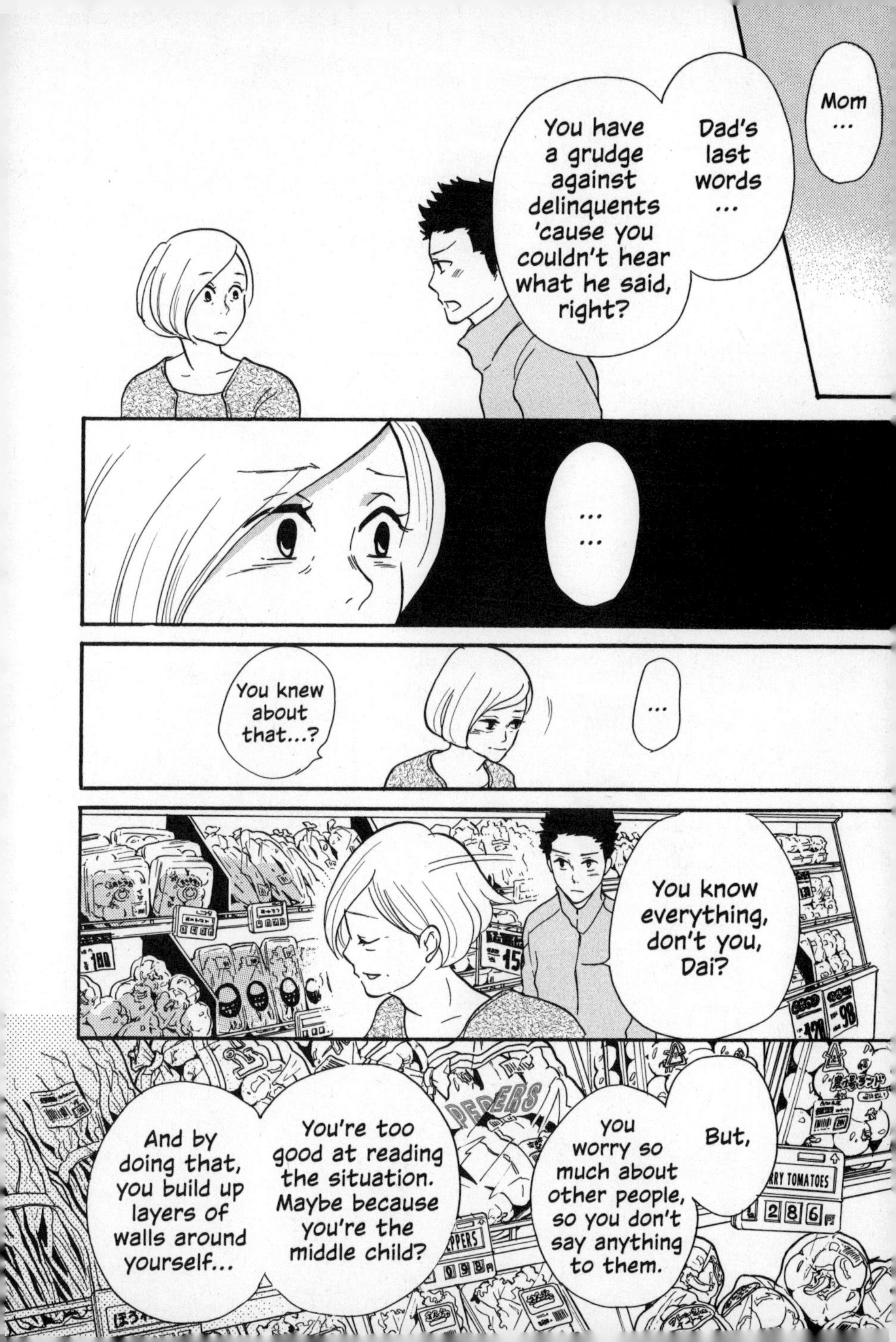
Mom ...
Dad's last words ...
You have a grudge against delinquents 'cause you couldn't hear what he said, right?
... ...
...
You knew about that...?
You know everything, don't you, Dai?
But,
you worry so much about other people, so you don't say anything to them.
You're too good at reading the situation. Maybe because you're the middle child?
And by doing that, you build up layers of walls around yourself...

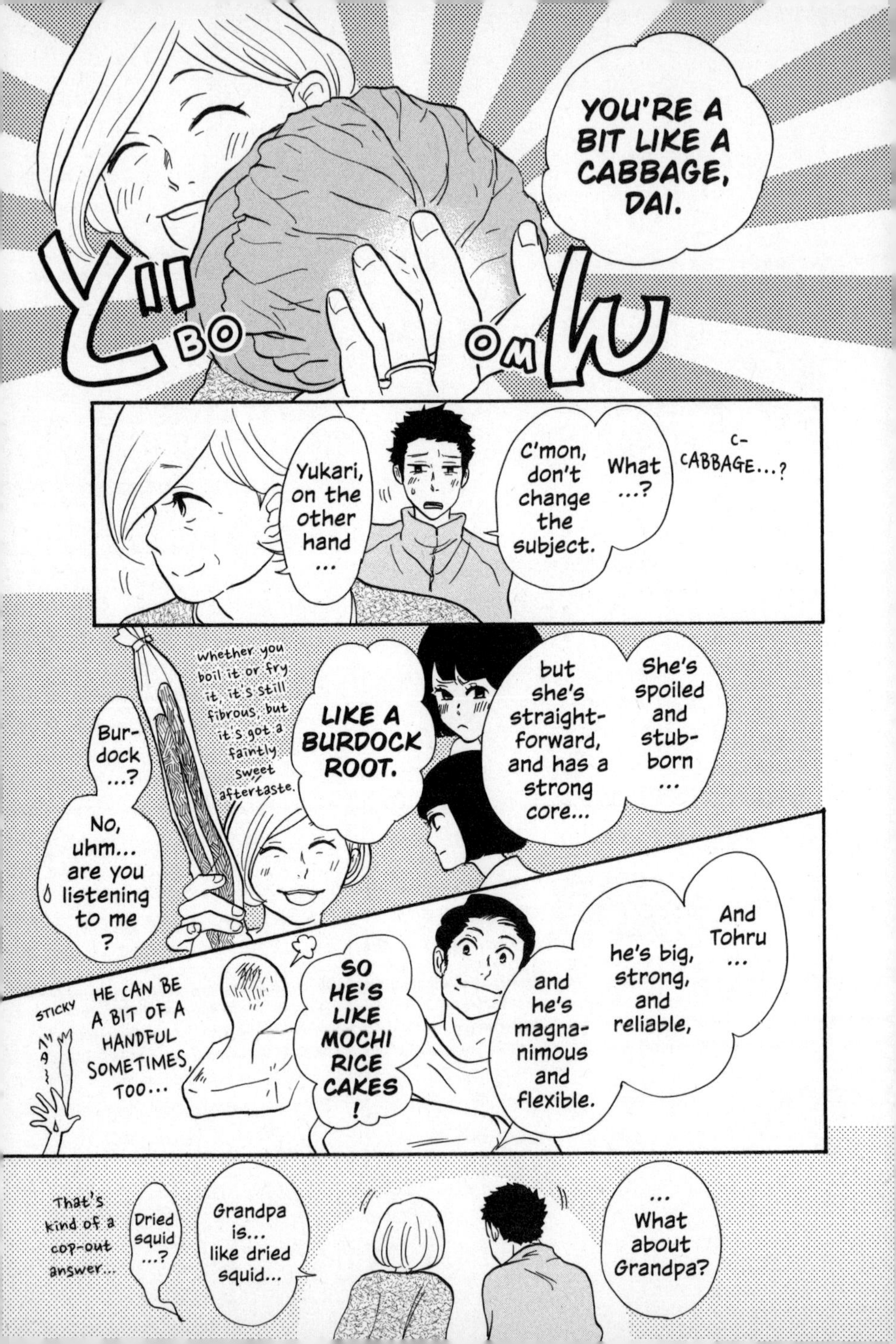
YOU'RE A BIT LIKE A CABBAGE, DAI.
BOOM
C-CABBAGE...?
What ...?
C'mon, don't change the subject.
Yukari, on the other hand ...
She's spoiled and stubborn ...
but she's straightforward, and has a strong core...
LIKE A BURDOCK ROOT.
Whether you boil it or fry it, it's still fibrous, but it's got a faintly sweet aftertaste.
Burdock ...?
No, uhm... are you listening to me ?
And Tohru ...
he's big, strong, and reliable,
and he's magnanimous and flexible.
SO HE'S LIKE MOCHI RICE CAKES !
HE CAN BE A BIT OF A HANDFUL SOMETIMES, TOO...
STICKY
... What about Grandpa?
Grandpa is... like dried squid...
Dried squid ...?
That's kind of a cop-out answer...

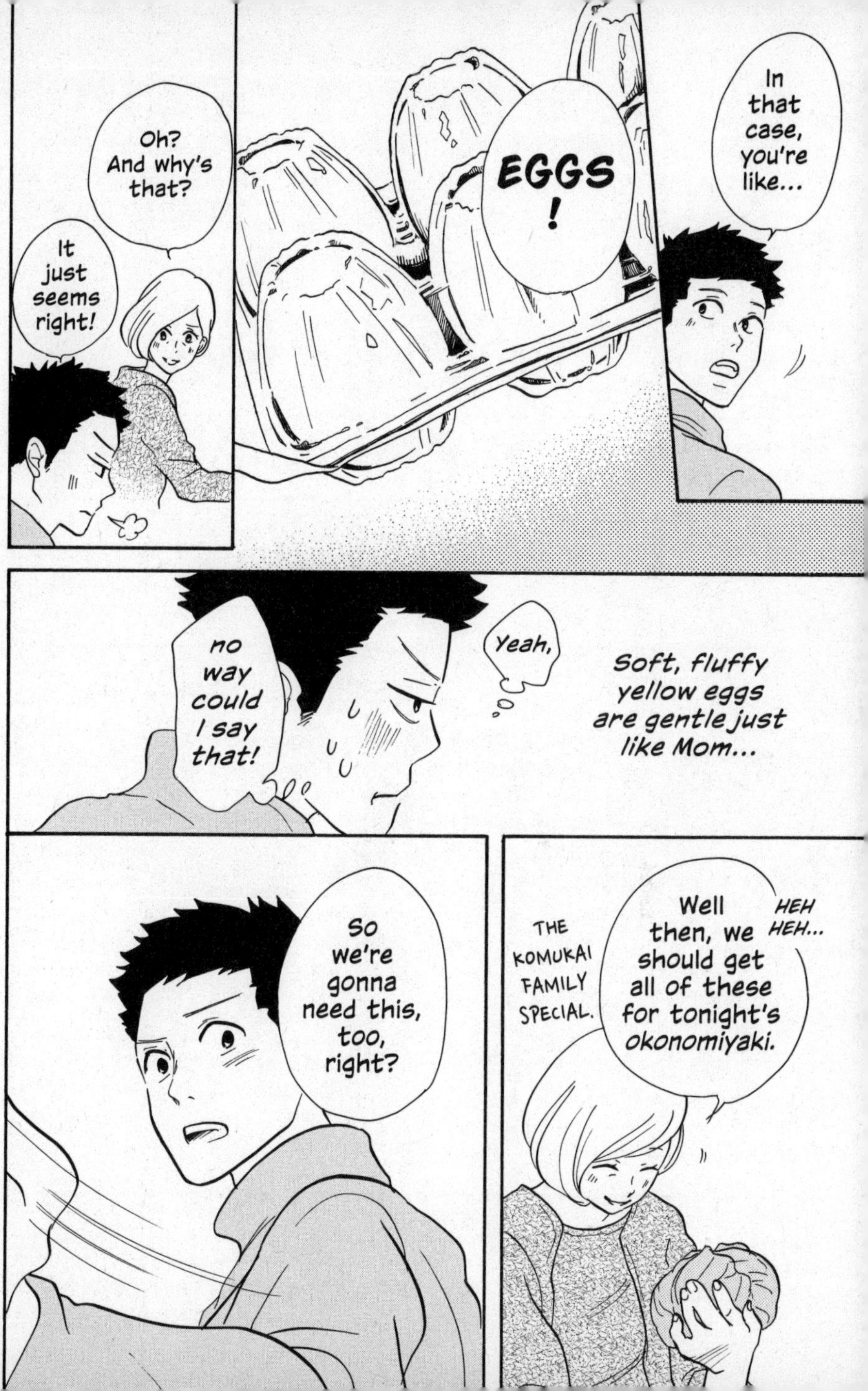
In that case, you're like...
EGGS!
Oh? And why's that?
It just seems right!
Soft, fluffy yellow eggs are gentle just like Mom...
Yeah,
no way could I say that!
Well then, we should get all of these for tonight's okonomiyaki.
HEH HEH...
THE KOMUKAI FAMILY SPECIAL.
So we're gonna need this, too, right?

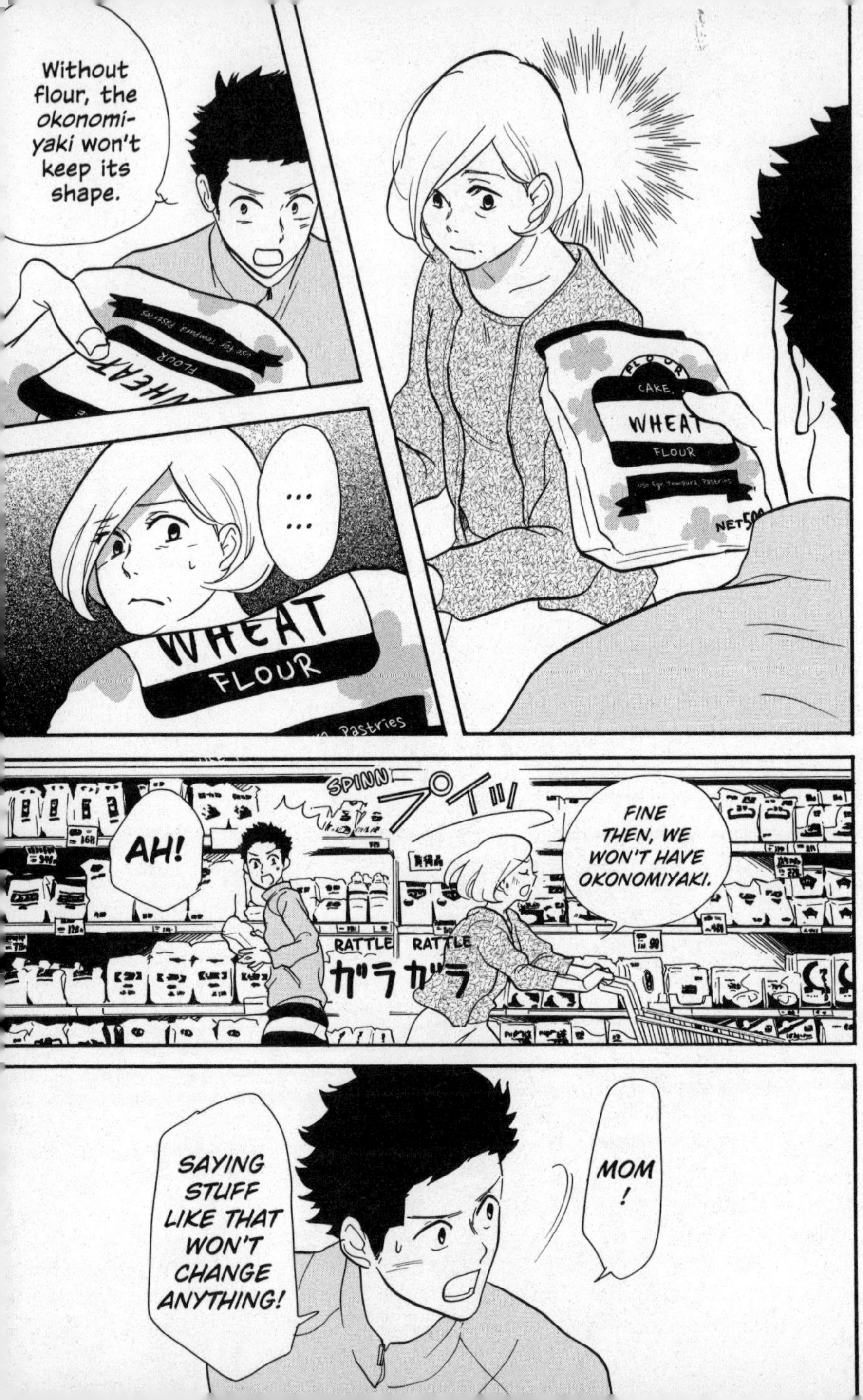
WHEAT
FLOUR
Use for Tempura, Pastries
Without flour, the okonomi-yaki won't keep its shape.
WHEAT
FLOUR
......
WHEAT
FLOUR
FINE THEN, WE WON'T HAVE OKONOMIYAKI.
SPINN
プイッ
AH!
RATTLE RATTLE
ガラガラ
MOM!
SAYING STUFF LIKE THAT WON'T CHANGE ANYTHING!

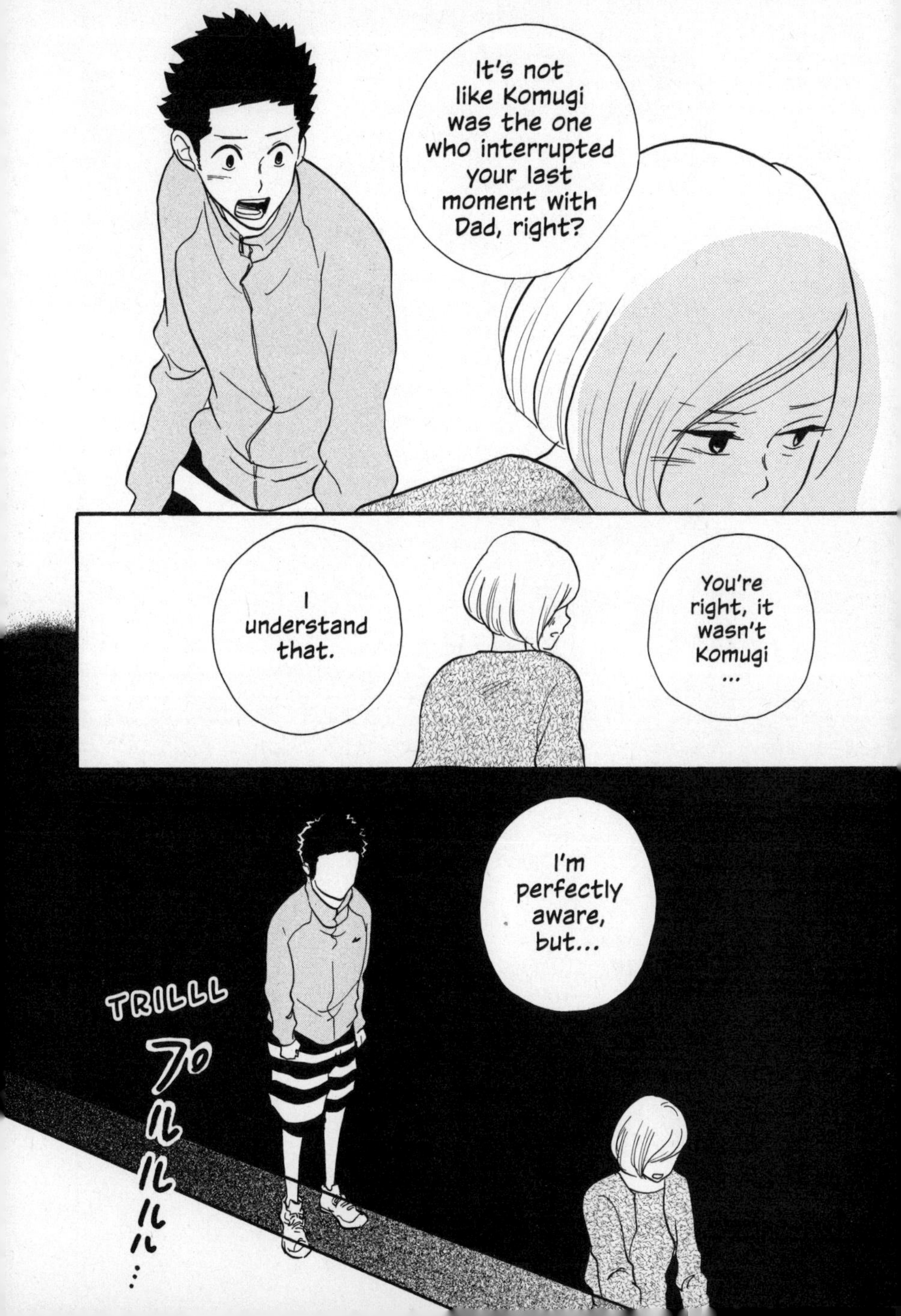
It's not like Komugi was the one who interrupted your last moment with Dad, right?
You're right, it wasn't Komugi ...
I understand that.
I'm perfectly aware, but...
TRILLL
プルルル…

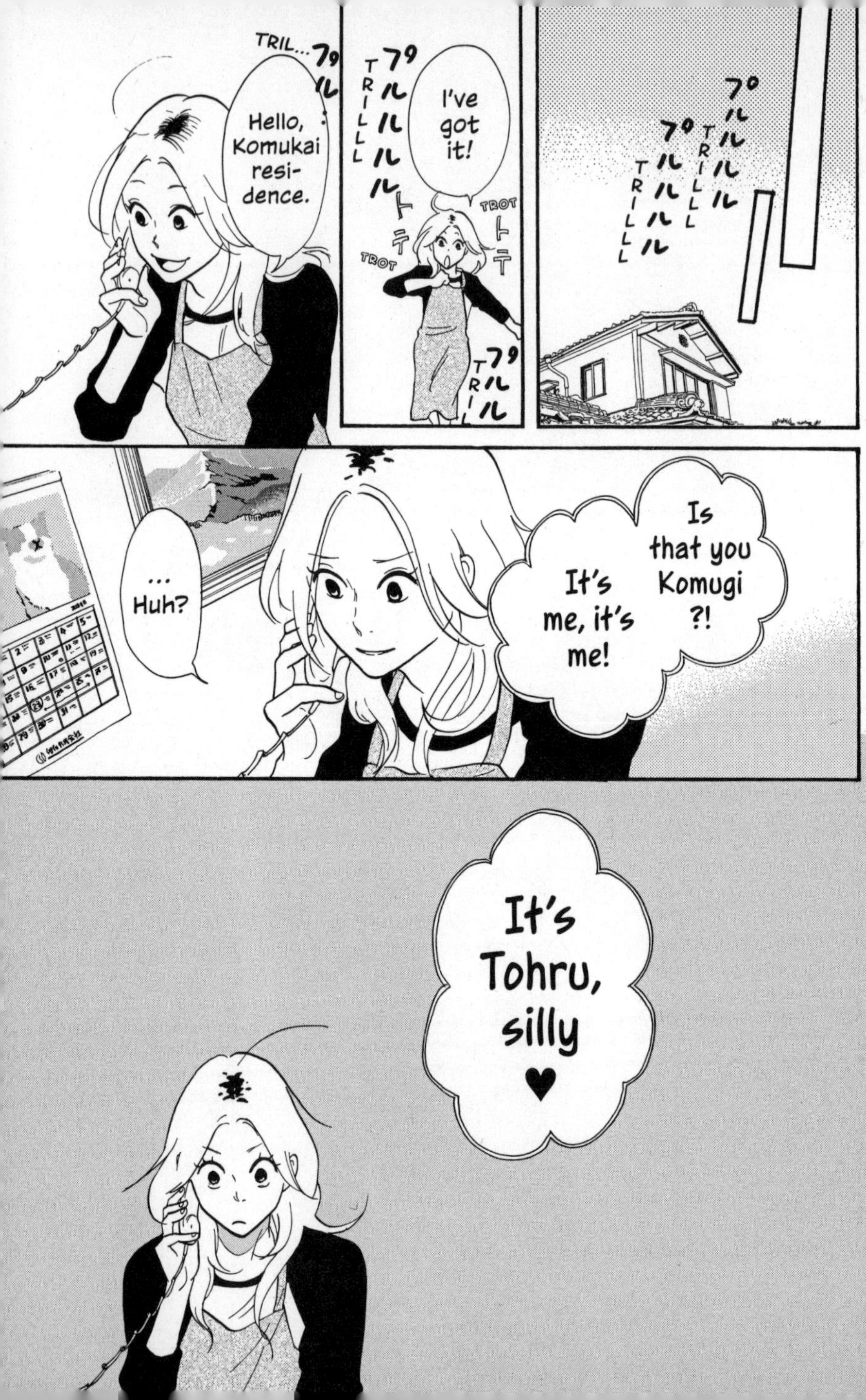
プルルル プルルルル
TRILLL TRILLL
I've got it!
TROT トテ TROT トテ
プルル TRIL
TRIL... プル
Hello, Komukai residence.
プルルルル TRILLL
Is that you Komugi?!
It's me, it's me!
... Huh?
It's Tohru, silly ♥

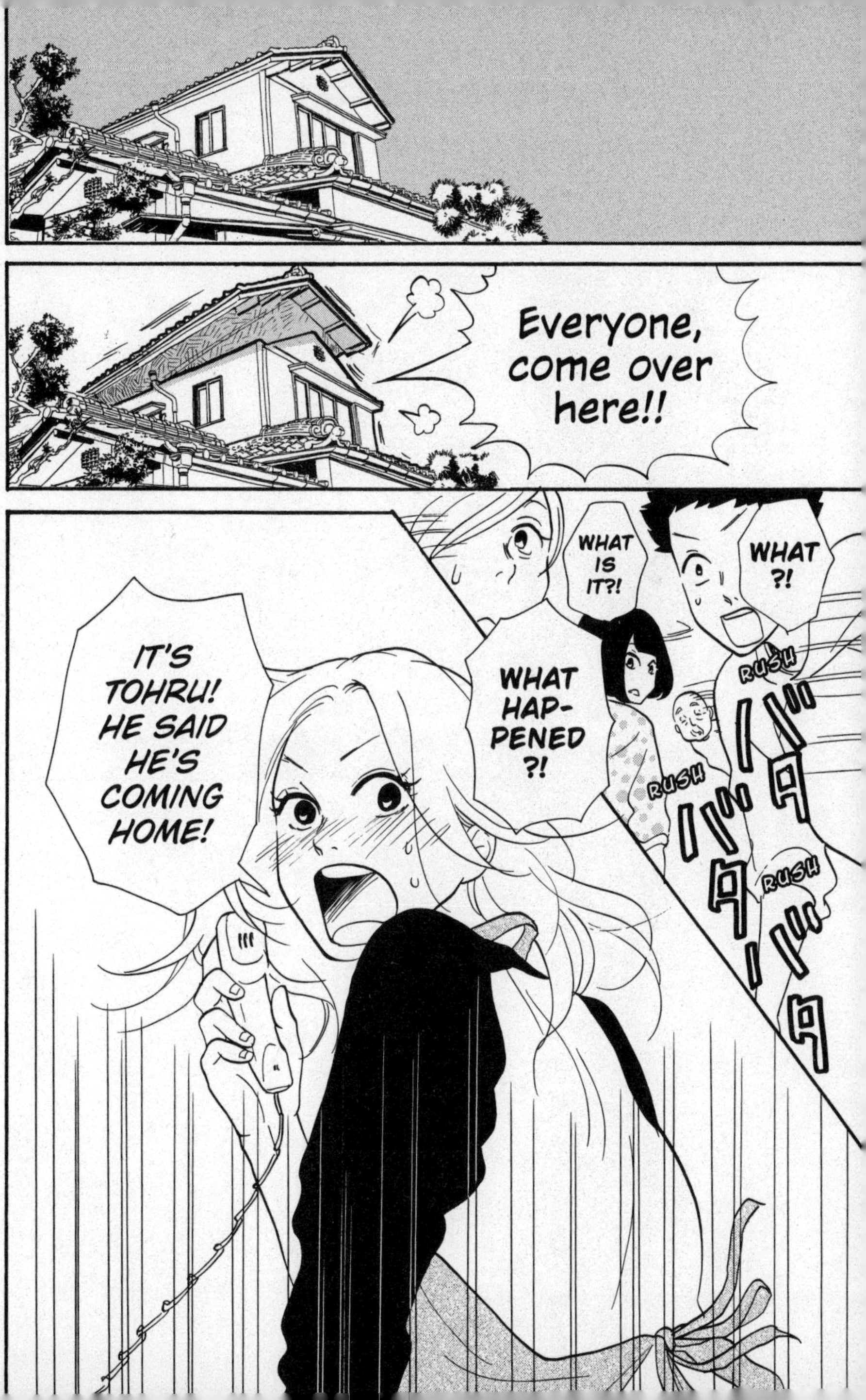
Everyone, come over here!!
WHAT ?!
WHAT IS IT?!
RUSH
RUSH
RUSH
WHAT HAPPENED ?!
IT'S TOHRU! HE SAID HE'S COMING HOME!

34 I TOTALLY HATE YOU, DAI

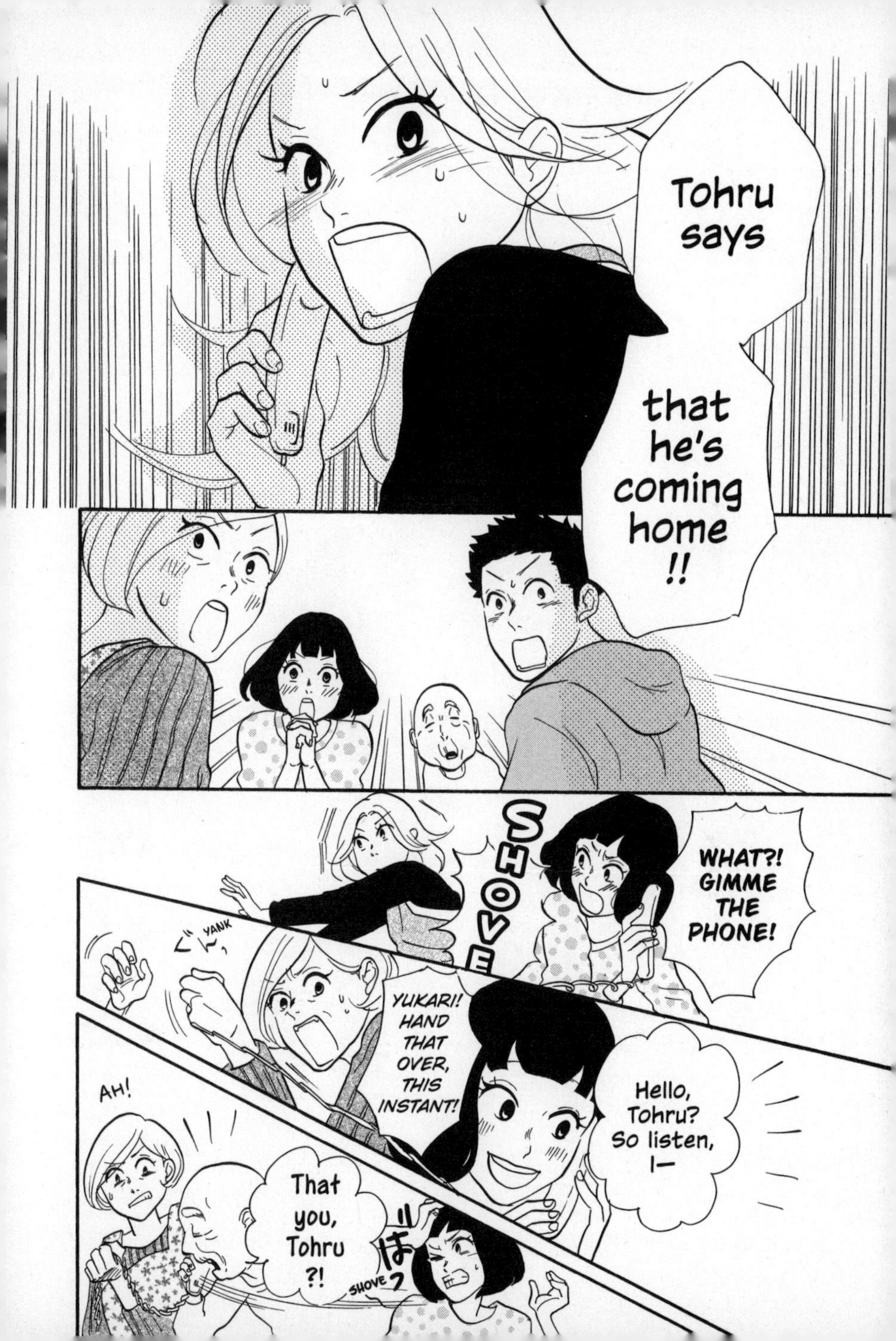
Tohru says that he's coming home !!
SHOVE
WHAT?! GIMME THE PHONE!
YANK
YUKARI! HAND THAT OVER, THIS INSTANT!
Hello, Tohru? So listen, I—
That you, Tohru?!
SHOVE
AH!

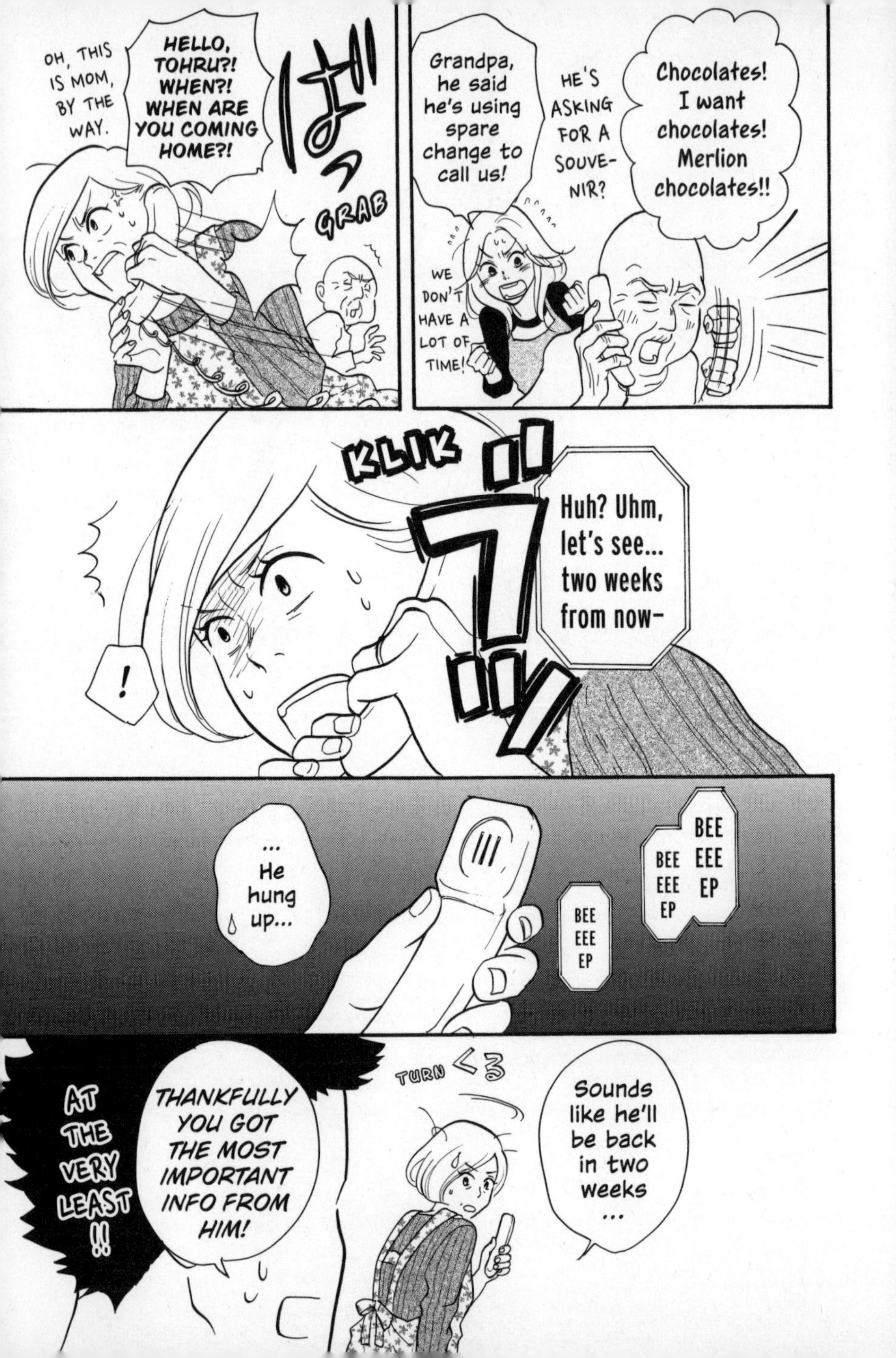

Chocolates! I want chocolates! Merlion chocolates!!
HE'S ASKING FOR A SOUVE-NIR?
Grandpa, he said he's using spare change to call us!
WE DON'T HAVE A LOT OF TIME!
ばっ
GRAB
HELLO, TOHRU?! WHEN?! WHEN ARE YOU COMING HOME?!
OH, THIS IS MOM, BY THE WAY.
Huh? Uhm, let's see... two weeks from now-
KLIK
!
BEE EEE EP
BEE EEE EP
BEE EEE EP
... He hung up...
Sounds like he'll be back in two weeks ...
くる
TURN
THANKFULLY YOU GOT THE MOST IMPORTANT INFO FROM HIM!
AT THE VERY LEAST!!

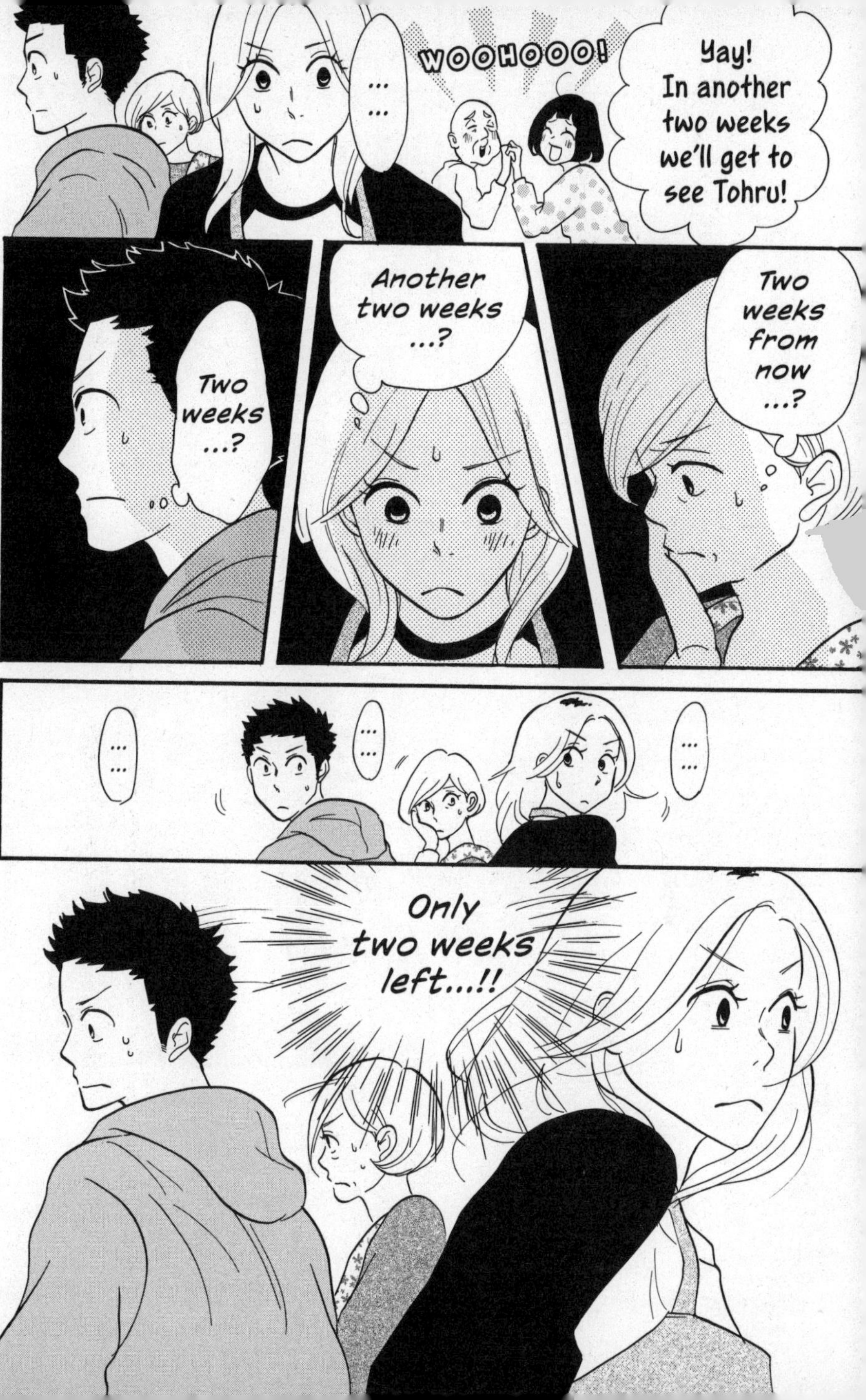
Yay! In another two weeks we'll get to see Tohru!
WOOHOOO!
... ...
Two weeks from now ...?
Another two weeks ...?
Two weeks ...?
... ...
... ...
... ...
Only two weeks left...!!

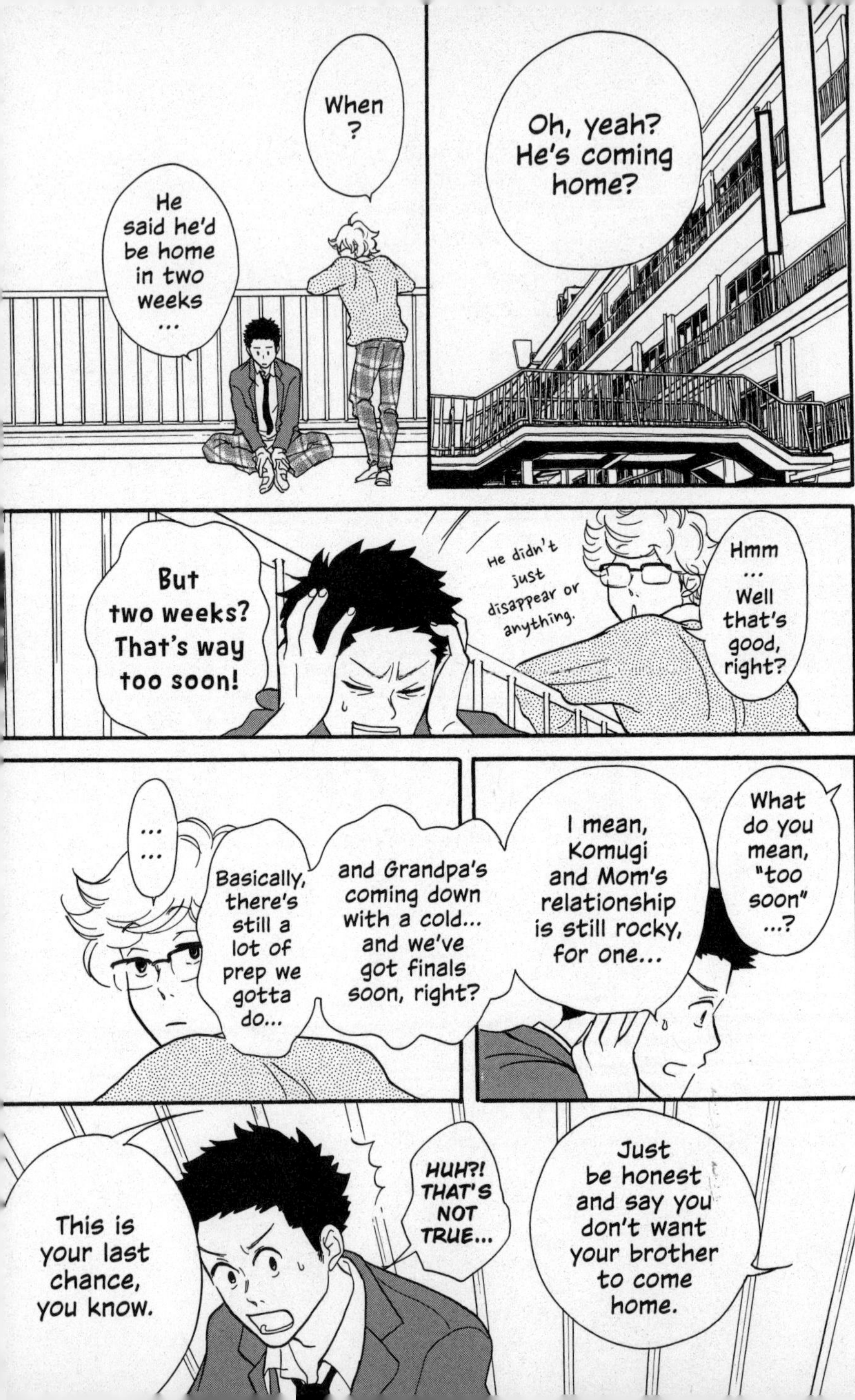

Oh, yeah? He's coming home?
When ?
He said he'd be home in two weeks ...
Hmm ... Well that's good, right?
He didn't just disappear or anything.
But two weeks? That's way too soon!
What do you mean, "too soon" ...?
I mean, Komugi and Mom's relationship is still rocky, for one...
and Grandpa's coming down with a cold... and we've got finals soon, right?
Basically, there's still a lot of prep we gotta do...
... ...
Just be honest and say you don't want your brother to come home.
HUH?! THAT'S NOT TRUE...
This is your last chance, you know.

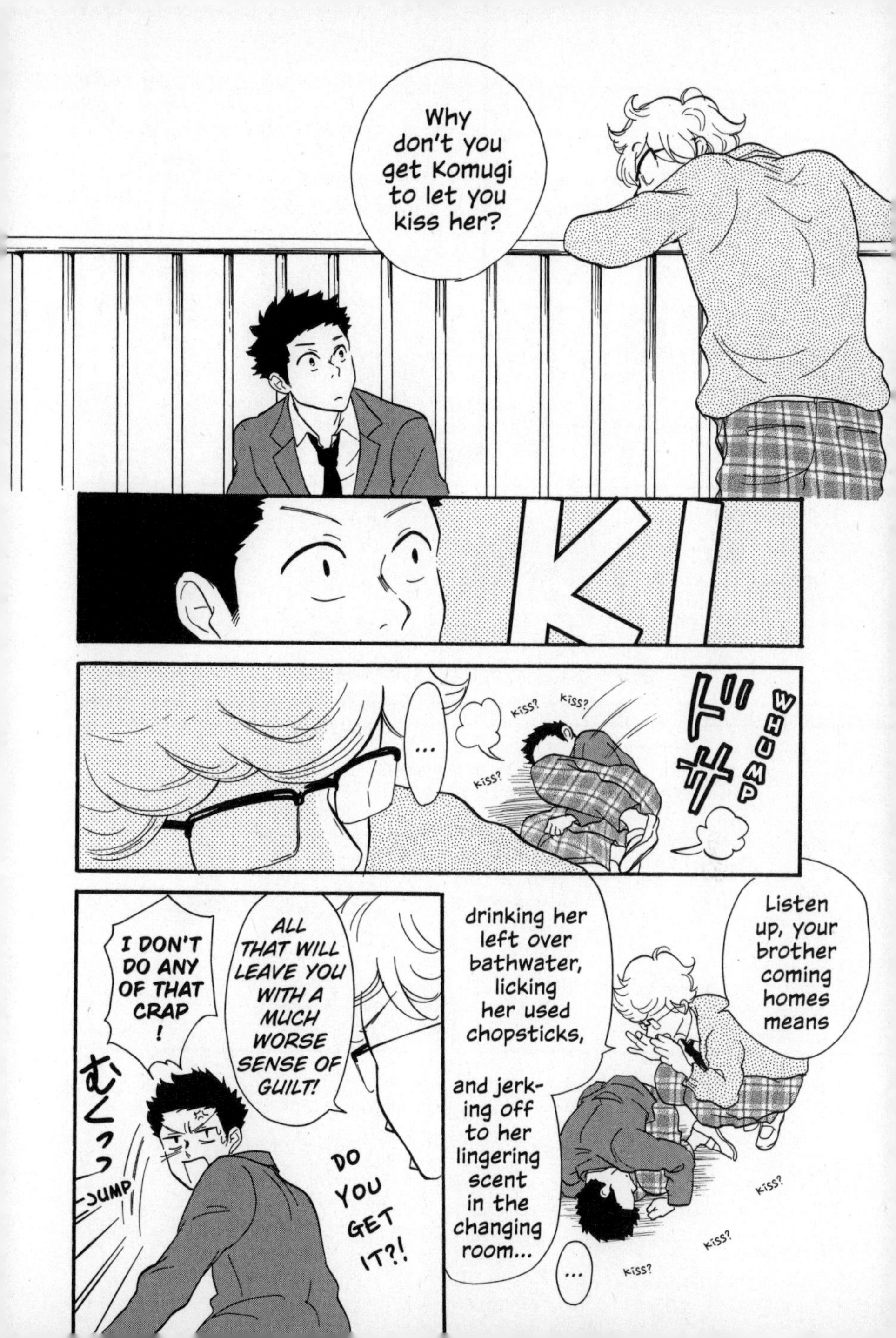
Why don't you get Komugi to let you kiss her?
KI
...
kiss?
kiss?
kiss?
WHUMP
Listen up, your brother coming homes means
drinking her left over bathwater, licking her used chopsticks,
and jerking off to her lingering scent in the changing room...
...
kiss?
kiss?
kiss?
ALL THAT WILL LEAVE YOU WITH A MUCH WORSE SENSE OF GUILT!
DO YOU GET IT?!
I DON'T DO ANY OF THAT CRAP!
むくっ
JUMP

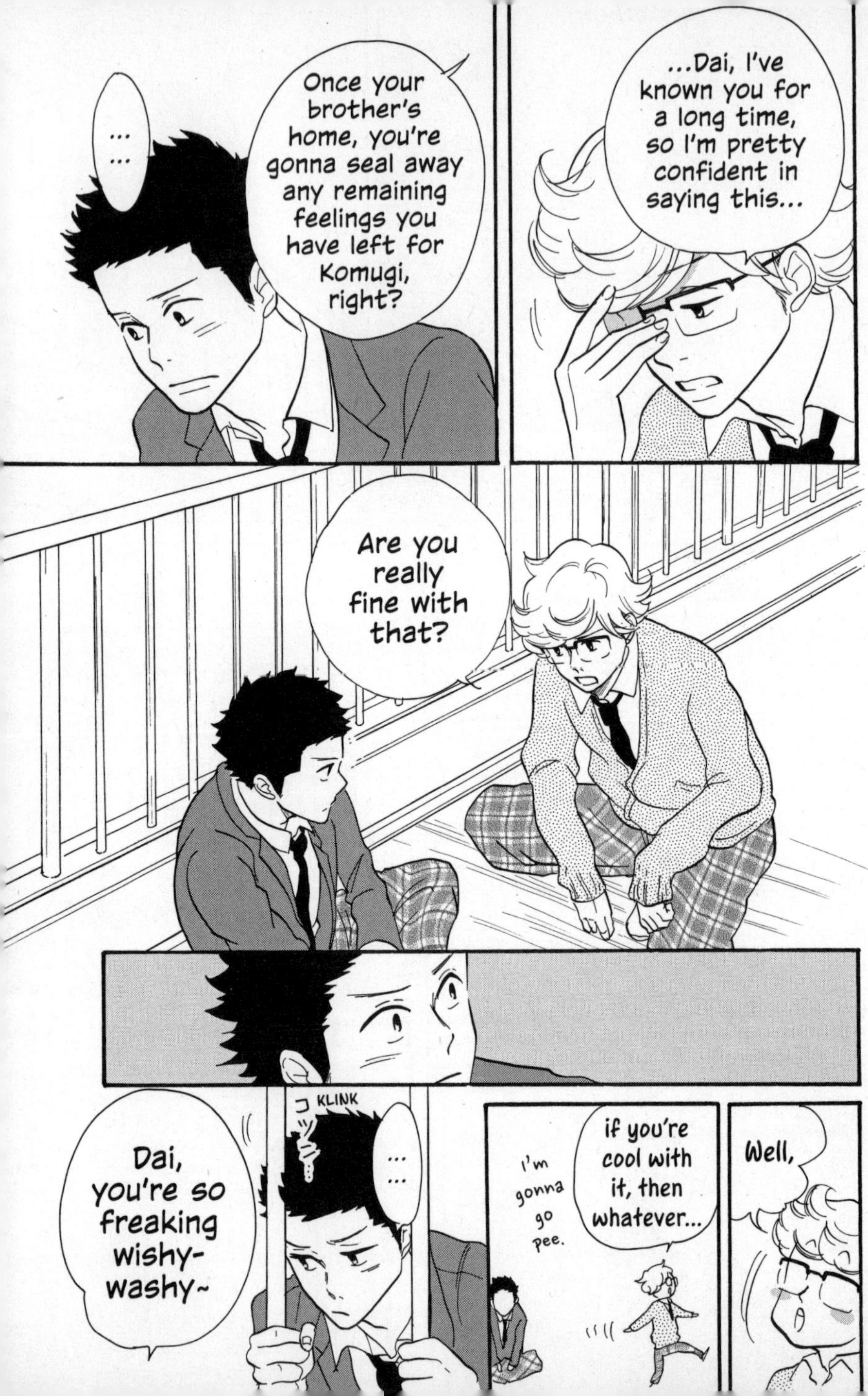
...Dai, I've known you for a long time, so I'm pretty confident in saying this...
Once your brother's home, you're gonna seal away any remaining feelings you have left for Komugi, right?
... ...
Are you really fine with that?
Well,
if you're cool with it, then whatever...
I'm gonna go pee.
... ...
KLINK
Dai, you're so freaking wishy-washy~

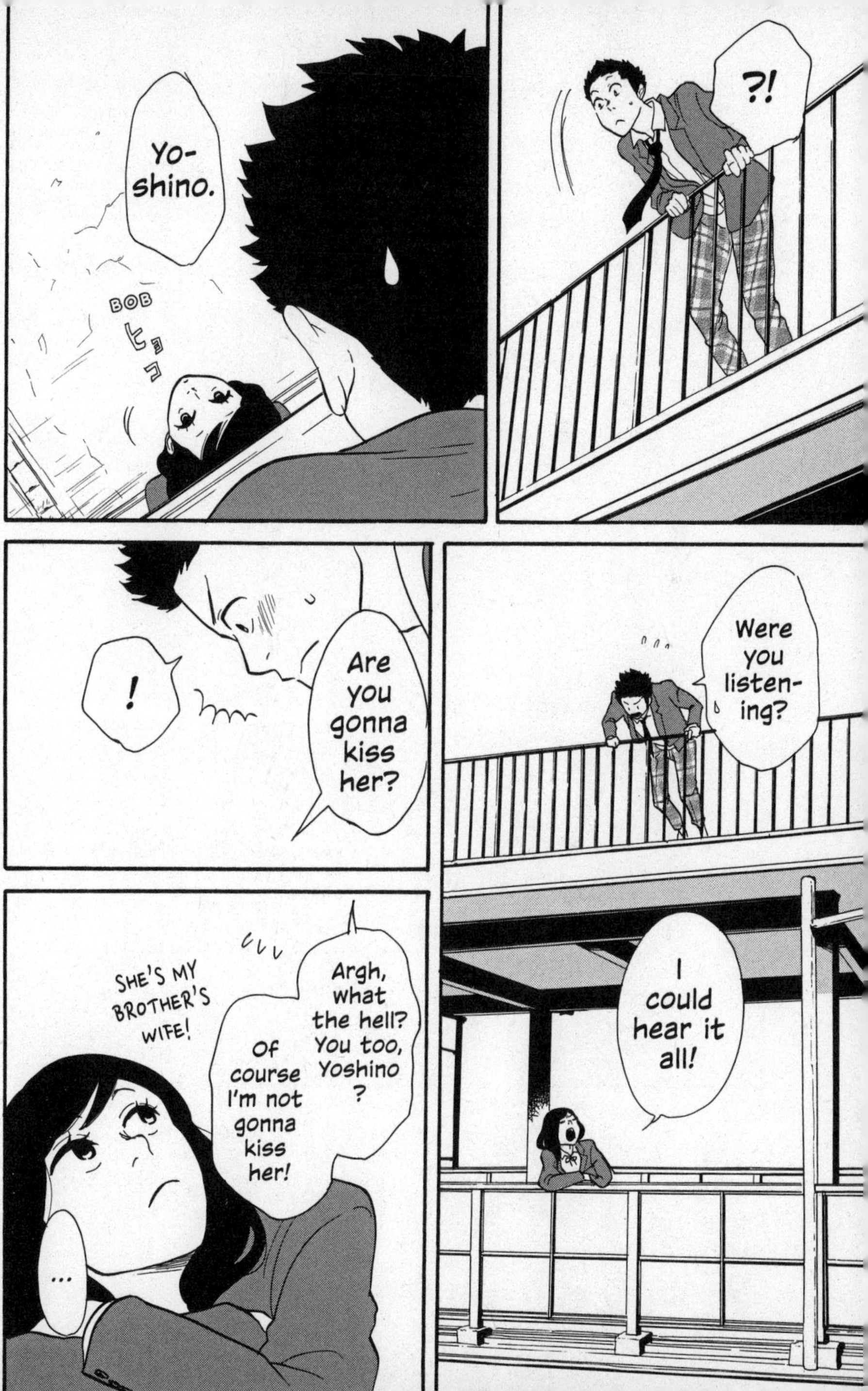
?!
Yo-shino.
BOB
ヒョコ
Were you listening?
I could hear it all!
Are you gonna kiss her?
!
Argh, what the hell? You too, Yoshino?
Of course I'm not gonna kiss her!
SHE'S MY BROTHER'S WIFE!
...

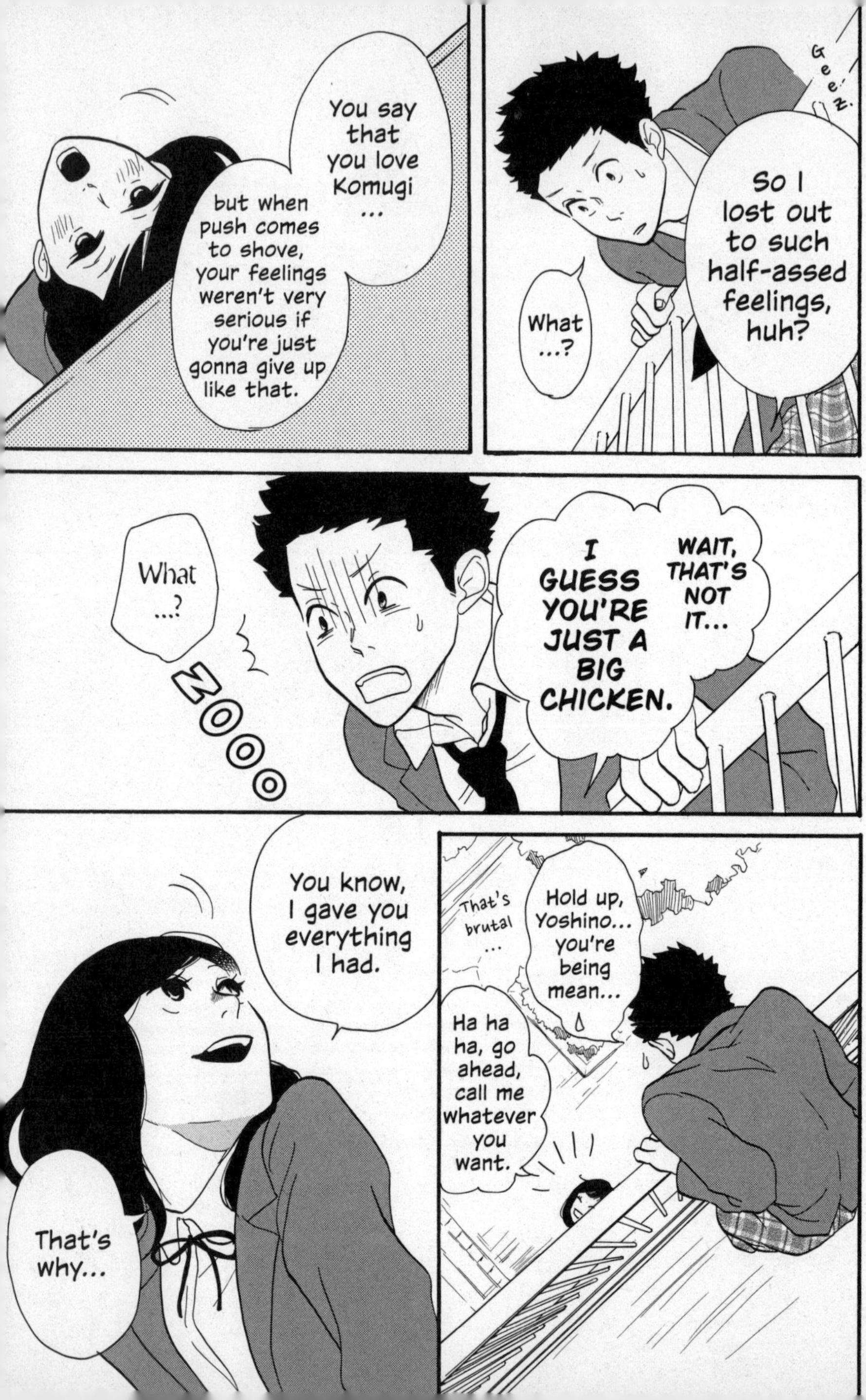
Geez.
So I lost out to such half-assed feelings, huh?
What...?
You say that you love Komugi...
but when push comes to shove, your feelings weren't very serious if you're just gonna give up like that.
WAIT, THAT'S NOT IT...
I GUESS YOU'RE JUST A BIG CHICKEN.
What...?
ZOOOO
Hold up, Yoshino... you're being mean...
That's brutal...
Ha ha ha, go ahead, call me whatever you want.
You know, I gave you everything I had.
That's why...

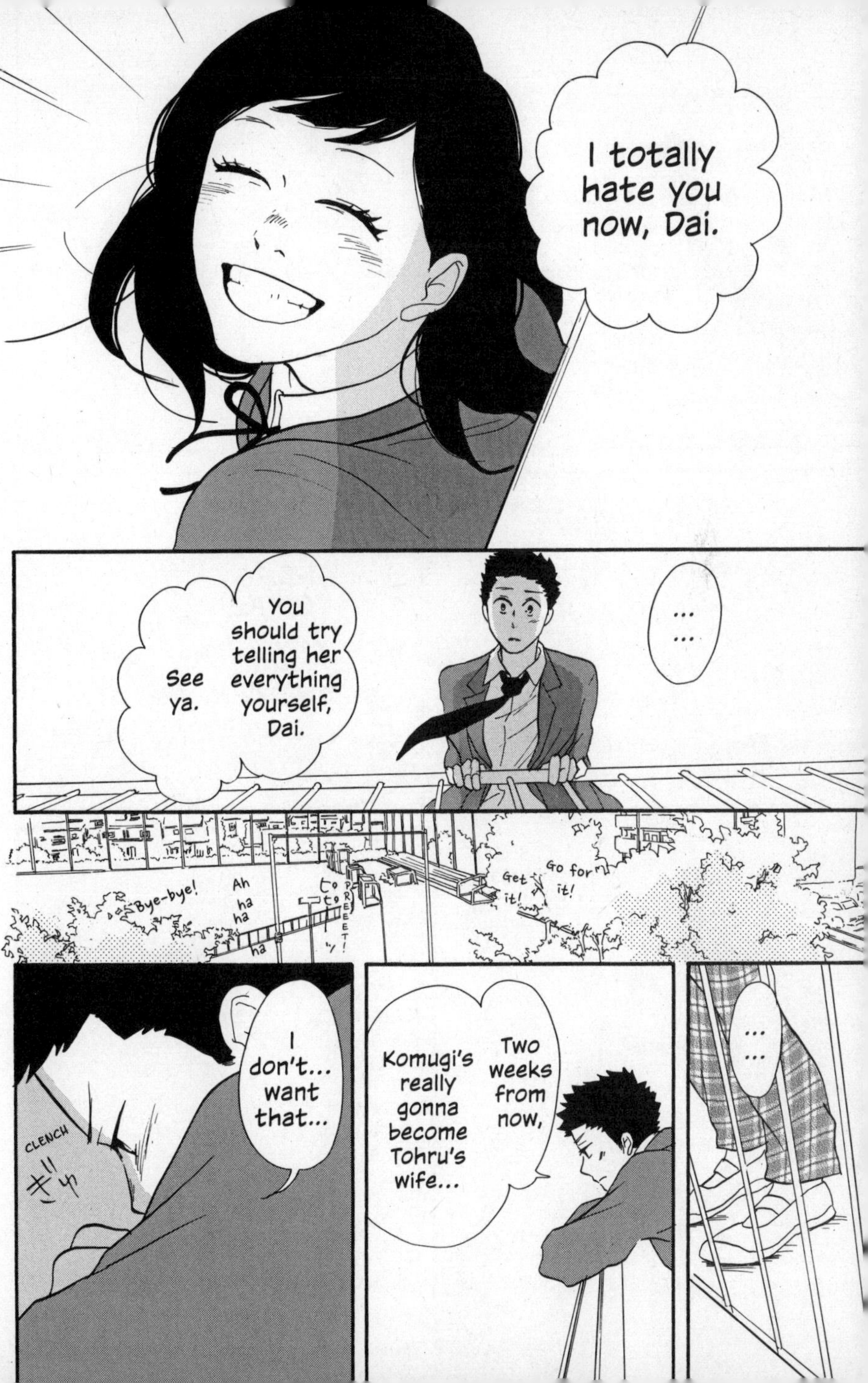
I totally hate you now, Dai.
... ...
You should try telling her everything yourself, Dai.
See ya.
Go for it!
Get it!
PREEEET!
to to
Ah ha ha ha
Bye-bye!
... ...
Two weeks from now,
Komugi's really gonna become Tohru's wife...
I don't... want that...
CLENCH

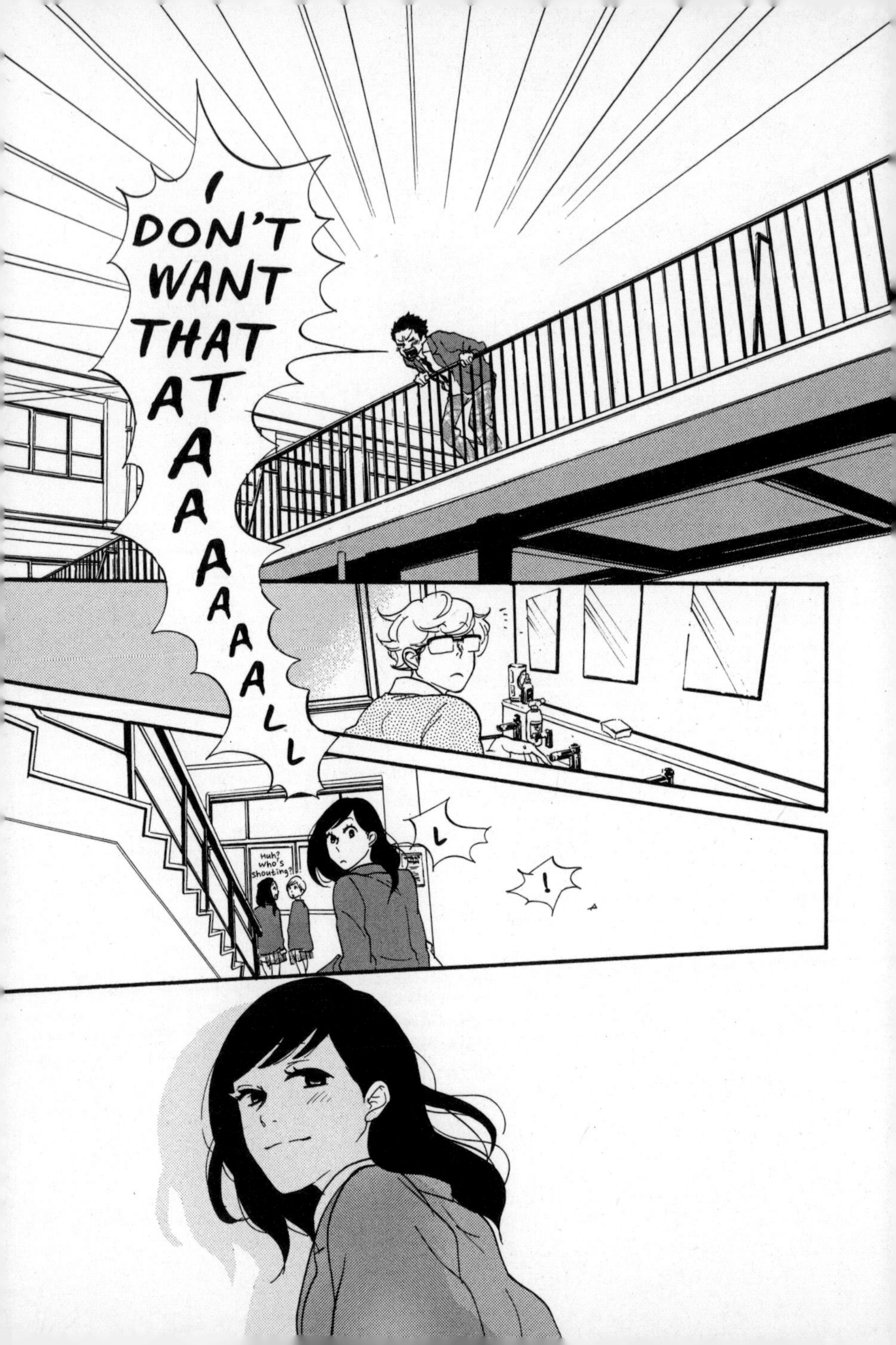
I DON'T WANT THAT AT AAAAAALLL
L
!
Huh? who's shouting?

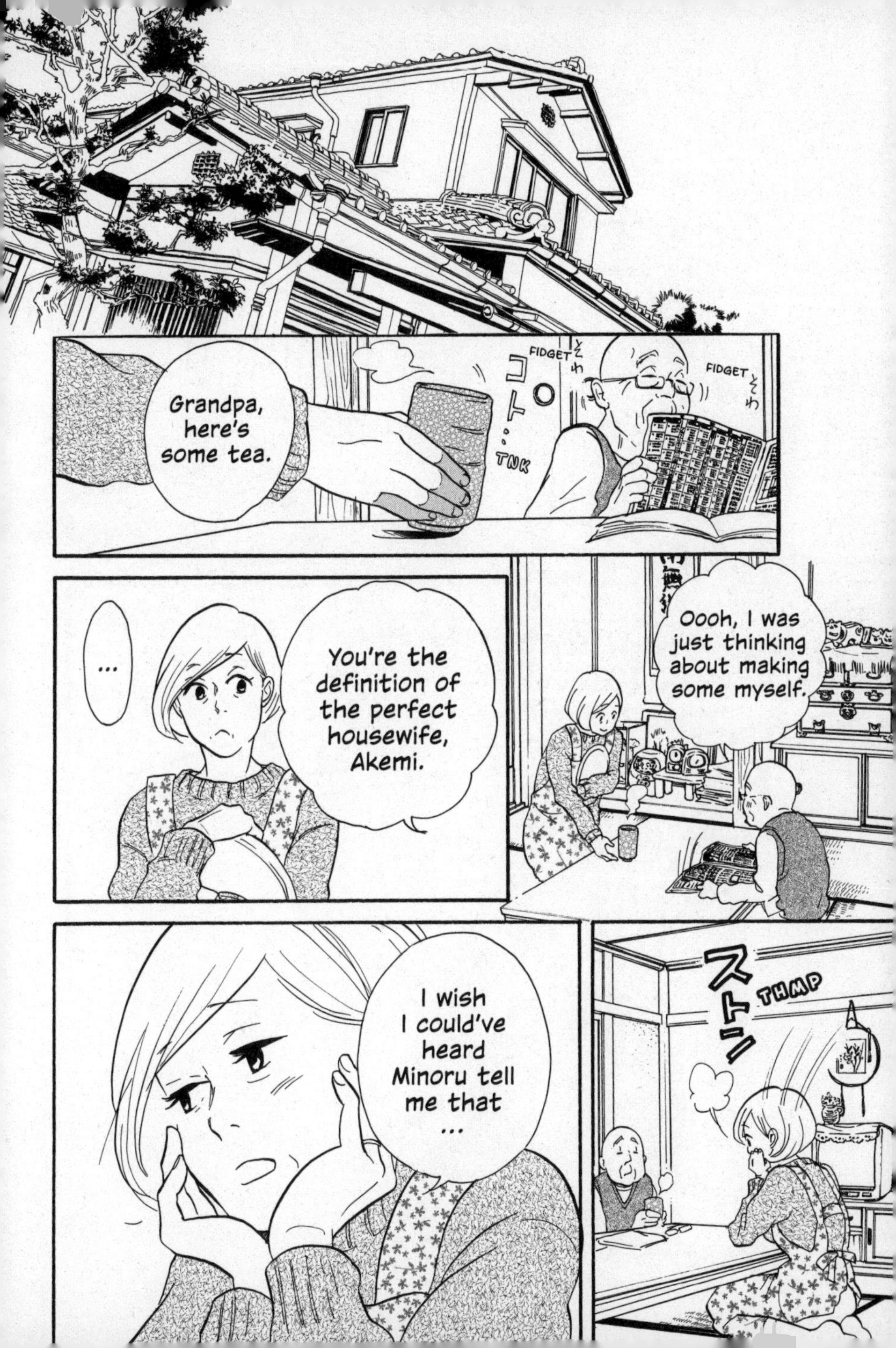
FIDGET
FIDGET
TNK
Grandpa, here's some tea.
Oooh, I was just thinking about making some myself.
You're the definition of the perfect housewife, Akemi.
...
THMP
I wish I could've heard Minoru tell me that ...

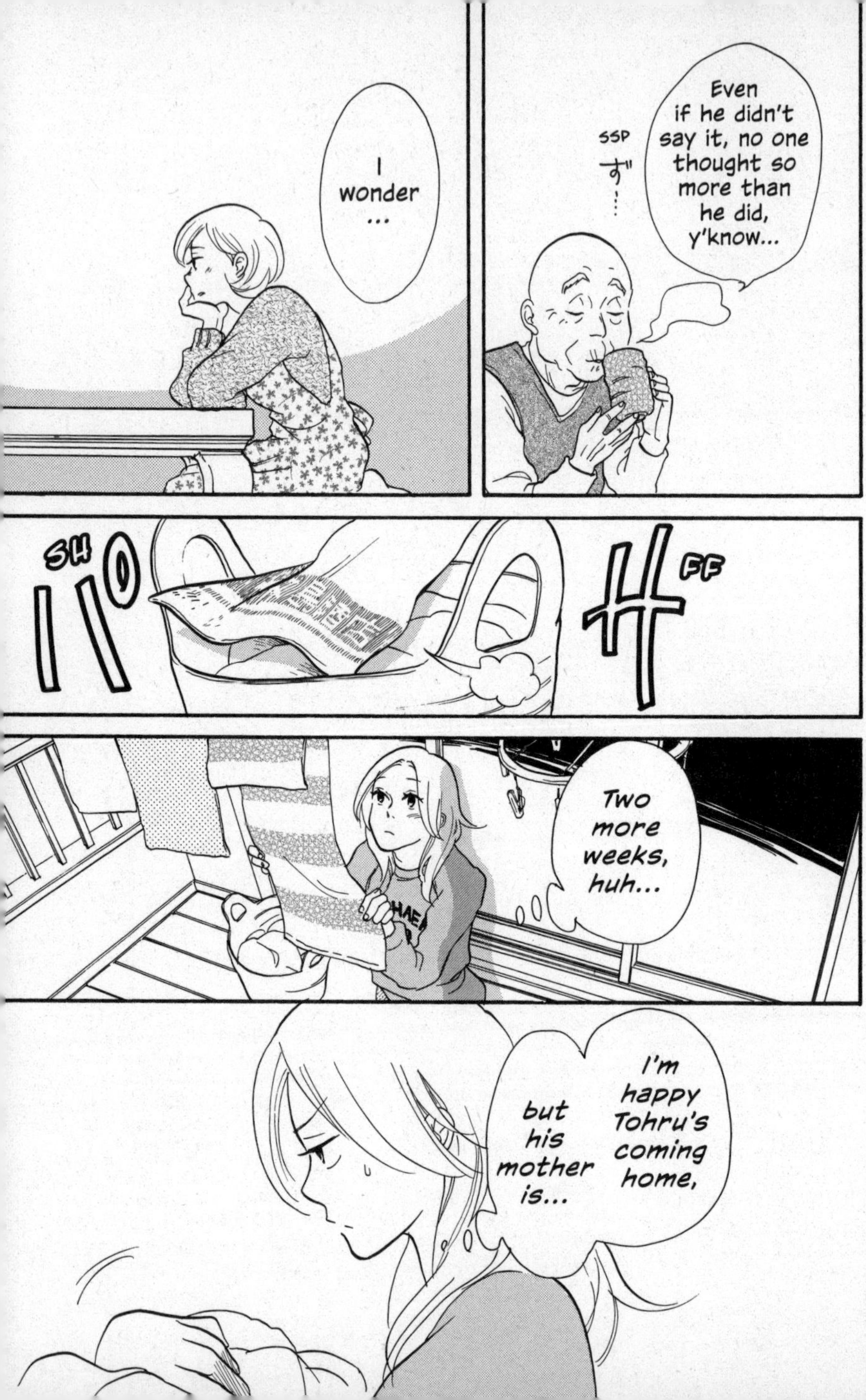
Even if he didn't say it, no one thought so more than he did, y'know...
SSP
ず…
I wonder ...
SH
FF
Two more weeks, huh...
I'm happy Tohru's coming home,
but his mother is...

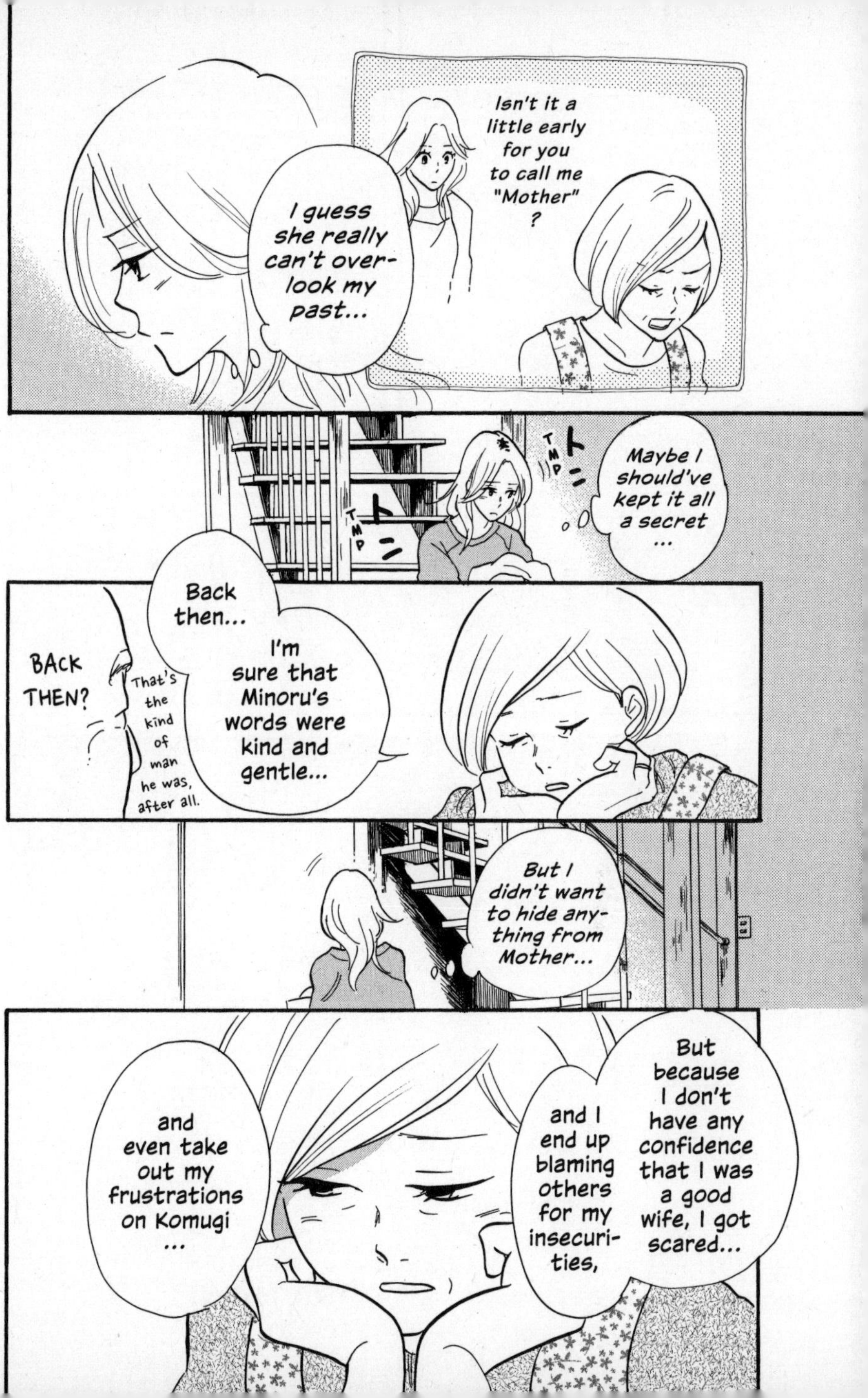
Isn't it a little early for you to call me "Mother" ?
I guess she really can't overlook my past...
TMP
TMP
Maybe I should've kept it all a secret ...
Back then...
I'm sure that Minoru's words were kind and gentle...
That's the kind of man he was, after all.
BACK THEN?
But I didn't want to hide anything from Mother...
But because I don't have any confidence that I was a good wife, I got scared...
and I end up blaming others for my insecurities,
and even take out my frustrations on Komugi ...

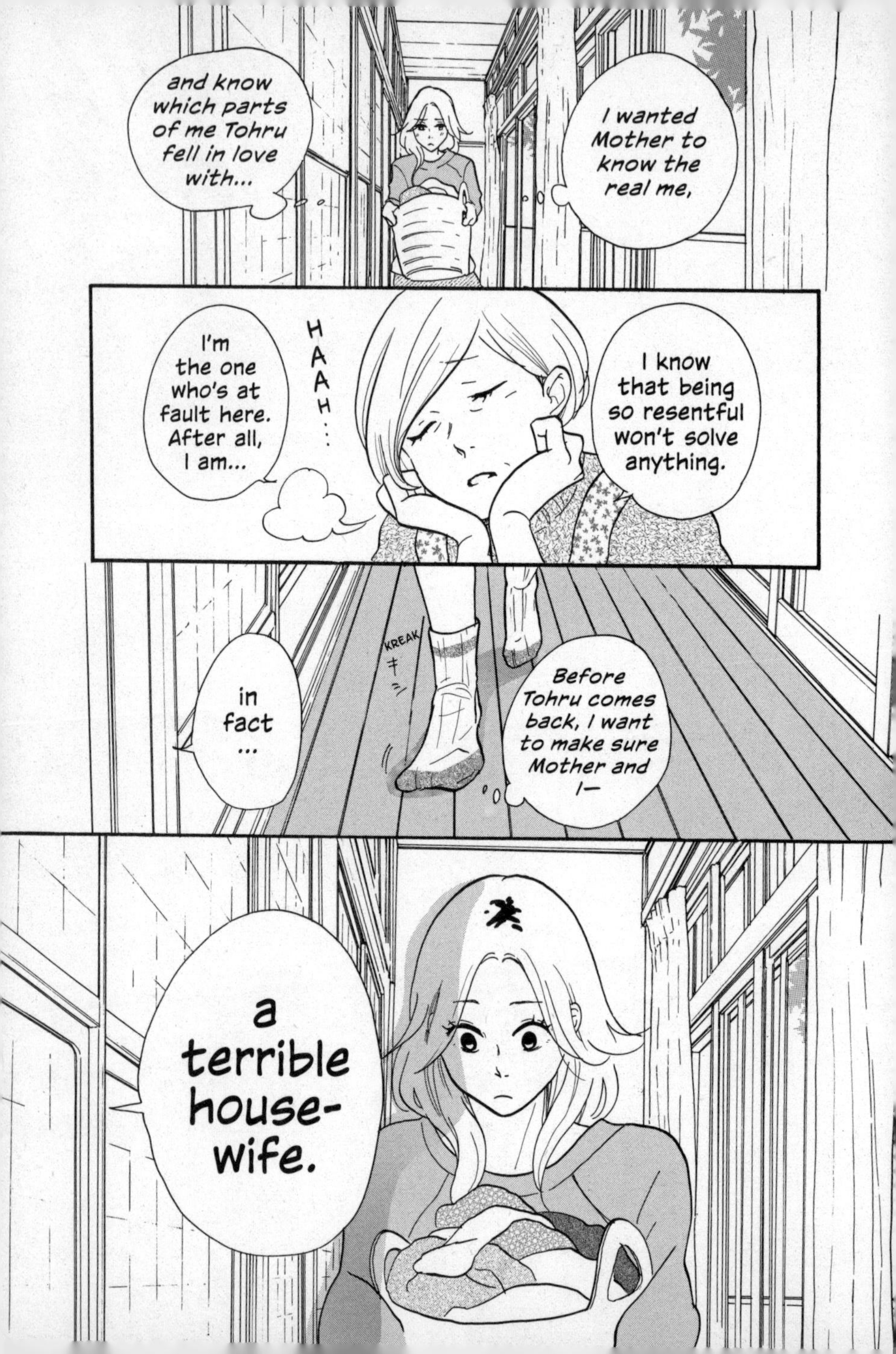
I wanted Mother to know the real me,
and know which parts of me Tohru fell in love with...
I know that being so resentful won't solve anything.
HAAH...
I'm the one who's at fault here. After all, I am...
Before Tohru comes back, I want to make sure Mother and I—
KREAK
in fact ...
a terrible house-wife.

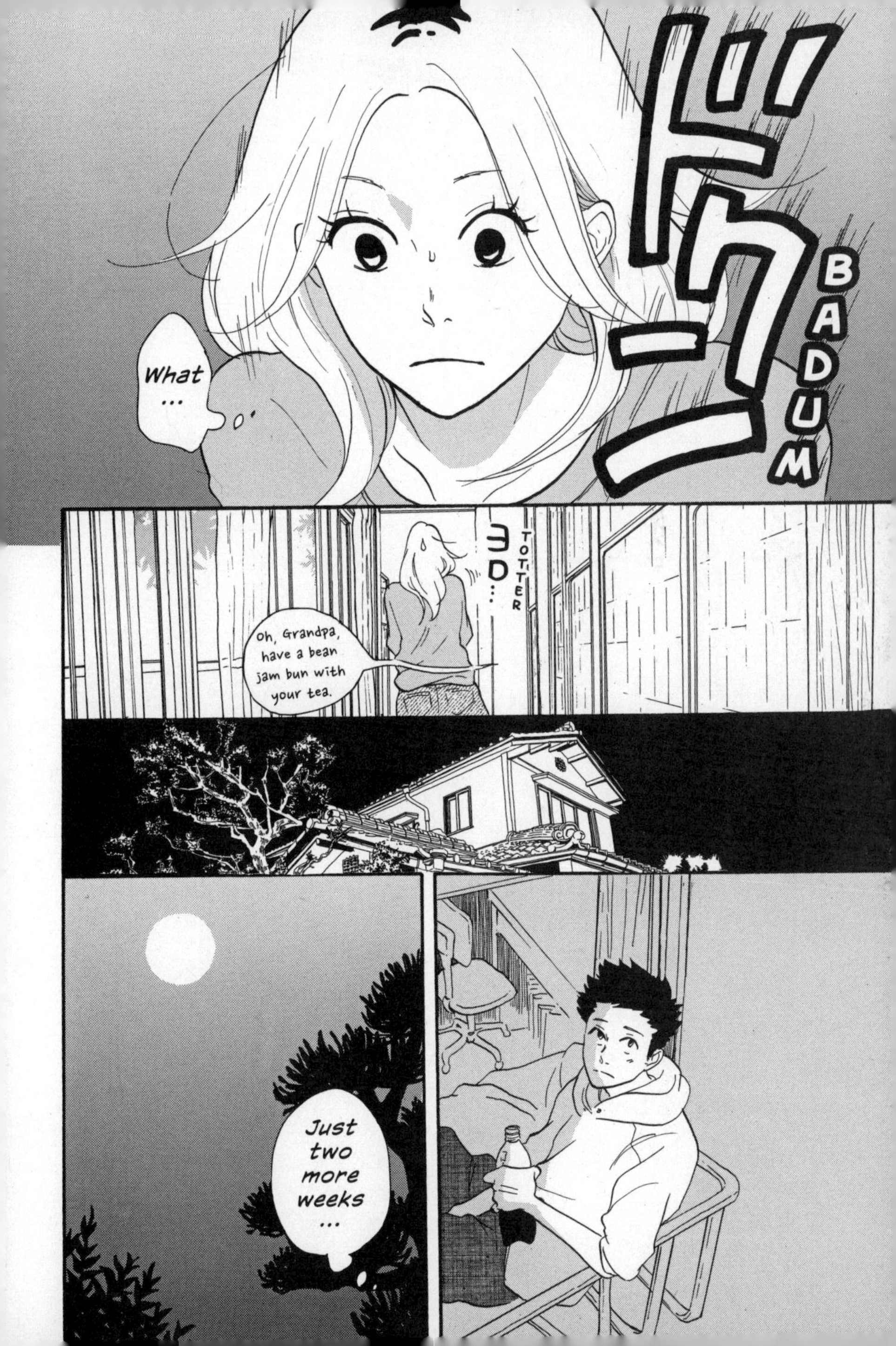

ドクン
BADUM
What ...
ヨロ…
TOTTER
Oh, Grandpa, have a bean jam bun with your tea.
Just two more weeks ...

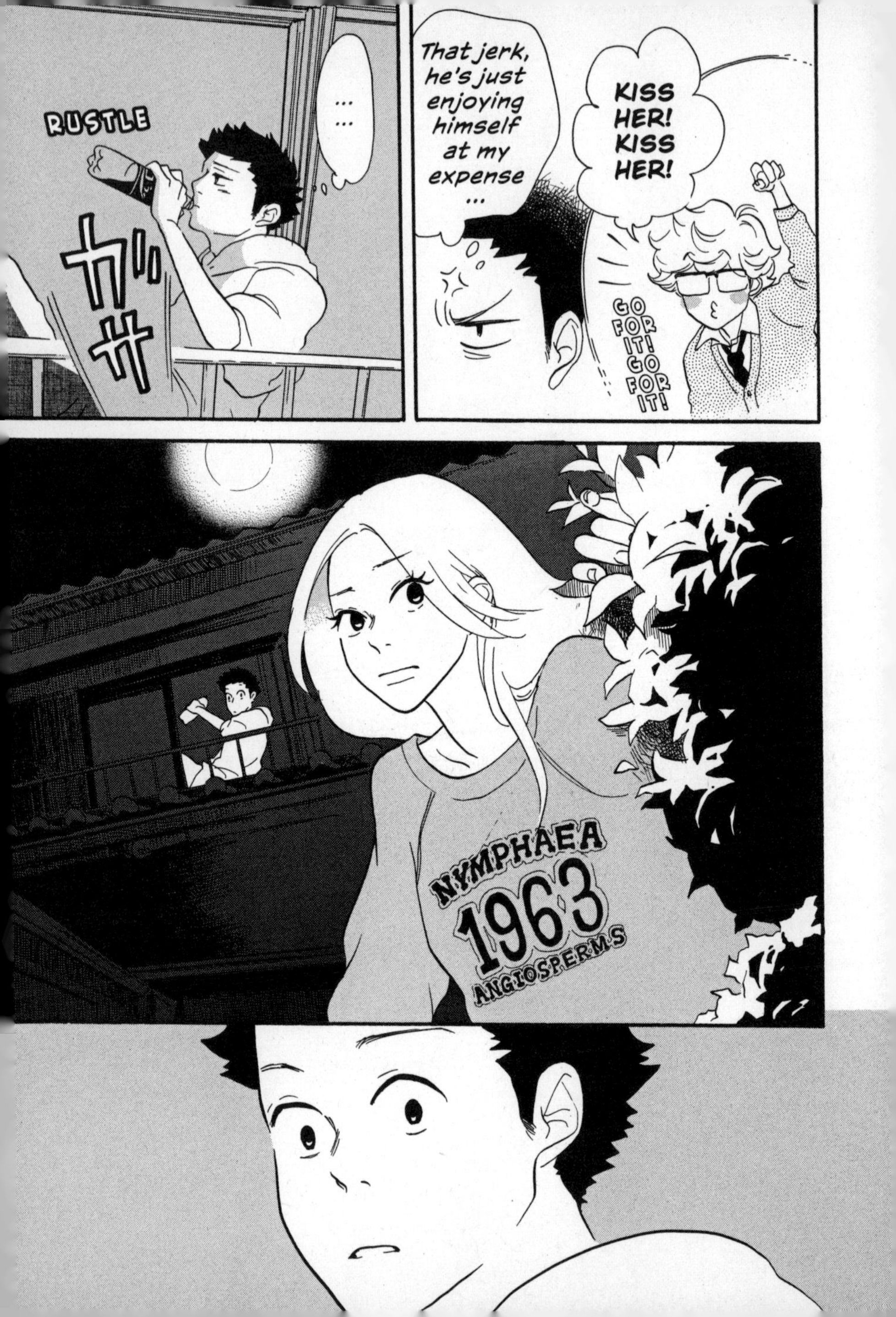
KISS HER! KISS HER!
That jerk, he's just enjoying himself at my expense ...
GO FOR IT! GO FOR IT!
... ...
RUSTLE
NYMPHAEA
1963
ANGIOSPERMS

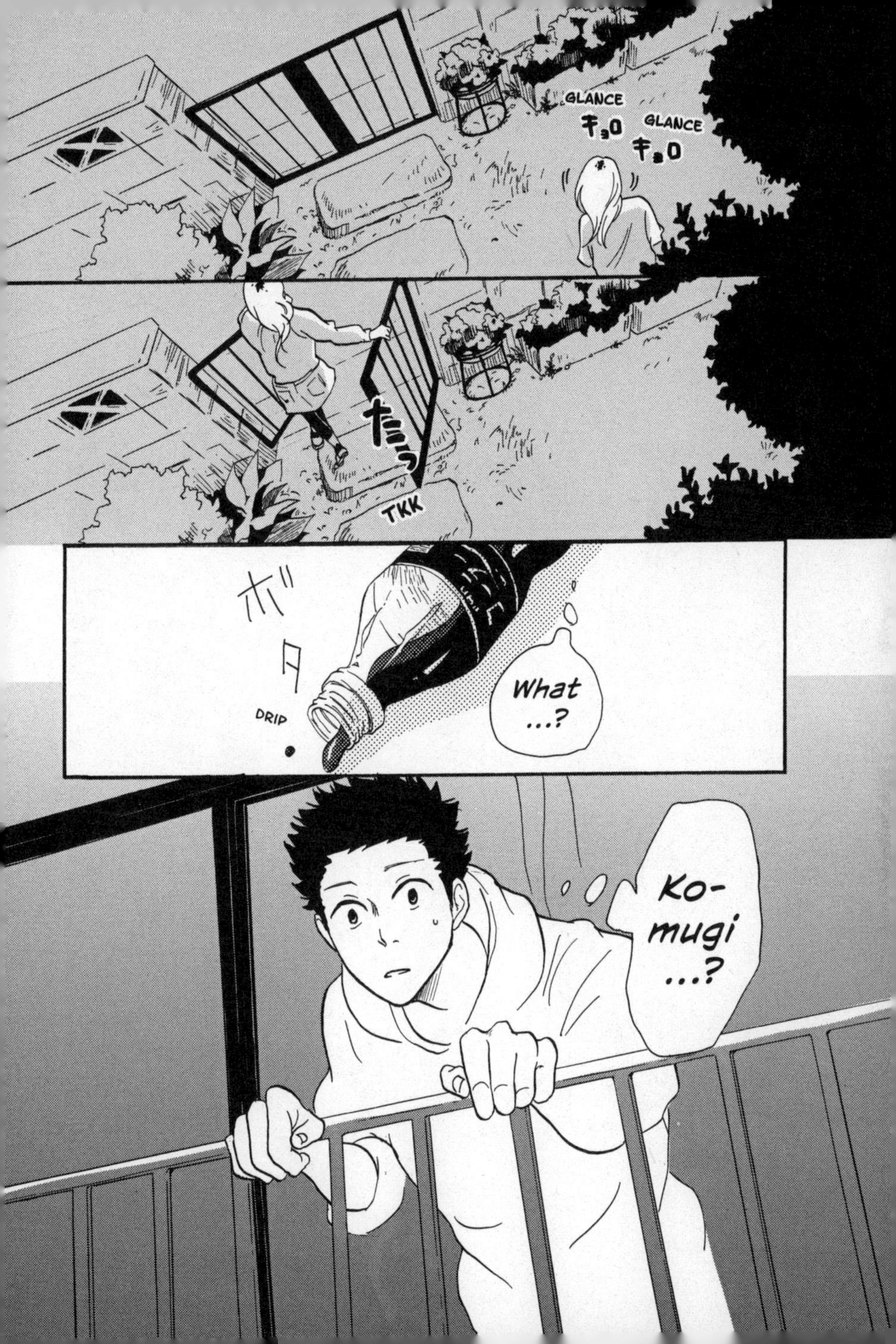
GLANCE
キョロ
GLANCE
キョロ
TKK
ボタ
DRIP
What ...?
Ko-mugi ...?

35 # SEASIDE AT NIGHT, TOGETHER

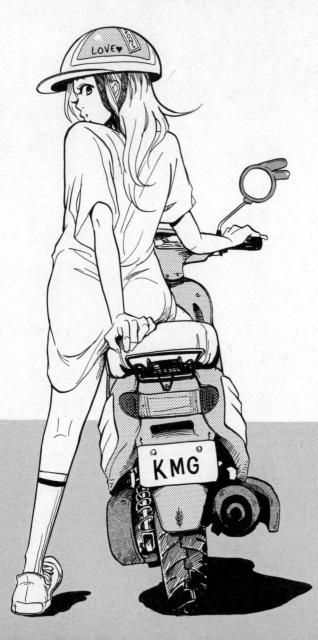

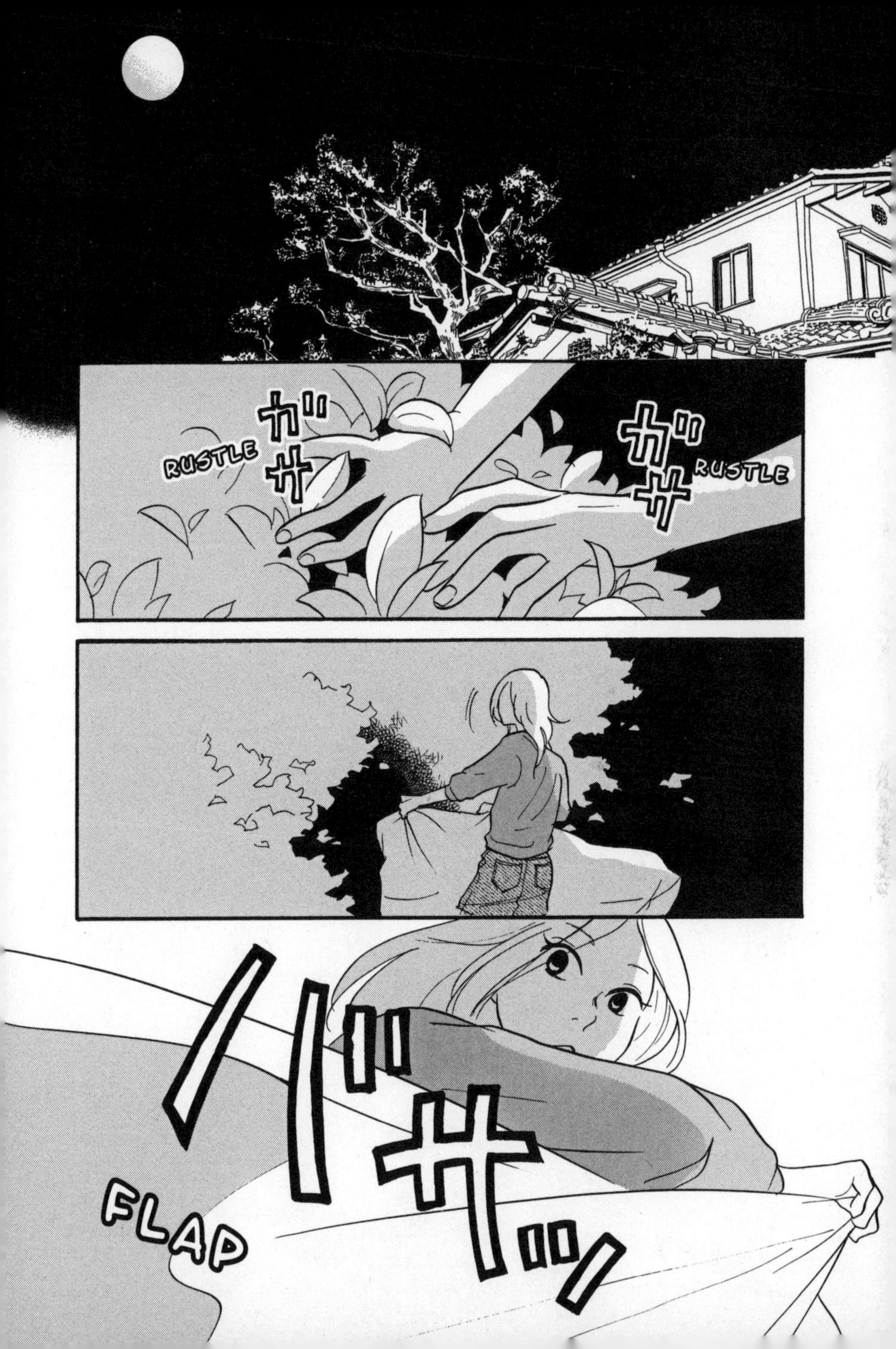
ガサ
RUSTLE
RUSTLE
ガサ
バサッ
FLAP

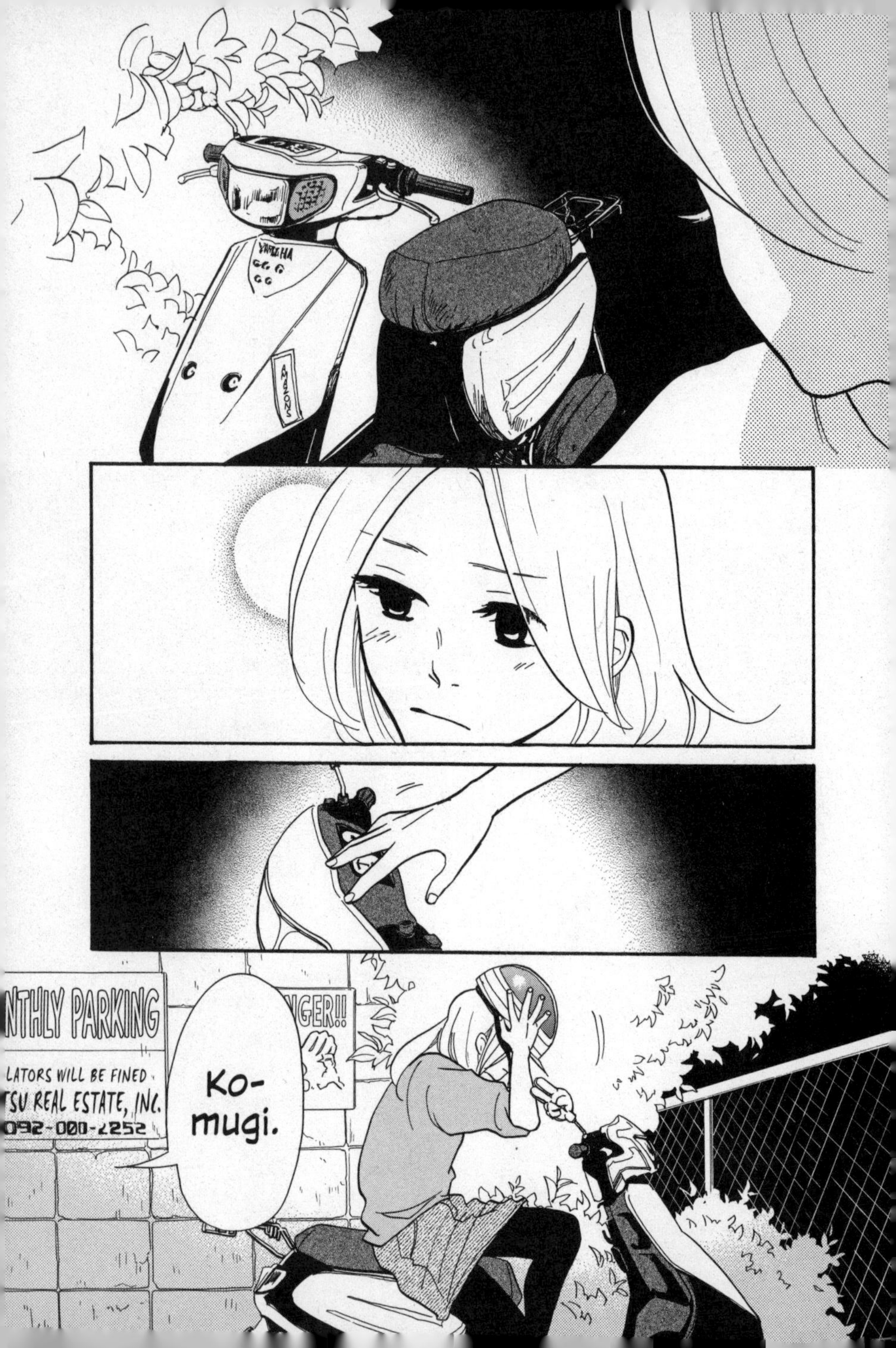
YAMAHA
AMAZONS
NTHLY PARKING
LATORS WILL BE FINED
TSU REAL ESTATE, INC.
092-000-2252
NGER!!
Ko-
mugi.

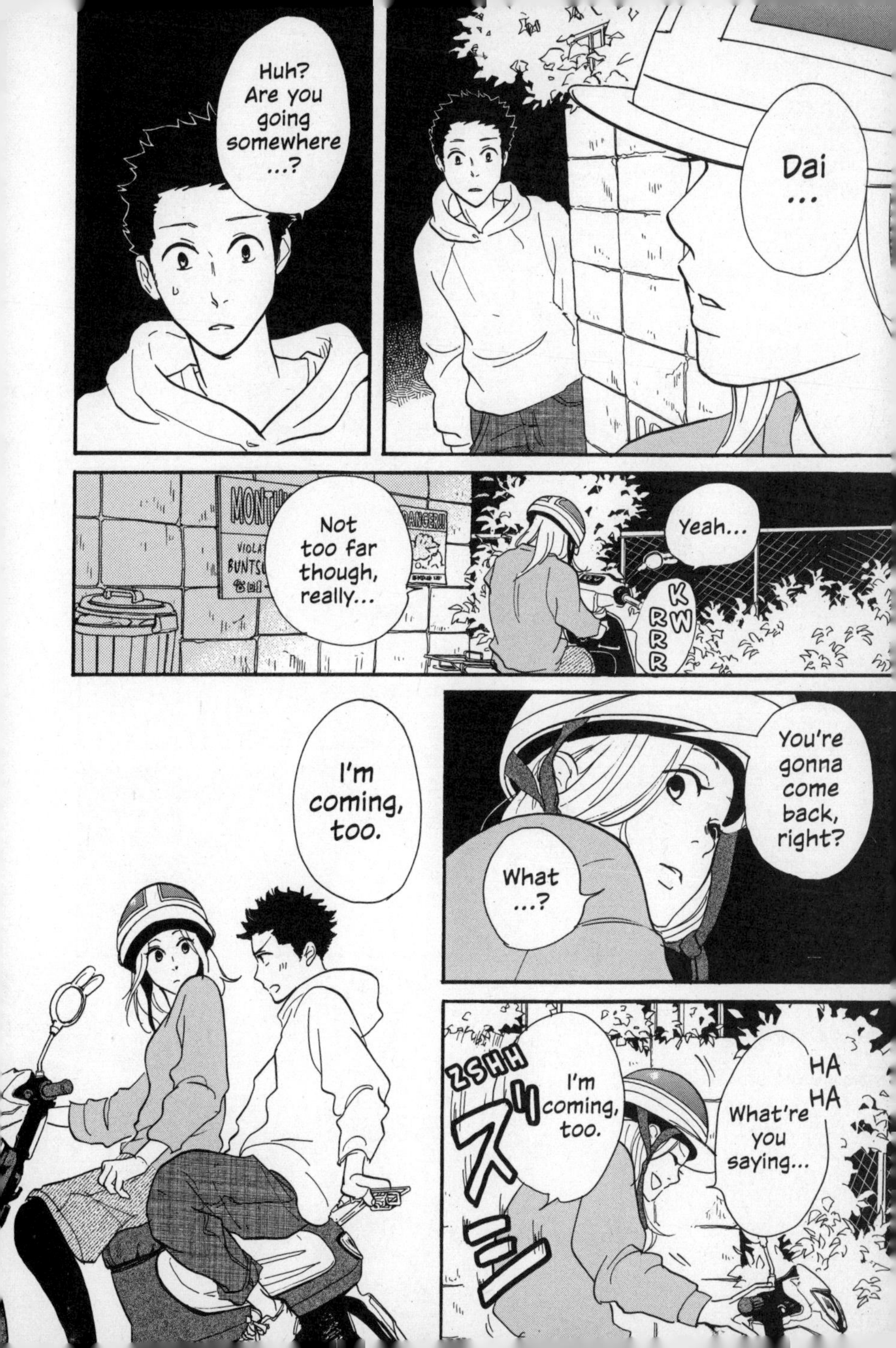
Dai
...
Huh? Are you going somewhere ...?
Yeah...
KWRRR
Not too far though, really...
DANGER!!
You're gonna come back, right?
What ...?
HA HA
What're you saying...
I'm coming, too.
ZSHH
I'm coming, too.

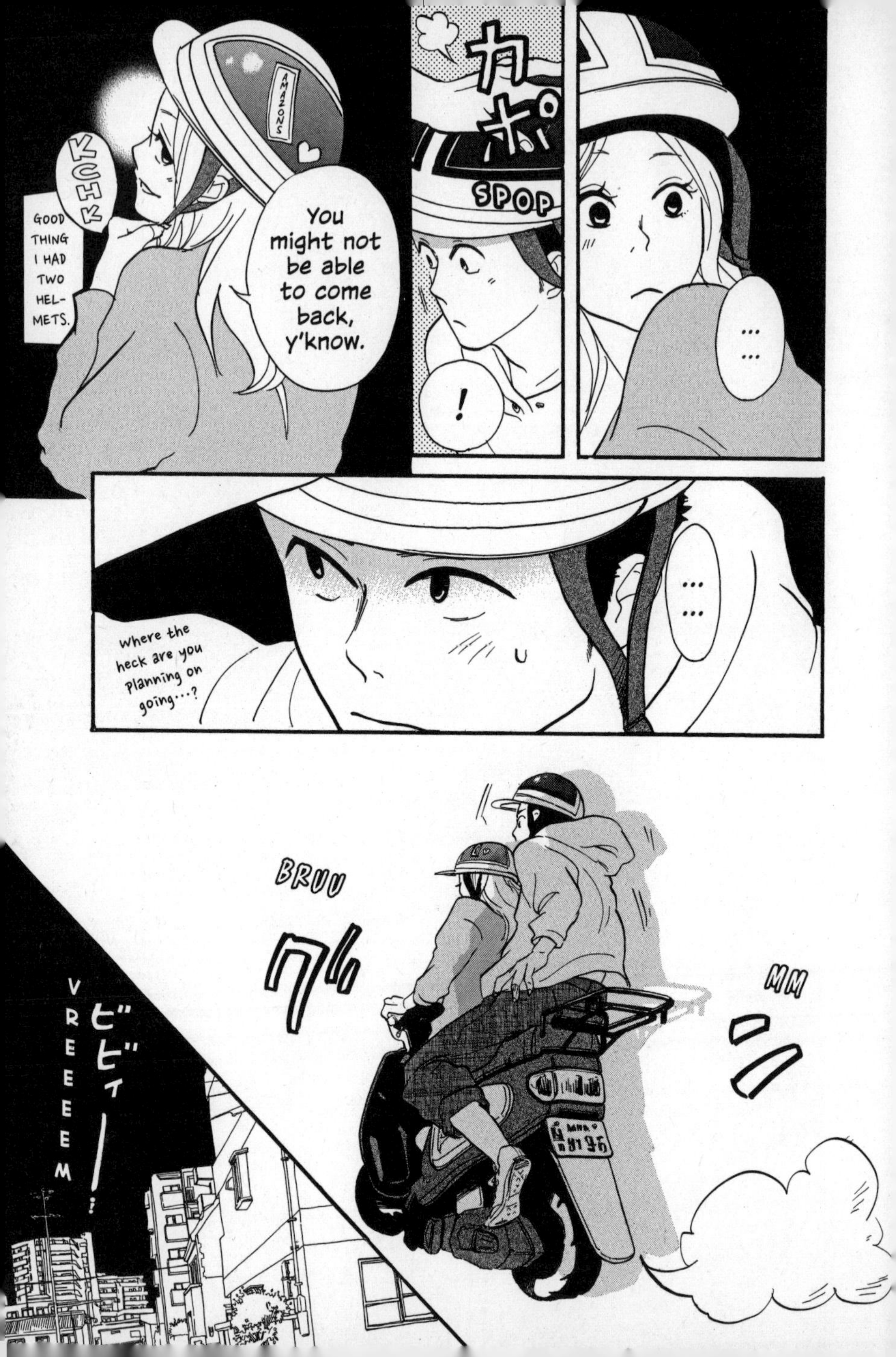

......
カポ
SPOP
!
KCHK
You might not be able to come back, y'know.
GOOD THING I HAD TWO HEL-METS.
......
Where the heck are you planning on going...?
ン
MM
ブル
BRUU
ビビィー!!
VREEEEEM

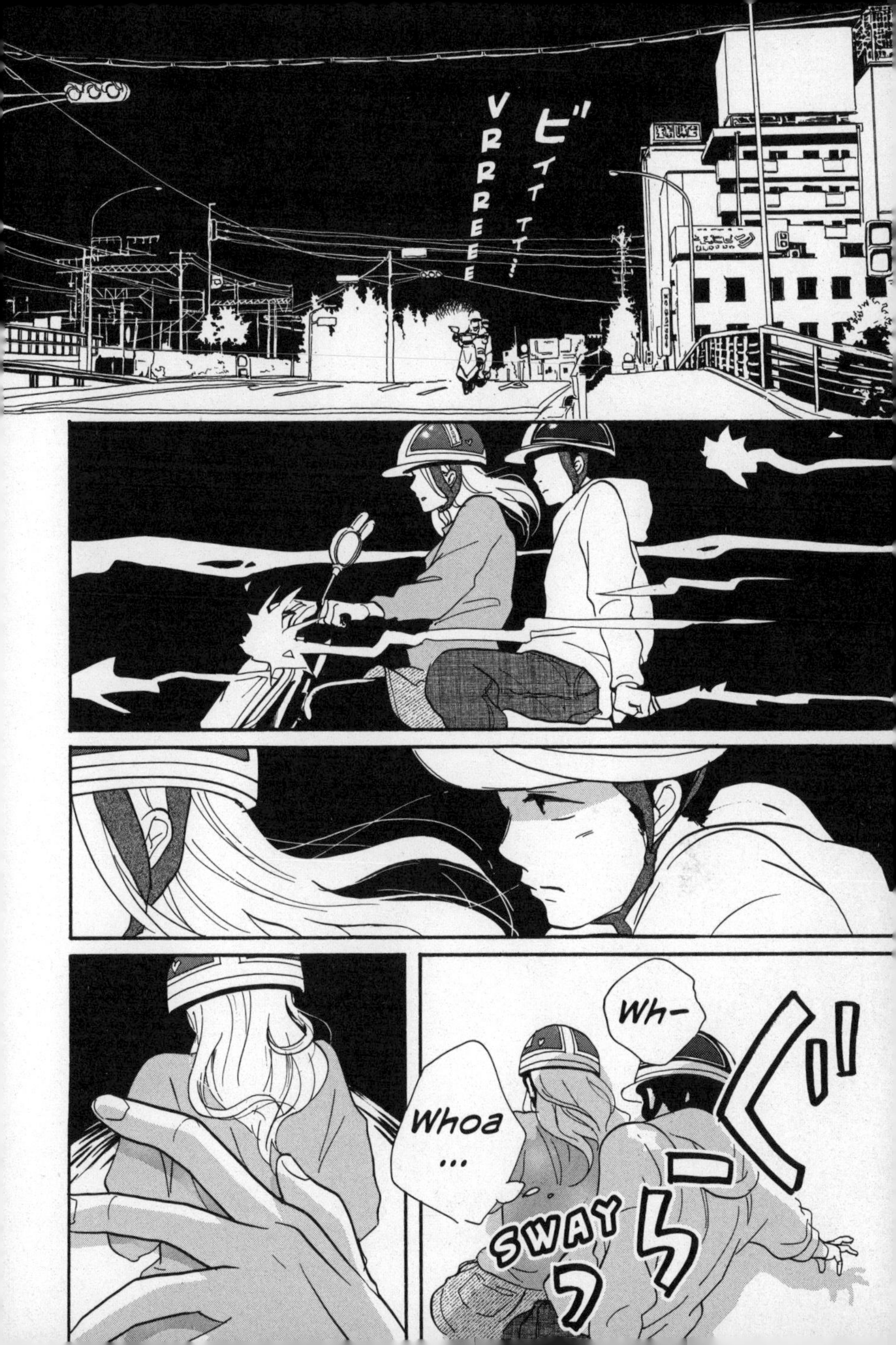
VRRREEE
Wh-
Whoa ...
SWAY

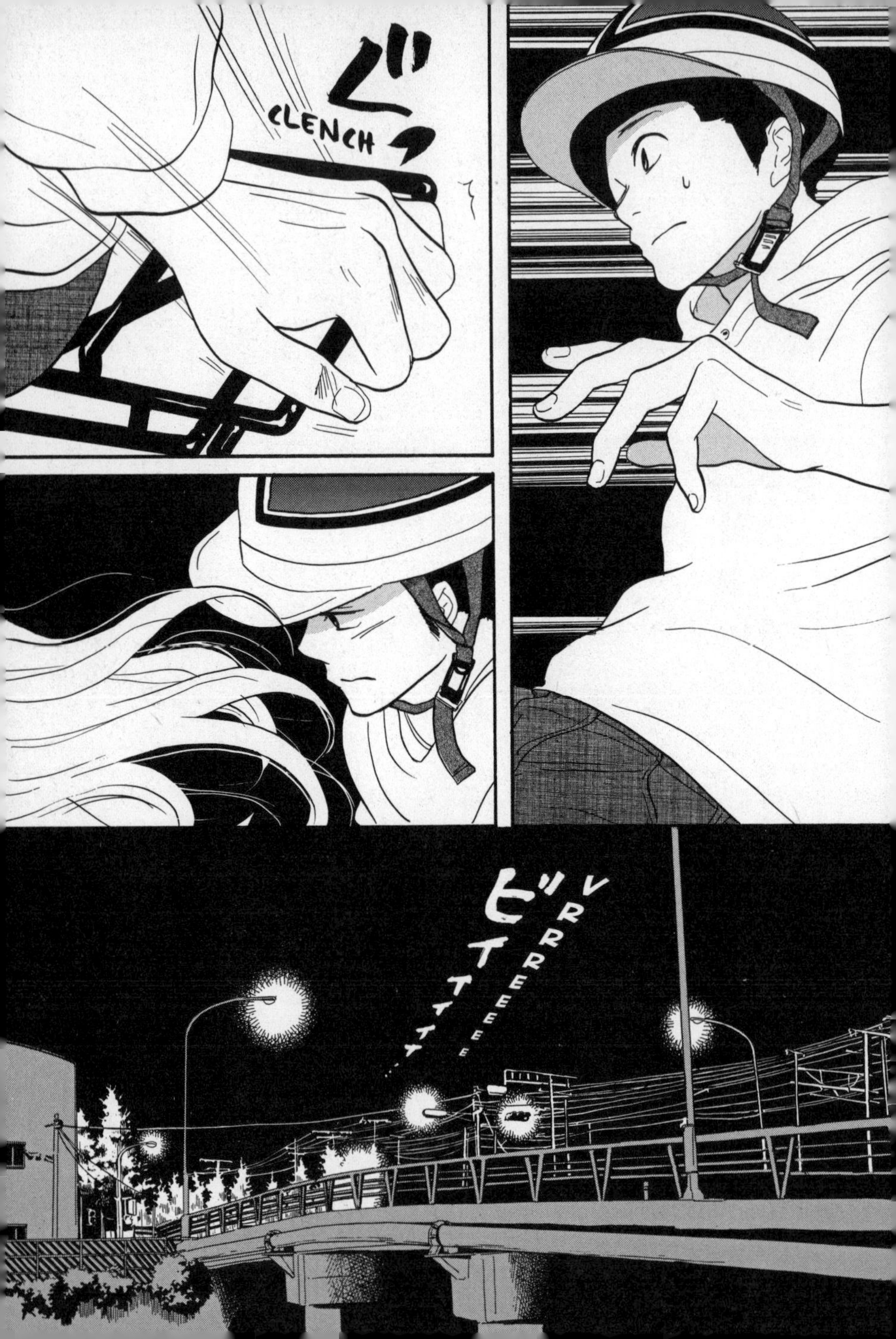
CLENCH
VRRREEEEE...

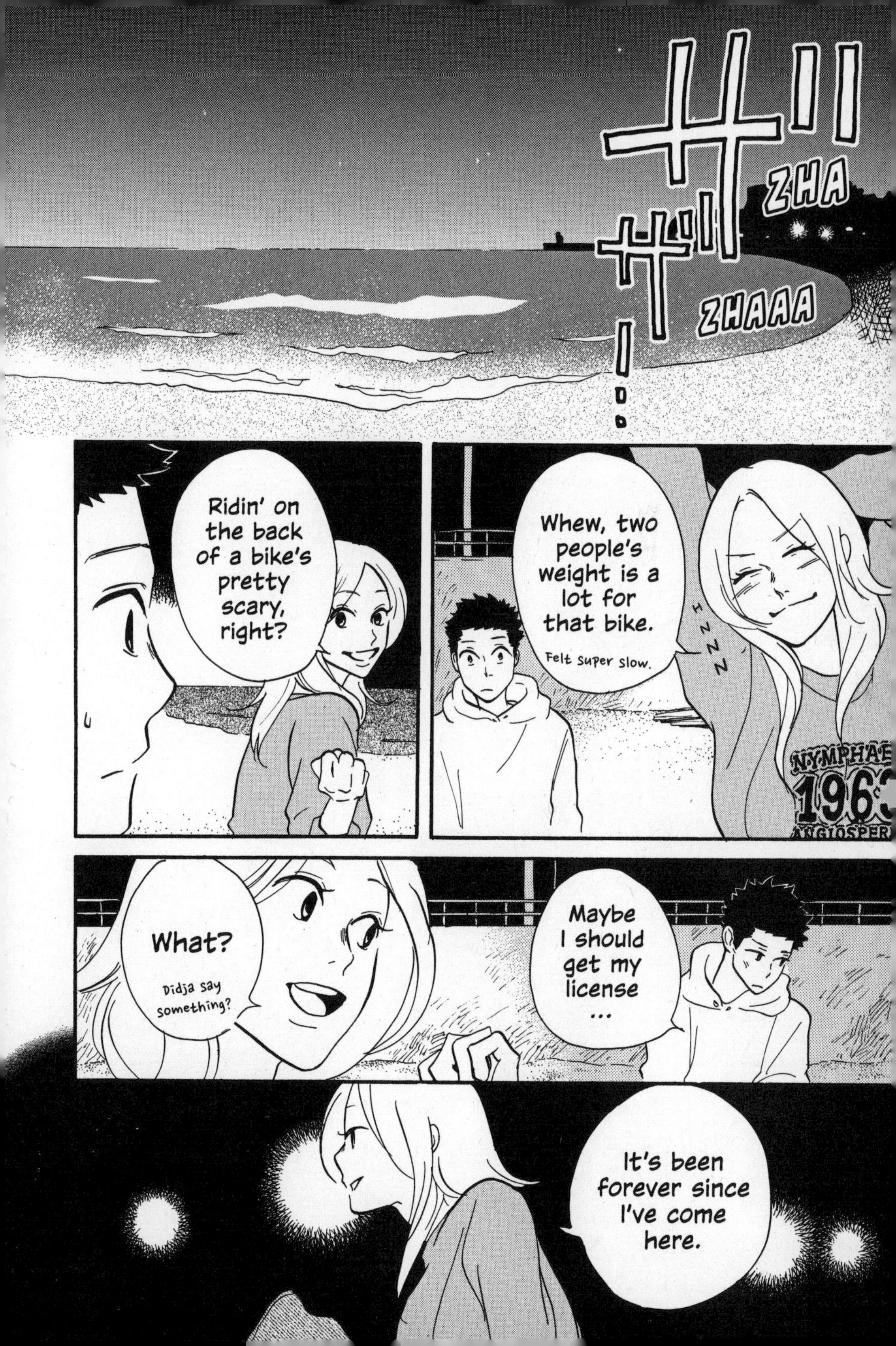
ZHA
ZHAAA
Whew, two people's weight is a lot for that bike.
Felt super slow.
Ridin' on the back of a bike's pretty scary, right?
Maybe I should get my license ...
What?
Didja say something?
It's been forever since I've come here.

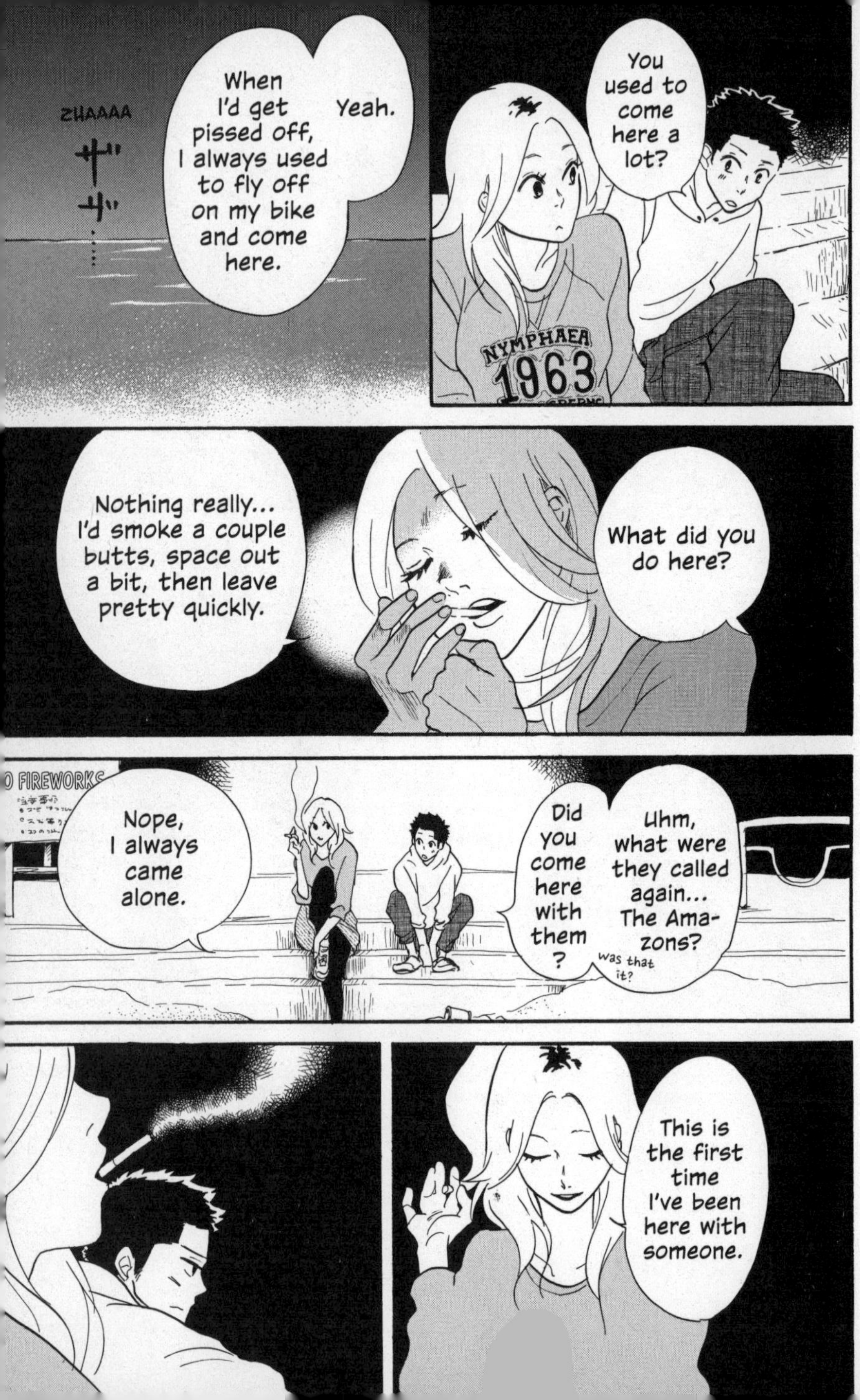
You used to come here a lot?
NYMPHAEA 1963
Yeah.
When I'd get pissed off, I always used to fly off on my bike and come here.
ZHAAAA
ザザ…
What did you do here?
Nothing really... I'd smoke a couple butts, space out a bit, then leave pretty quickly.
Uhm, what were they called again... The Ama-zons?
was that it?
Did you come here with them?
Nope, I always came alone.
This is the first time I've been here with someone.

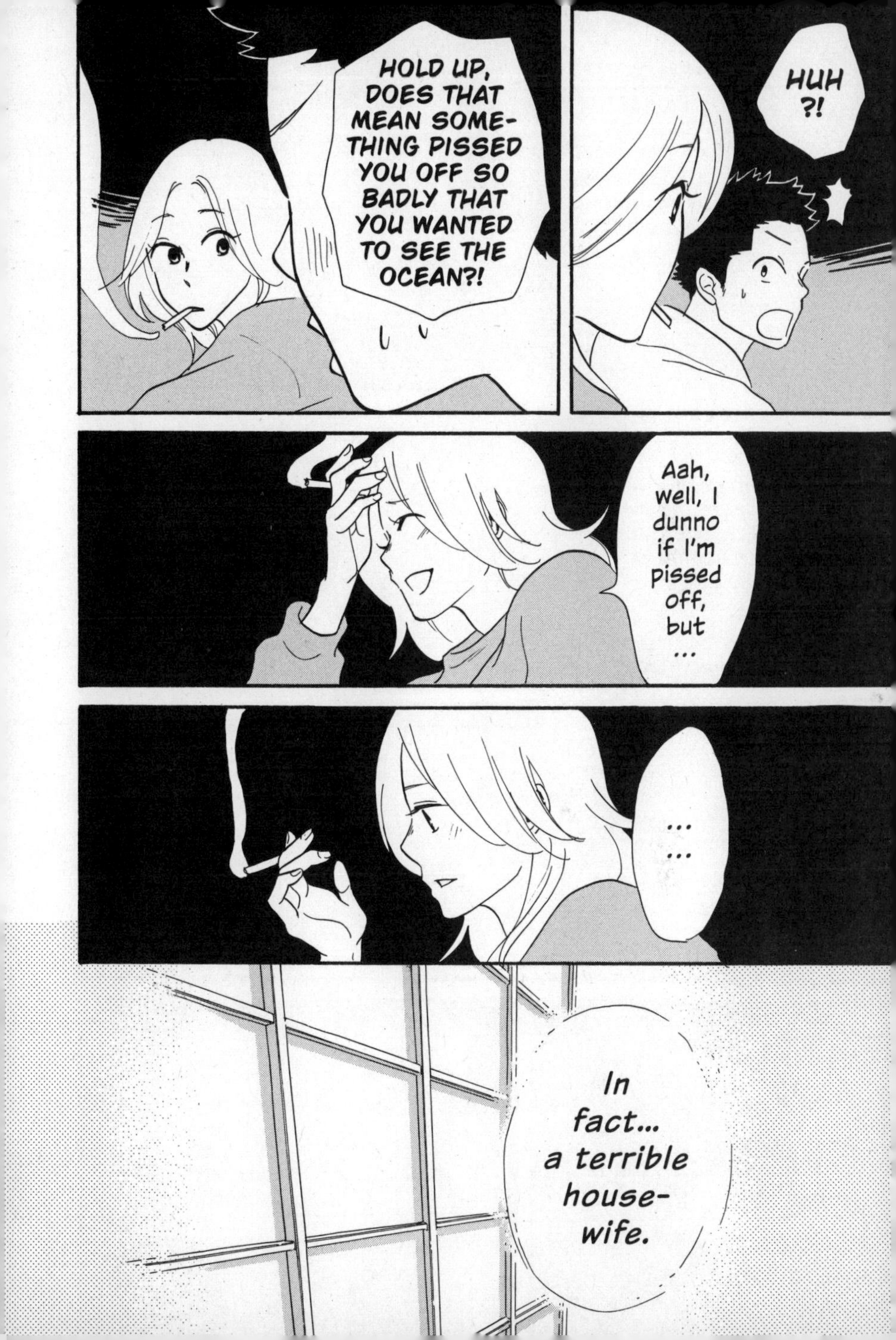
HUH ?!
HOLD UP, DOES THAT MEAN SOME-THING PISSED YOU OFF SO BADLY THAT YOU WANTED TO SEE THE OCEAN?!
Aah, well, I dunno if I'm pissed off, but ...
... ...
In fact... a terrible house-wife.

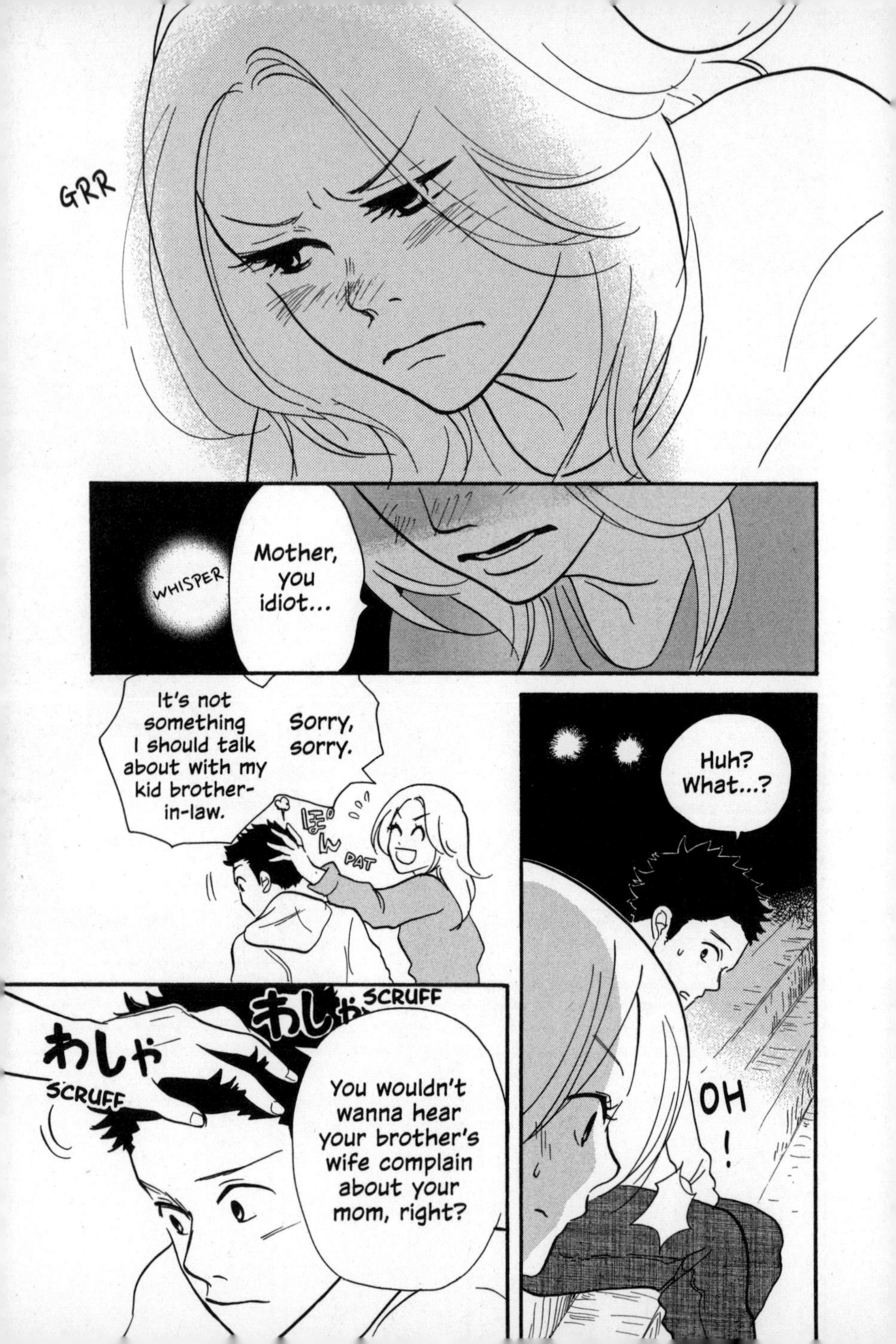
GRR
WHISPER
Mother, you idiot...
Huh? What...?
OH!
Sorry, sorry.
It's not something I should talk about with my kid brother-in-law.
ぽん
PAT
わしゃ
SCRUFF
わしゃ
SCRUFF
You wouldn't wanna hear your brother's wife complain about your mom, right?

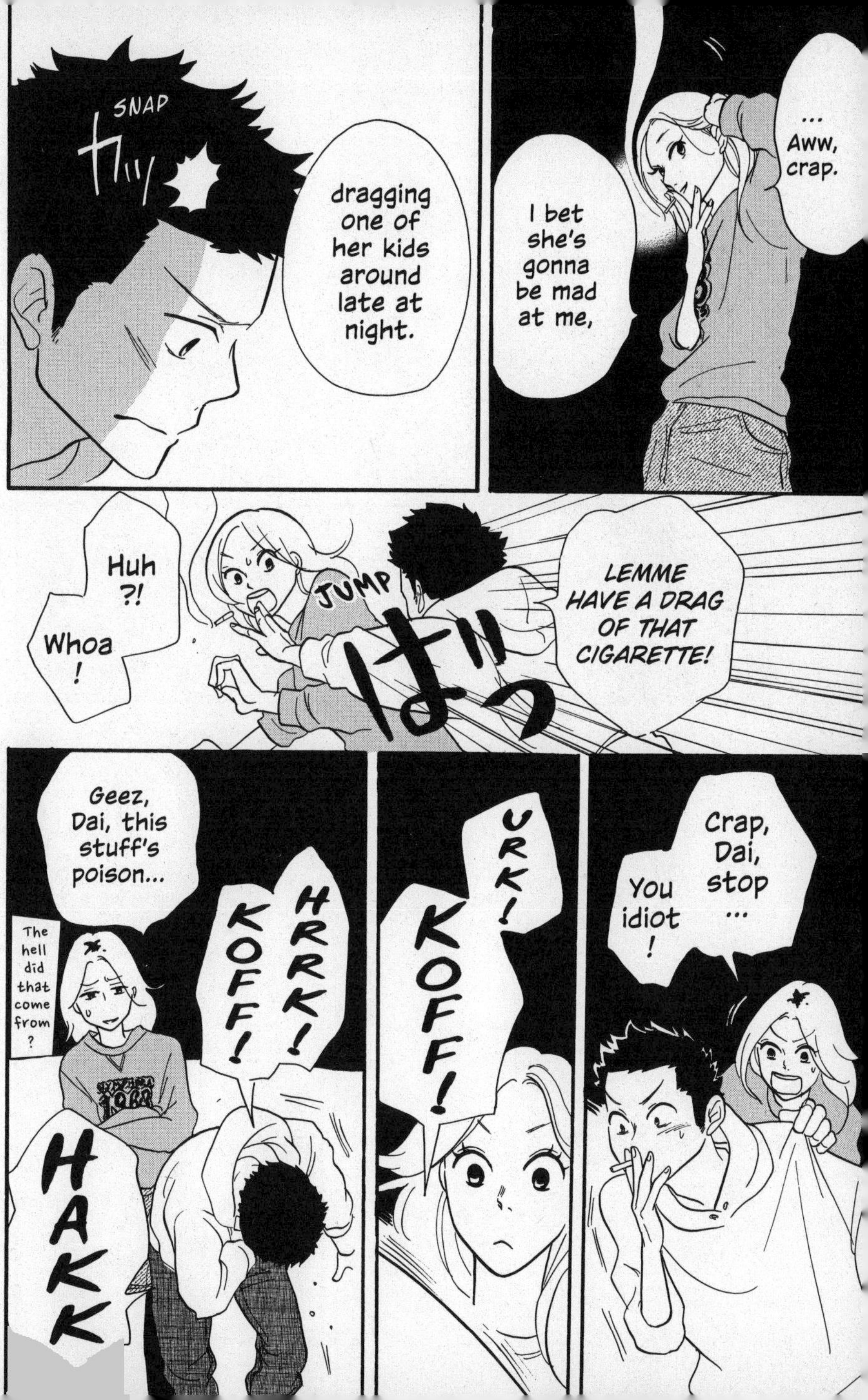
... Aww, crap.
I bet she's gonna be mad at me,
SNAP
dragging one of her kids around late at night.
LEMME HAVE A DRAG OF THAT CIGARETTE!
JUMP
Huh?!
Whoa!
Crap, Dai, stop ...
You idiot!
URK!
KOFF!
HRRK!
KOFF!
Geez, Dai, this stuff's poison...
The hell did that come from?
HAKK

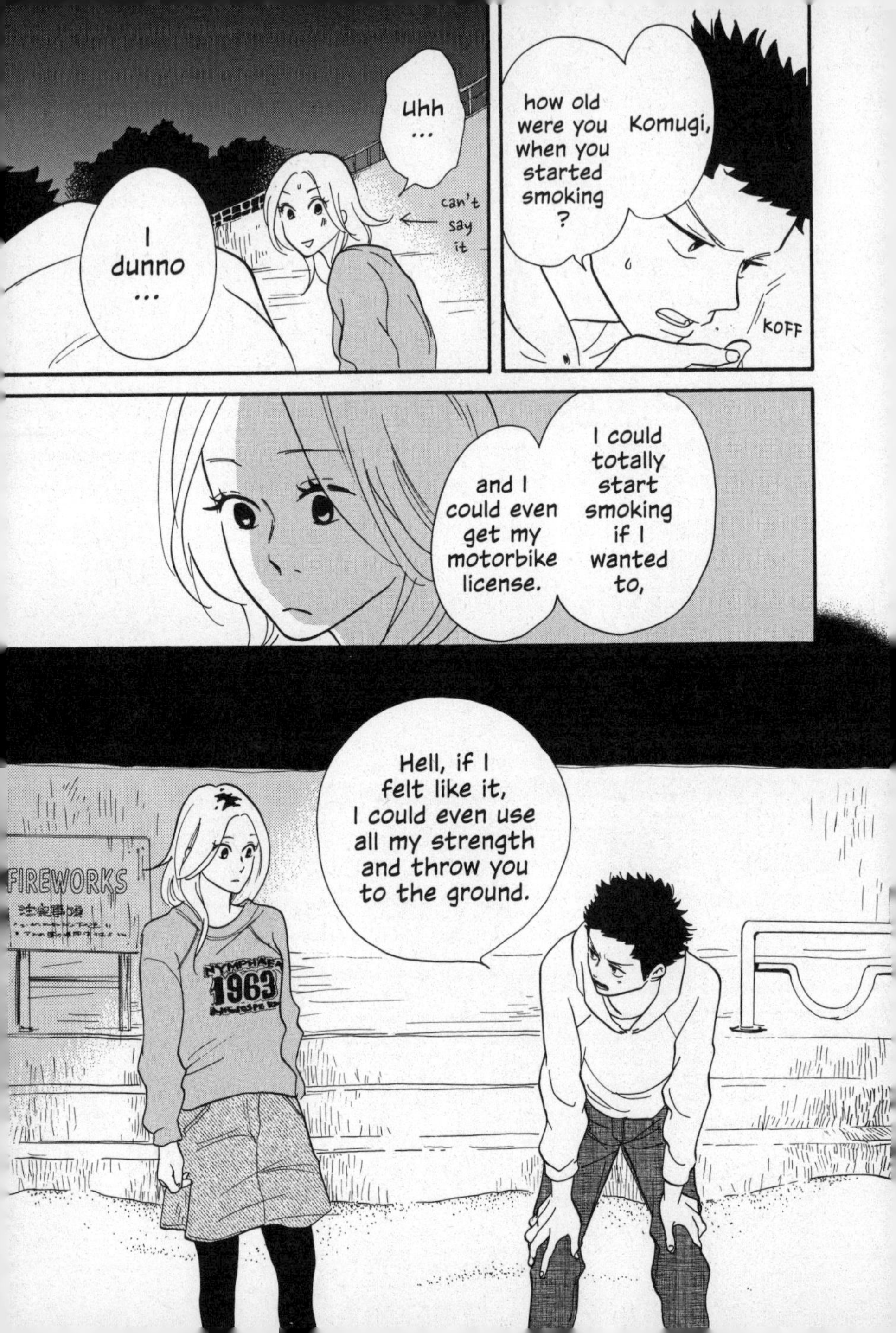
Komugi,
how old were you when you started smoking?
KOFF
Uhh ...
can't say it
I dunno ...
I could totally start smoking if I wanted to,
and I could even get my motorbike license.
Hell, if I felt like it, I could even use all my strength and throw you to the ground.
FIREWORKS
NYMPHAEA
1963

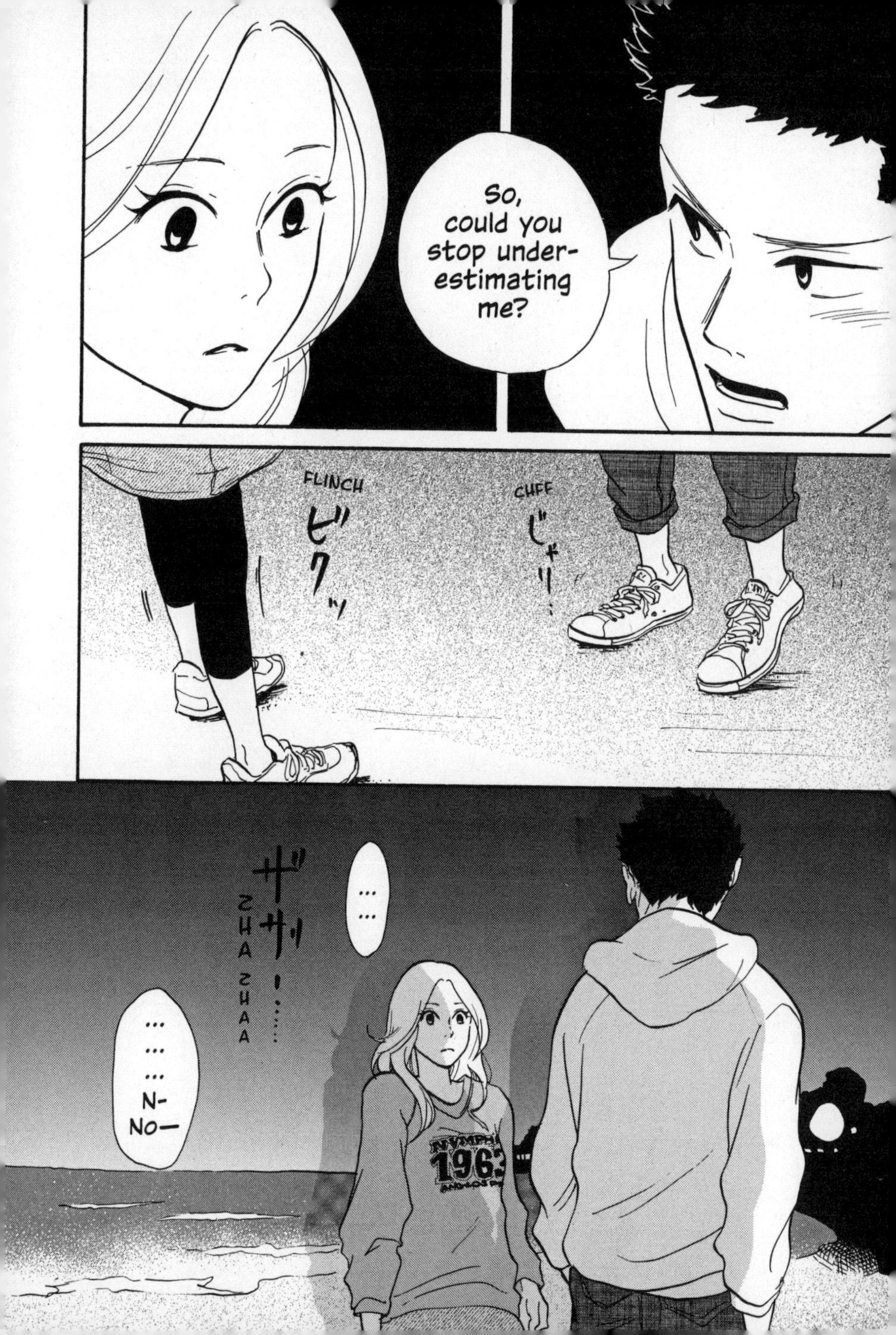
So, could you stop under-estimating me?
CUFF
じゃり…
FLINCH
ビクッ
……
……
ザザッ……
ZHA ZHAA
……
……
……
N-
No—

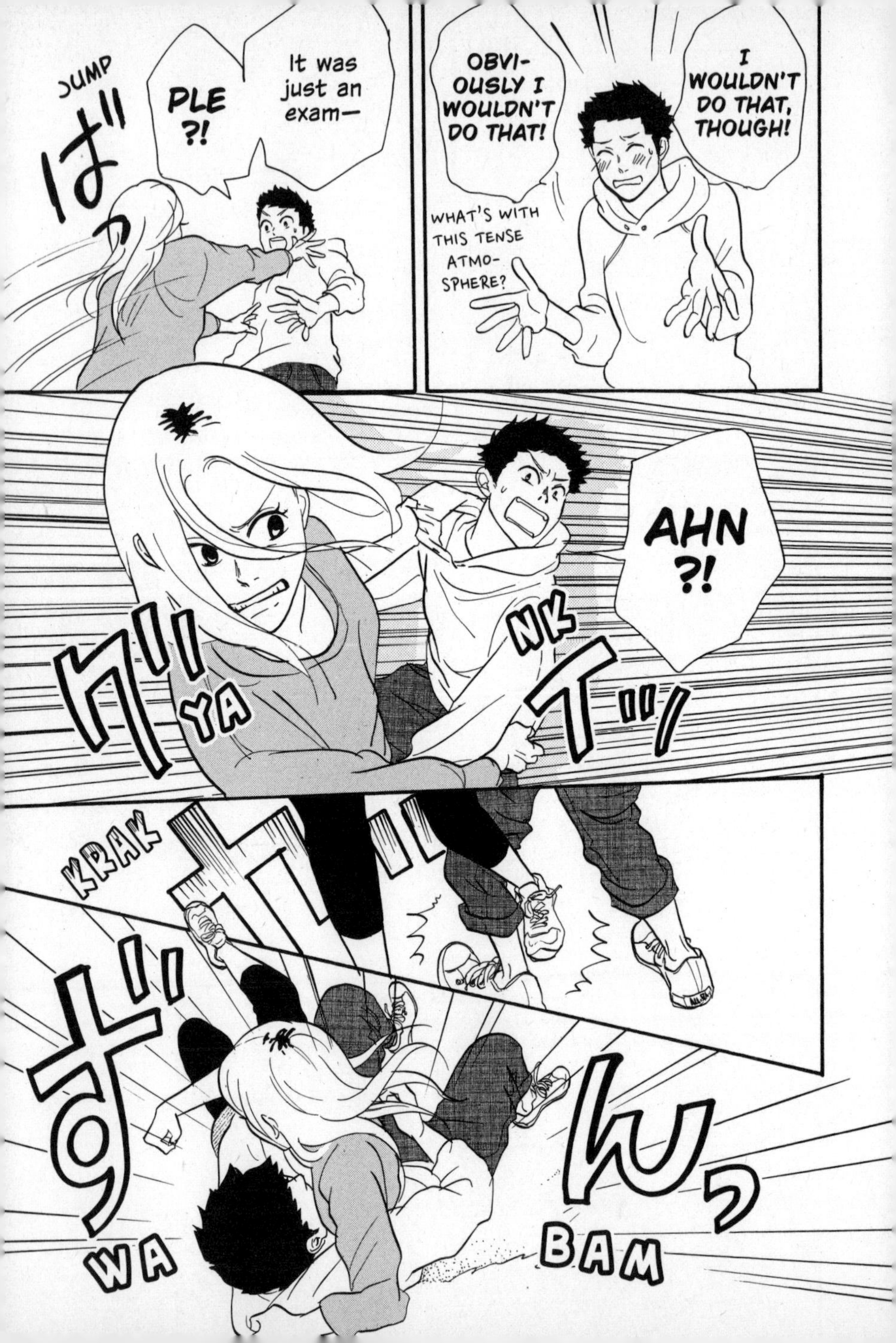
I WOULDN'T DO THAT, THOUGH!
OBVI-OUSLY I WOULDN'T DO THAT!
WHAT'S WITH THIS TENSE ATMO-SPHERE?
It was just an exam—
PLE ?!
JUMP
AHN ?!
NK
YA
KRAK
BAM
WA

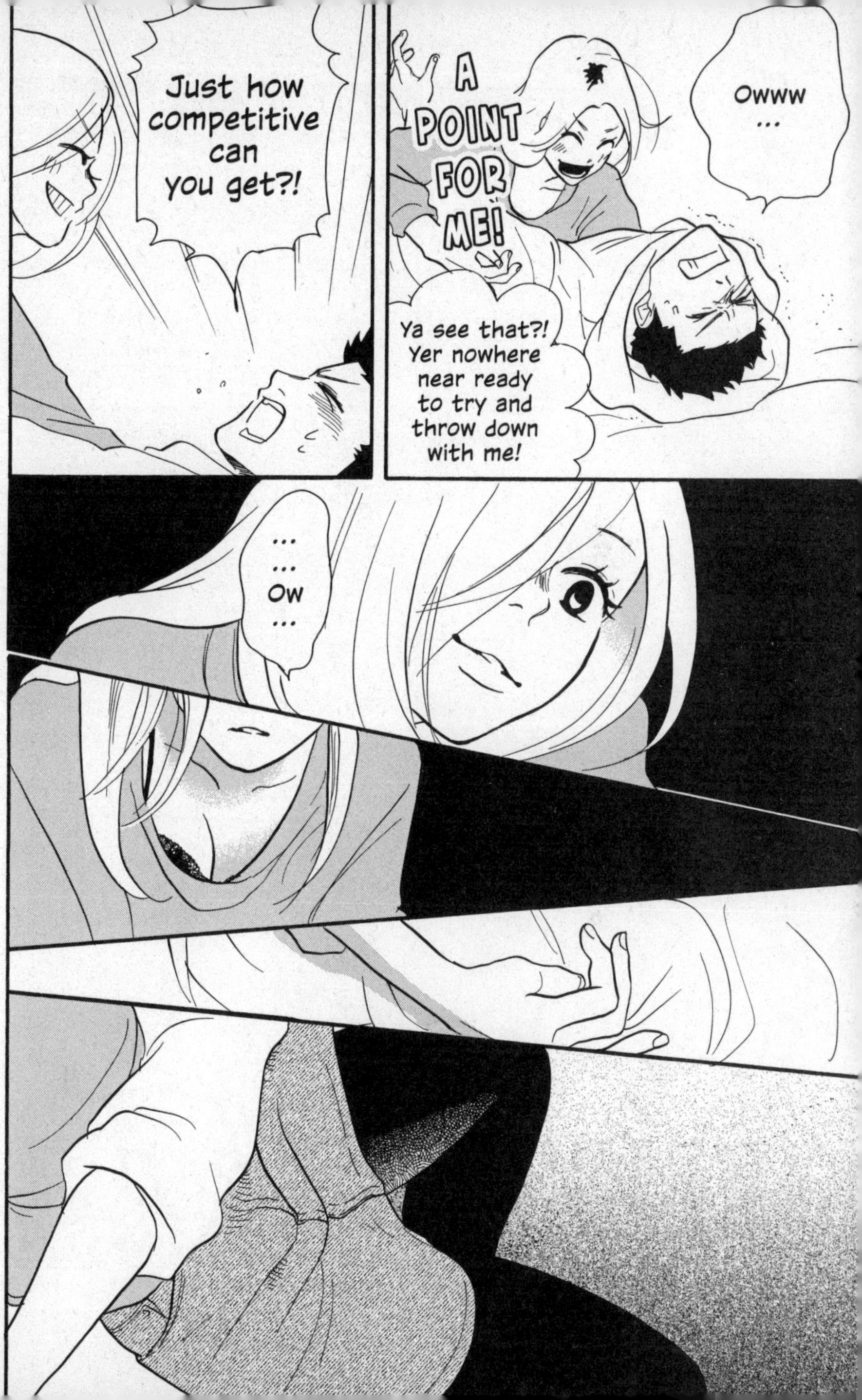
Owww ...
A POINT FOR ME!
Ya see that?! Yer nowhere near ready to try and throw down with me!
Just how competitive can you get?!
... ... Ow ...

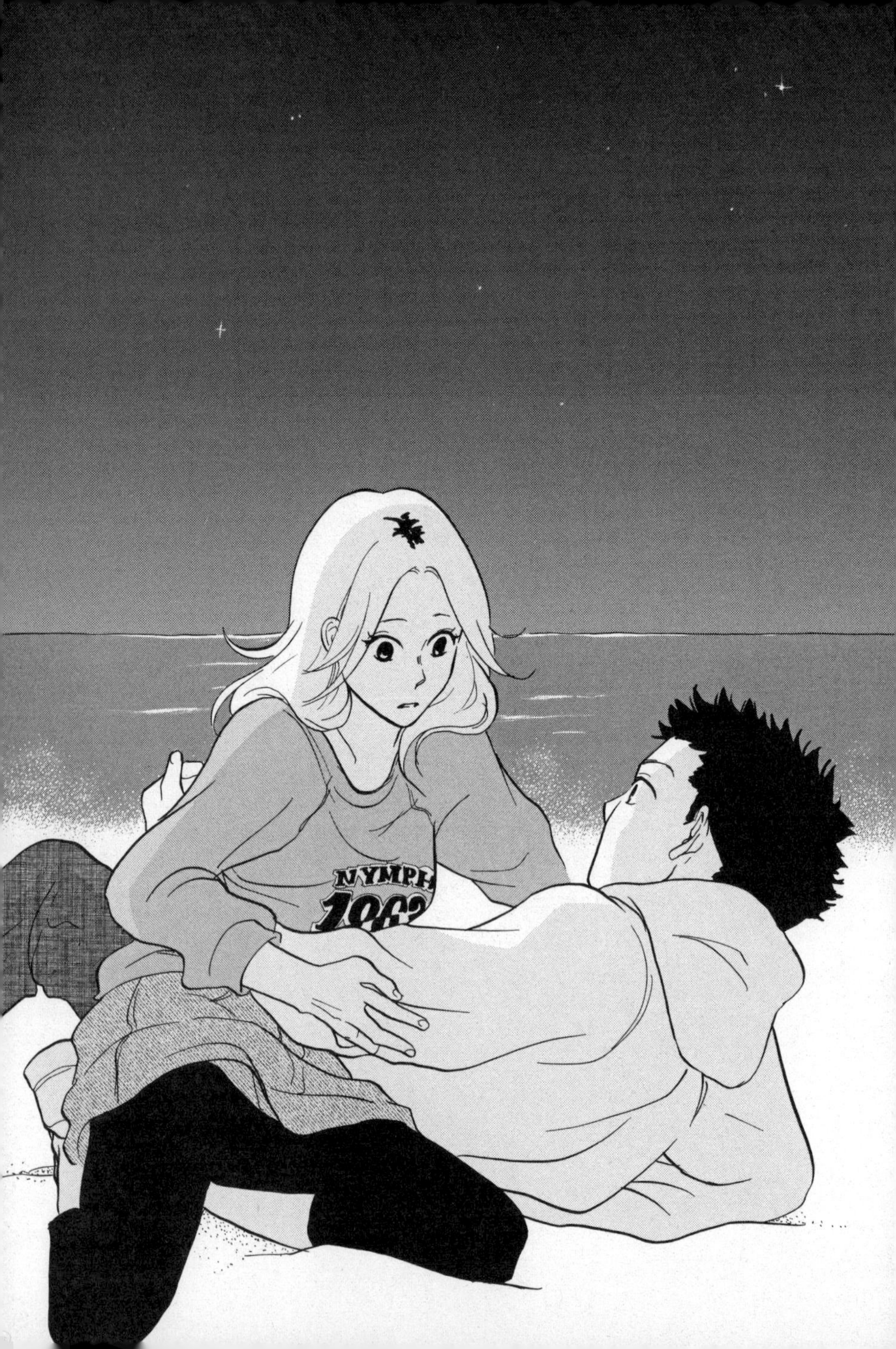
NYMPH

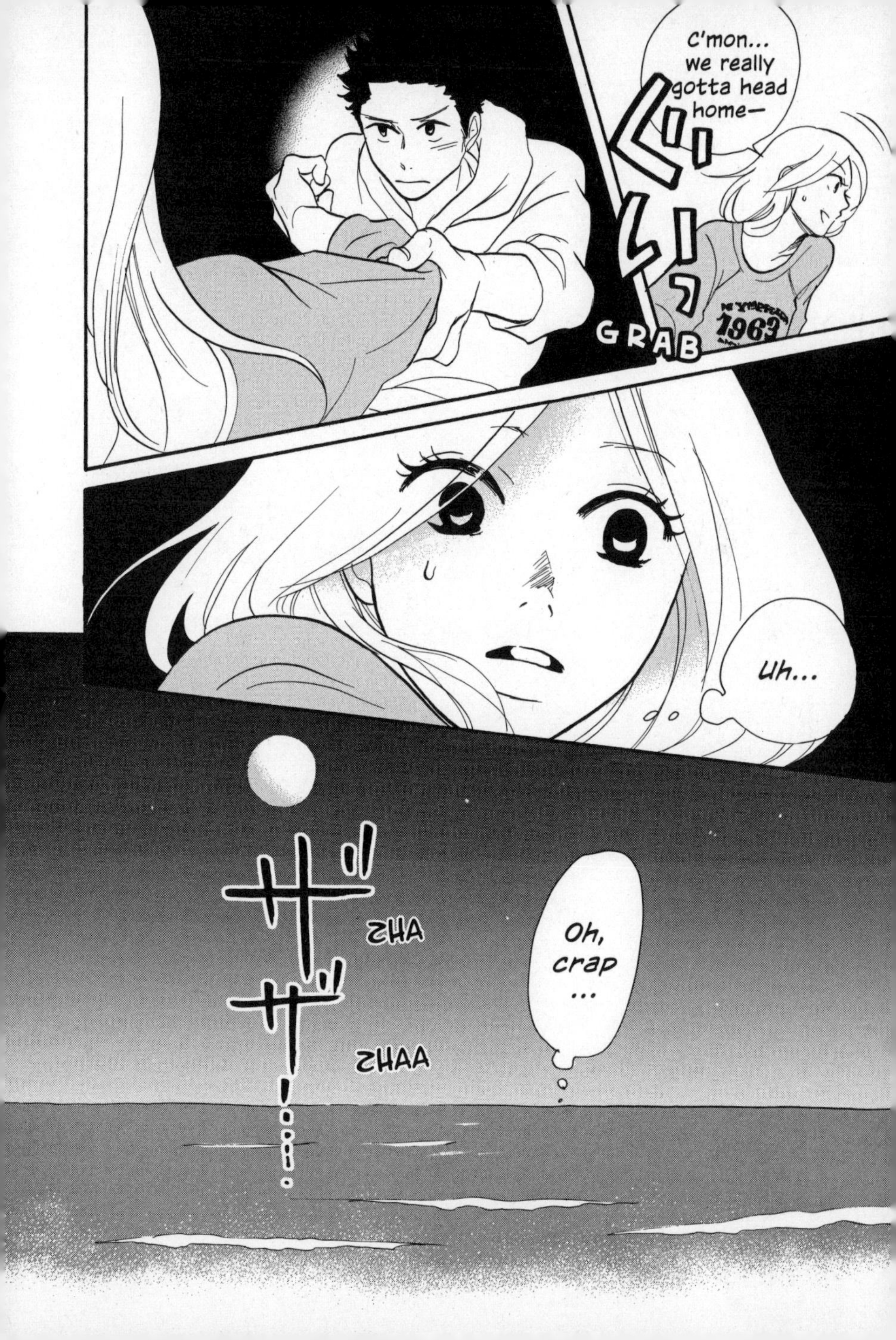
C'mon... we really gotta head home—
ぐいっ
GRAB
uh...
Oh, crap...
ザッ
ZHA
ザー
ZHAA

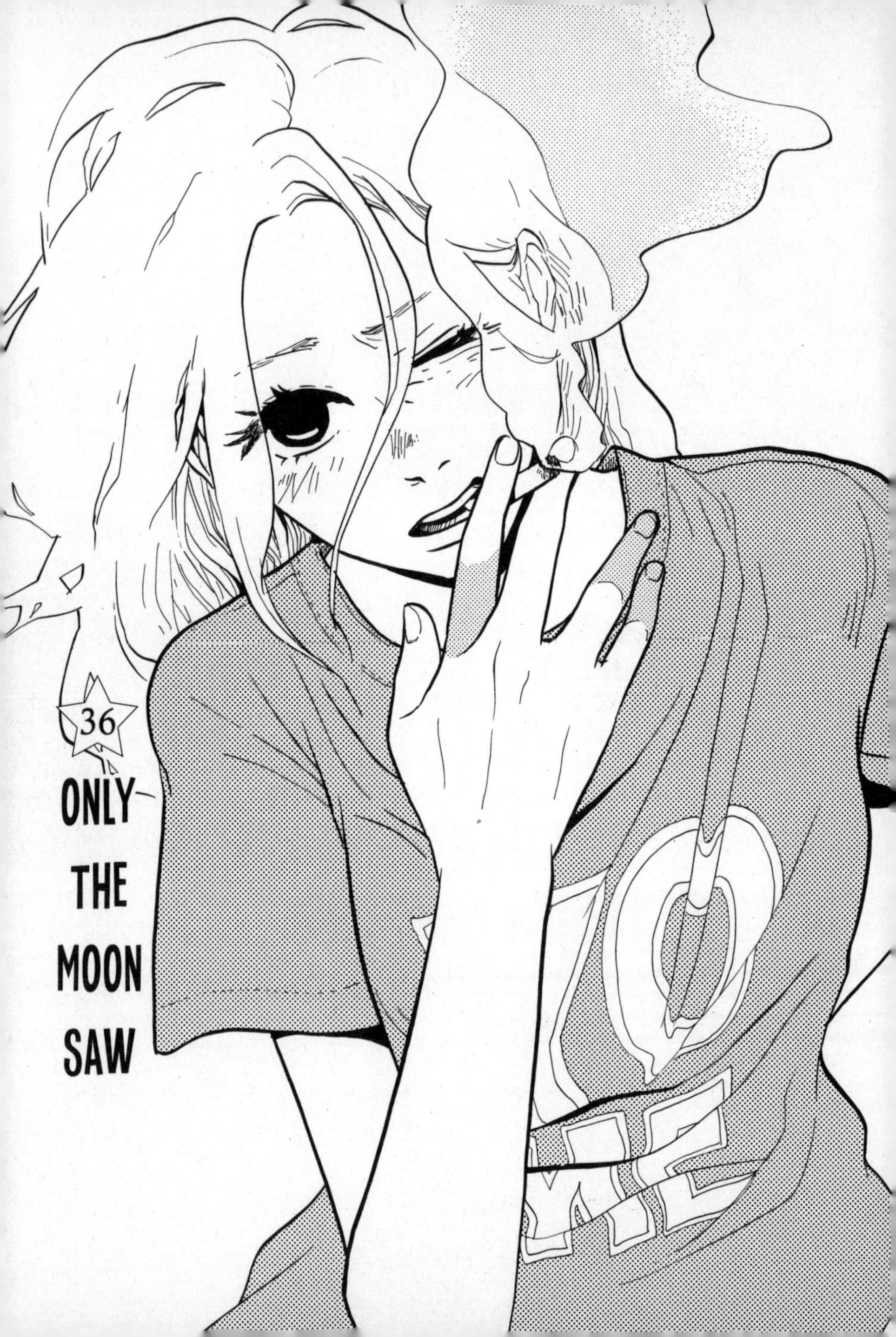
36
ONLY THE MOON SAW

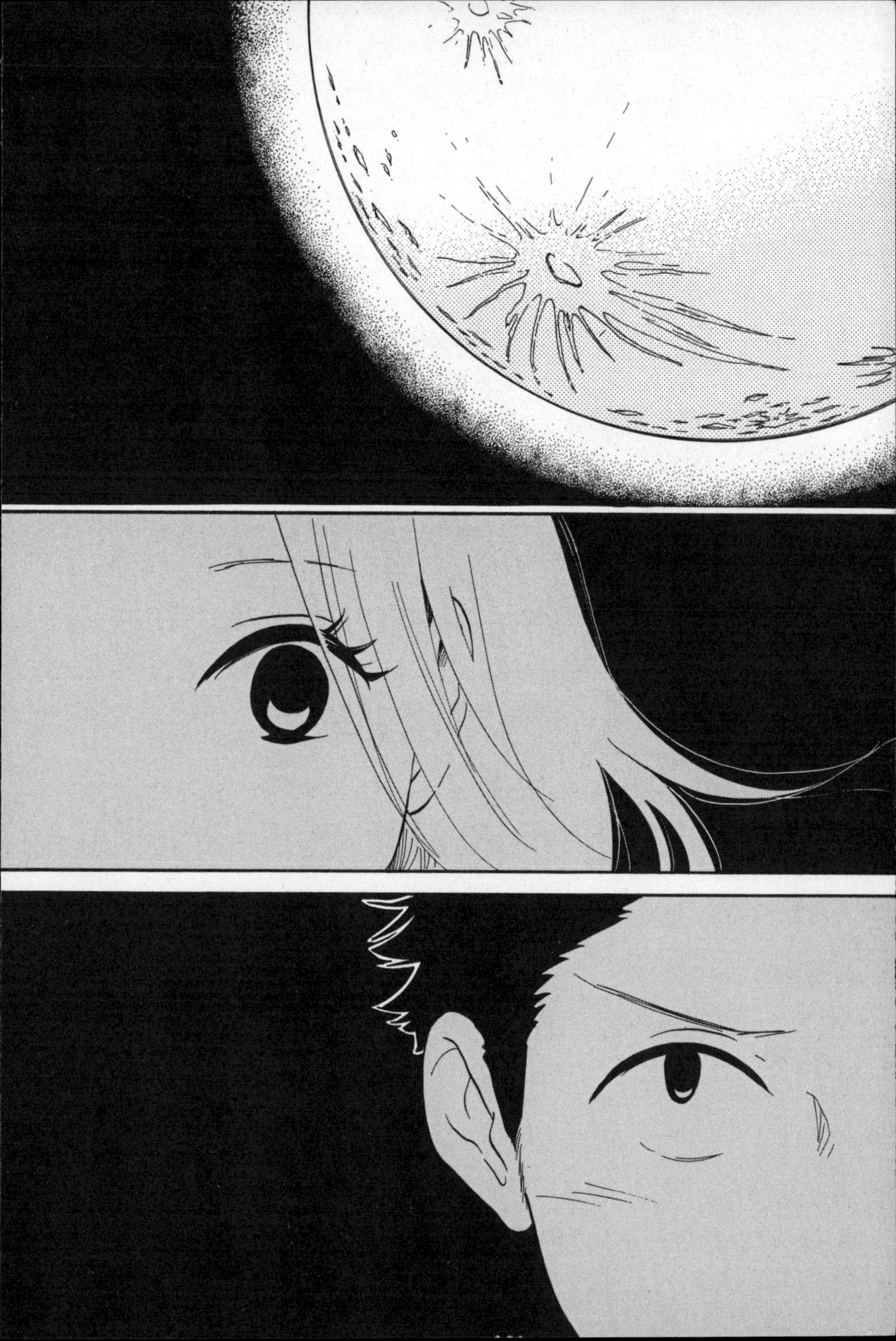

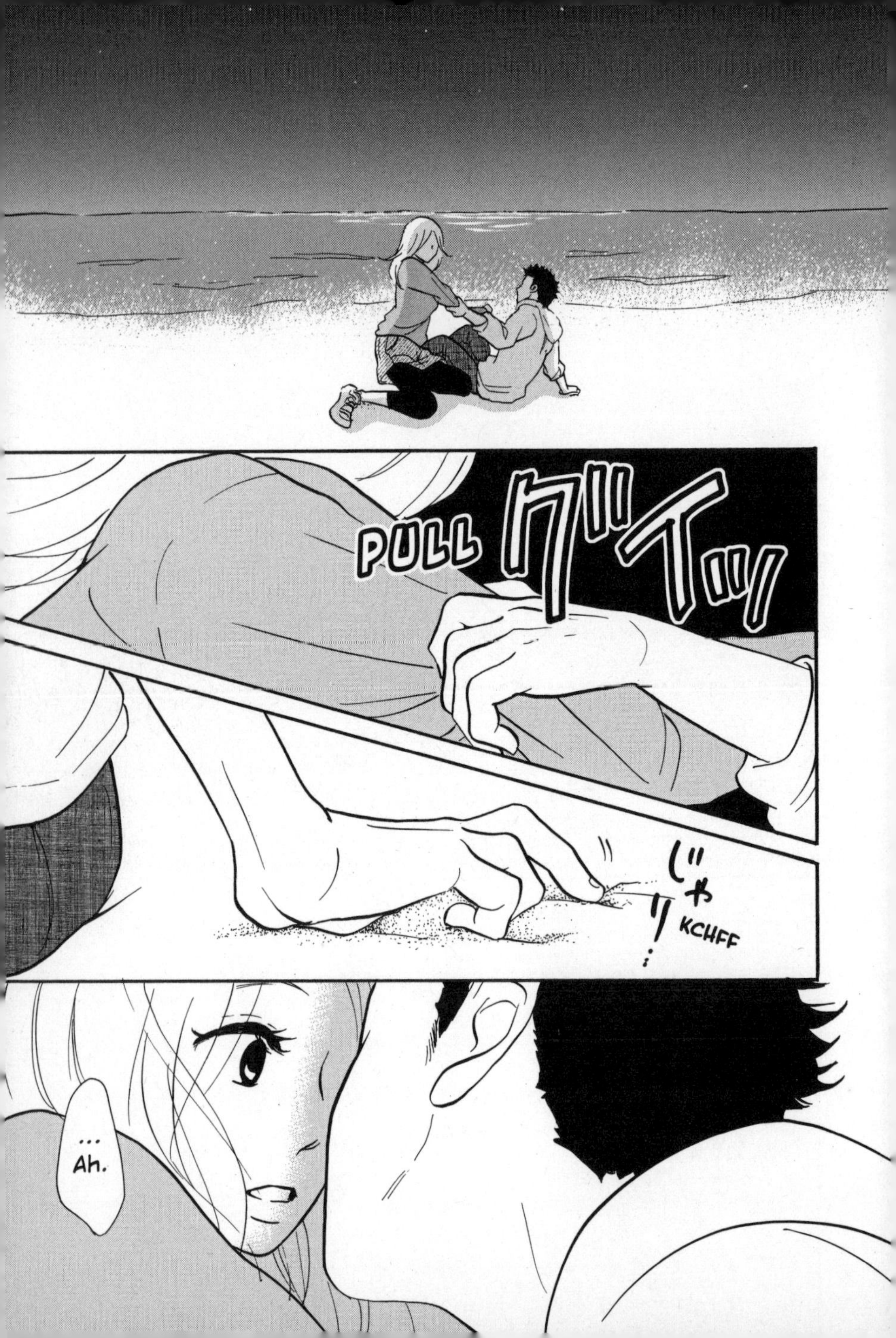
PULL
グイッ
じゃり
KCHFF
... Ah.

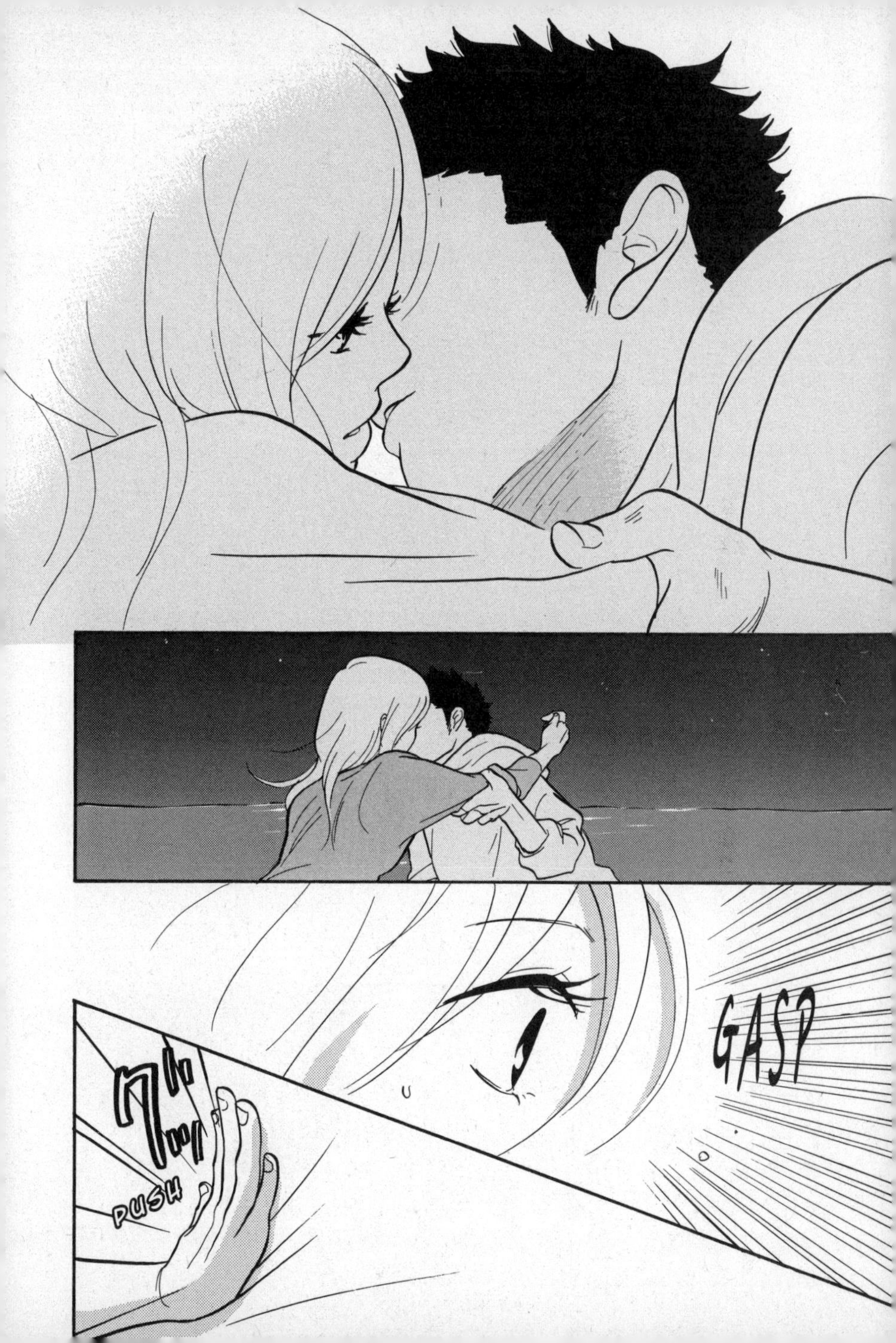
GASP
PUSH

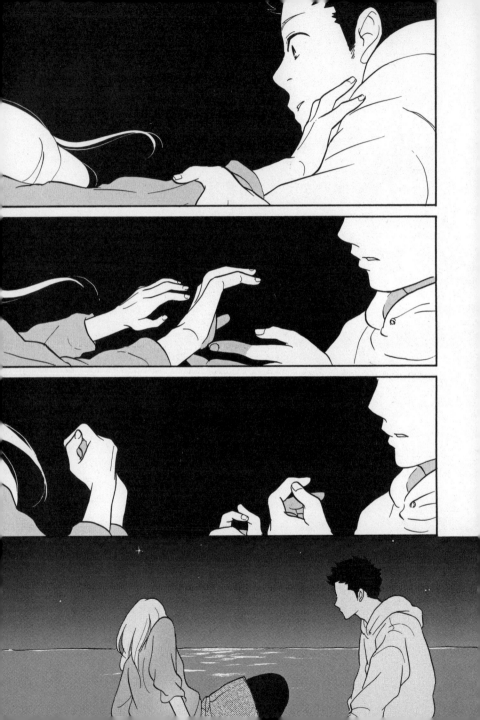

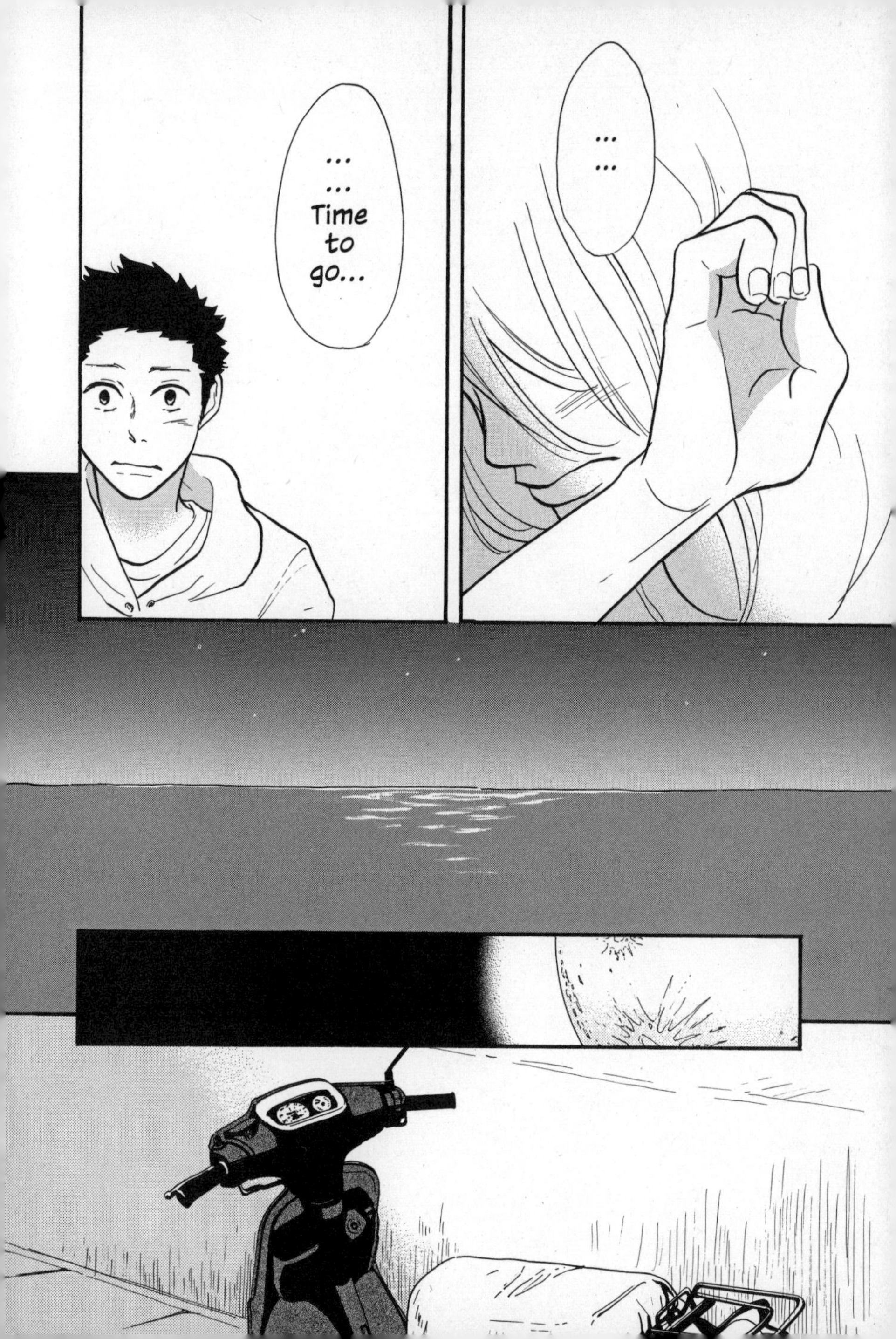
... ...
... ... Time to go...

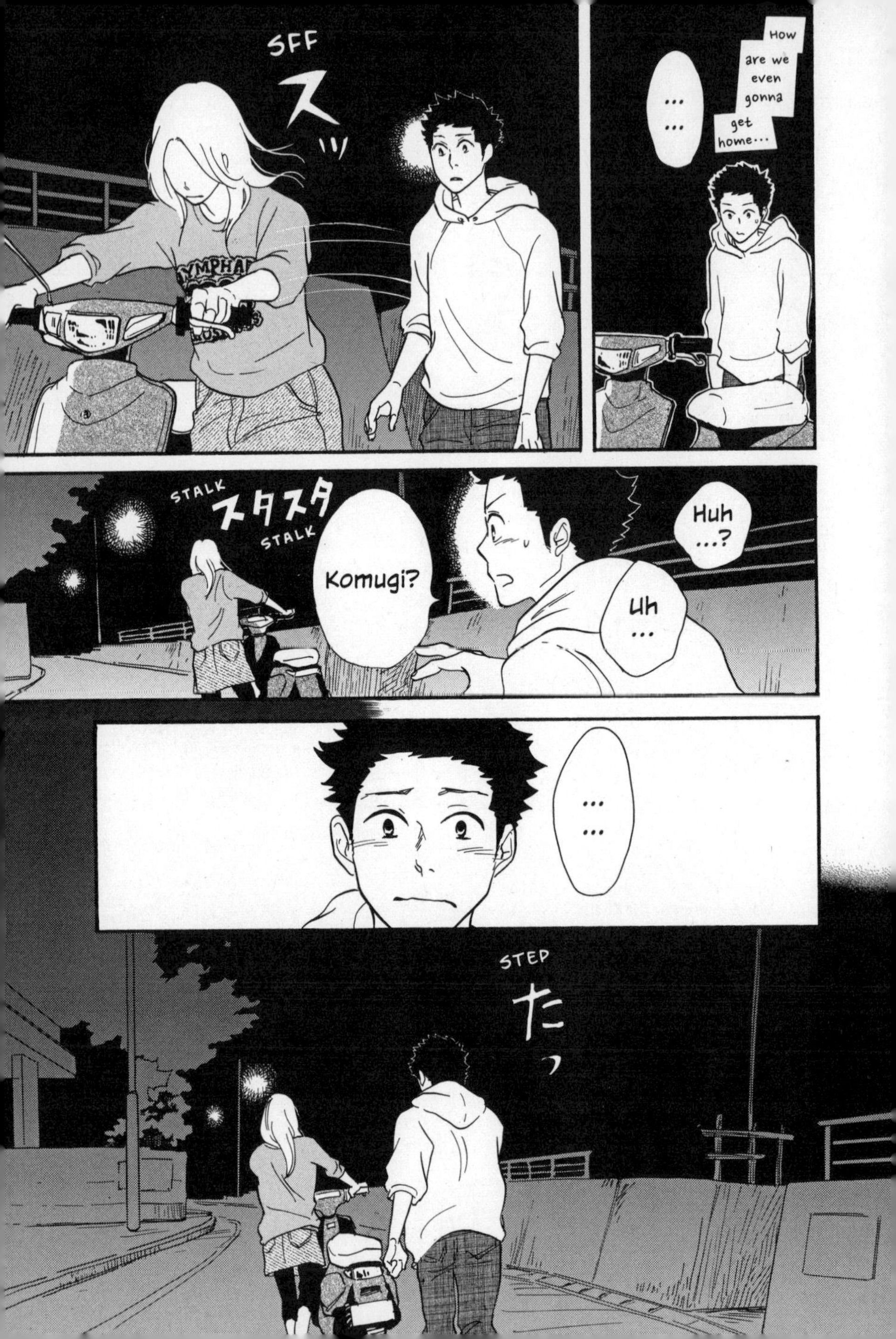
How are we even gonna get home...
......
SFF
スッ
Huh ...?
Uh ...
Komugi?
STALK
スタスタ
STALK
......
STEP
たっ

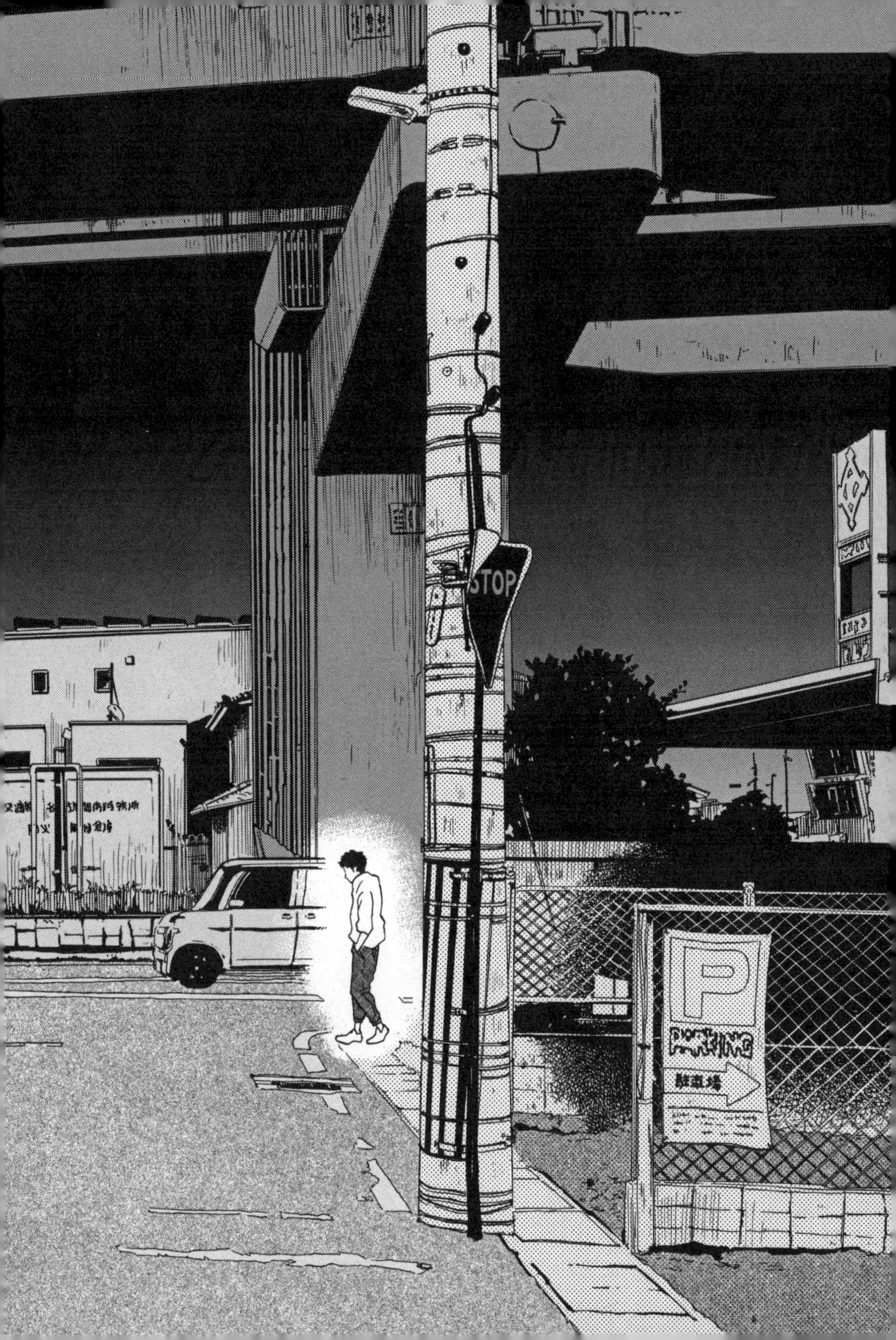
STOP
P
駐車場

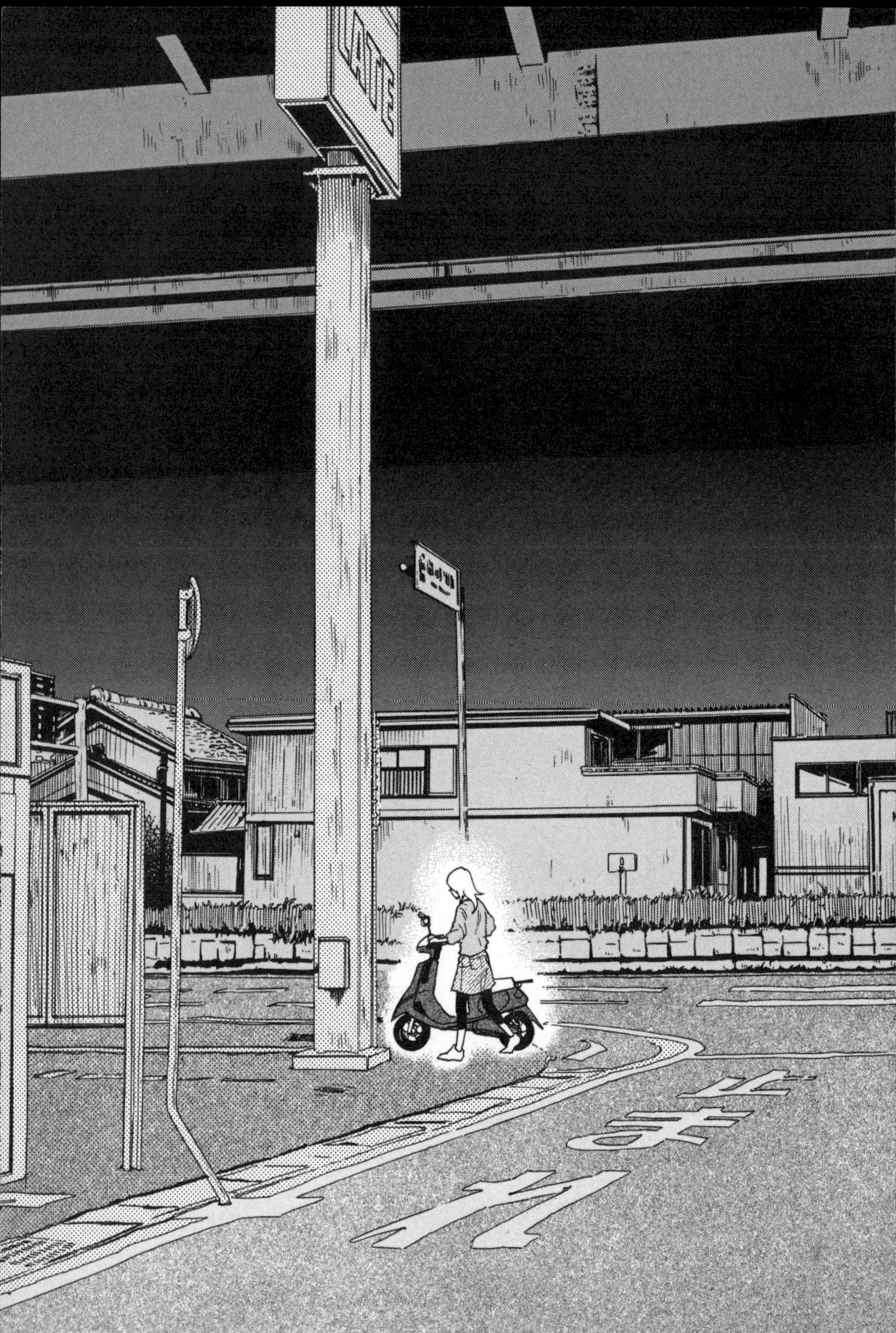
止まれ

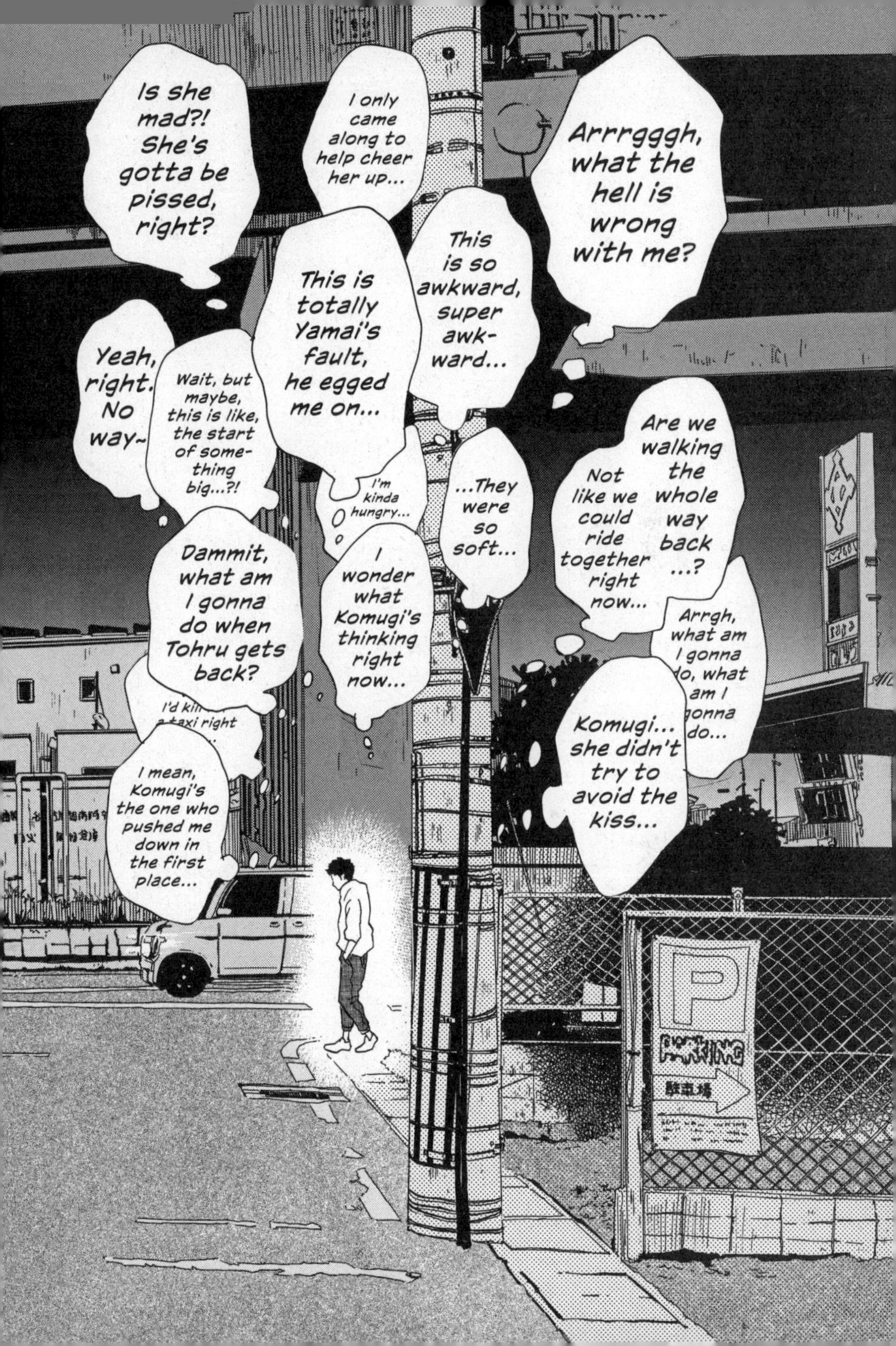
Arrrgggh, what the hell is wrong with me?
I only came along to help cheer her up...
Is she mad?! She's gotta be pissed, right?
This is so awkward, super awk-ward...
This is totally Yamai's fault, he egged me on...
Wait, but maybe, this is like, the start of some-thing big...?!
Yeah, right. No way~
Are we walking the whole way back ...?
Not like we could ride together right now...
...They were so soft...
I'm kinda hungry...
I wonder what Komugi's thinking right now...
Dammit, what am I gonna do when Tohru gets back?
I'd kil
taxi right
Arrgh, what am I gonna do, what am I gonna do...
Komugi... she didn't try to avoid the kiss...
I mean, Komugi's the one who pushed me down in the first place...

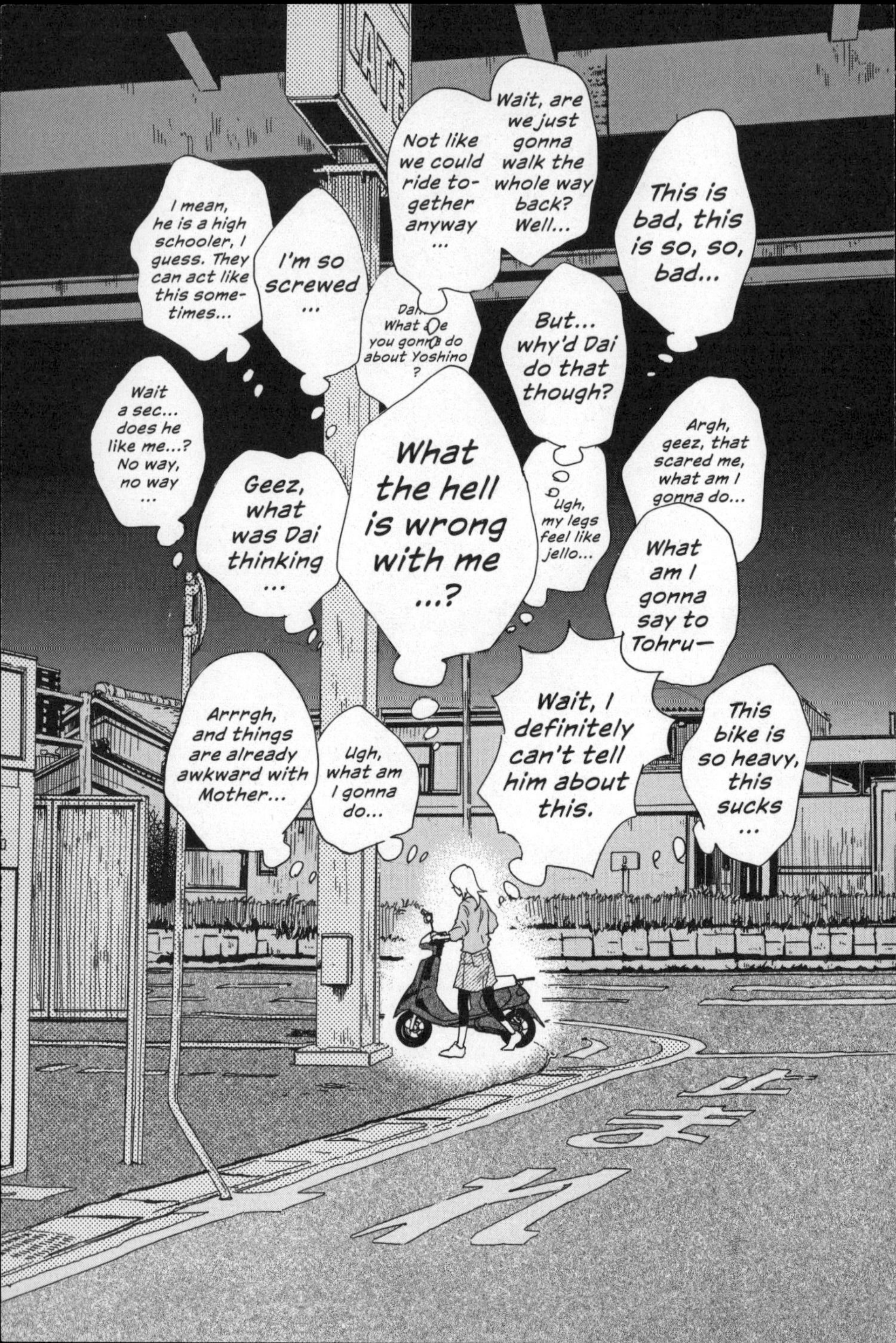
This is bad, this is so, so, bad...
Wait, are we just gonna walk the whole way back? Well...
Not like we could ride to-gether anyway ...
But... why'd Dai do that though?
Dai... What are you gonna do about Yoshino ?
I'm so screwed ...
I mean, he is a high schooler, I guess. They can act like this some-times...
Argh, geez, that scared me, what am I gonna do...
Ugh, my legs feel like jello...
What the hell is wrong with me ...?
Geez, what was Dai thinking ...
Wait a sec... does he like me...? No way, no way ...
What am I gonna say to Tohru—
This bike is so heavy, this sucks ...
Wait, I definitely can't tell him about this.
Ugh, what am I gonna do...
Arrrgh, and things are already awkward with Mother...

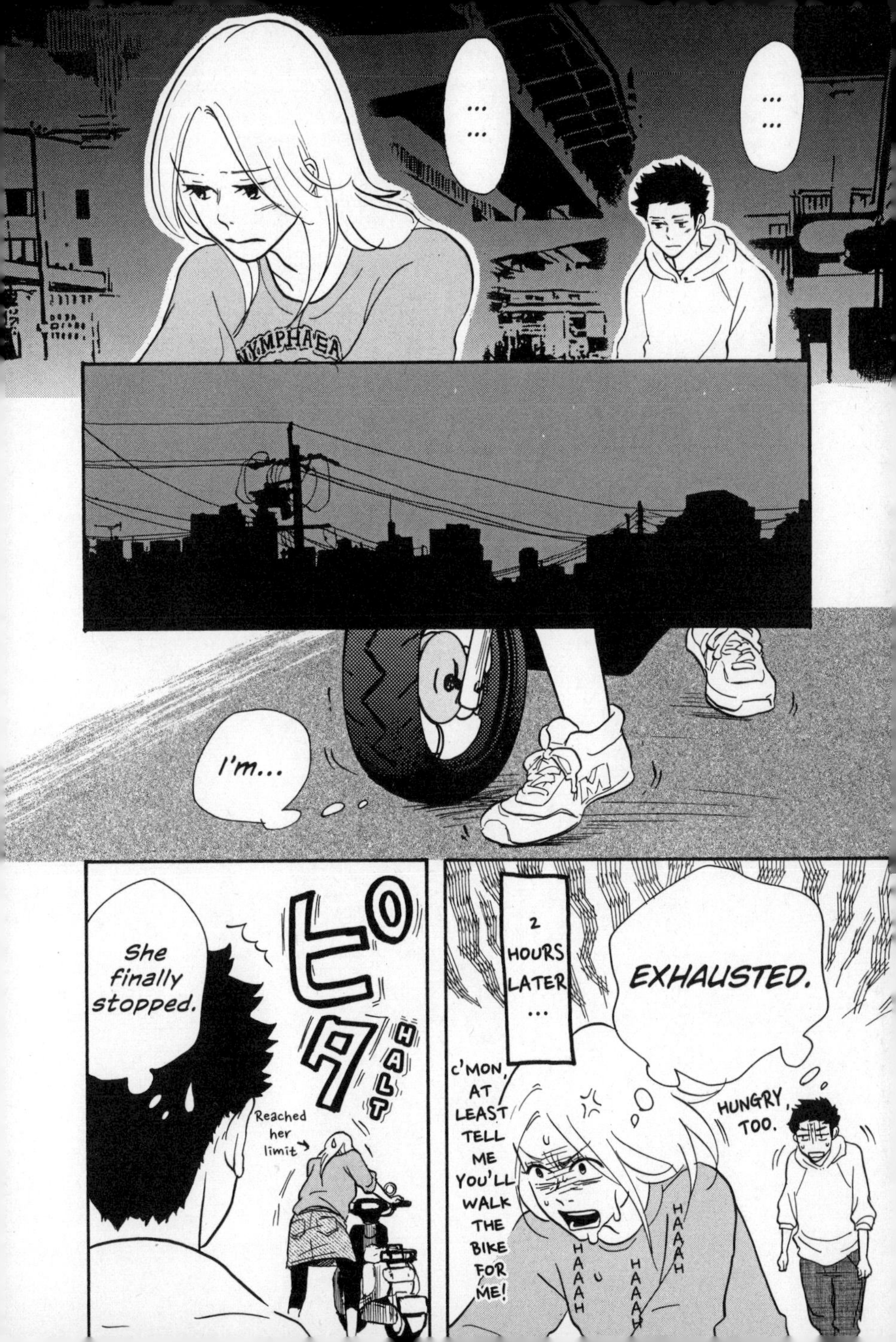

... ...
... ...
I'm...
2 HOURS LATER ...
EXHAUSTED.
HUNGRY, TOO.
C'MON, AT LEAST TELL ME YOU'LL WALK THE BIKE FOR ME!
HAAAH HAAAH HAAAH
She finally stopped.
ピタ
HALT
Reached her limit

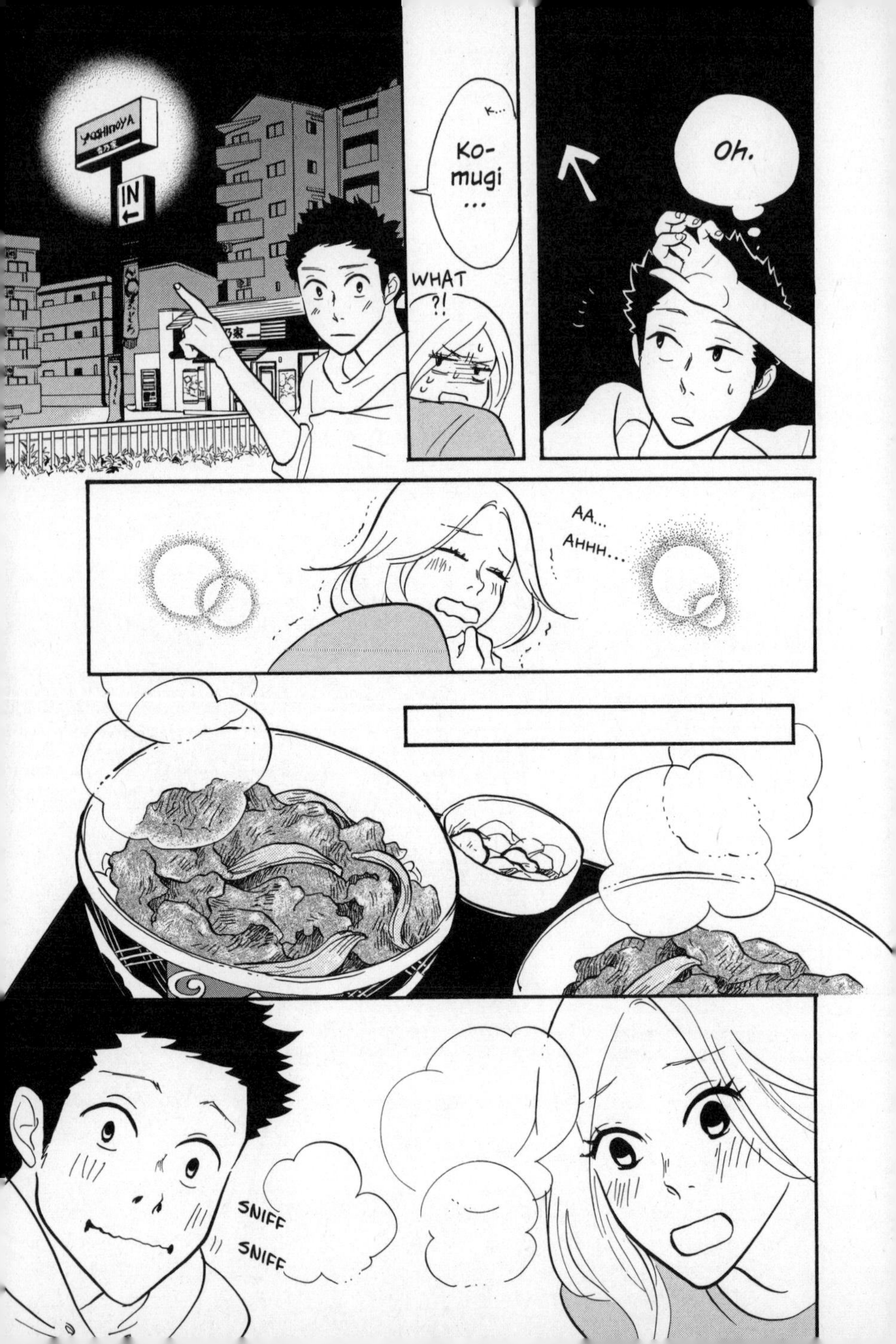
Oh.
K... Ko-mugi ...
WHAT ?!
YOSHINOYA
IN
AA... AHHH...
SNIFF
SNIFF

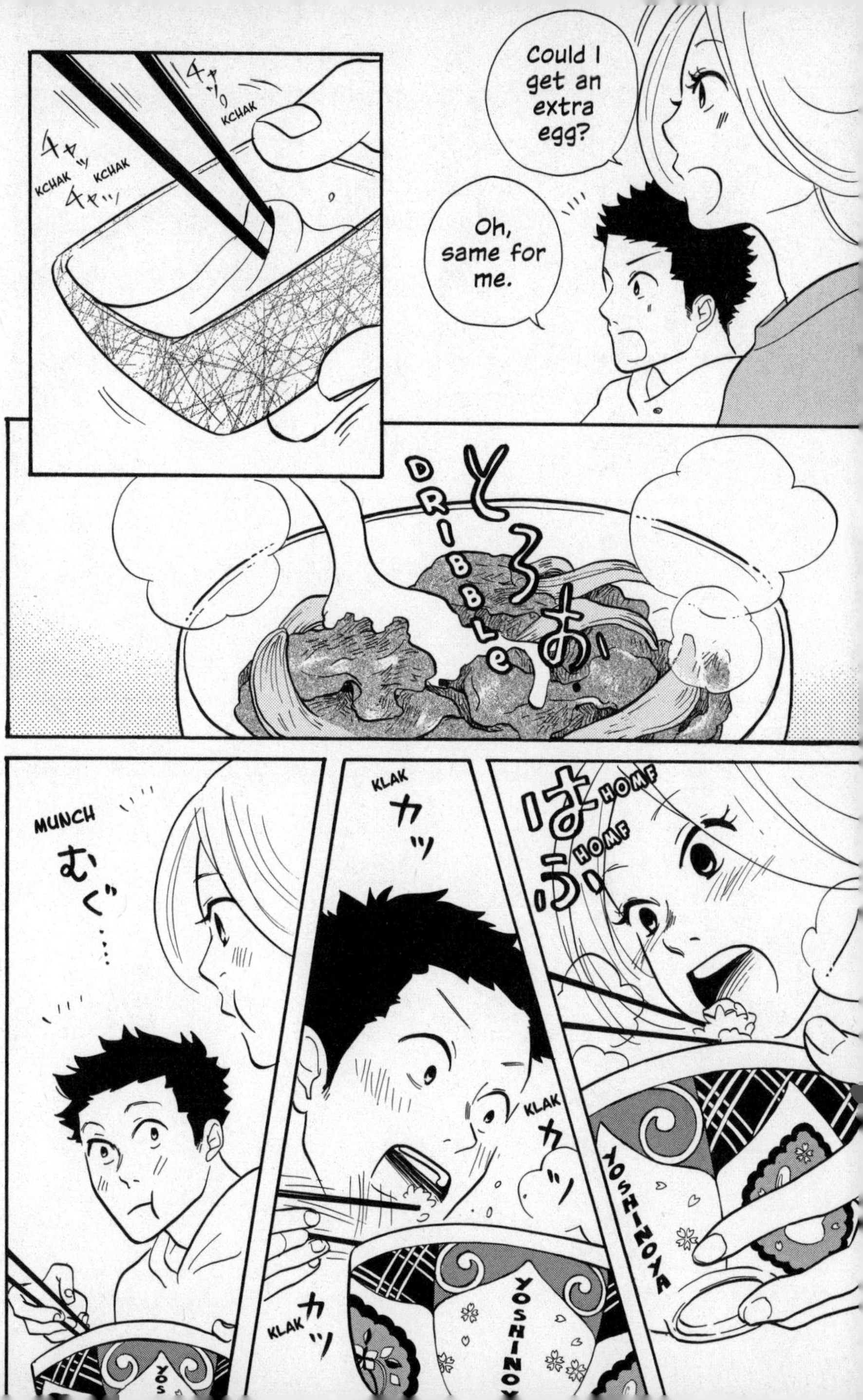
Could I get an extra egg?
Oh, same for me.
KCHAK
KCHAK
KCHAK
DRIBBLE
とろぉ
HOMF
HOMF
はふ
YOSHINOYA
KLAK
カッ
KLAK
カッ
YOSHINOYA
MUNCH
むぐ…
KLAK
カッ

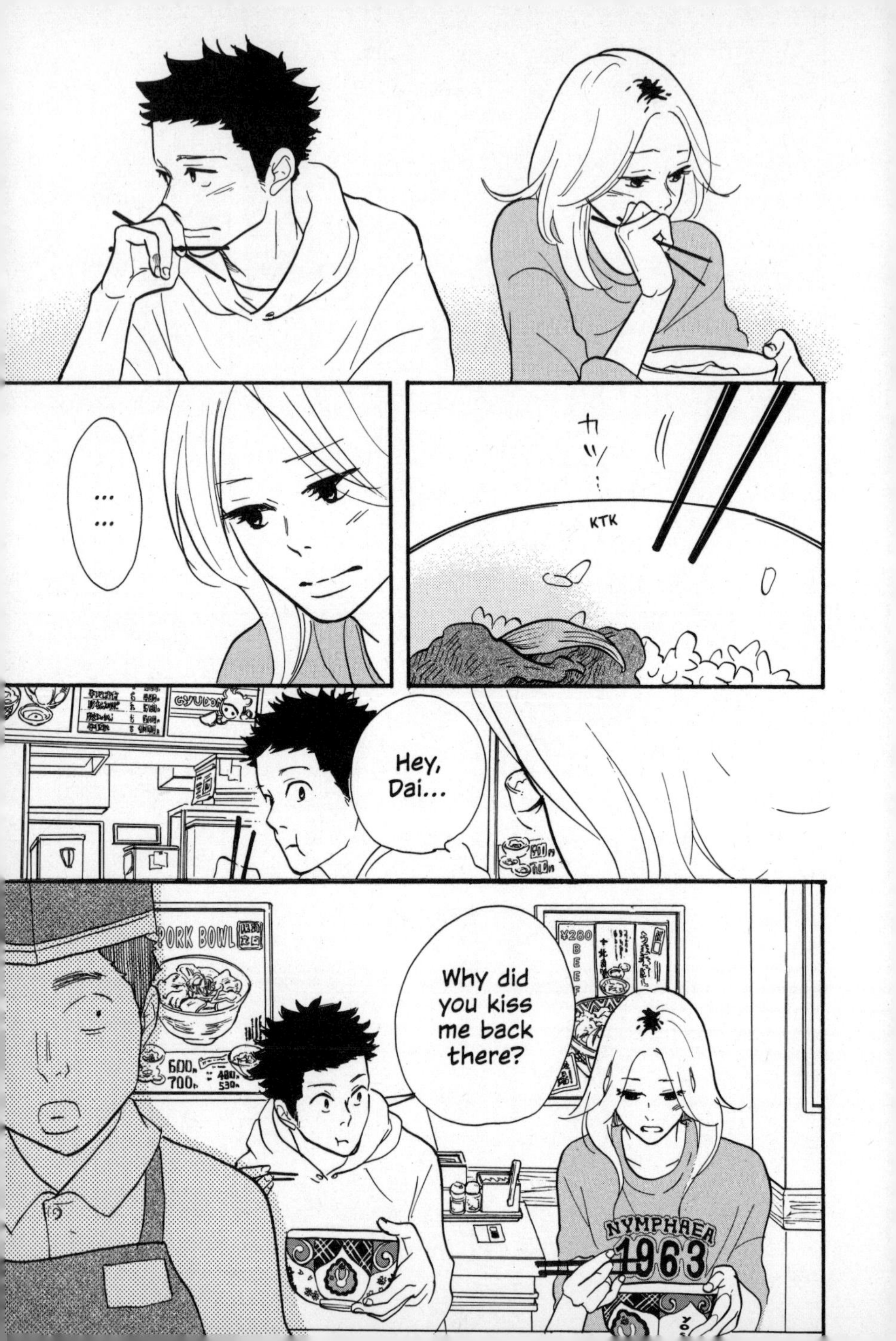

カッ…
KTK
…
…
GYUDON
Hey, Dai...
PORK BOWL
¥280 BEEF
Why did you kiss me back there?
NYMPHAEA 1963

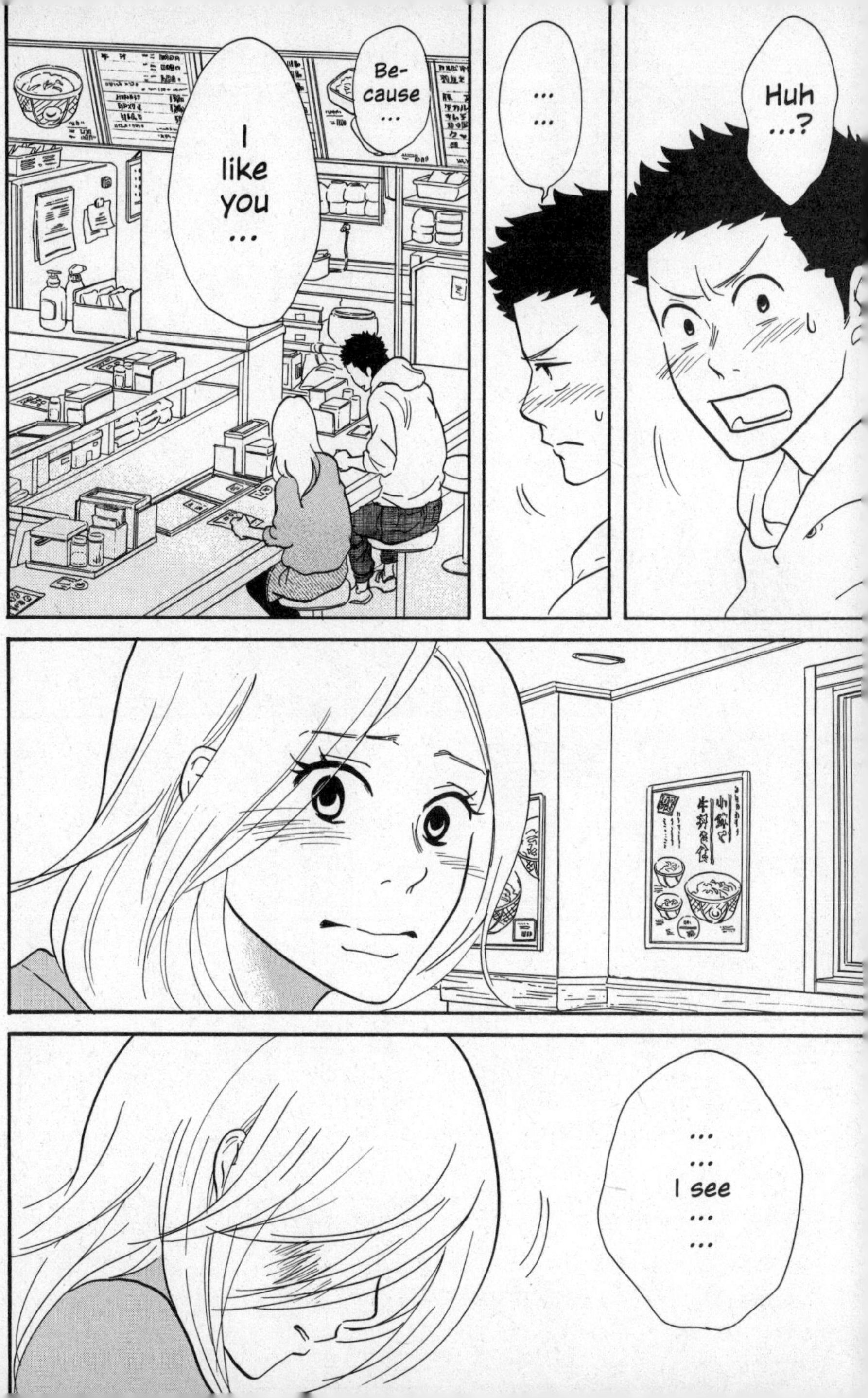
Huh ...?
... ...
Be- cause ...
I like you ...
... ... I see ... ...

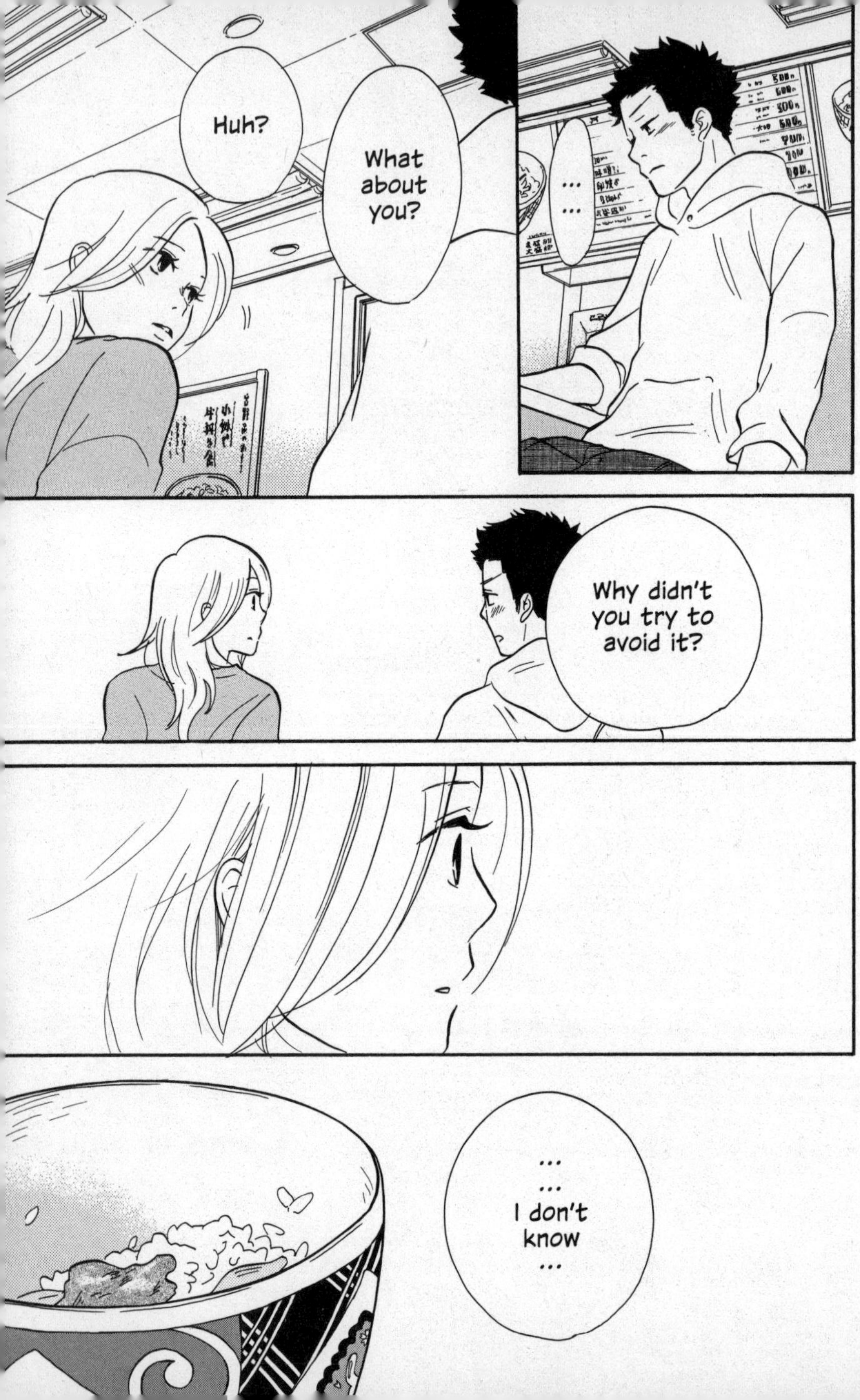
……
What about you?
Huh?
Why didn't you try to avoid it?
…
…
I don't know
…

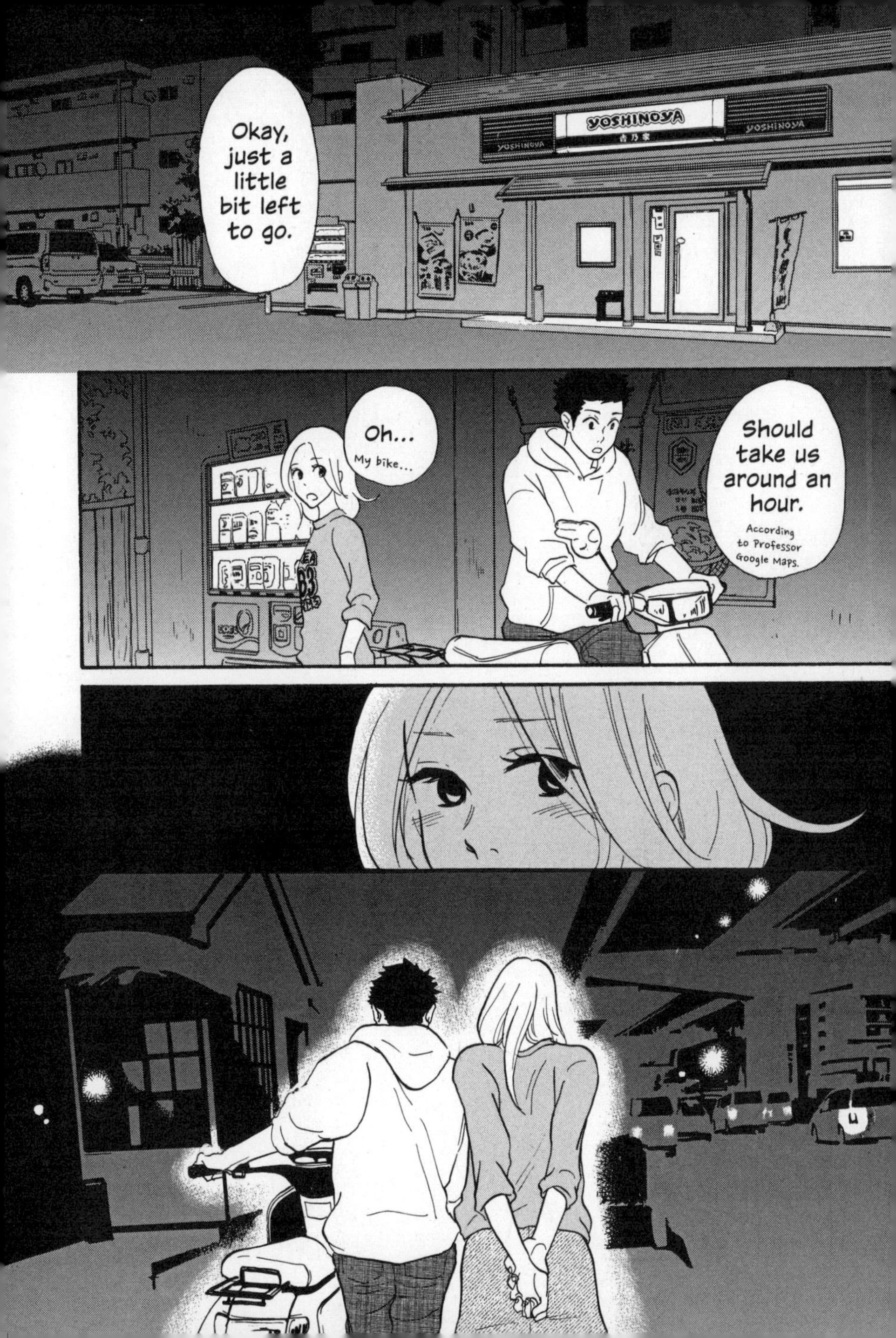
Okay, just a little bit left to go.
YOSHINOYA
Should take us around an hour.
According to Professor Google Maps.
Oh...
My bike...

The _Delinquent_
HOUSEWIFE!

37

THE DAY AFTER: TWO VERSIONS

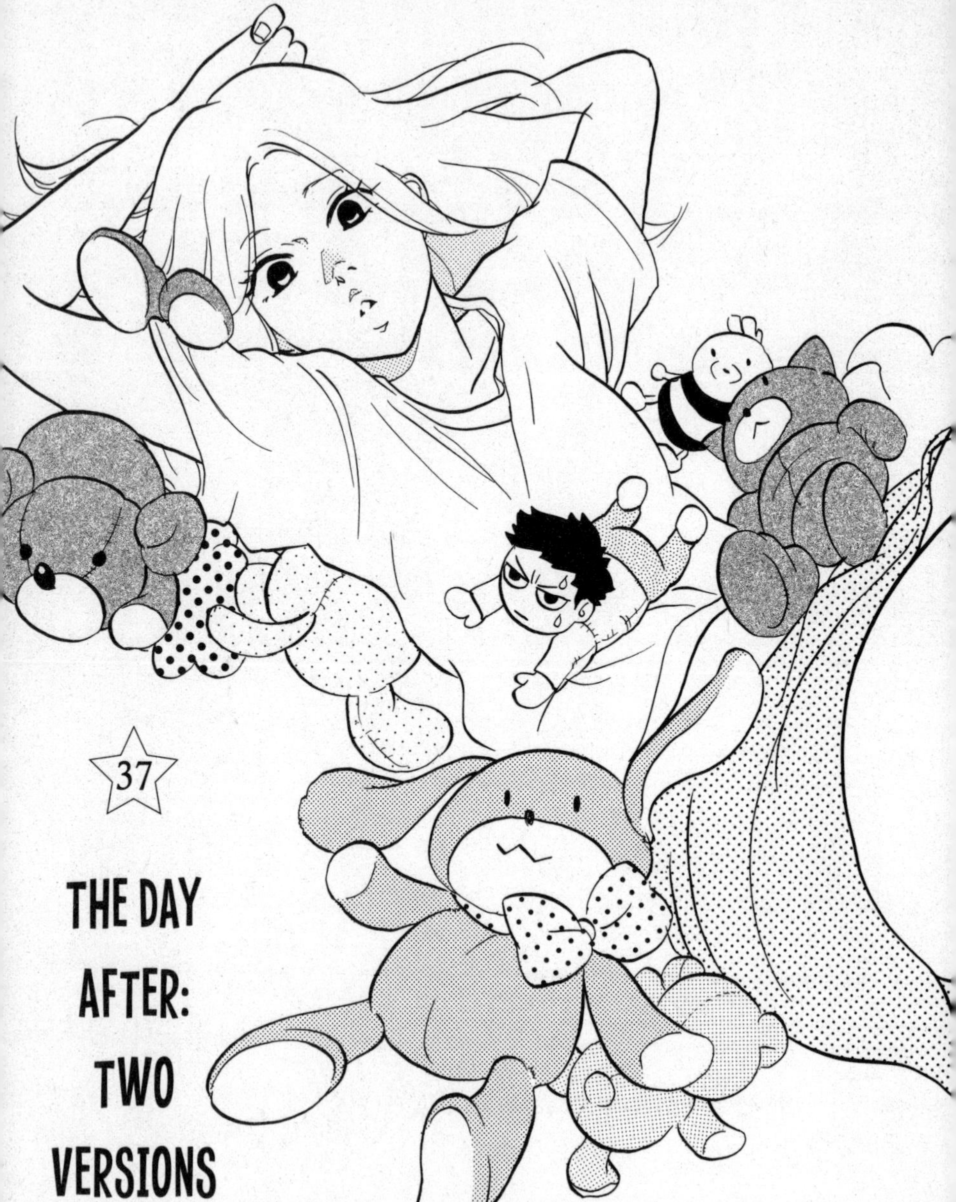

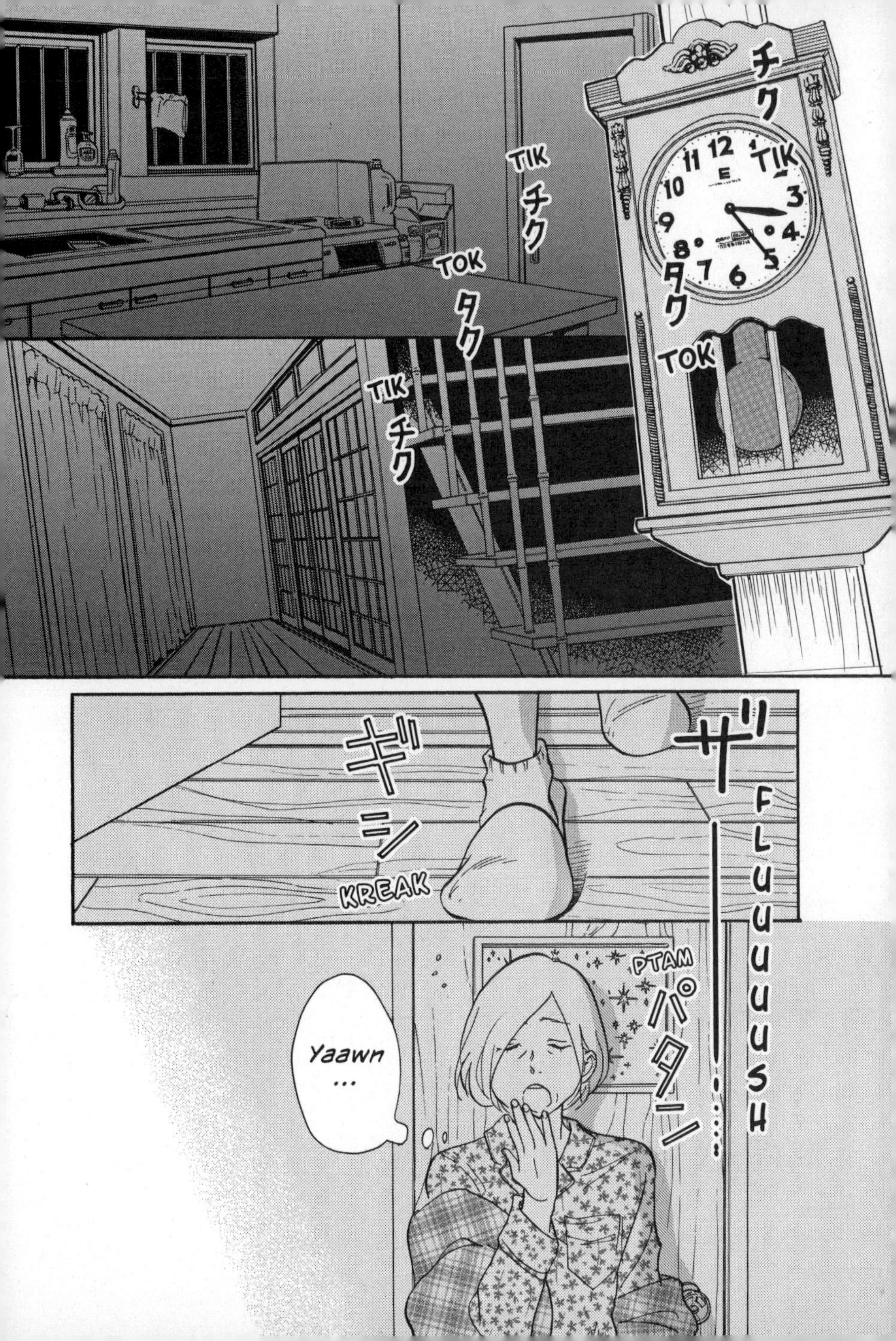

チク
TIK
タク
TOK
TIK
チク
TOK
タク
TIK
チク
ザーー……
FLUUUUUSH
ギシーン
KREAK
PTAM
パターン
Yaawn ...

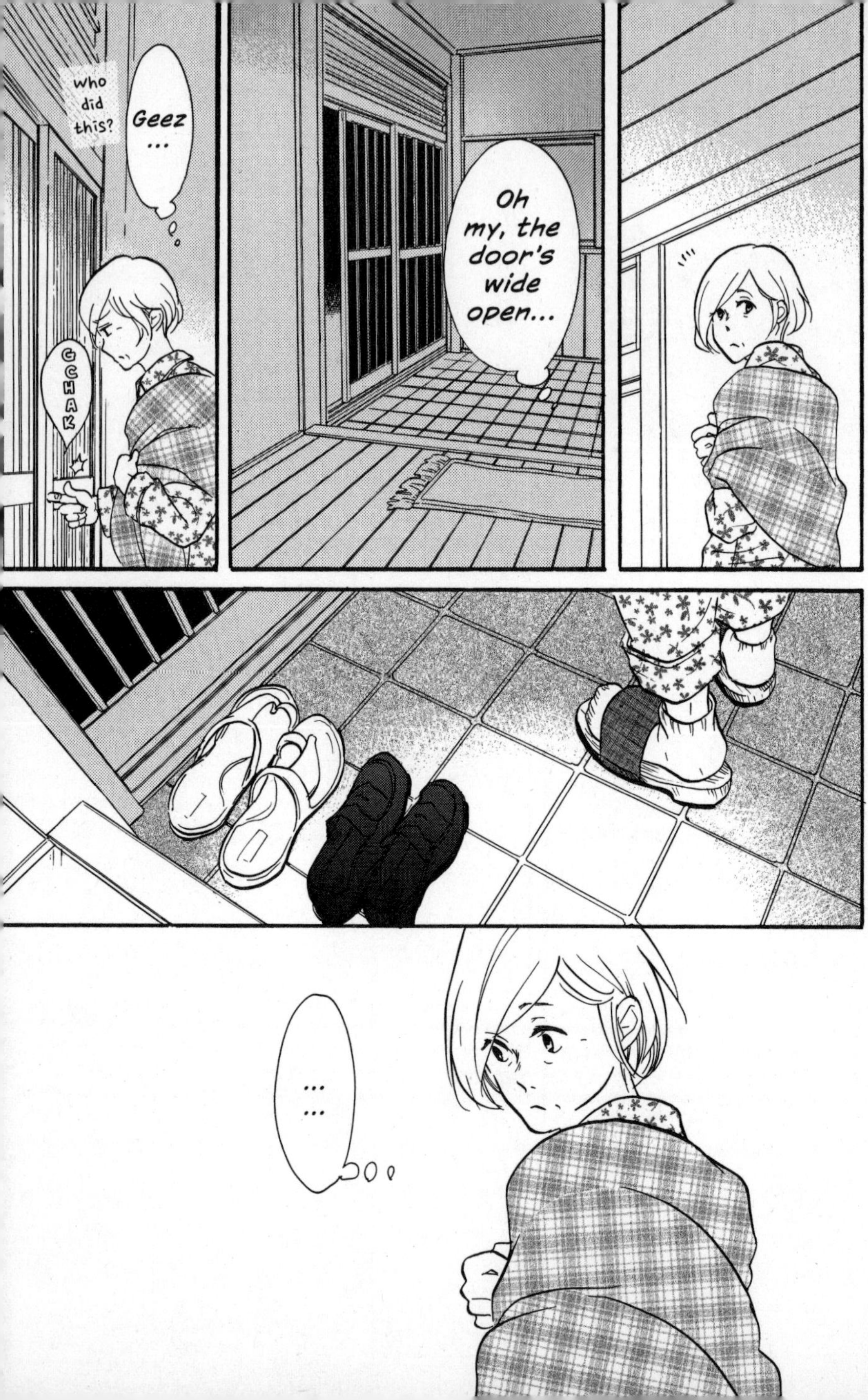
Oh my, the door's wide open...
Geez ...
who did this?
GCHAK
......

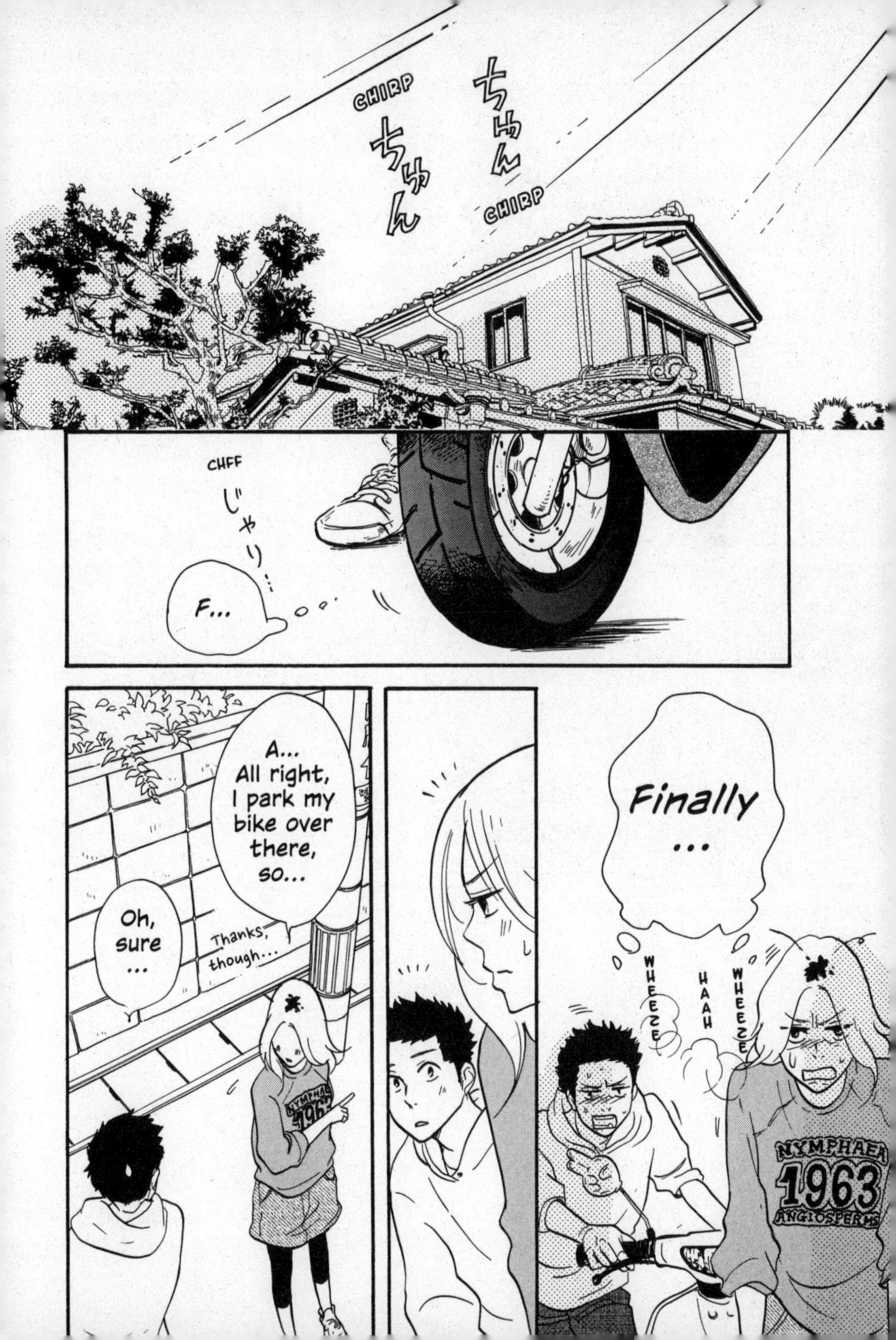

ちゅん
CHIRP
ちゅん
CHIRP
じゃり…
CHFF
F...
Finally ...
WHEEZE
HAAH
WHEEZE
A... All right, I park my bike over there, so...
Thanks, though...
Oh, sure ...

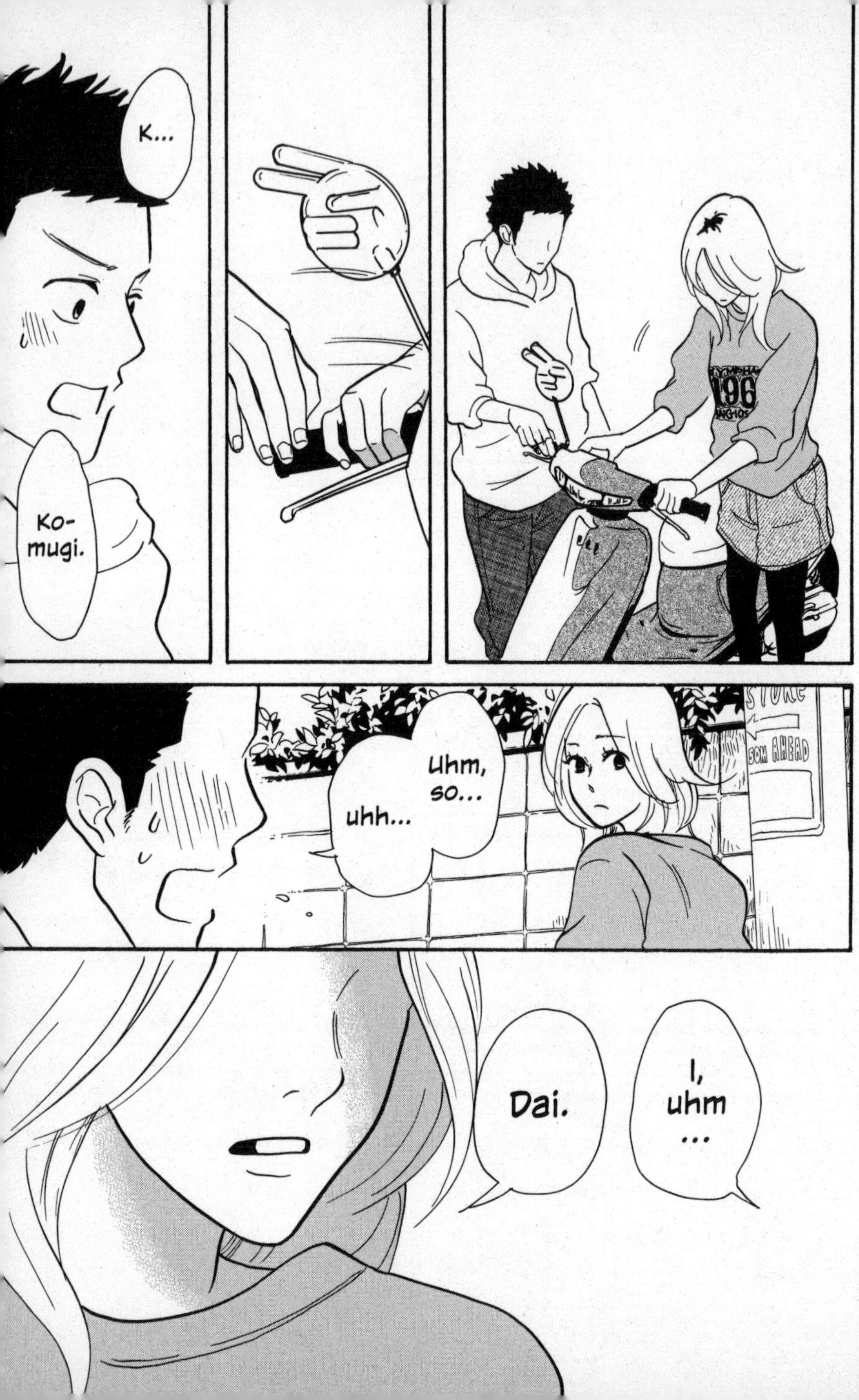
K...
Ko-mugi.
Uhm, so...
uhh...
I, uhm ...
Dai.

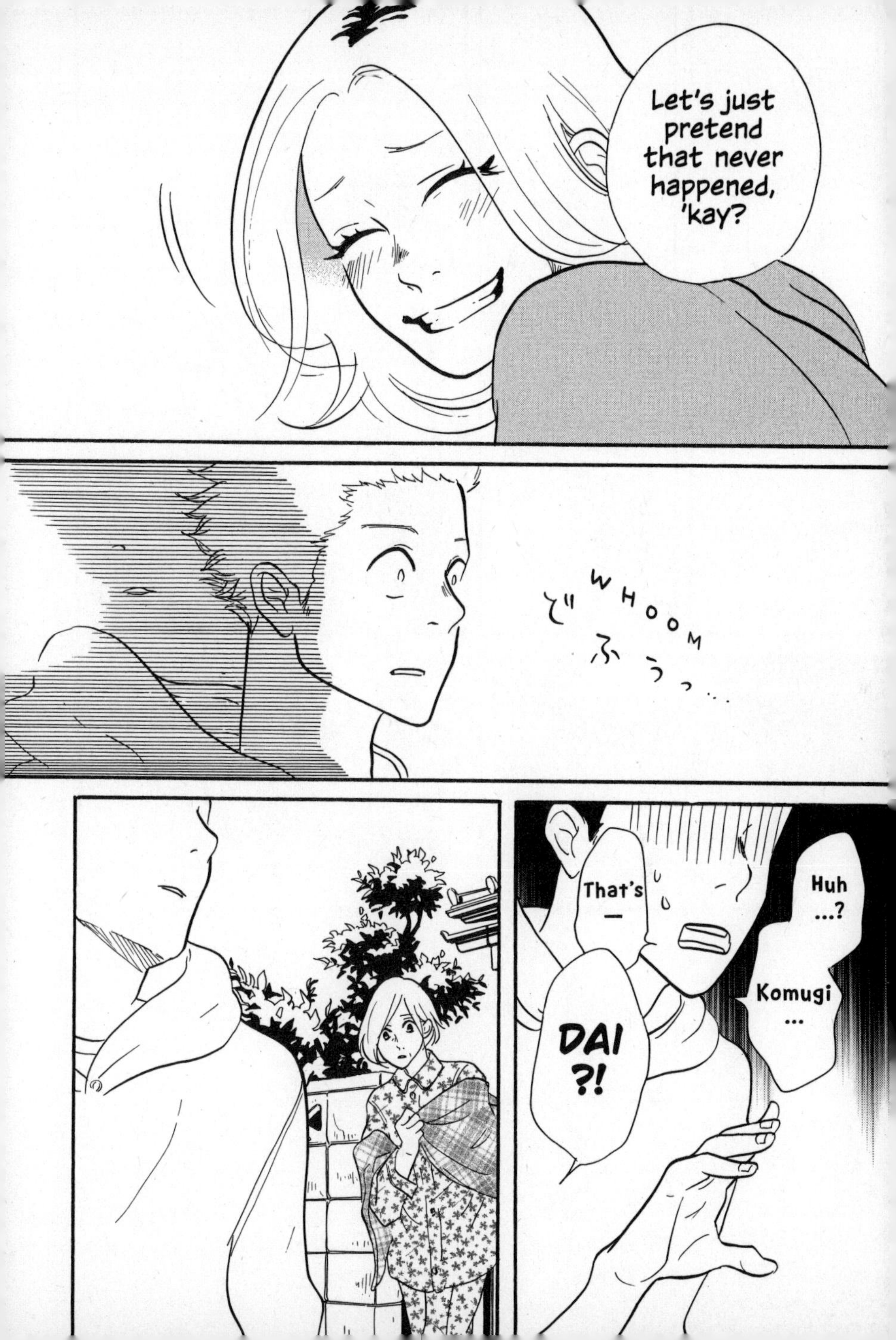
Let's just pretend that never happened, 'kay?
WHOOM
Huh ...?
That's —
Komugi ...
DAI ?!

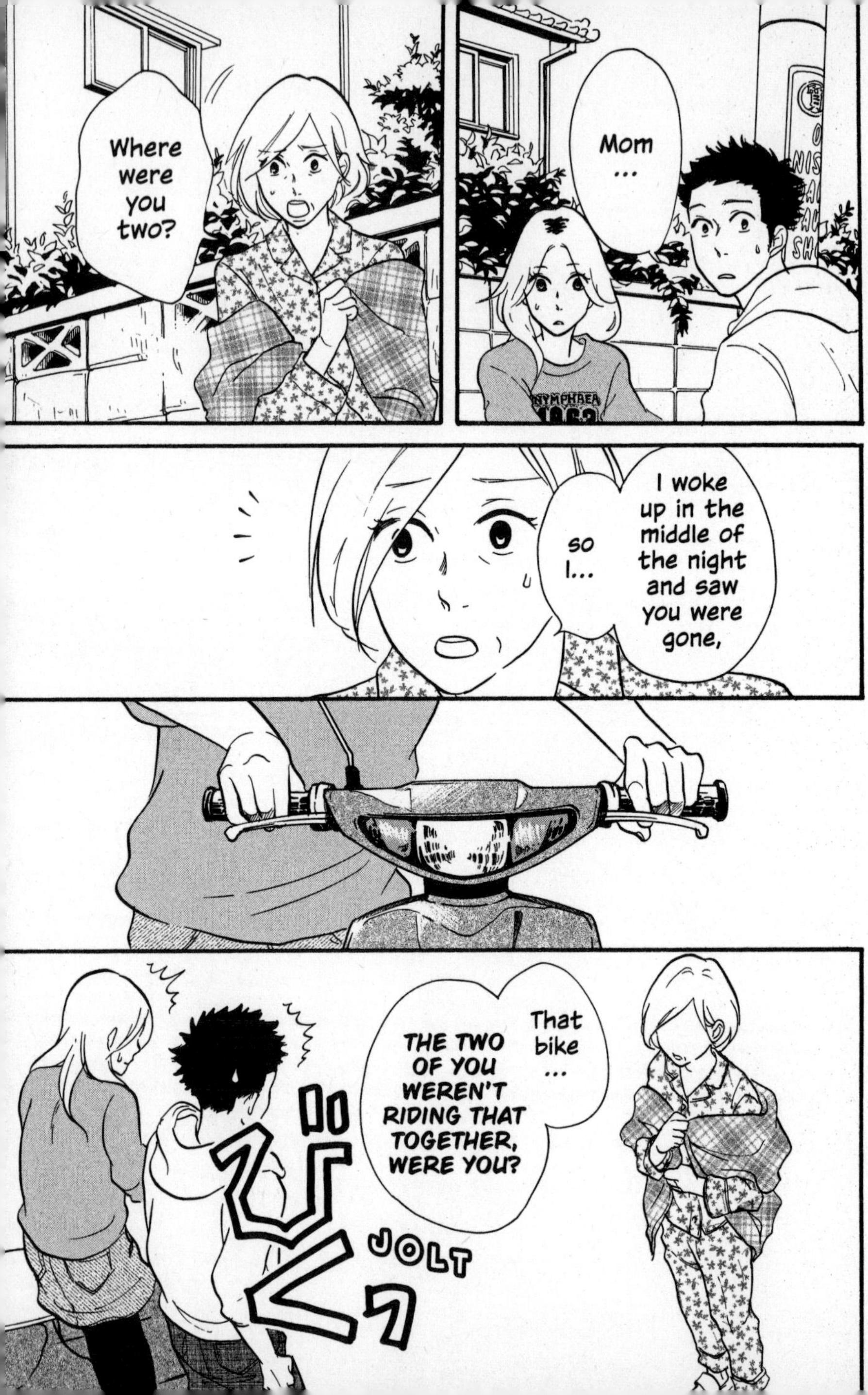
Mom ...
Where were you two?
I woke up in the middle of the night and saw you were gone,
so I...
That bike ...
THE TWO OF YOU WEREN'T RIDING THAT TOGETHER, WERE YOU?
JOLT

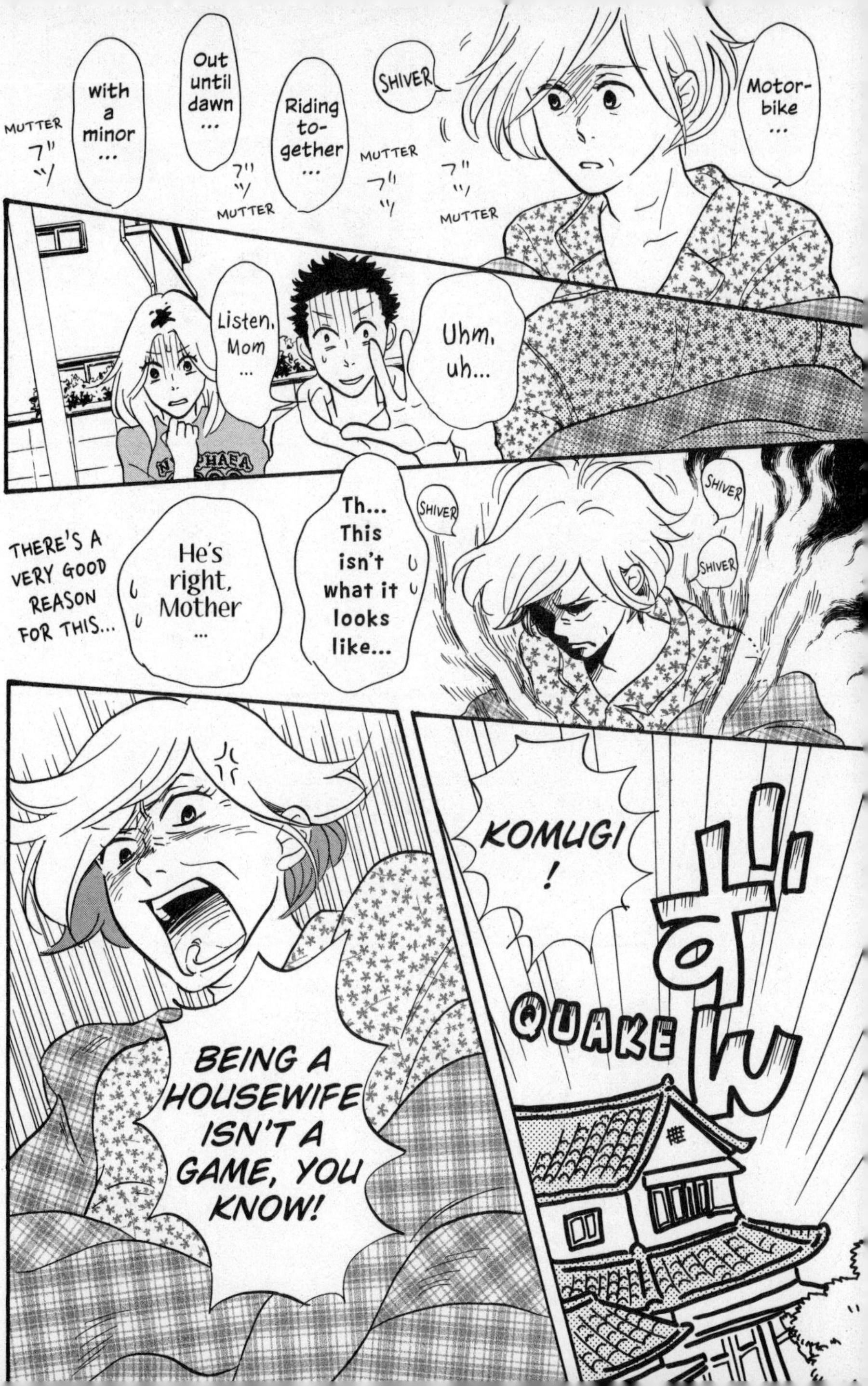

Motor-bike...
MUTTER
SHIVER
MUTTER
Riding to-gether...
MUTTER
Out until dawn...
MUTTER
with a minor...
Uhm, uh...
Listen, Mom...
SHIVER
SHIVER
SHIVER
Th... This isn't what it looks like...
He's right, Mother...
THERE'S A VERY GOOD REASON FOR THIS...
KOMUGI!
QUAKE
ずん
BEING A HOUSEWIFE ISN'T A GAME, YOU KNOW!

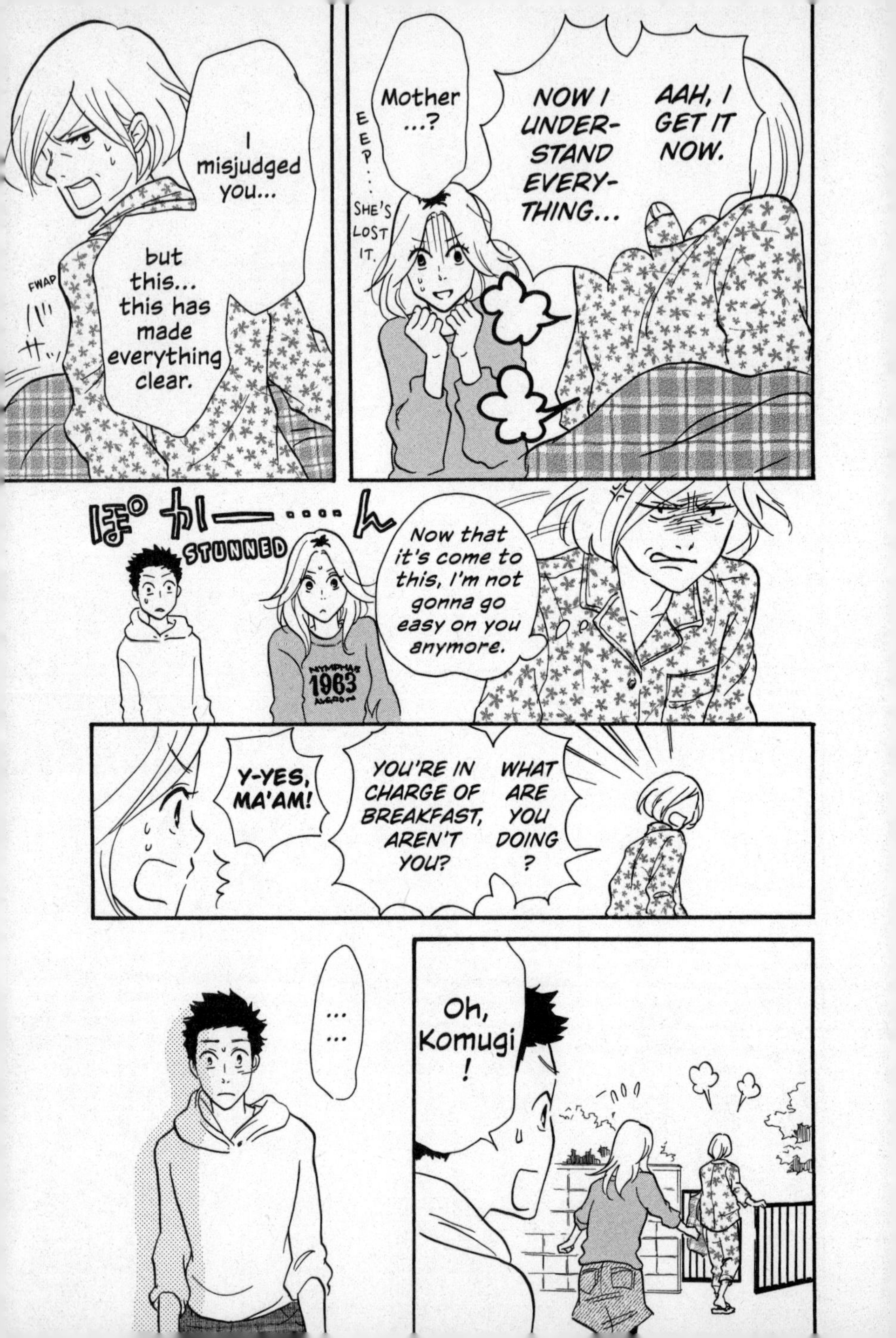
AAH, I GET IT NOW.
NOW I UNDERSTAND EVERYTHING...
Mother ...?
EEP...
SHE'S LOST IT.
I misjudged you...
but this... this has made everything clear.
FWAP
バサッ
Now that it's come to this, I'm not gonna go easy on you anymore.
ぽかーー....ん
STUNNED
WHAT ARE YOU DOING?
YOU'RE IN CHARGE OF BREAKFAST, AREN'T YOU?
Y-YES, MA'AM!
Oh, Komugi!
......

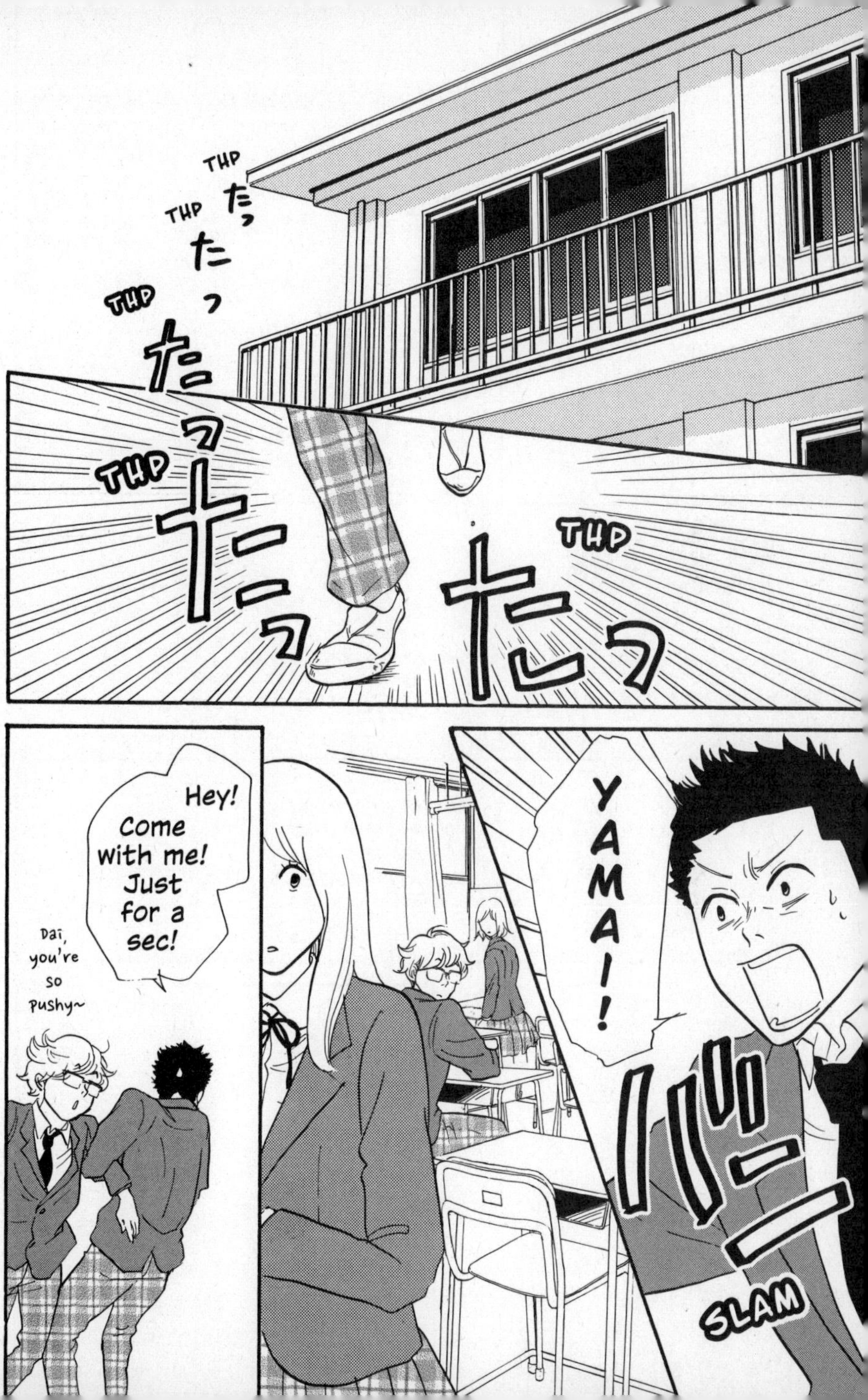
THP
たっ
THP
たっ
THP
たっ
THP
たっ
THP
たっ
YAMA!!
バーン
SLAM
Hey! Come with me! Just for a sec!
Dai, you're so pushy~

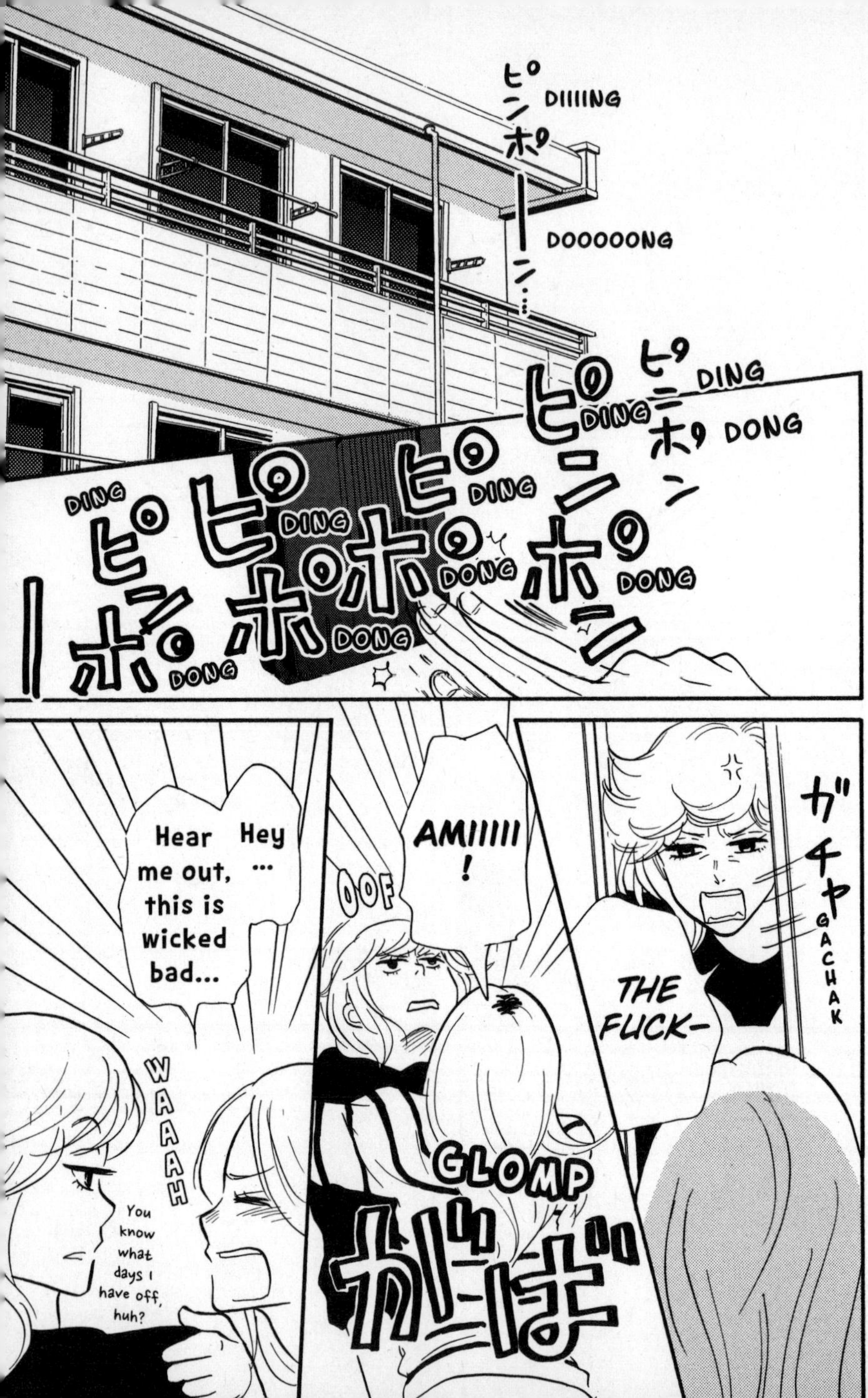
ピンポーン…
DIIIING
DOOOOONG
ピンポン
DING
DONG
ピンポンピンポンピンポンピンポン
DING
DONG
DING
DONG
DING
DONG
DING
DONG
ガチャ
GACHAK
THE FUCK-
AMIIIII!
OOF
GLOMP
がばっ
Hey…
Hear me out, this is wicked bad…
WAAAAH
You know what days I have off, huh?

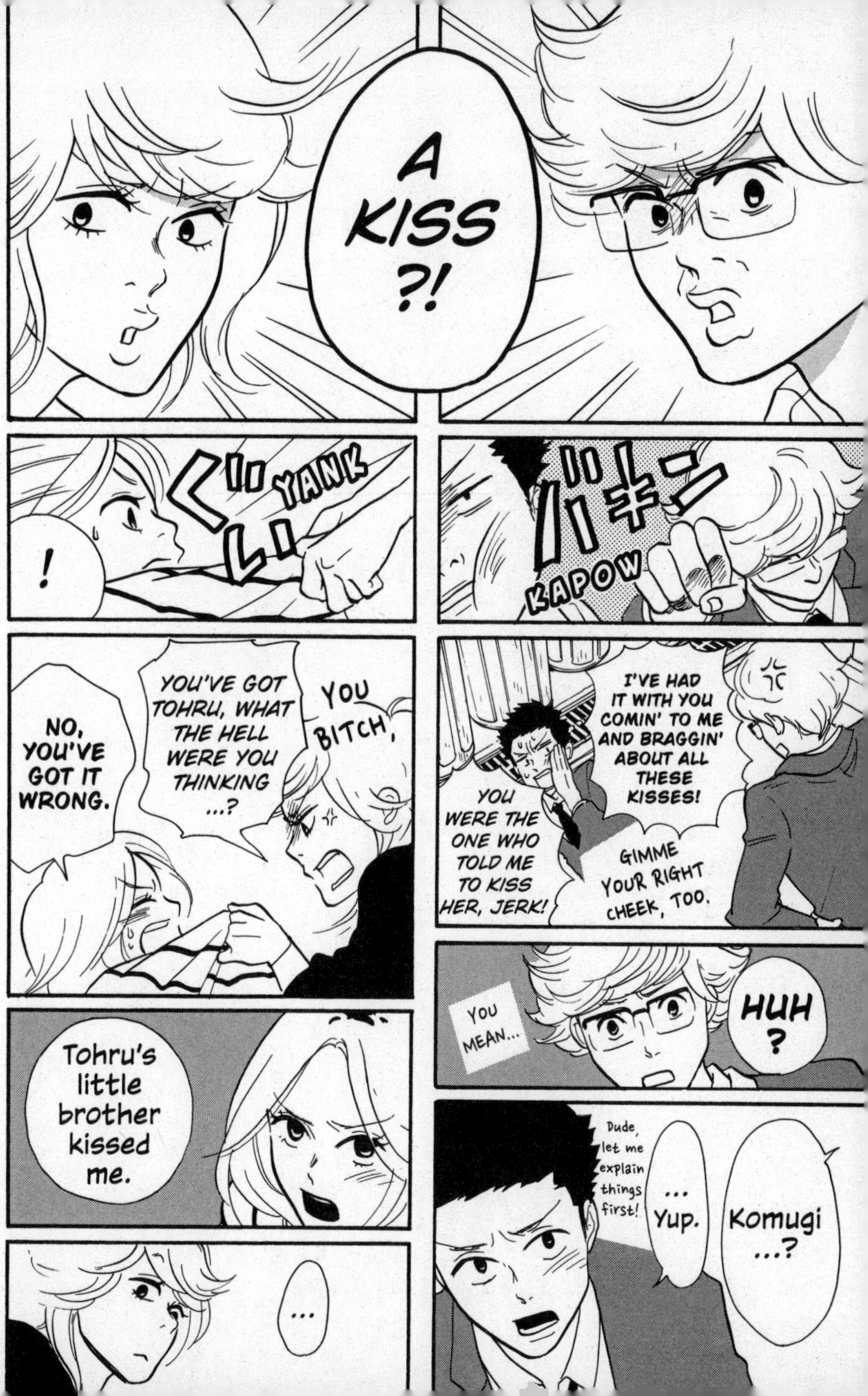
A KISS ?!
バキン
KAPOW
グイ
YANK
!
I'VE HAD IT WITH YOU COMIN' TO ME AND BRAGGIN' ABOUT ALL THESE KISSES!
GIMME YOUR RIGHT CHEEK, TOO.
YOU WERE THE ONE WHO TOLD ME TO KISS HER, JERK!
HUH ?
YOU MEAN...
YOU BITCH,
YOU'VE GOT TOHRU, WHAT THE HELL WERE YOU THINKING ...?
NO, YOU'VE GOT IT WRONG.
Komugi ...?
... Yup.
Dude, let me explain things first!
Tohru's little brother kissed me.
...

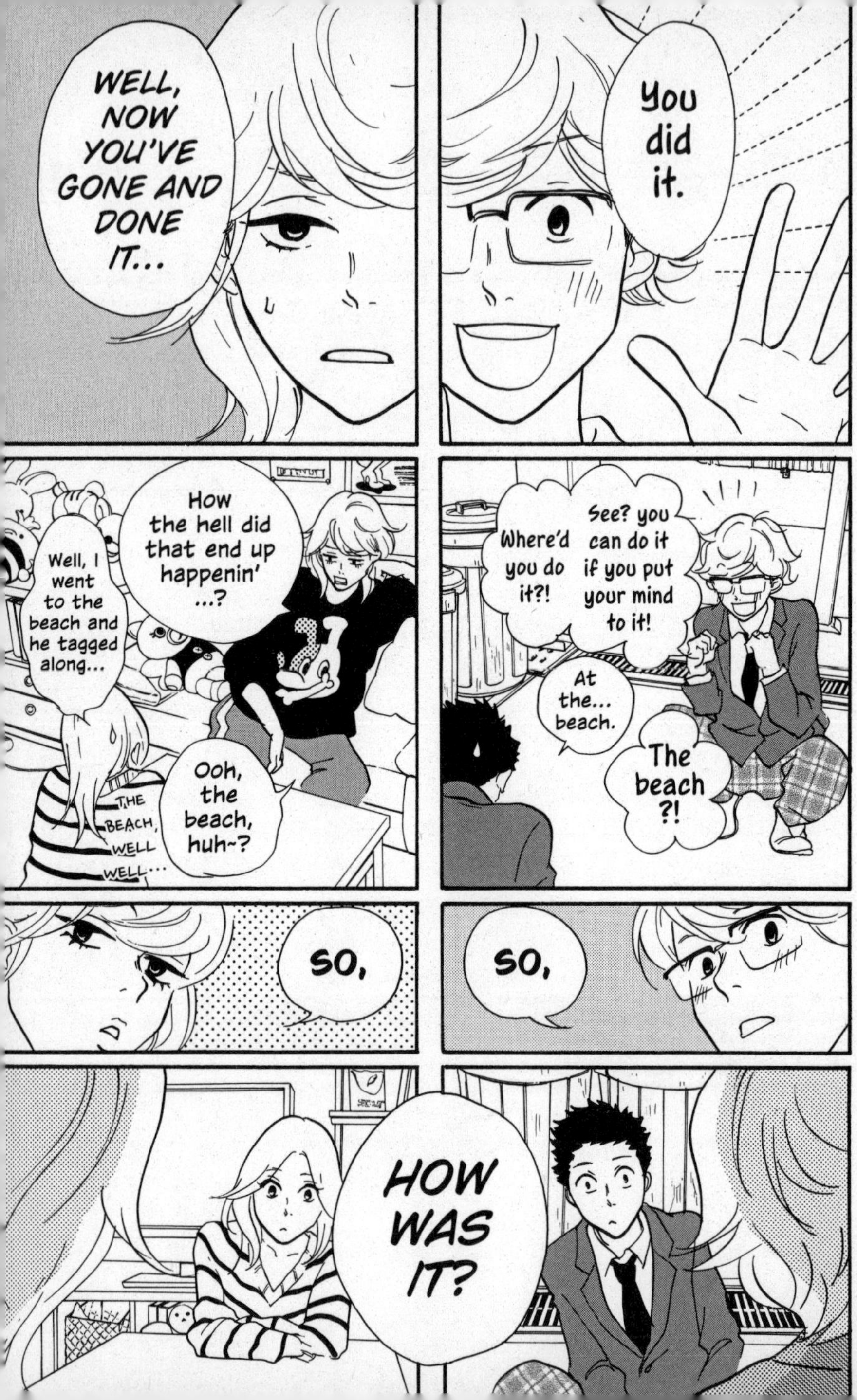
You did it.
WELL, NOW YOU'VE GONE AND DONE IT...
See? you can do it if you put your mind to it!
Where'd you do it?!
At the... beach.
The beach?!
How the hell did that end up happenin' ...?
Well, I went to the beach and he tagged along...
Ooh, the beach, huh~?
THE BEACH, WELL WELL...
SO,
SO,
HOW WAS IT?

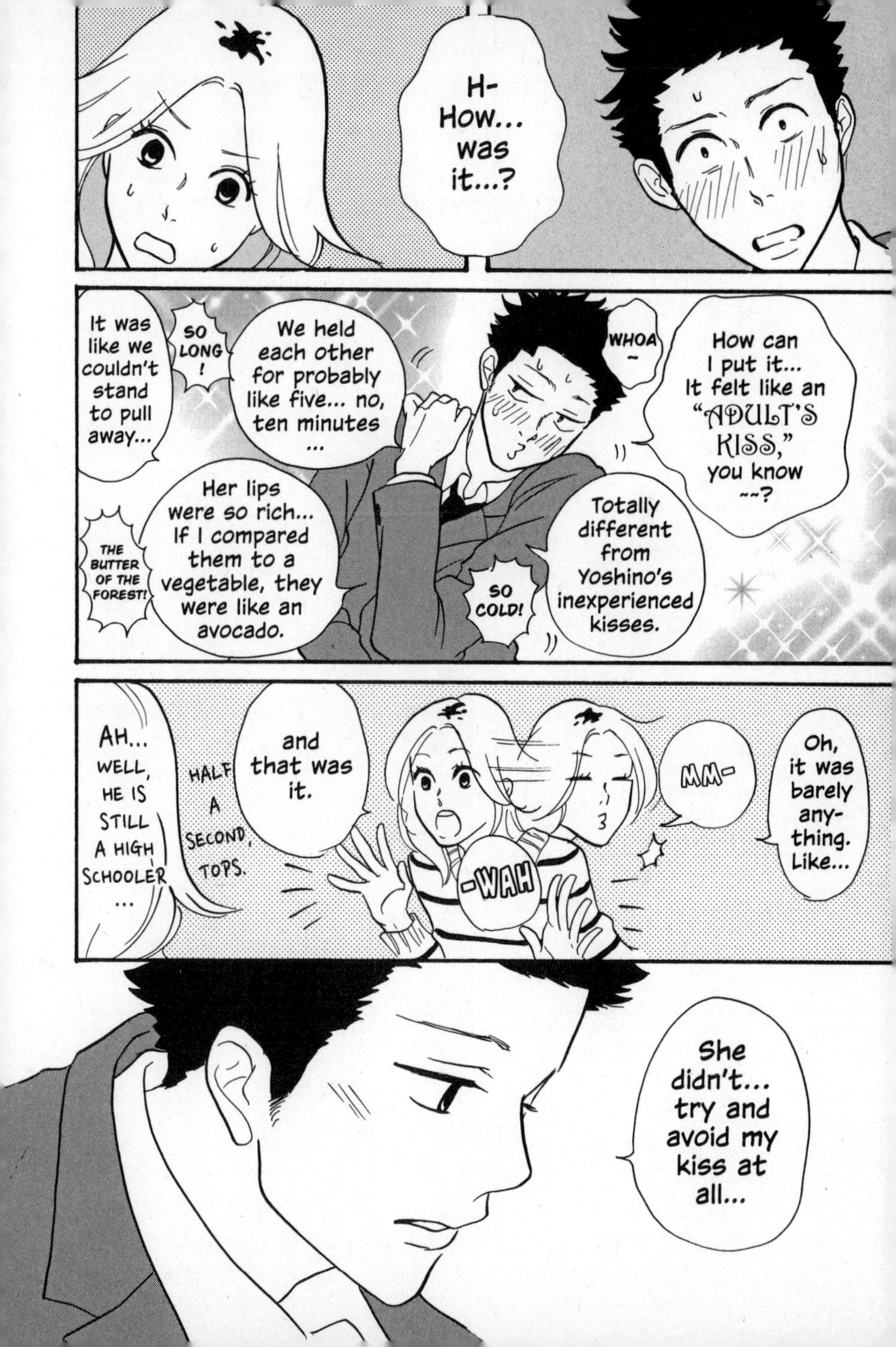
H- How... was it...?
WHOA ~
How can I put it... It felt like an "ADULT'S KISS," you know ~~?
We held each other for probably like five... no, ten minutes ...
SO LONG!
It was like we couldn't stand to pull away...
Totally different from Yoshino's inexperienced kisses.
SO COLD!
Her lips were so rich... If I compared them to a vegetable, they were like an avocado.
THE BUTTER OF THE FOREST!
Oh, it was barely any-thing. Like...
MM-
-WAH
and that was it.
HALF A SECOND, TOPS.
AH... WELL, HE IS STILL A HIGH SCHOOLER ...
She didn't... try and avoid my kiss at all...

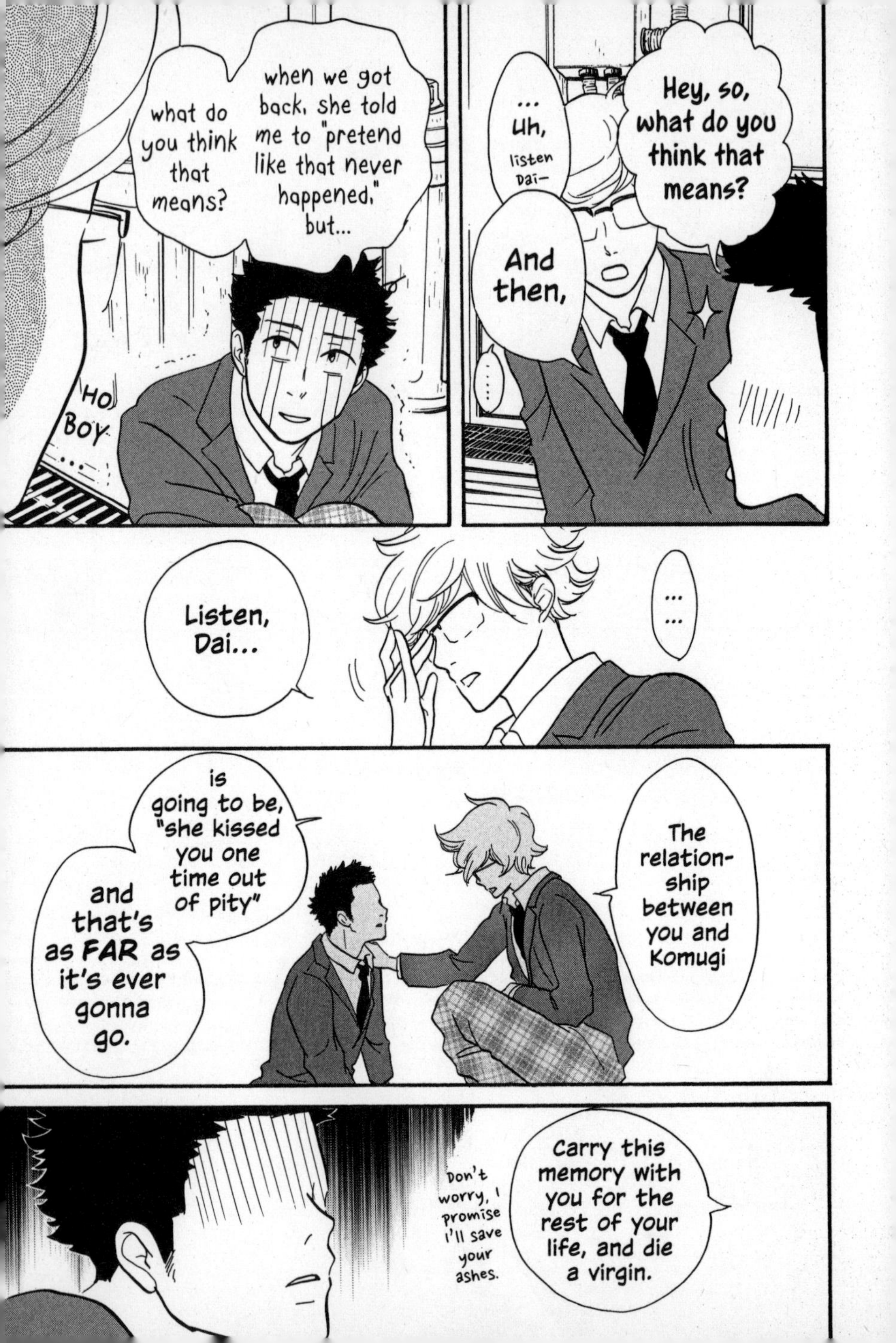
Hey, so, what do you think that means?
... Uh, listen Dai—
And then,
......
when we got back, she told me to "pretend like that never happened," but...
what do you think that means?
HO BOY...
...
...
Listen, Dai...
The relationship between you and Komugi
is going to be, "she kissed you one time out of pity"
and that's as FAR as it's ever gonna go.
Carry this memory with you for the rest of your life, and die a virgin.
Don't worry, I promise I'll save your ashes.

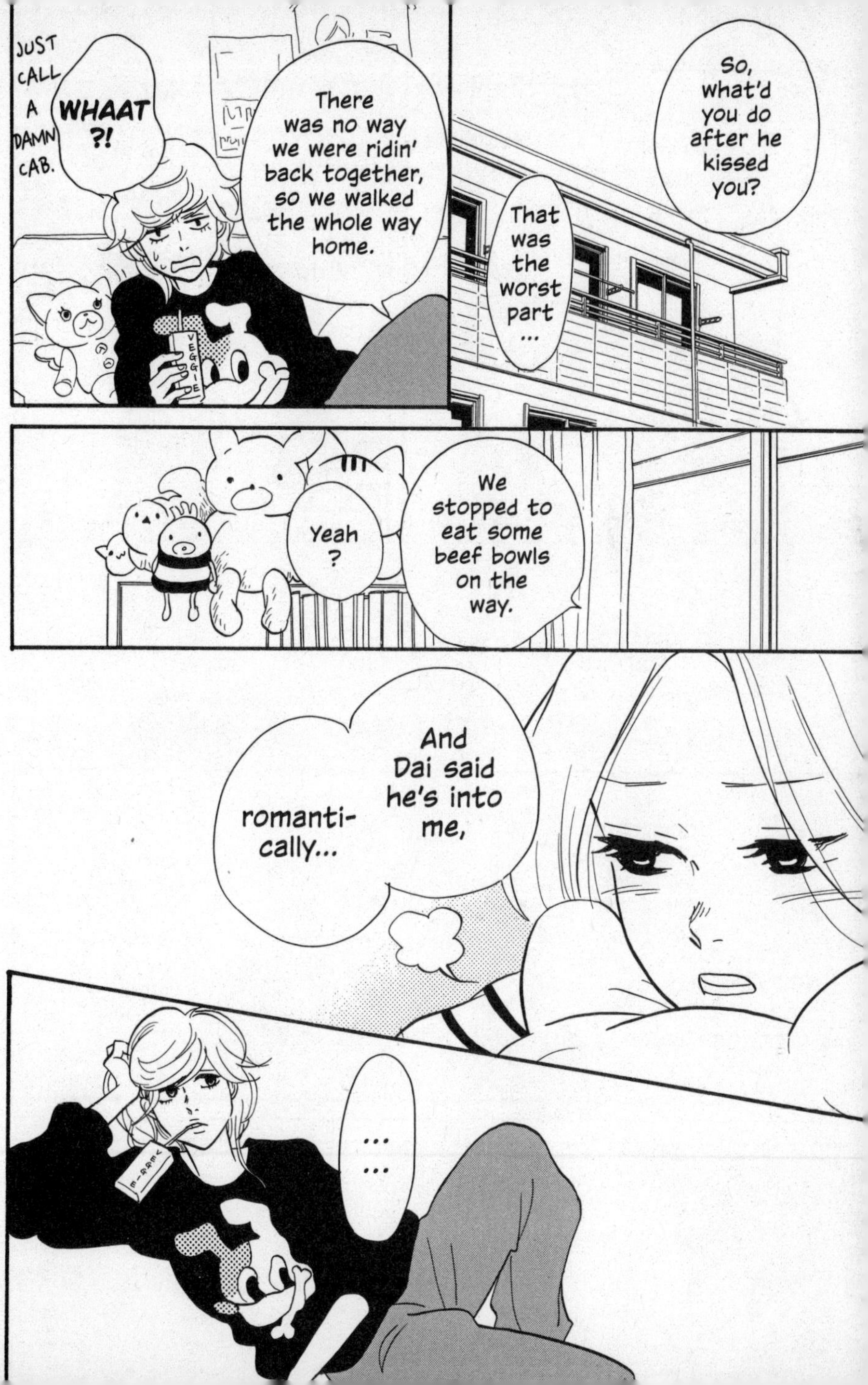
So, what'd you do after he kissed you?
That was the worst part ...
There was no way we were ridin' back together, so we walked the whole way home.
WHAAT ?!
JUST CALL A DAMN CAB.
VEGGIE
We stopped to eat some beef bowls on the way.
Yeah ?
And Dai said he's into me,
romanti-cally...
... ...

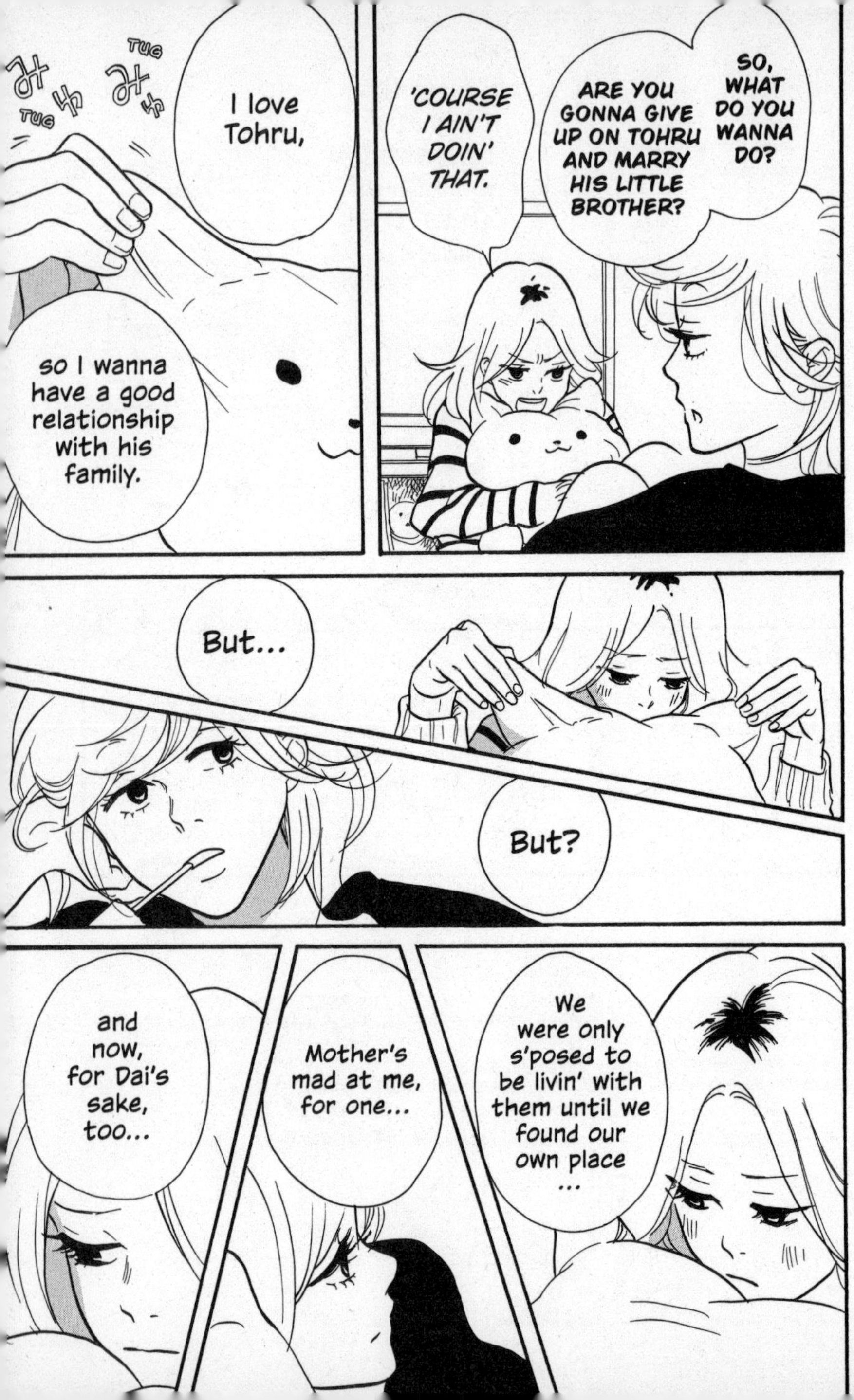
SO, WHAT DO YOU WANNA DO?
ARE YOU GONNA GIVE UP ON TOHRU AND MARRY HIS LITTLE BROTHER?
'COURSE I AIN'T DOIN' THAT.
みゅ TUG
みゅ TUG
I love Tohru,
so I wanna have a good relationship with his family.
But...
But?
We were only s'posed to be livin' with them until we found our own place ...
Mother's mad at me, for one...
and now, for Dai's sake, too...

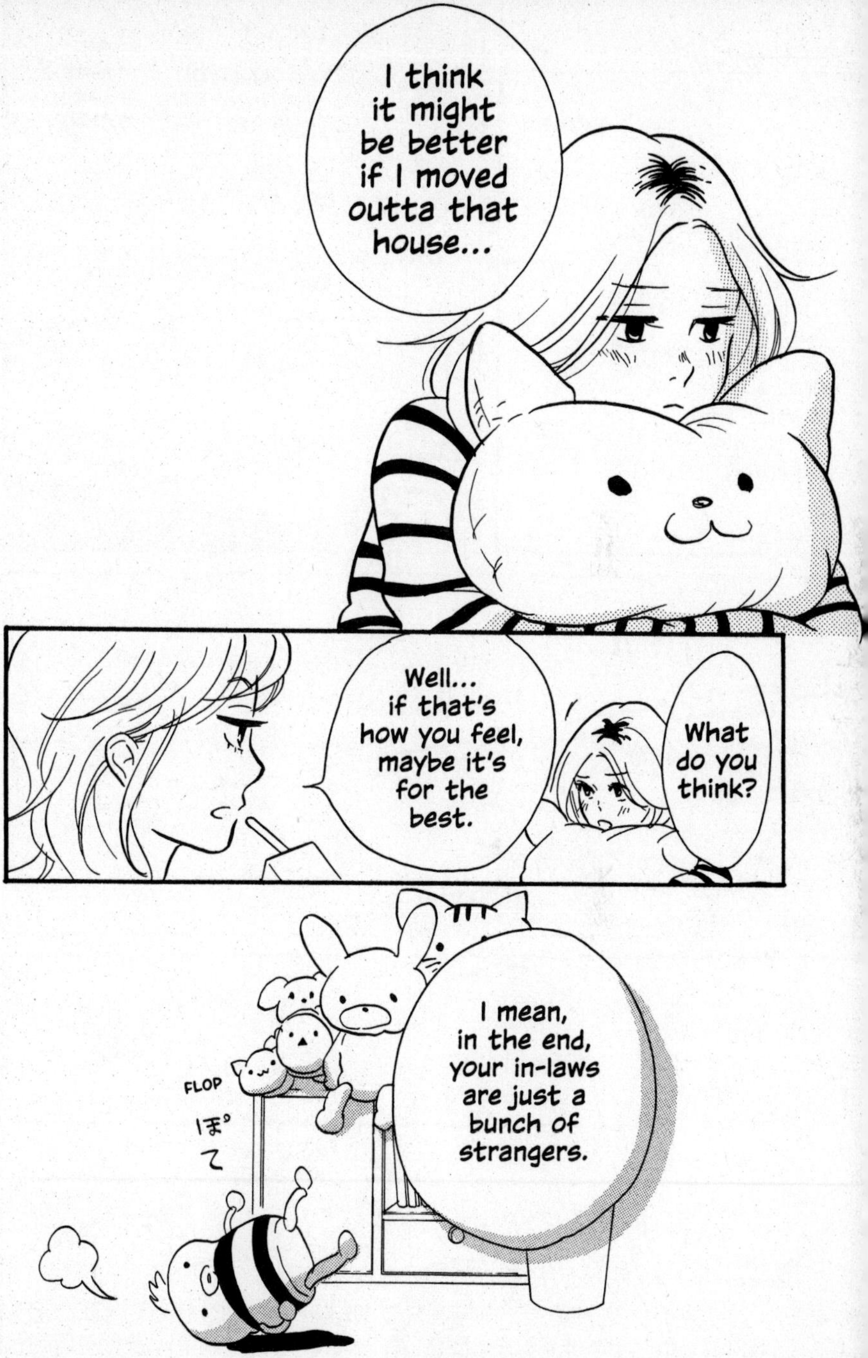
I think it might be better if I moved outta that house...
What do you think?
Well... if that's how you feel, maybe it's for the best.
I mean, in the end, your in-laws are just a bunch of strangers.
FLOP
ぽて

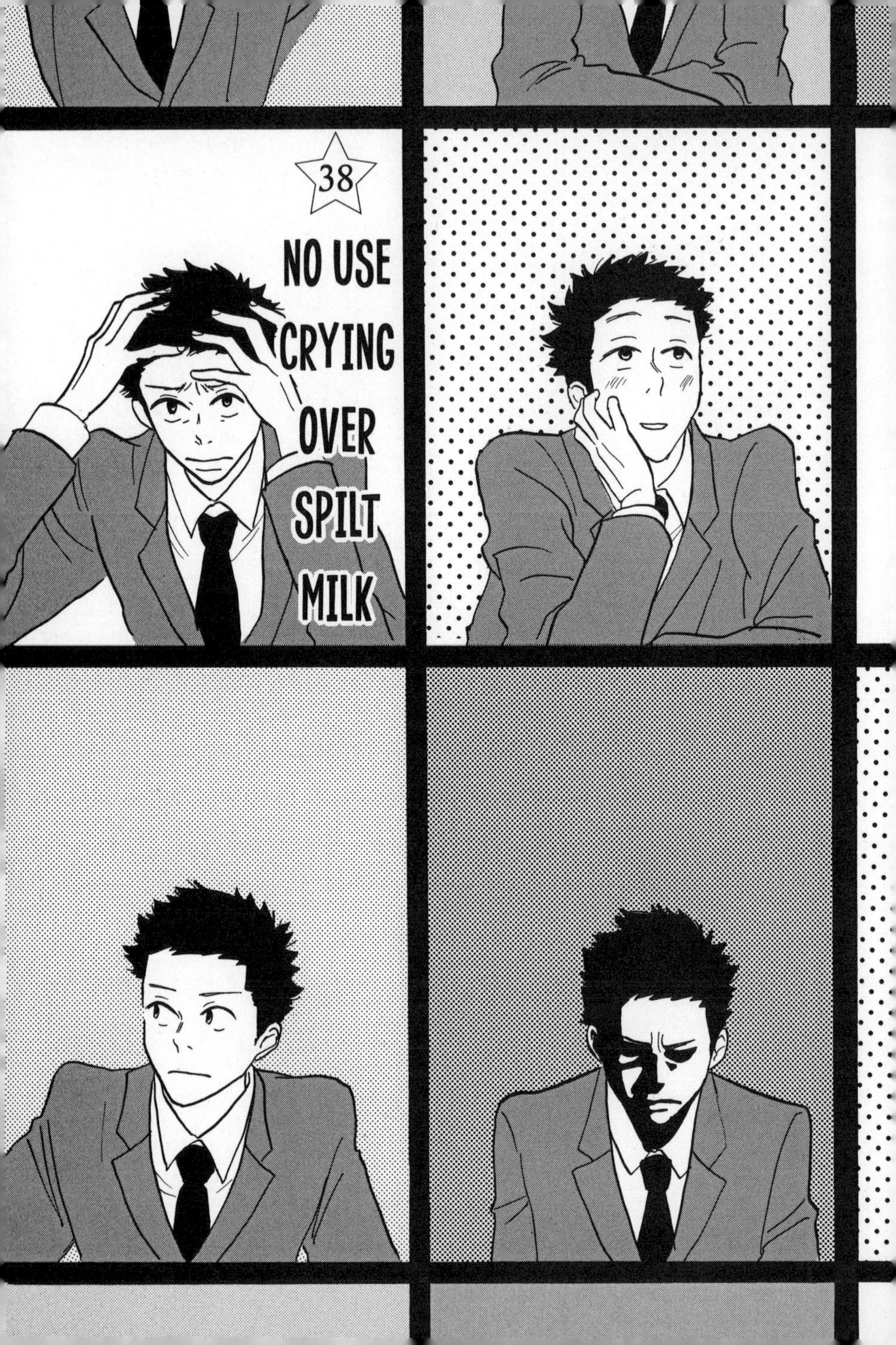
38
NO USE CRYING OVER SPILT MILK

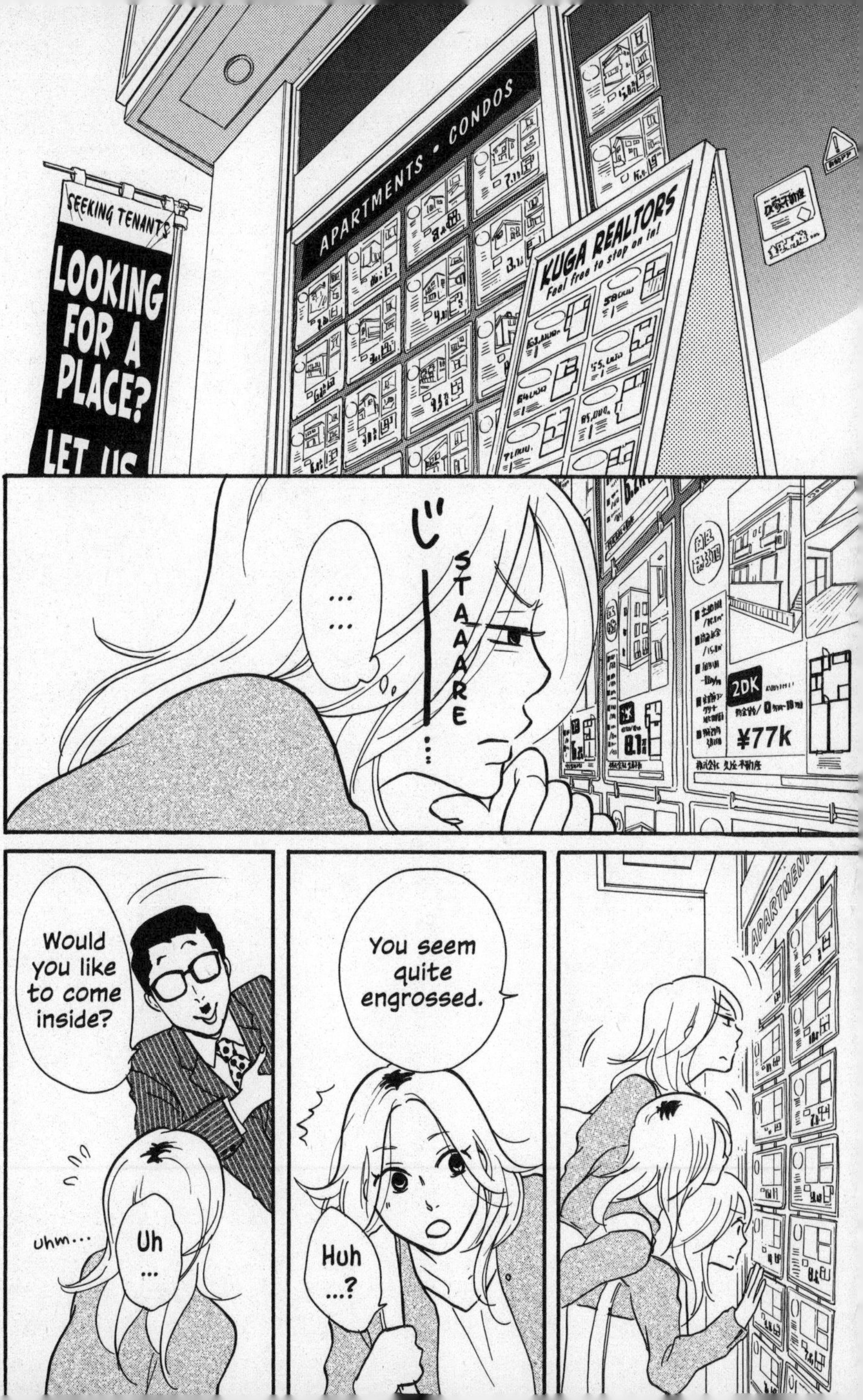
SEEKING TENANTS
LOOKING FOR A PLACE?
LET US
APARTMENTS • CONDOS
KUGA REALTORS
Feel free to stop on in!
......
じ STAAARE...
2DK
¥77k
You seem quite engrossed.
Huh ...?
Would you like to come inside?
Uh ...
uhm...

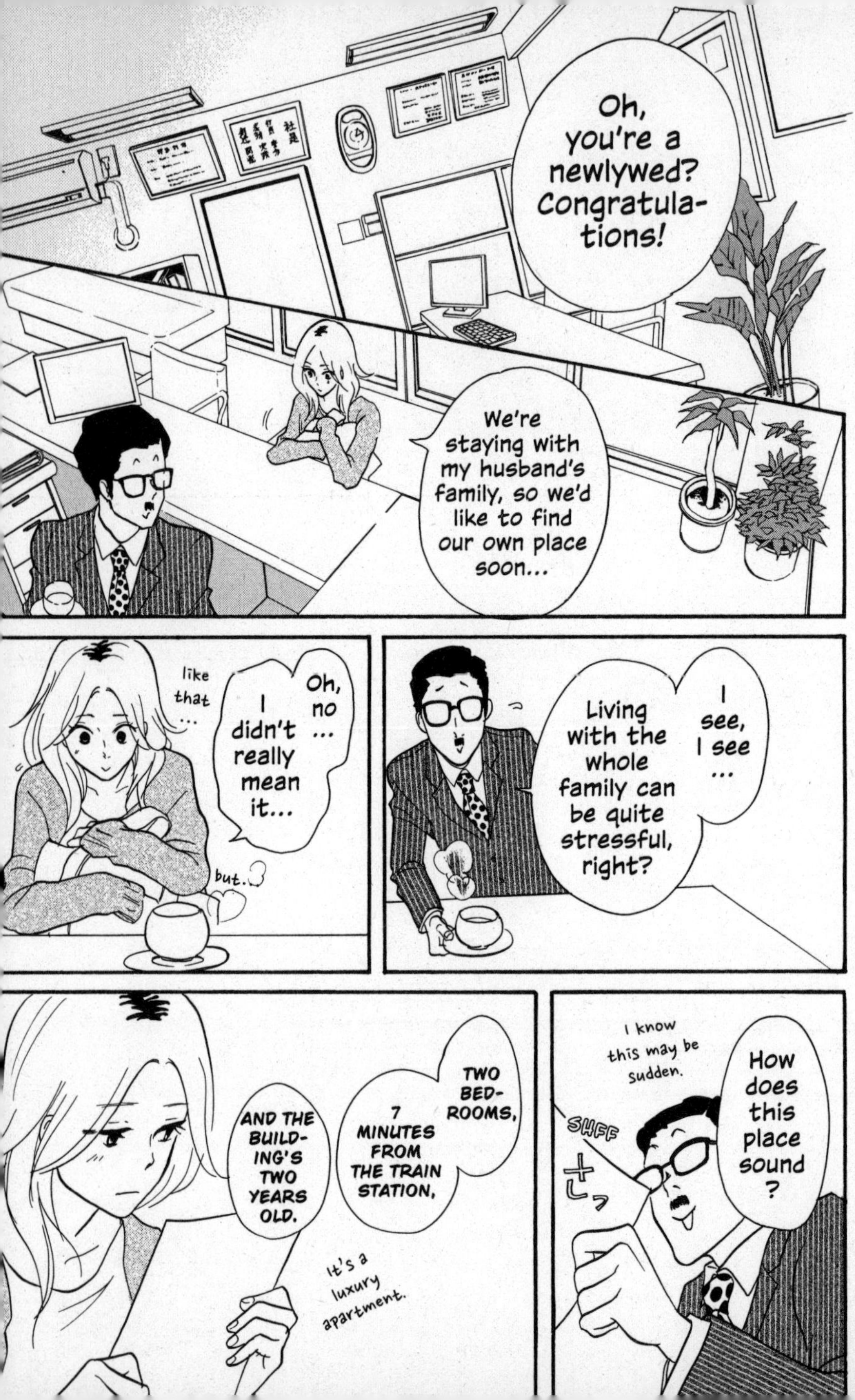
Oh, you're a newlywed? Congratulations!
We're staying with my husband's family, so we'd like to find our own place soon...
I see, I see...
Living with the whole family can be quite stressful, right?
Oh, no...
I didn't really mean it...
like that...
but...
I know this may be sudden.
How does this place sound?
SHFF
TWO BED-ROOMS,
7 MINUTES FROM THE TRAIN STATION,
AND THE BUILD-ING'S TWO YEARS OLD.
It's a luxury apartment.

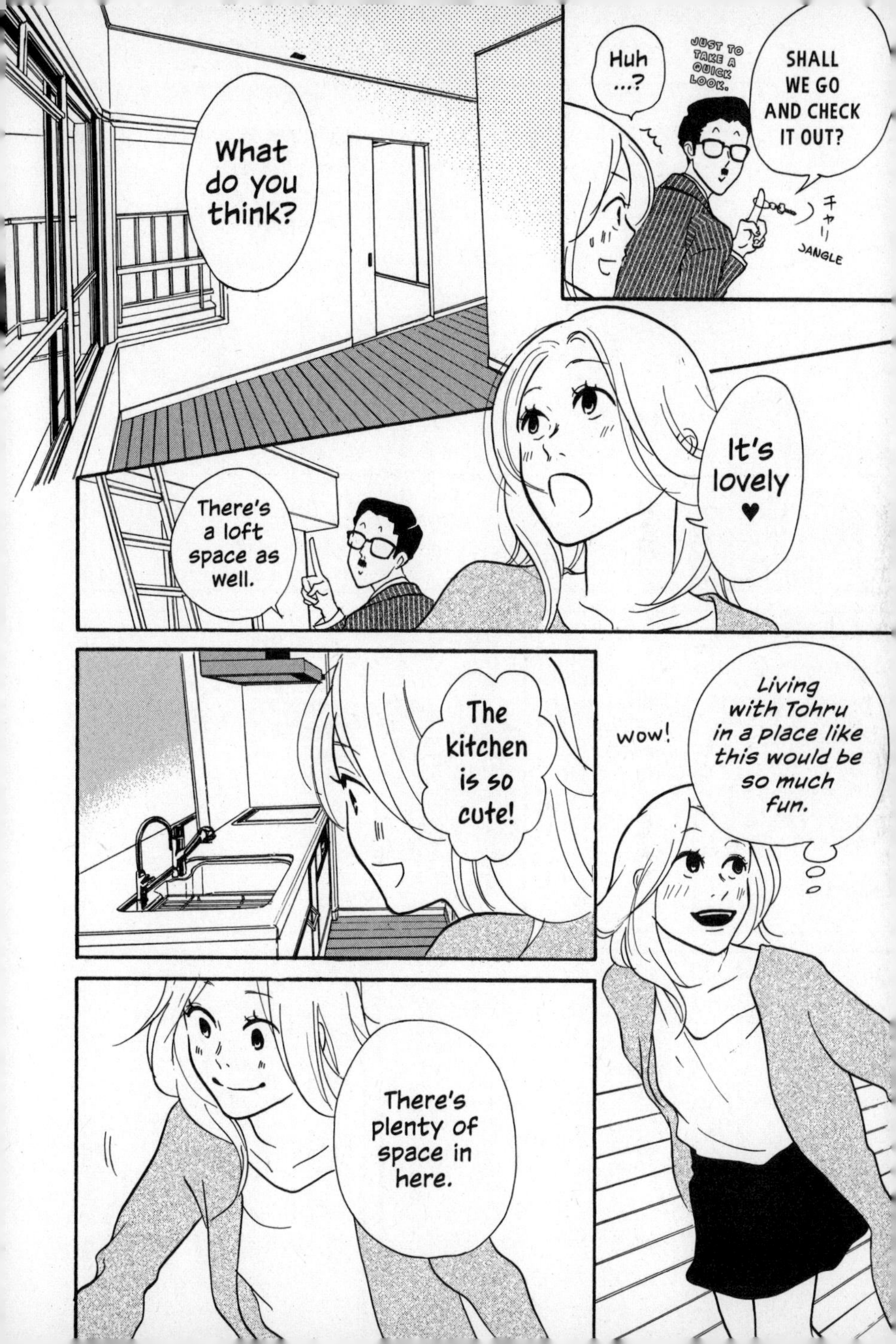
SHALL WE GO AND CHECK IT OUT?
JUST TO TAKE A QUICK LOOK.
Huh ...?
チャリ
JANGLE
What do you think?
It's lovely ♥
There's a loft space as well.
Living with Tohru in a place like this would be so much fun.
wow!
The kitchen is so cute!
There's plenty of space in here.

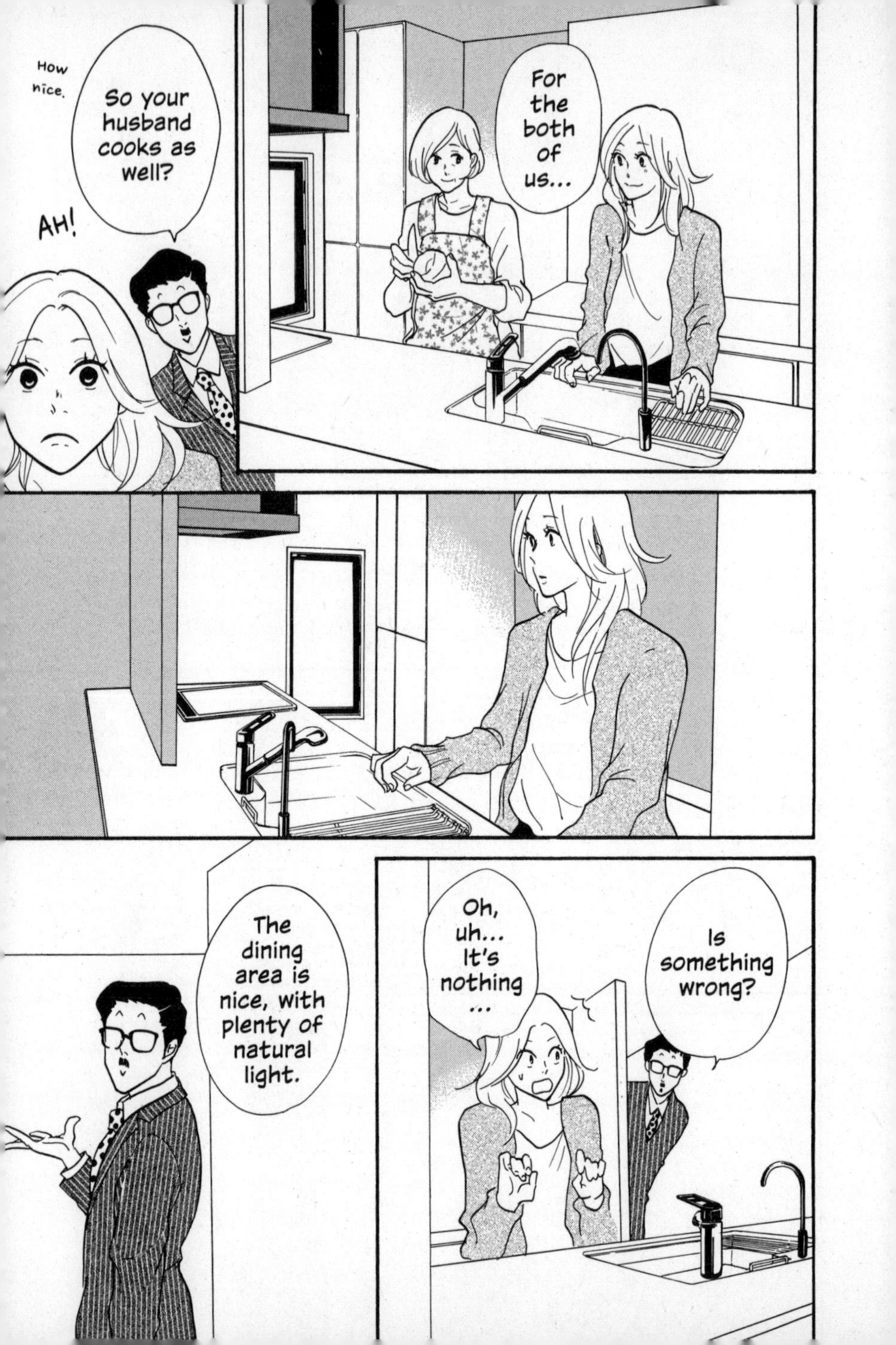
For the both of us...
So your husband cooks as well?
How nice.
AH!
Is something wrong?
Oh, uh... It's nothing...
The dining area is nice, with plenty of natural light.

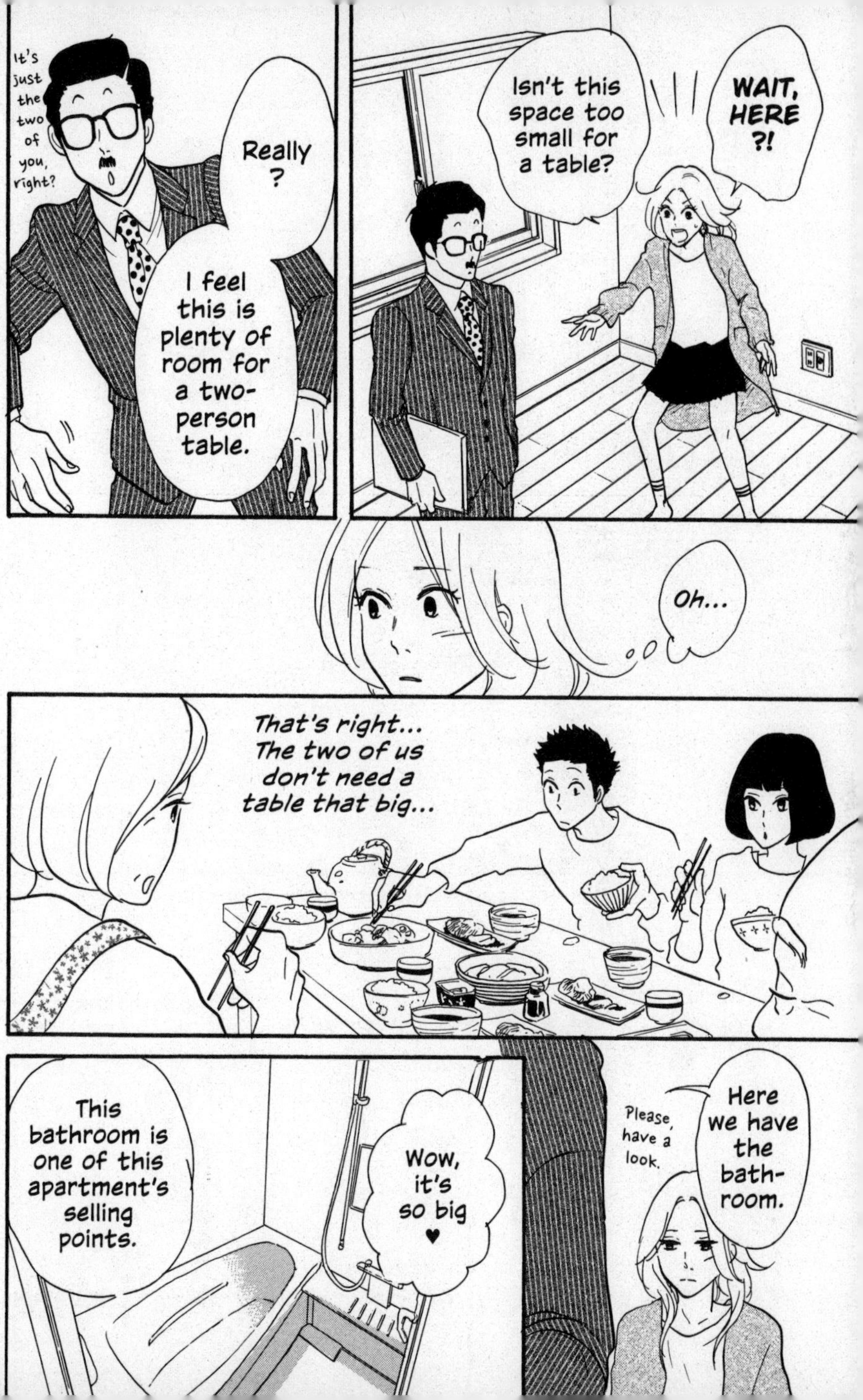
WAIT, HERE ?!
Isn't this space too small for a table?
Really ?
It's just the two of you, right?
I feel this is plenty of room for a two-person table.
Oh...
That's right... The two of us don't need a table that big...
Here we have the bath-room.
Please, have a look.
Wow, it's so big ♥
This bathroom is one of this apartment's selling points.

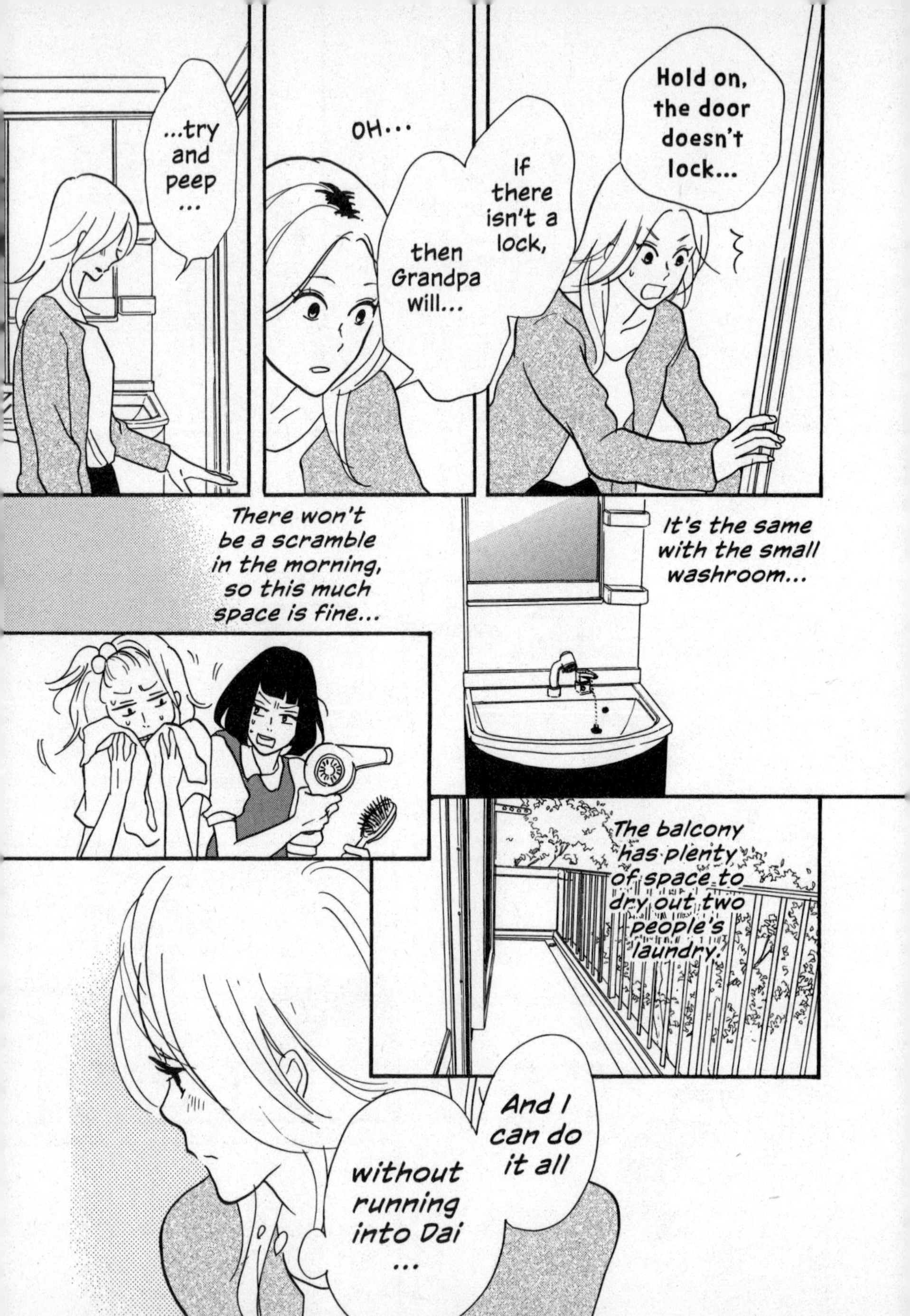
Hold on, the door doesn't lock...
If there isn't a lock,
then Grandpa will...
OH...
...try and peep ...
It's the same with the small washroom...
There won't be a scramble in the morning, so this much space is fine...
The balcony has plenty of space to dry out two people's laundry.
And I can do it all
without running into Dai ...

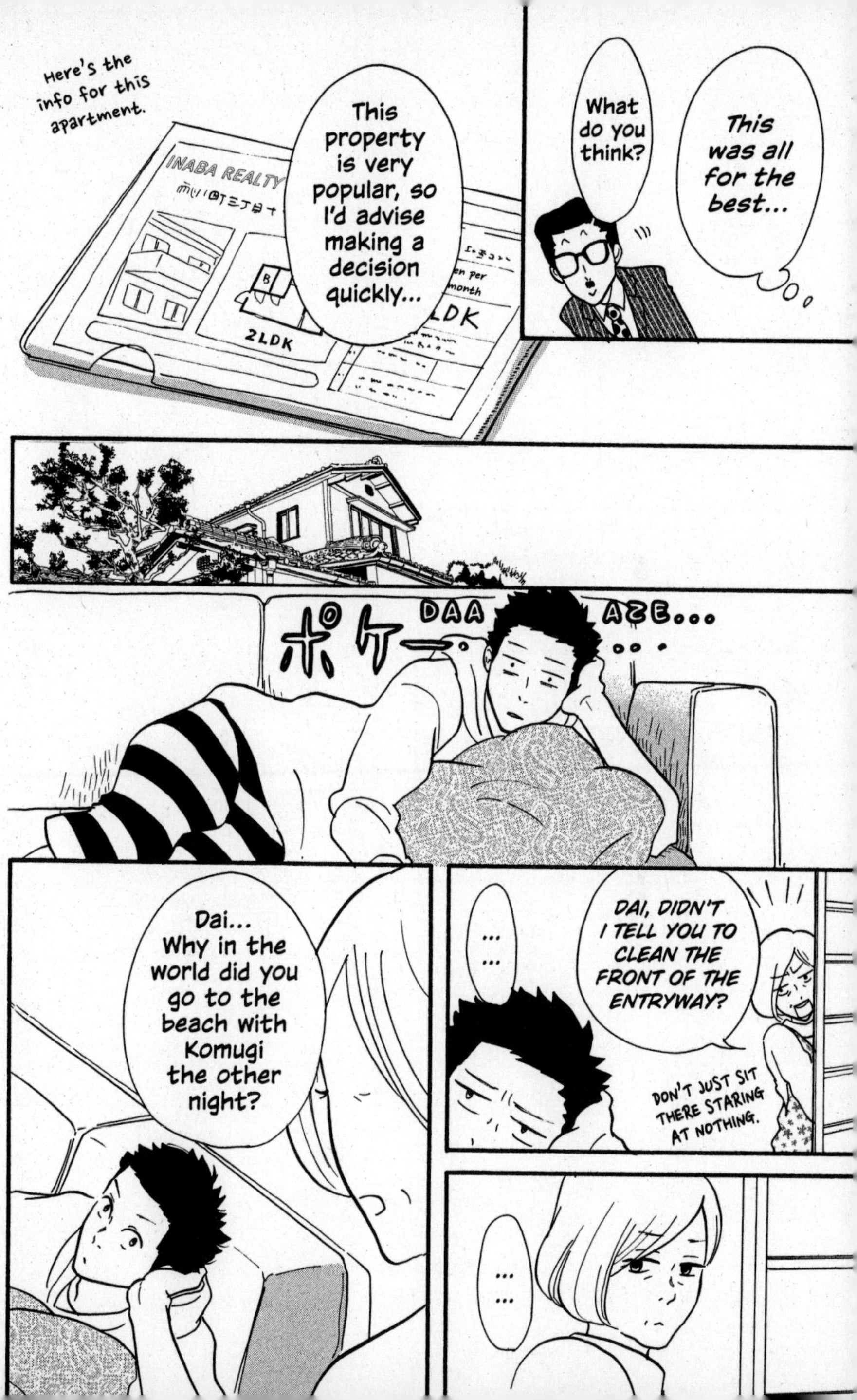
This was all for the best...
What do you think?
This property is very popular, so I'd advise making a decision quickly...
Here's the info for this apartment.
INABA REALTY
2LDK
ポケー
DAA AZE.........
DAI, DIDN'T I TELL YOU TO CLEAN THE FRONT OF THE ENTRYWAY?
......
DON'T JUST SIT THERE STARING AT NOTHING.
......
Dai... Why in the world did you go to the beach with Komugi the other night?

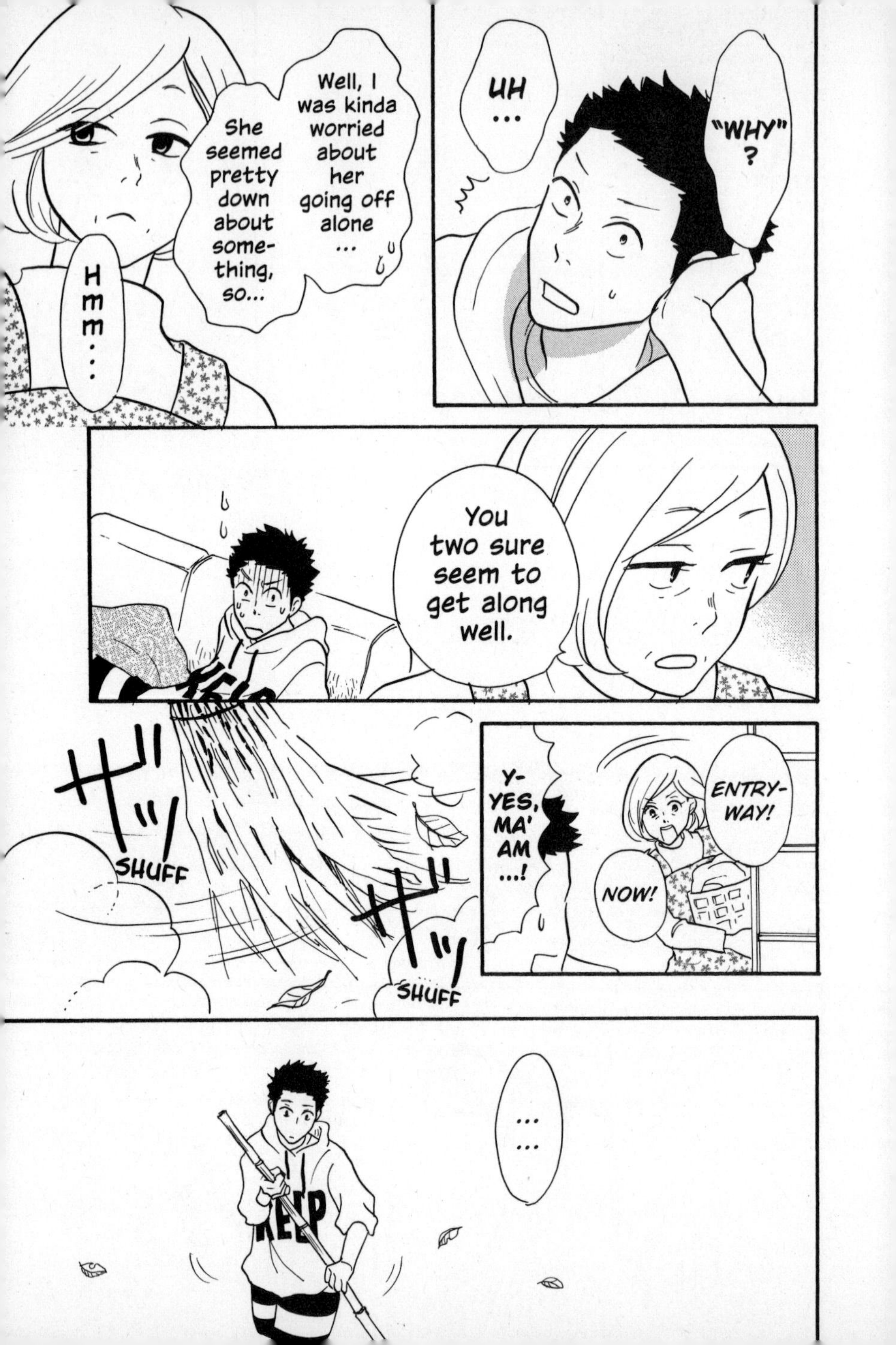
"WHY"?
UH...
Well, I was kinda worried about her going off alone...
She seemed pretty down about something, so...
Hmm...
You two sure seem to get along well.
ENTRY-WAY!
NOW!
Y-YES, MA'AM...!
ザッ
SHUFF
ザッ
SHUFF
......

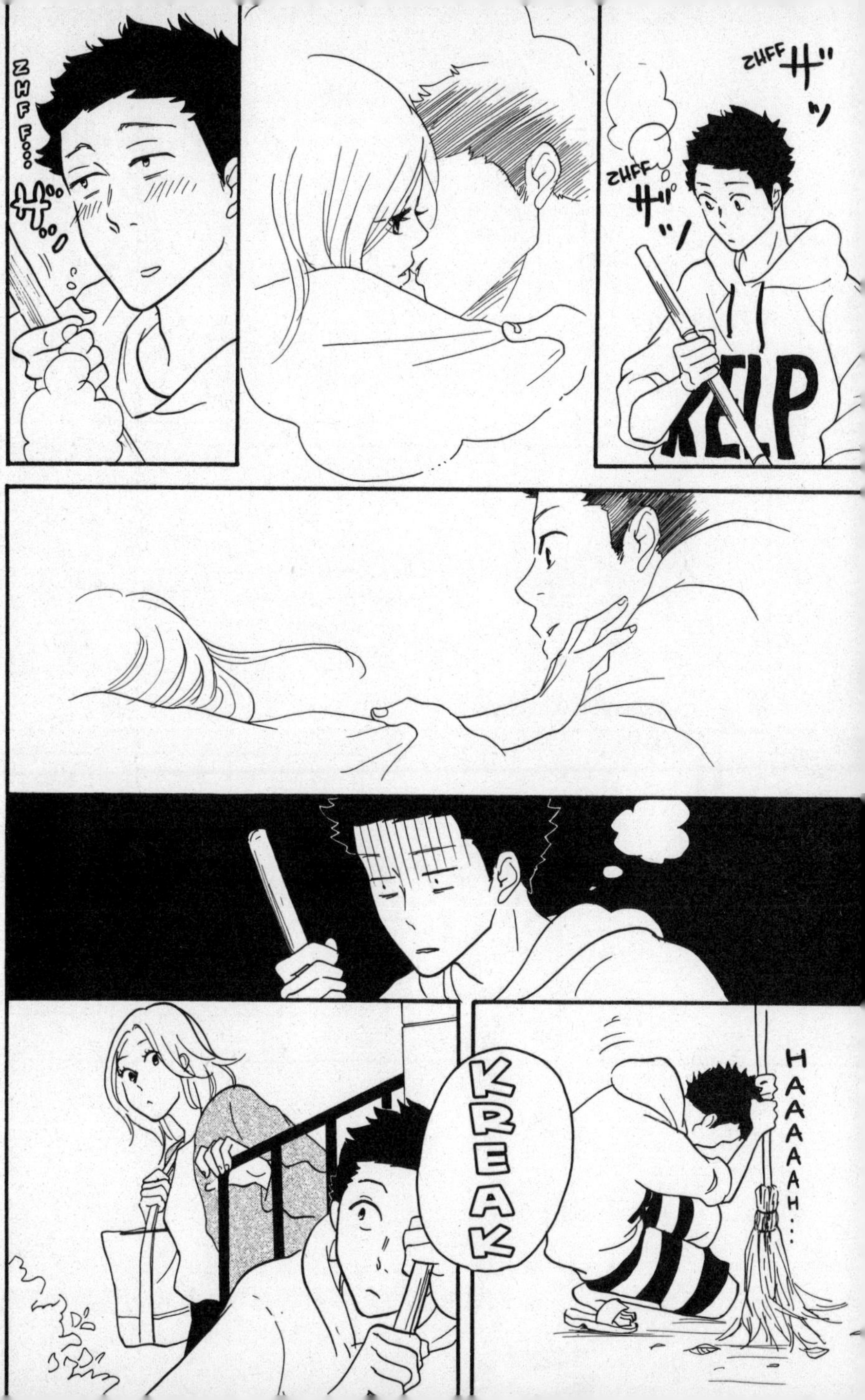

ZHFF
ザッ
ZHFF
ザッ
ZHFF...
ザッ...
HAAAAAH...
KREAK

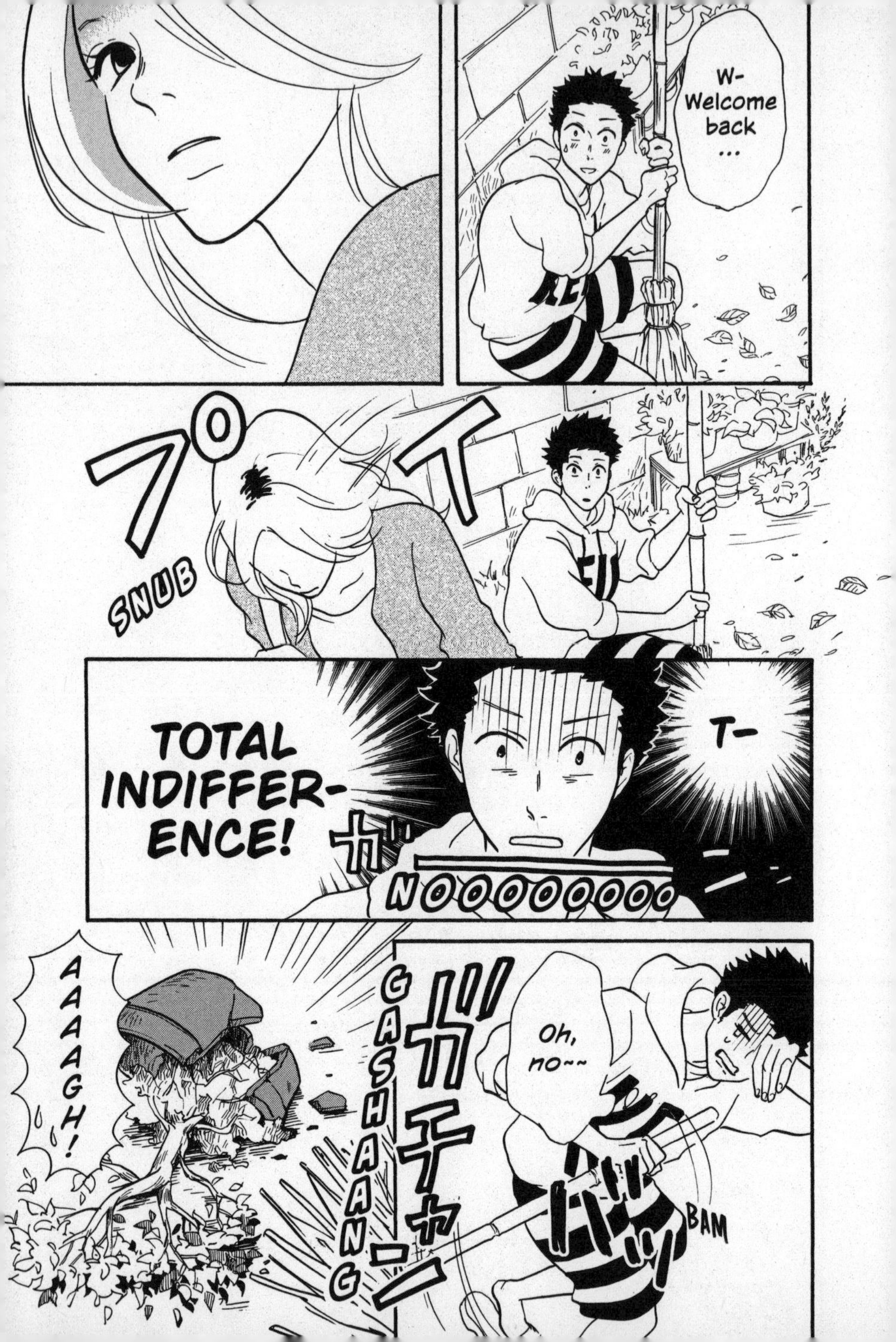
W-
Welcome
back
...
プイ
SNUB
T-
TOTAL
INDIFFER-
ENCE!
ガ
NOOOOOOOOO
Oh,
no~~
BAM
ガシャーン
GASHAAANG
AAAAAGH!

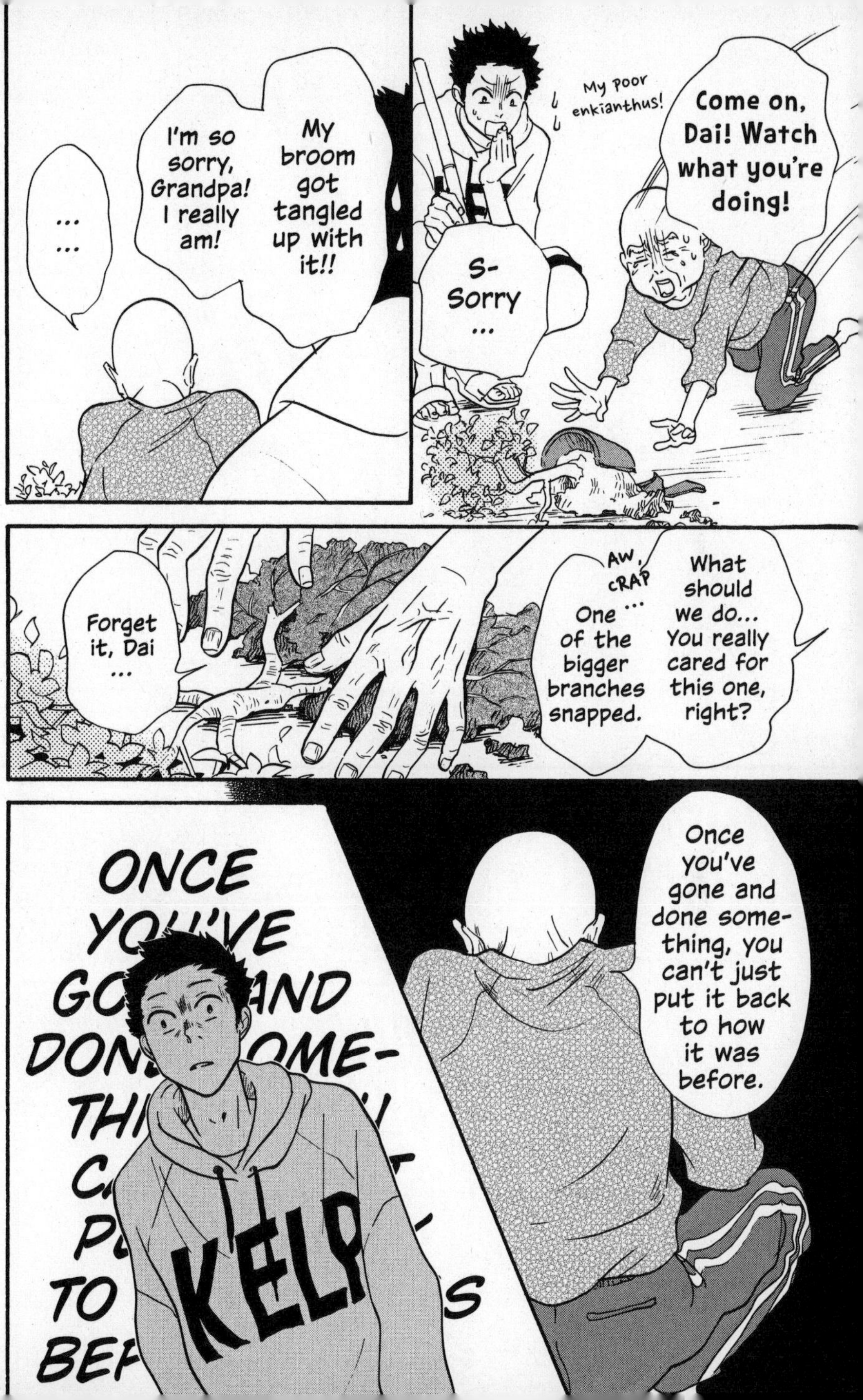

Come on, Dai! Watch what you're doing!
My poor enkianthus!
S-Sorry...
My broom got tangled up with it!!
I'm so sorry, Grandpa! I really am!
......
What should we do... You really cared for this one, right?
AW, CRAP...
One of the bigger branches snapped.
Forget it, Dai...
Once you've gone and done some-thing, you can't just put it back to how it was before.
ONCE

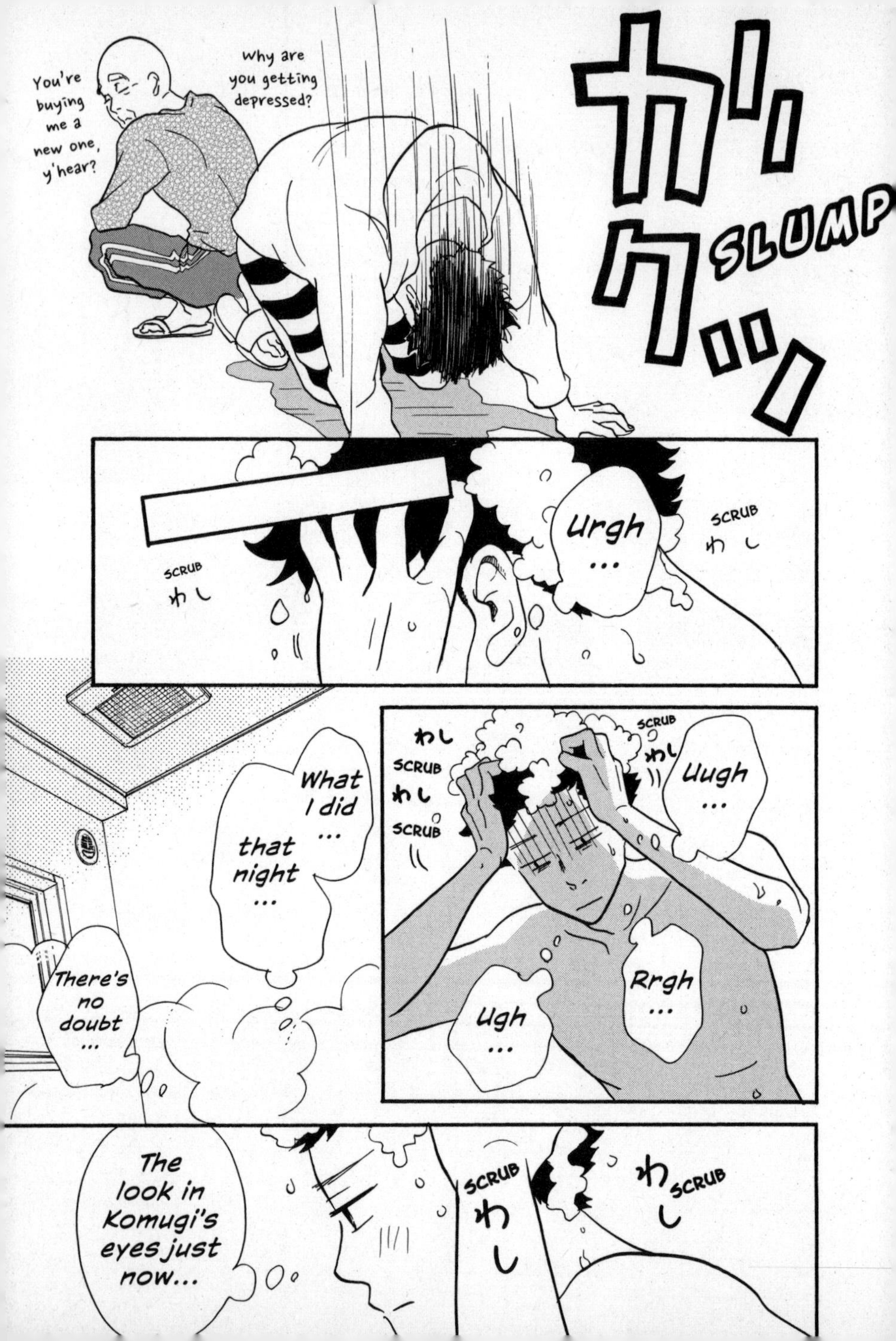
カクッ
SLUMP
Why are you getting depressed?
You're buying me a new one, y'hear?
SCRUB
わし
Urgh ...
SCRUB
わし
SCRUB
わし
Uugh ...
わし
SCRUB
わし
SCRUB
Rrgh ...
Ugh ...
What I did ...
that night ...
There's no doubt ...
SCRUB
わし
SCRUB
わし
The look in Komugi's eyes just now...

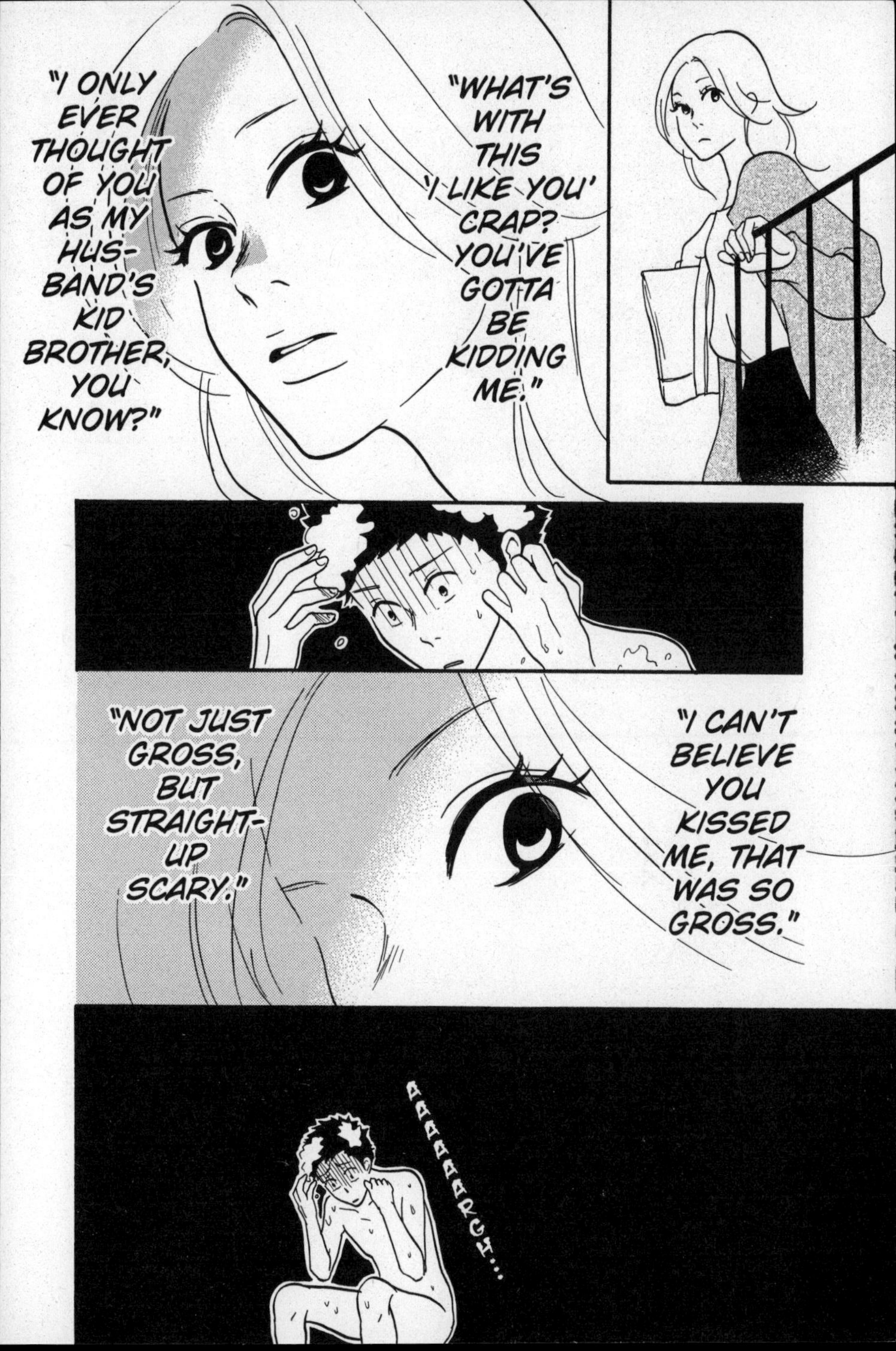
"WHAT'S WITH THIS 'I LIKE YOU' CRAP? YOU'VE GOTTA BE KIDDING ME."
"I ONLY EVER THOUGHT OF YOU AS MY HUS-BAND'S KID BROTHER, YOU KNOW?"
"I CAN'T BELIEVE YOU KISSED ME, THAT WAS SO GROSS."
"NOT JUST GROSS, BUT STRAIGHT-UP SCARY."
AAAAAARGH...

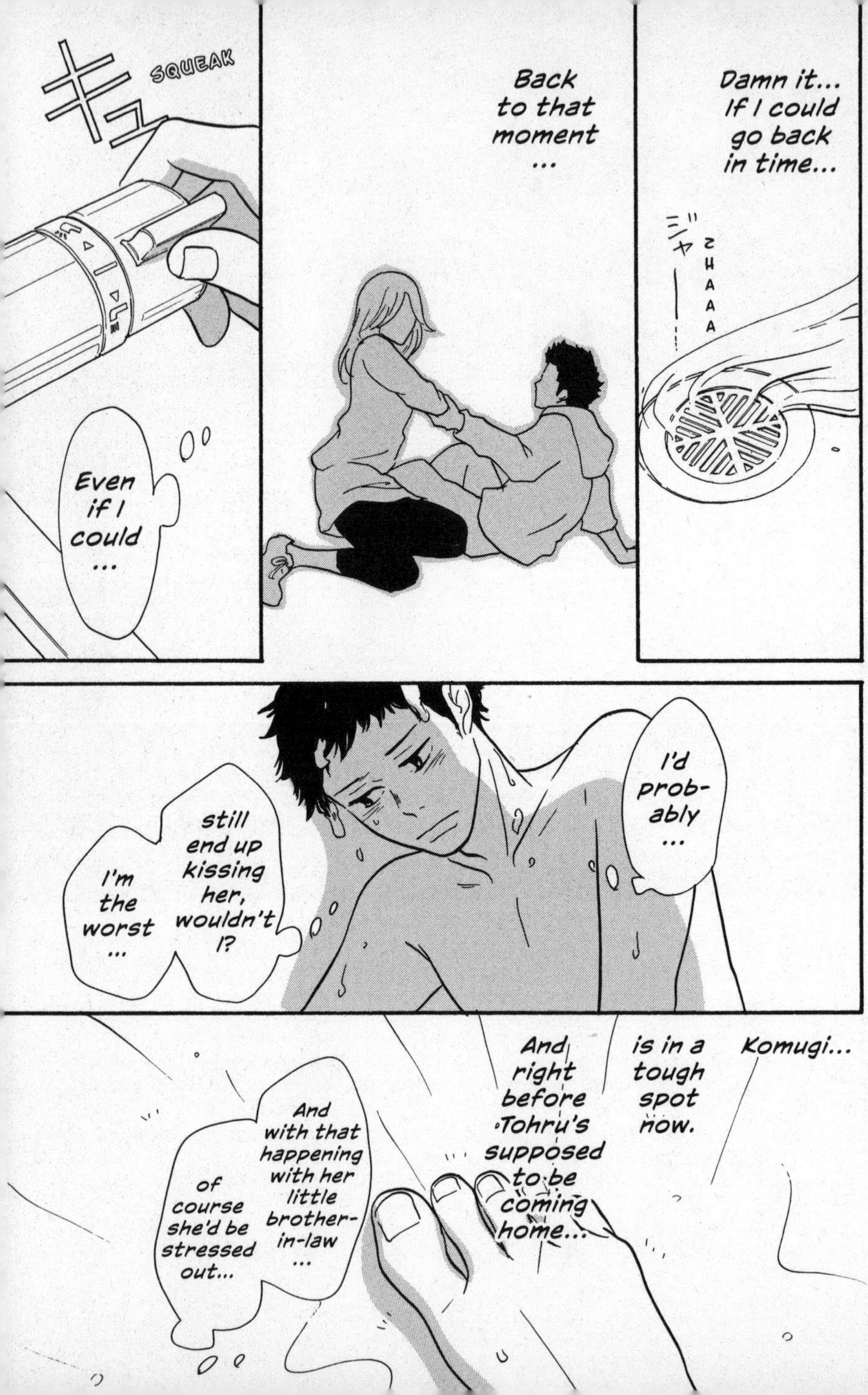
Damn it... If I could go back in time...
ジャー
ZHAAA
Back to that moment...
キュ
SQUEAK
Even if I could...
I'd probably...
still end up kissing her, wouldn't I?
I'm the worst...
Komugi...
is in a tough spot now.
And right before Tohru's supposed to be coming home...
And with that happening with her little brother-in-law...
of course she'd be stressed out...

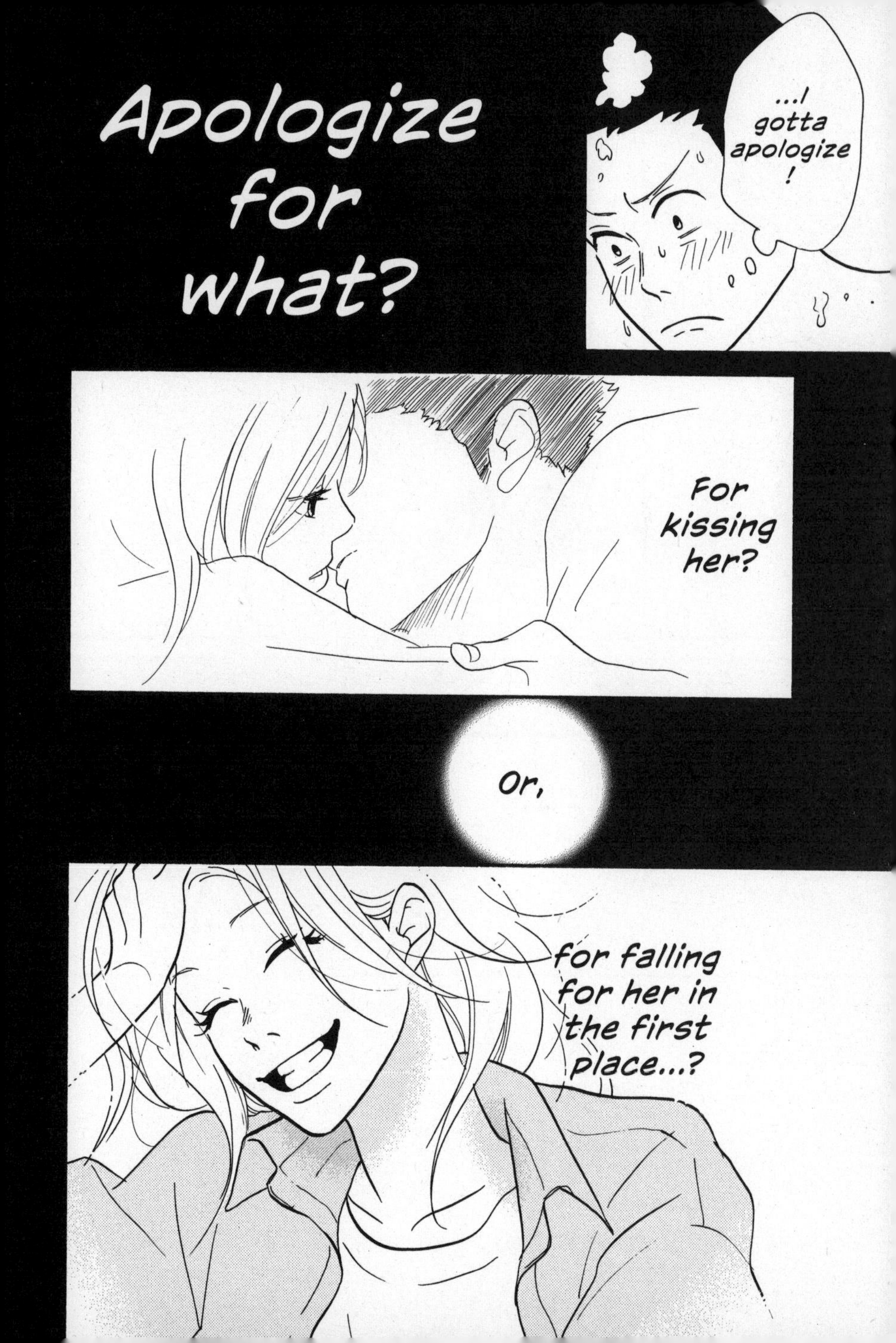
...I gotta apologize!
Apologize for what?
For kissing her?
Or,
for falling for her in the first place...?

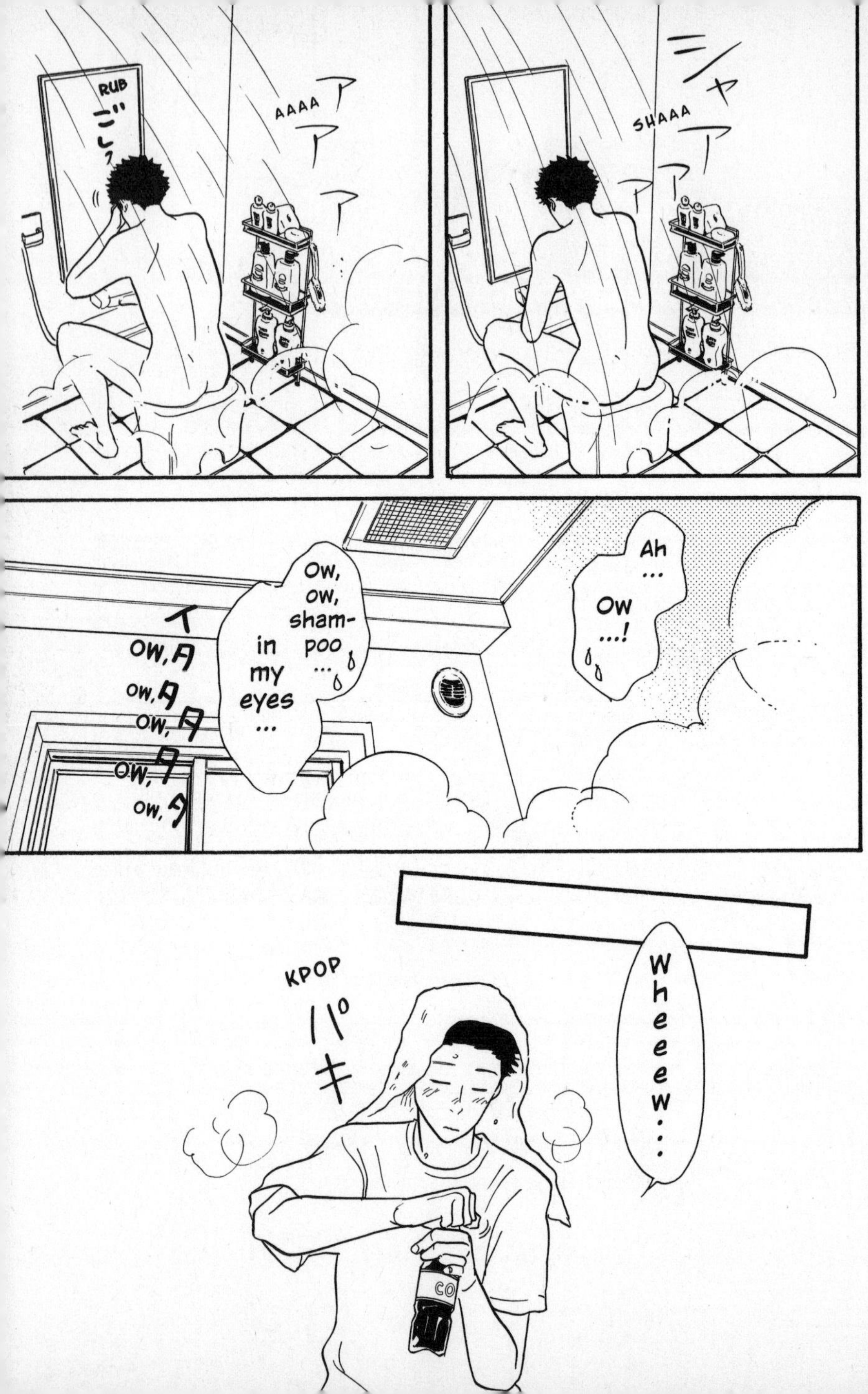
SHAAA
シャアアア
RUB
ごしっ
AAAA
アアア
Ah... Ow...!
Ow, ow, shampoo in my eyes...
イ
ow, タ
ow, タ
ow, タ
ow, タ
ow, タ
Wheeew...
KPOP
パキ
CO

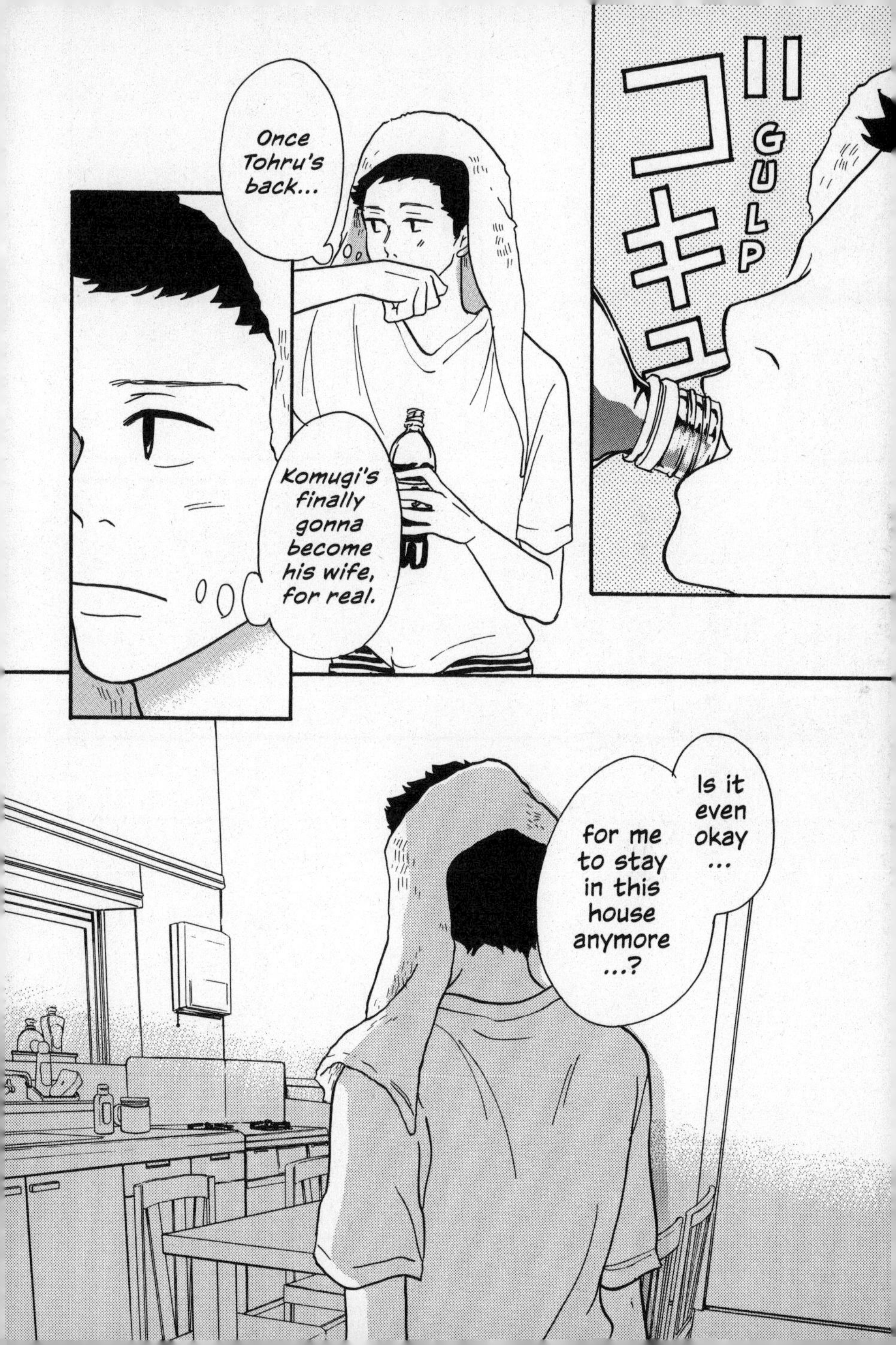
コキュ
GULP
Once Tohru's back...
Komugi's finally gonna become his wife, for real.
Is it even okay...
for me to stay in this house anymore...?

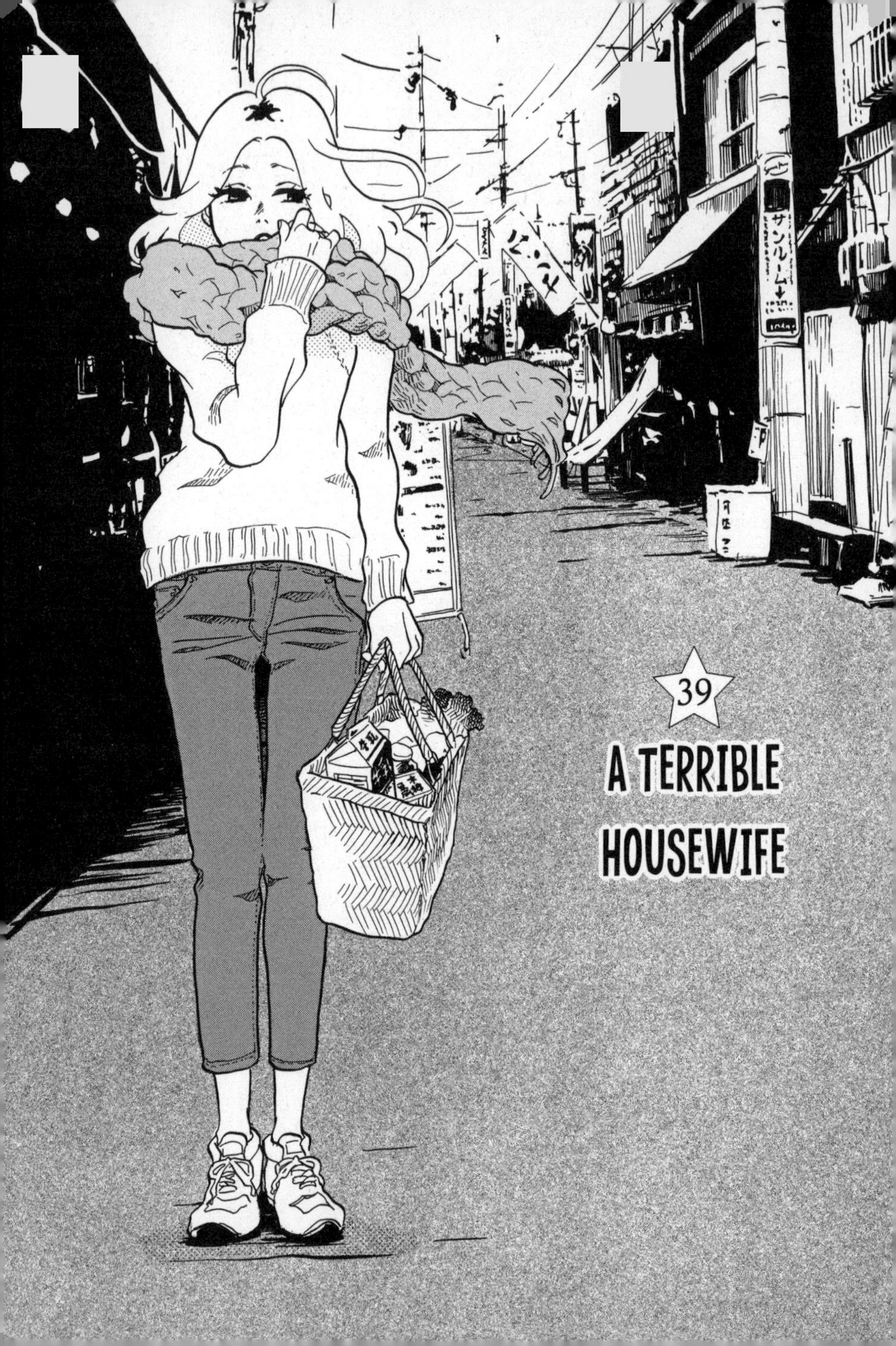
39
A TERRIBLE HOUSEWIFE
サンルーム

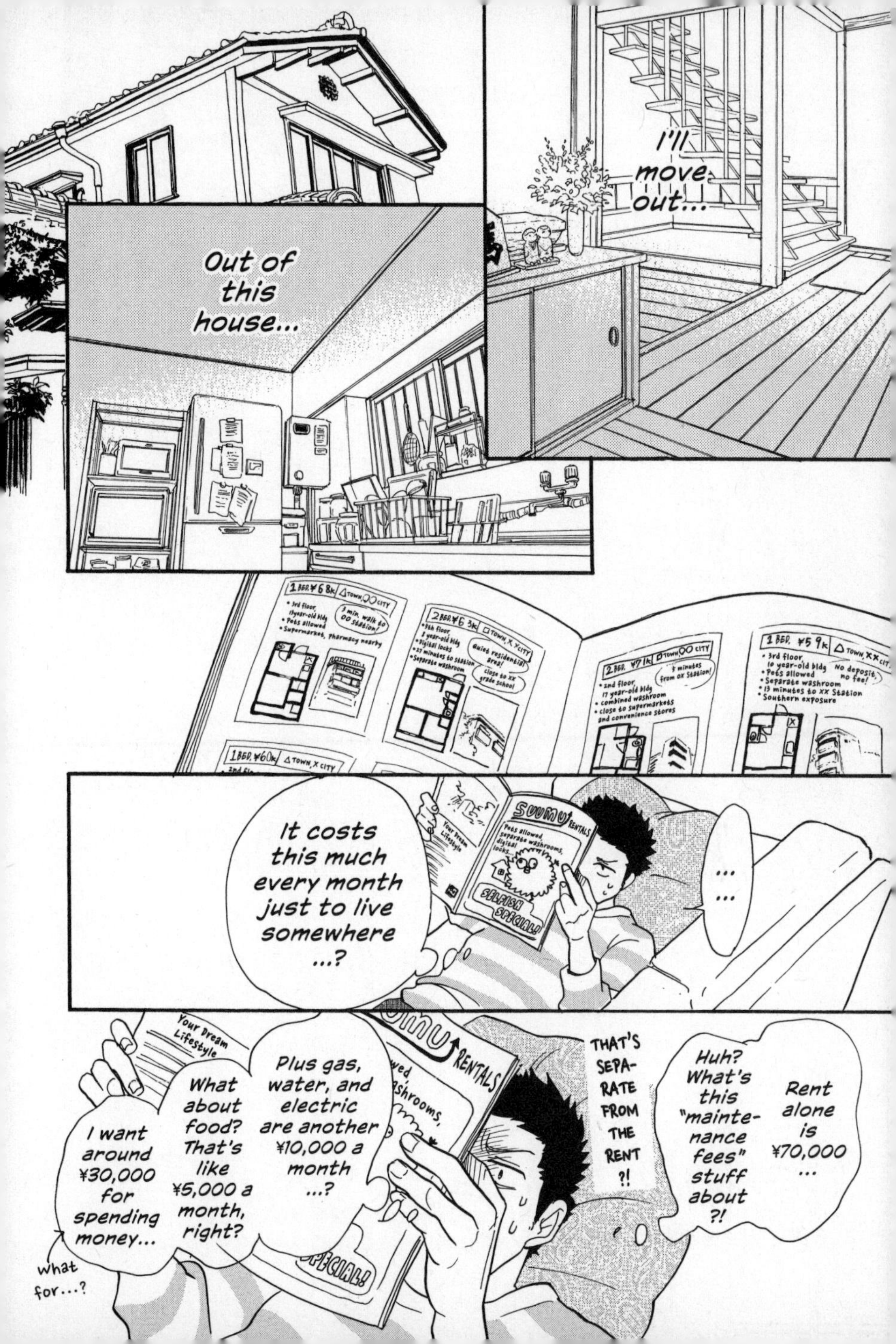
I'll move out...
Out of this house...
1 BED. ¥59K △TOWN, XX CITY
• 3rd floor, 10 year-old bldg
• Pets allowed
• Separate washroom
• 13 minutes to XX Station
• Southern exposure
No deposit, no fee!
2 BED. ¥71K □TOWN, OO CITY
• 2nd floor, 17 year-old bldg
• combined washroom
• close to supermarkets and convenience stores
5 minutes from OX Station!
2BED. ¥63K □TOWN, X X CITY
• 9th floor, 8 year-old bldg
• Digital locks
• 27 minutes to station
• Separate washroom
Quiet residential area!
close to XX grade school
1BED. ¥68K △TOWN, OO CITY
• 3rd floor, 13year-old bldg
• Pets allowed
• Supermarket, pharmacy nearby
3 min. walk to OO Station!
1BED. ¥60K △TOWN, X CITY
... ...
It costs this much every month just to live somewhere ...?
SUUMO RENTALS
Pets allowed, separate washrooms, digital locks...
SELFISH SPECIAL!
Your Dream Lifestyle
Rent alone is ¥70,000 ...
Huh? What's this "mainte-nance fees" stuff about ?!
THAT'S SEPA-RATE FROM THE RENT ?!
Plus gas, water, and electric are another ¥10,000 a month ...?
What about food? That's like ¥5,000 a month, right?
I want around ¥30,000 for spending money...
what for...?

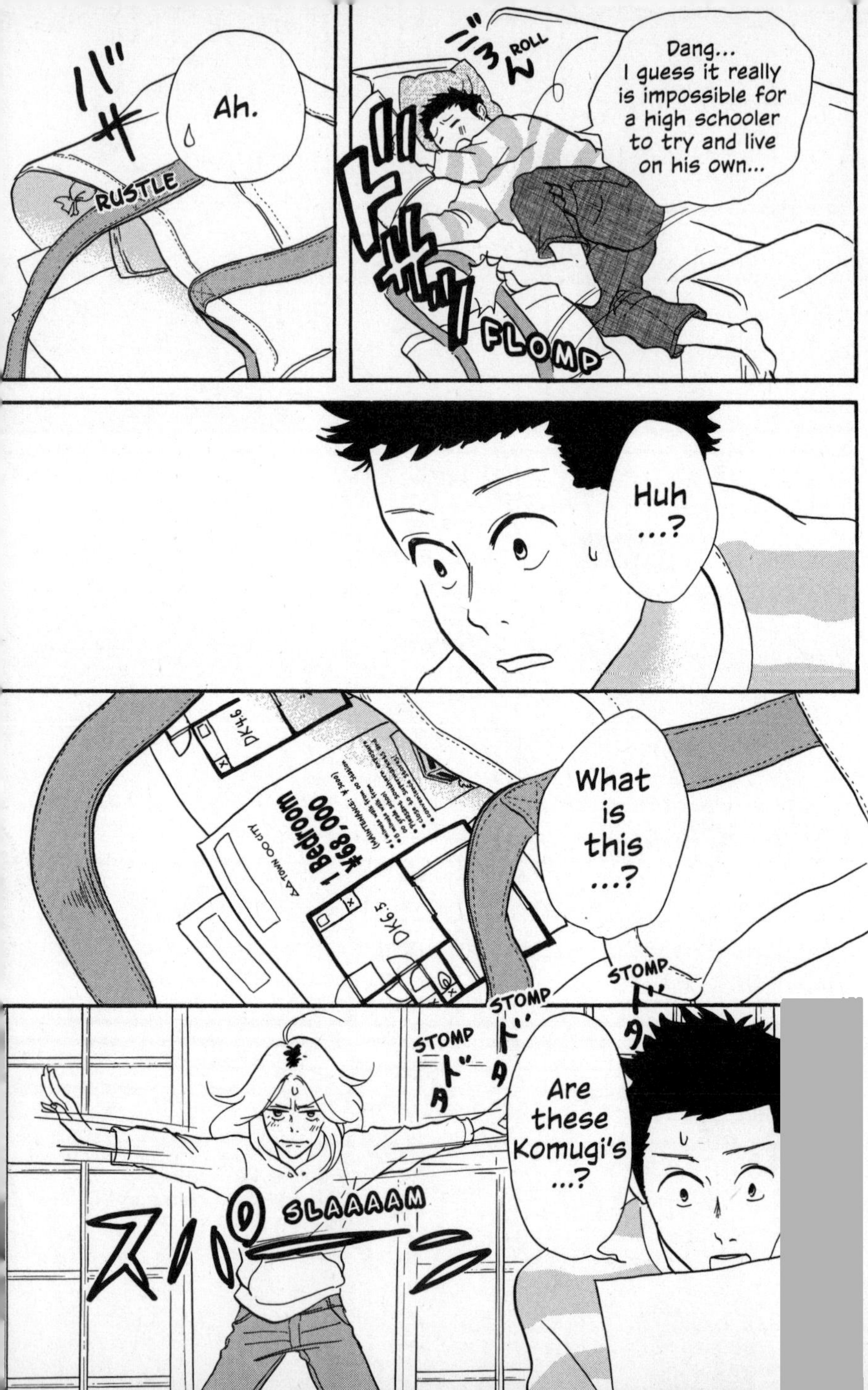
Dang... I guess it really is impossible for a high schooler to try and live on his own...
ROLL
FLOMP
Ah.
RUSTLE
Huh ...?
1 Bedroom
¥68,000
DK6.5
DK4.6
What is this ...?
STOMP
STOMP
STOMP
Are these Komugi's ...?
SLAAAAM

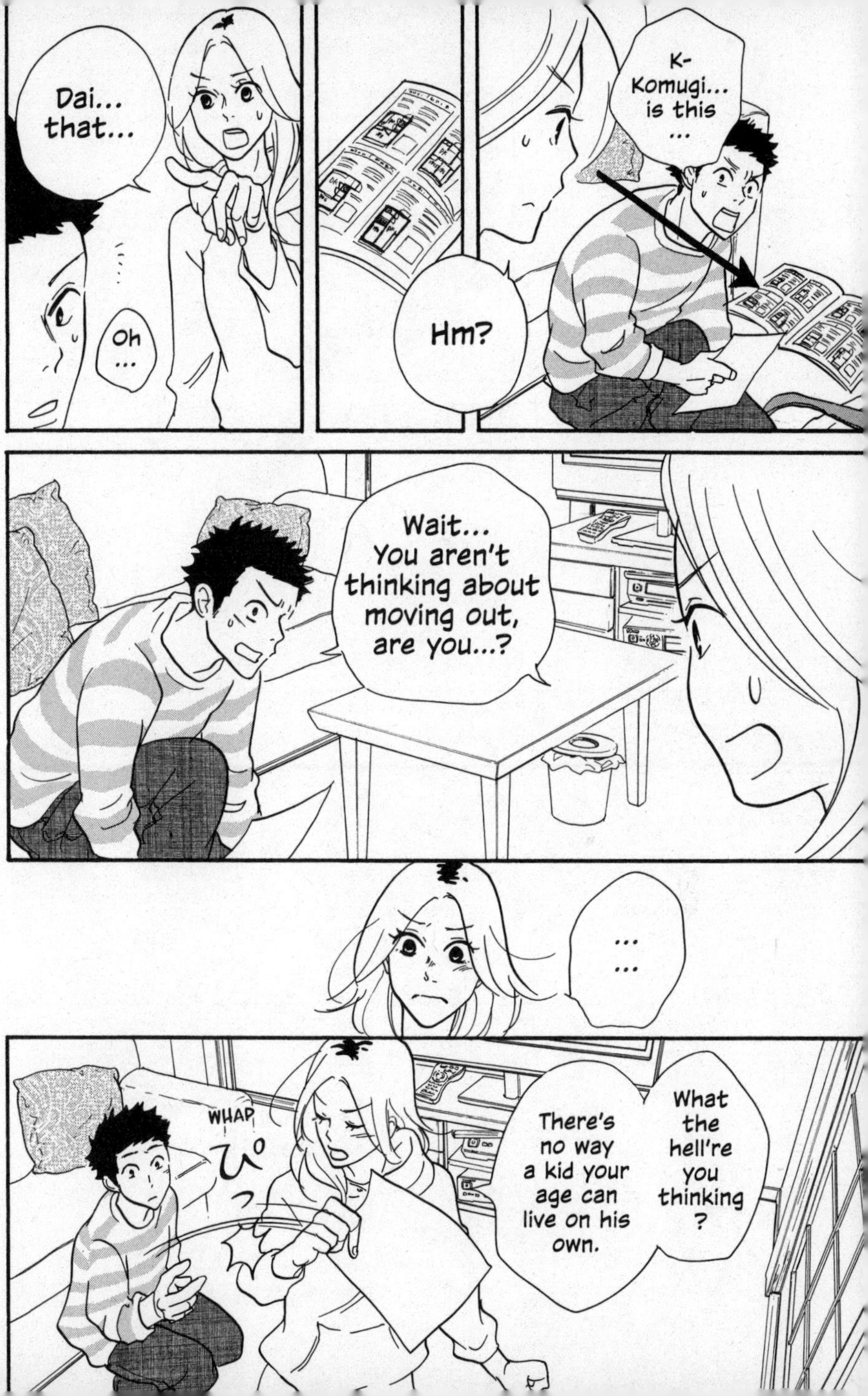
K- Komugi... is this ...
Hm?
Dai... that...
Oh ...
Wait... You aren't thinking about moving out, are you...?
... ...
What the hell're you thinking ?
There's no way a kid your age can live on his own.
WHAP
ぴっ

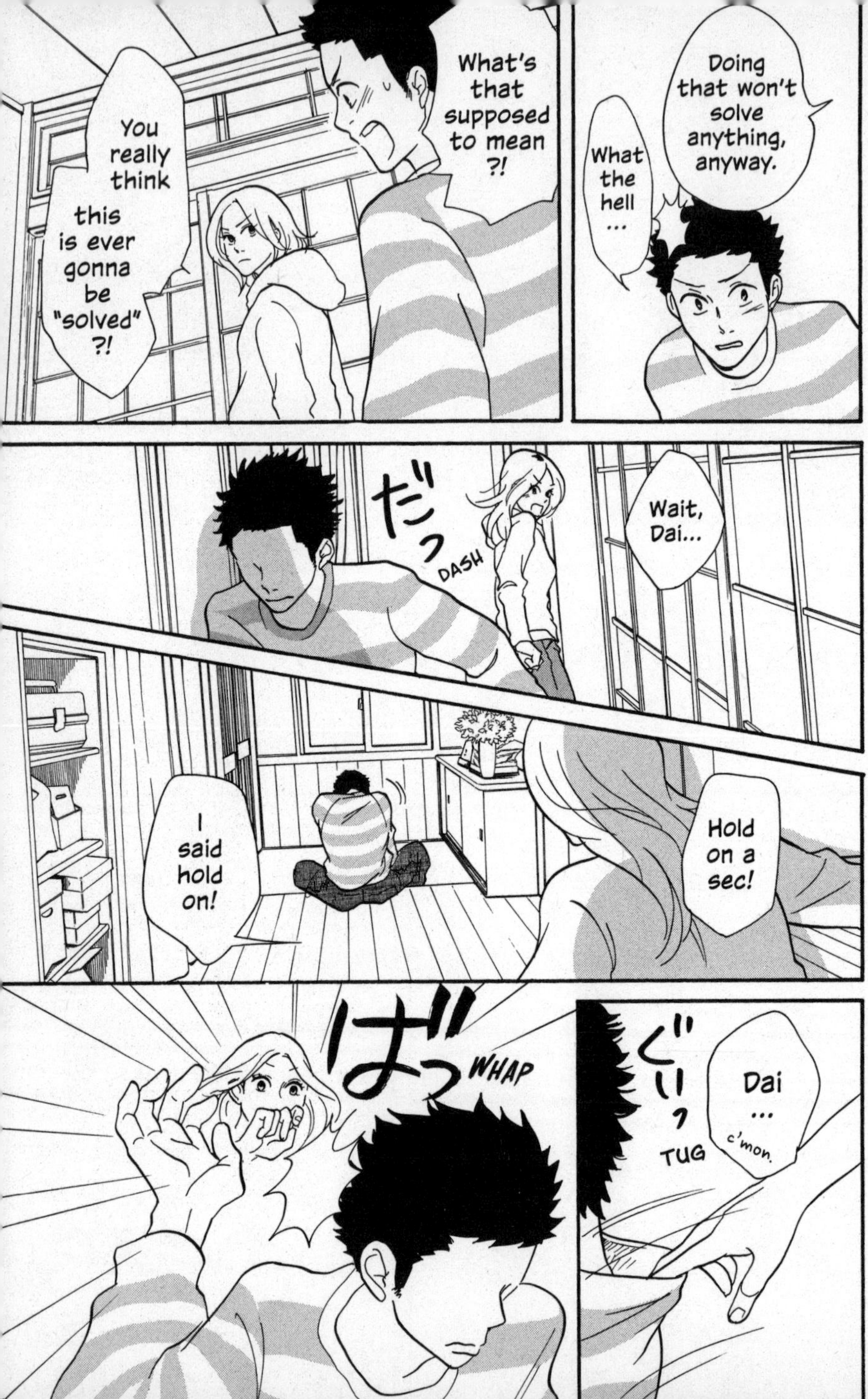
Doing that won't solve anything, anyway.
What the hell...
What's that supposed to mean?!
You really think this is ever gonna be "solved"?!
だっ DASH
Wait, Dai...
Hold on a sec!
I said hold on!
ぐいっ TUG
Dai... c'mon.
ばっ WHAP

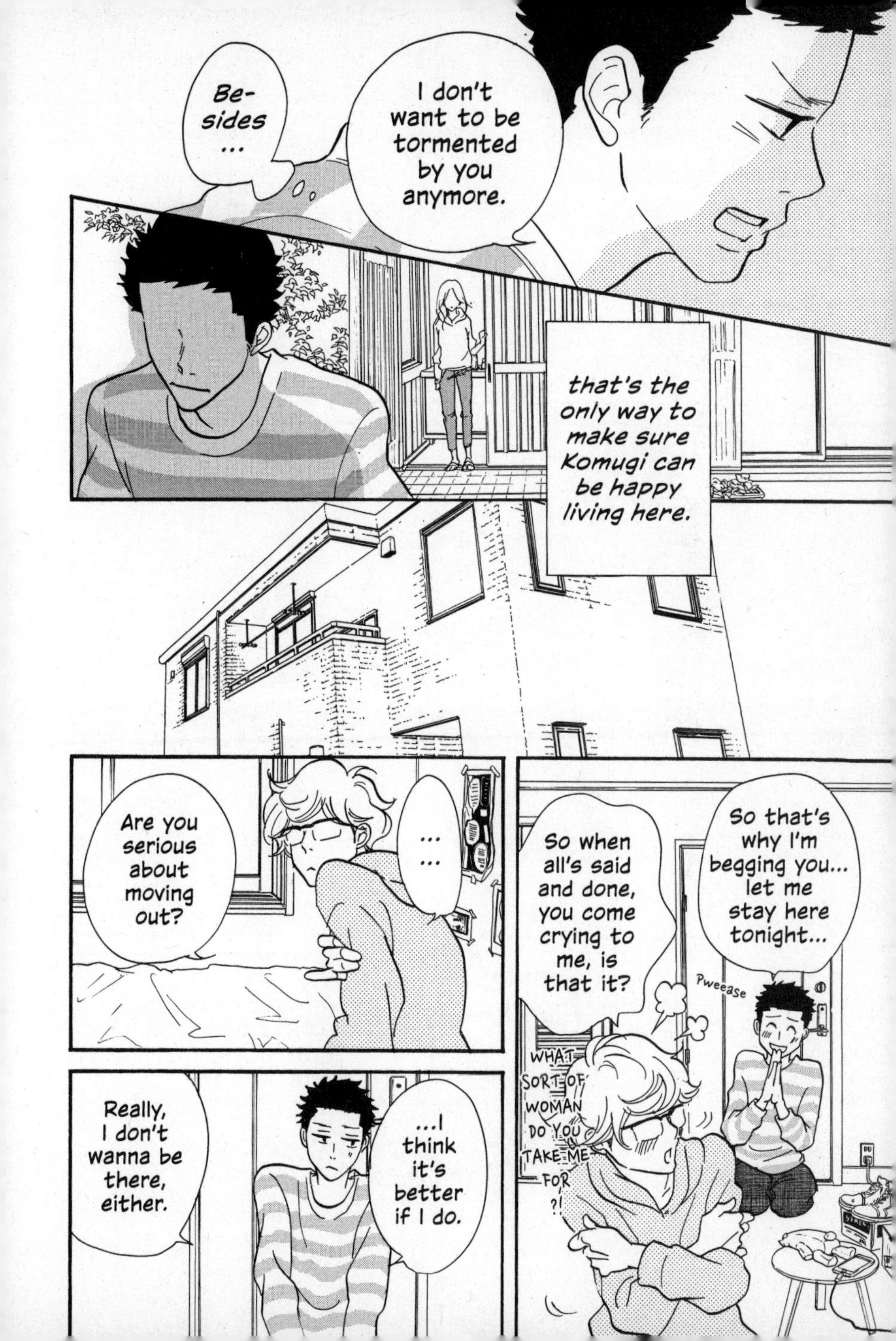
I don't want to be tormented by you anymore.
Be-sides ...
that's the only way to make sure Komugi can be happy living here.
So that's why I'm begging you... let me stay here tonight...
Pweease
So when all's said and done, you come crying to me, is that it?
WHAT SORT OF WOMAN DO YOU TAKE ME FOR ?!
Are you serious about moving out?
... ...
...I think it's better if I do.
Really, I don't wanna be there, either.

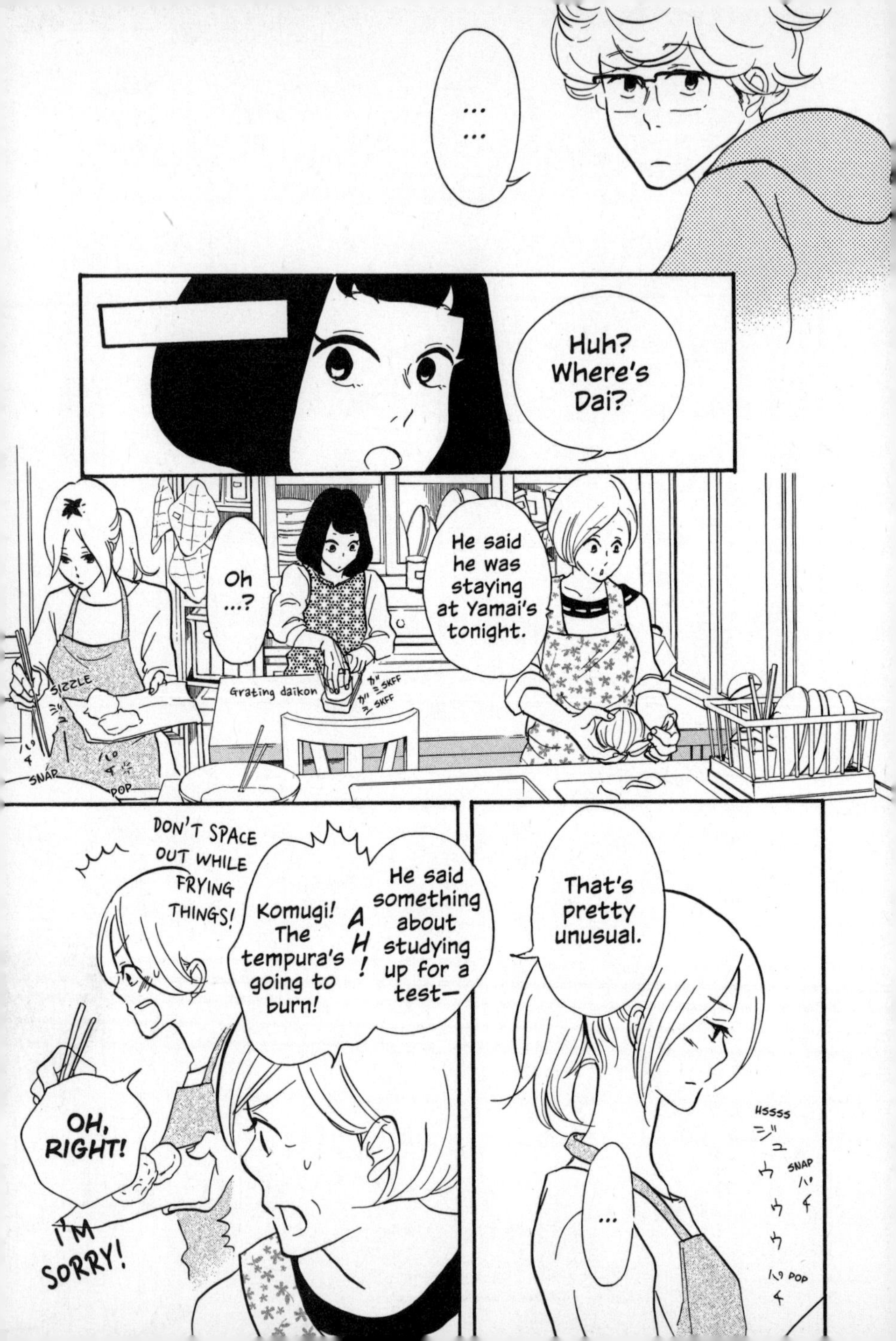
……
Huh? Where's Dai?
He said he was staying at Yamai's tonight.
Grating daikon
SKFF
SKFF
Oh ...?
SIZZLE
SNAP
POP
That's pretty unusual.
...
HSSSS
SNAP
POP
He said something about studying up for a test—
AH!
Komugi! The tempura's going to burn!
DON'T SPACE OUT WHILE FRYING THINGS!
OH, RIGHT!
I'M SORRY!

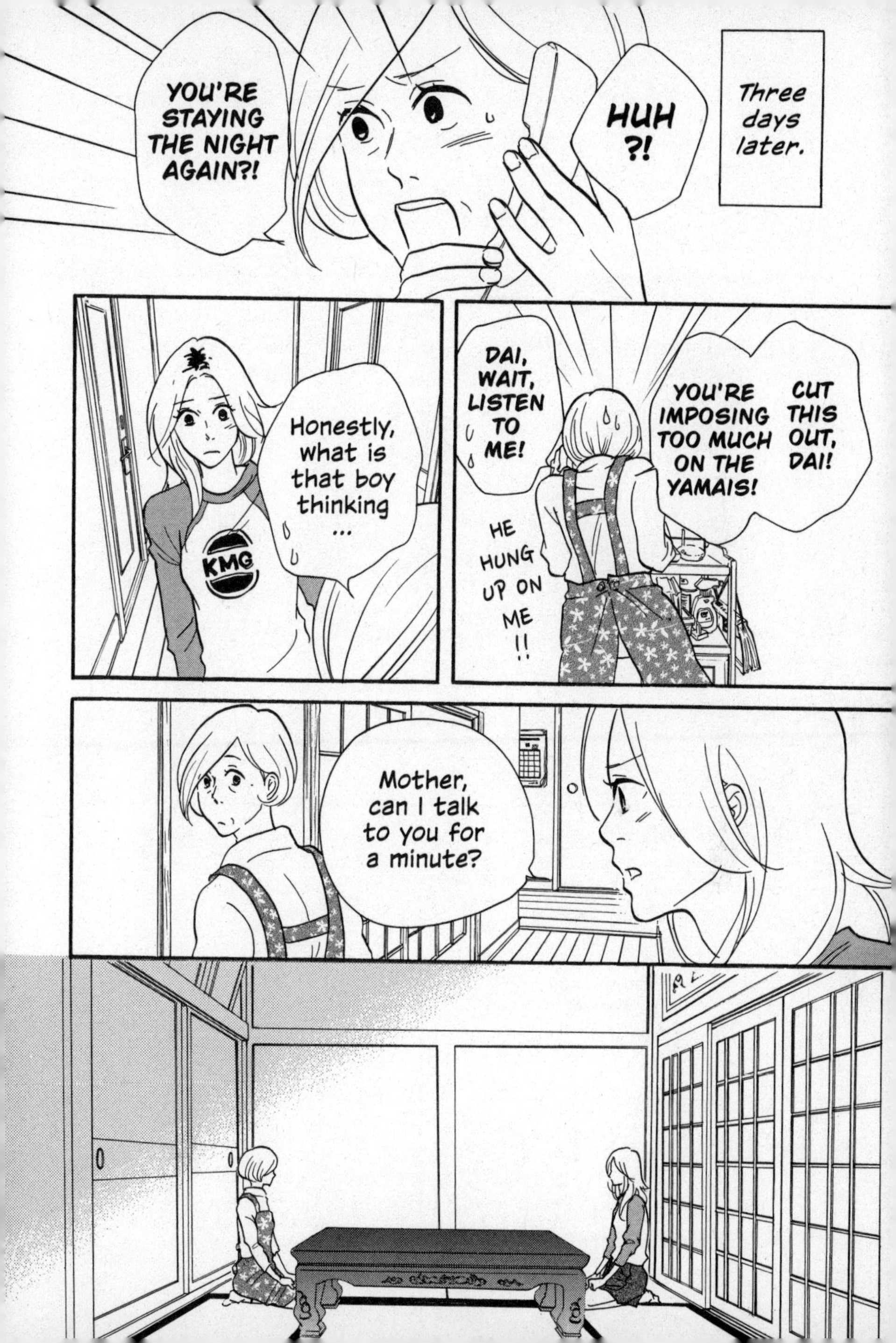
Three days later.
HUH ?!
YOU'RE STAYING THE NIGHT AGAIN?!
CUT THIS OUT, DAI!
YOU'RE IMPOSING TOO MUCH ON THE YAMAIS!
DAI, WAIT, LISTEN TO ME!
HE HUNG UP ON ME !!
Honestly, what is that boy thinking ...
Mother, can I talk to you for a minute?

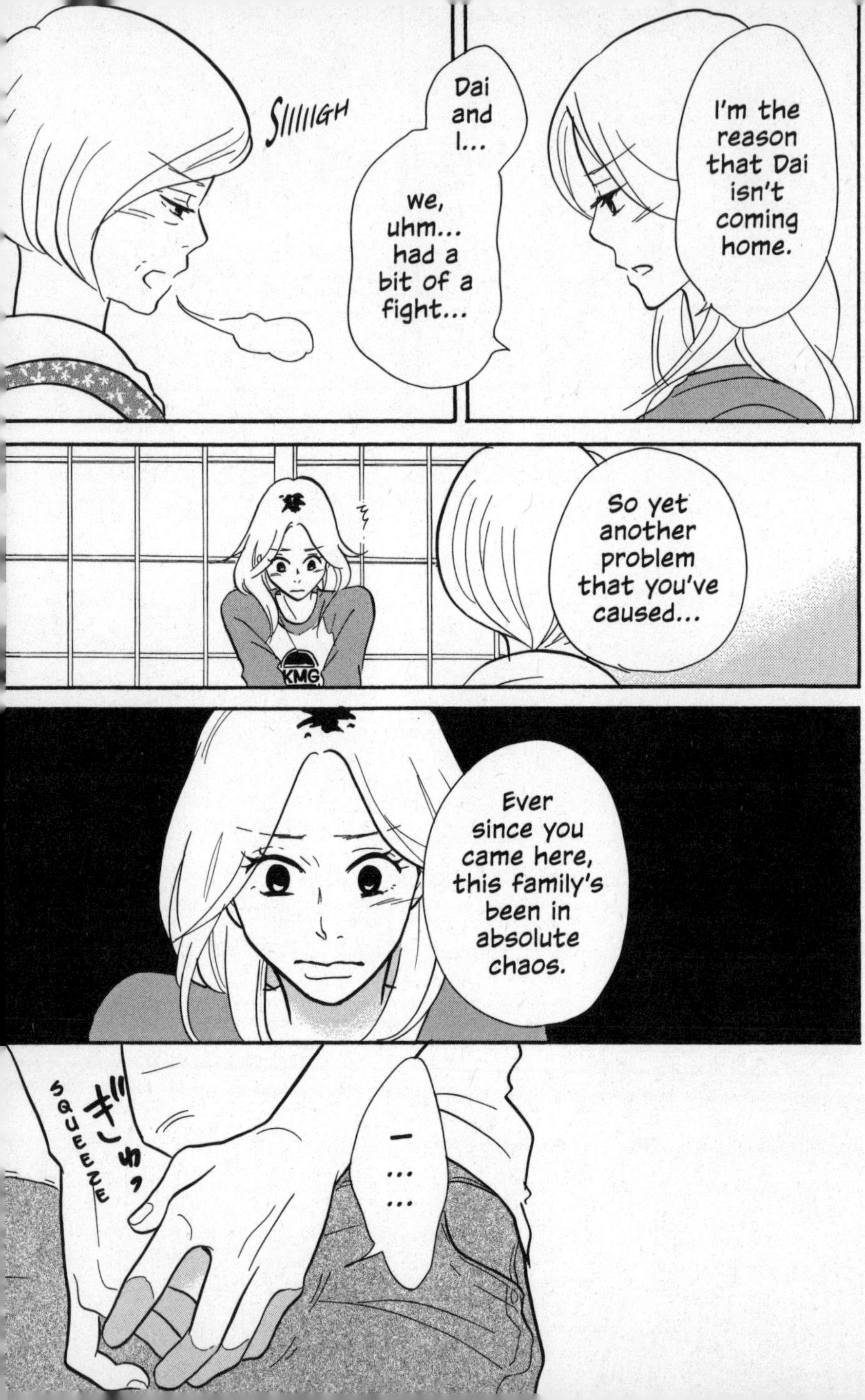
I'm the reason that Dai isn't coming home.
Dai and I... we, uhm... had a bit of a fight...
SIIIIIGH
So yet another problem that you've caused...
Ever since you came here, this family's been in absolute chaos.
— ... ...
ぎゅっ
SQUEEZE

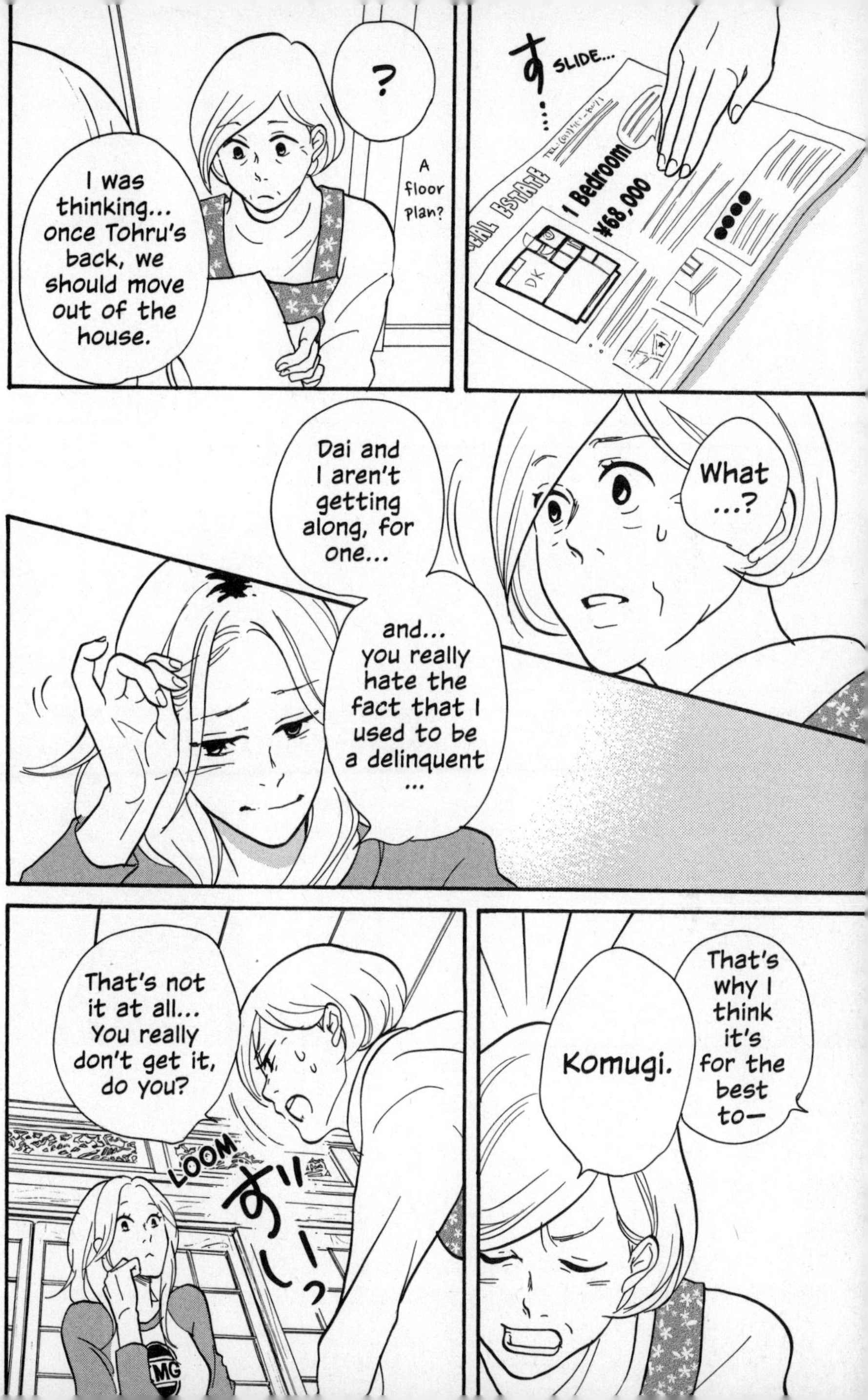
す SLIDE...
1 Bedroom
¥68,000
?
A floor plan?
I was thinking... once Tohru's back, we should move out of the house.
What ...?
Dai and I aren't getting along, for one...
and... you really hate the fact that I used to be a delinquent ...
That's why I think it's for the best to—
Komugi.
That's not it at all... You really don't get it, do you?
LOOM

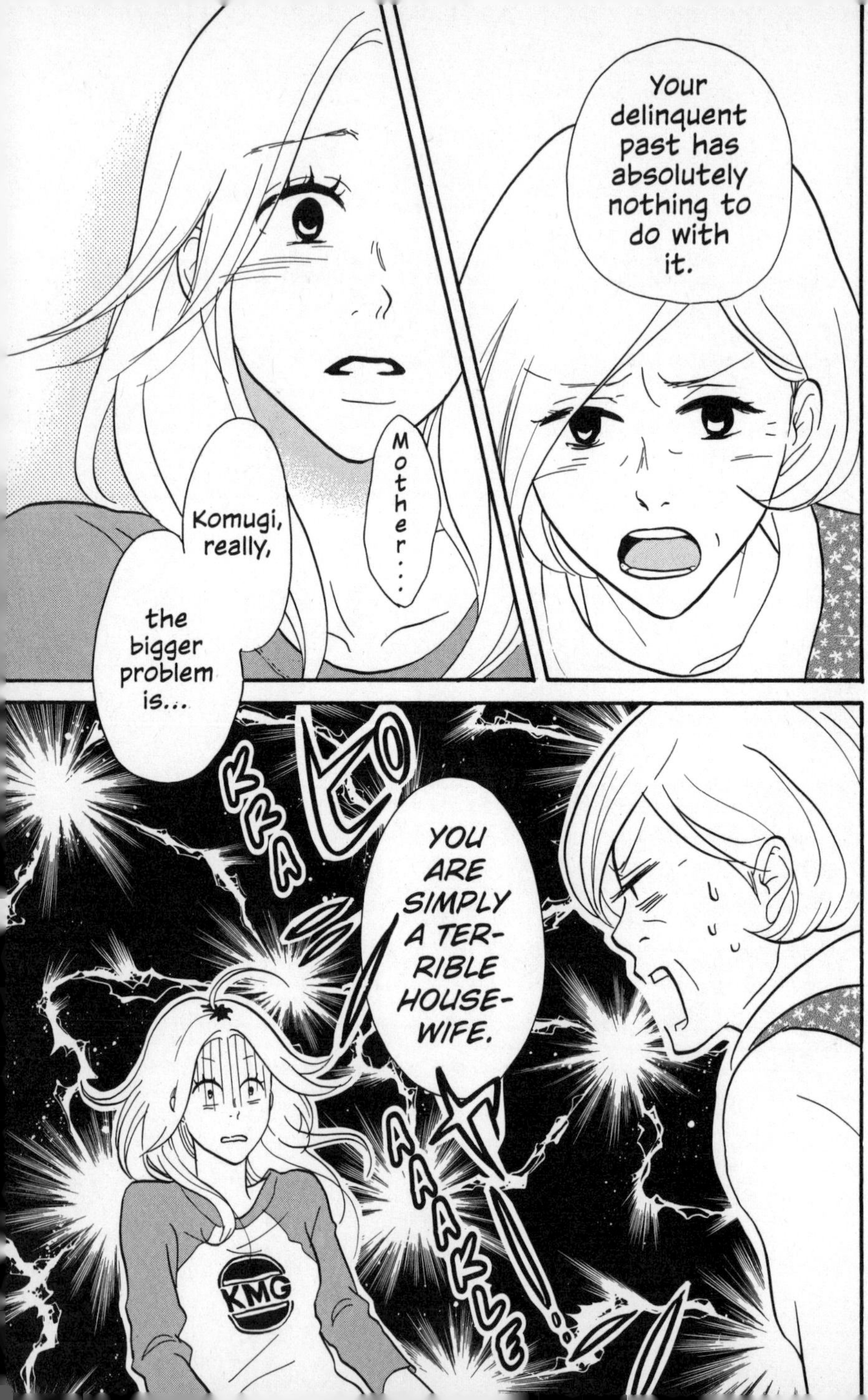
Your delinquent past has absolutely nothing to do with it.
Mother...
Komugi, really,
the bigger problem is...
KRA
YOU ARE SIMPLY A TERRIBLE HOUSEWIFE.
AAAKLE

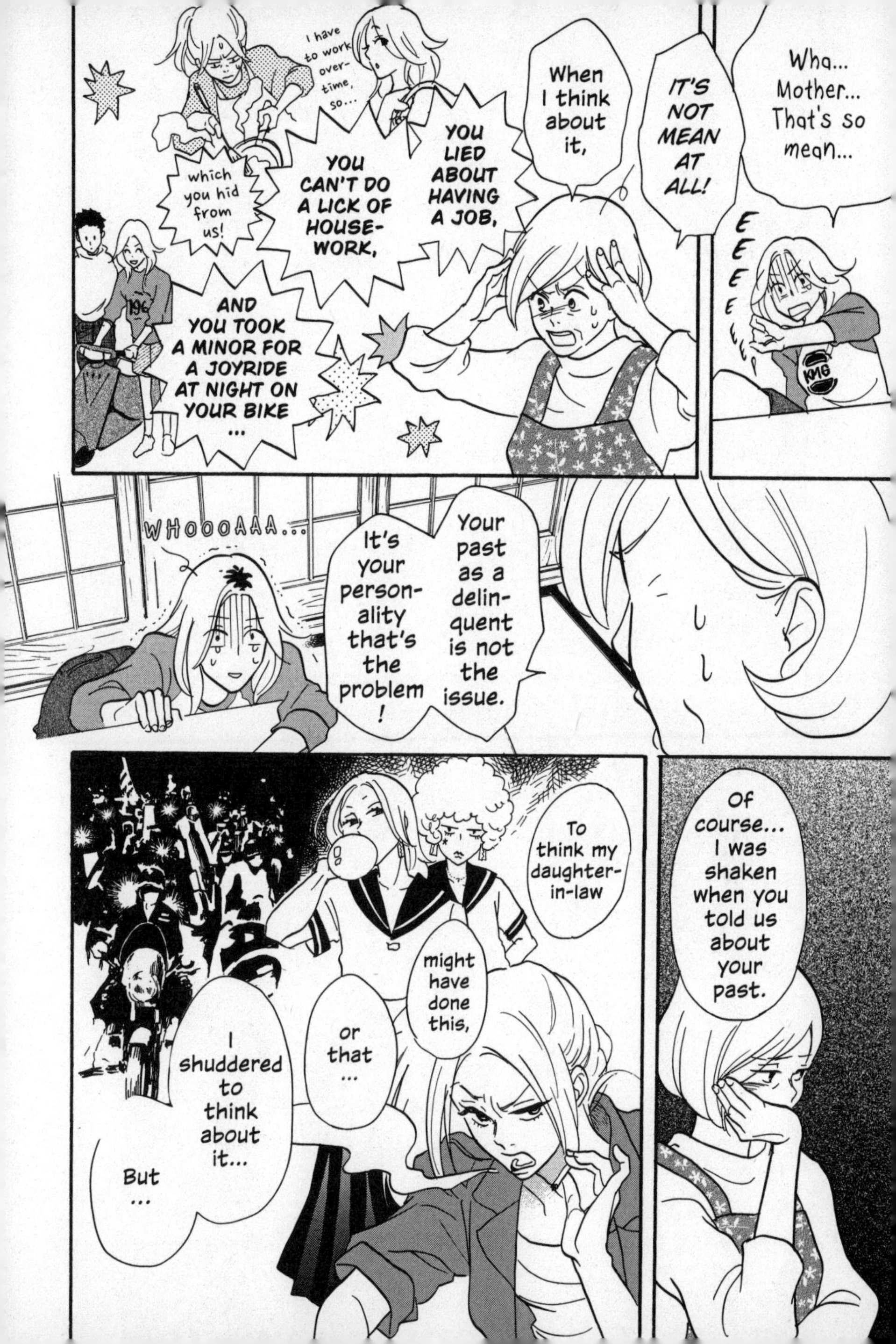
Wha... Mother... That's so mean...
EEEEEEE
IT'S NOT MEAN AT ALL!
When I think about it,
YOU LIED ABOUT HAVING A JOB,
I have to work over-time, so...
YOU CAN'T DO A LICK OF HOUSE-WORK,
which you hid from us!
AND YOU TOOK A MINOR FOR A JOYRIDE AT NIGHT ON YOUR BIKE ...
Your past as a delin-quent is not the issue.
It's your person-ality that's the problem!
WHOOOAAA...
Of course... I was shaken when you told us about your past.
To think my daughter-in-law
might have done this,
or that ...
I shuddered to think about it...
But ...

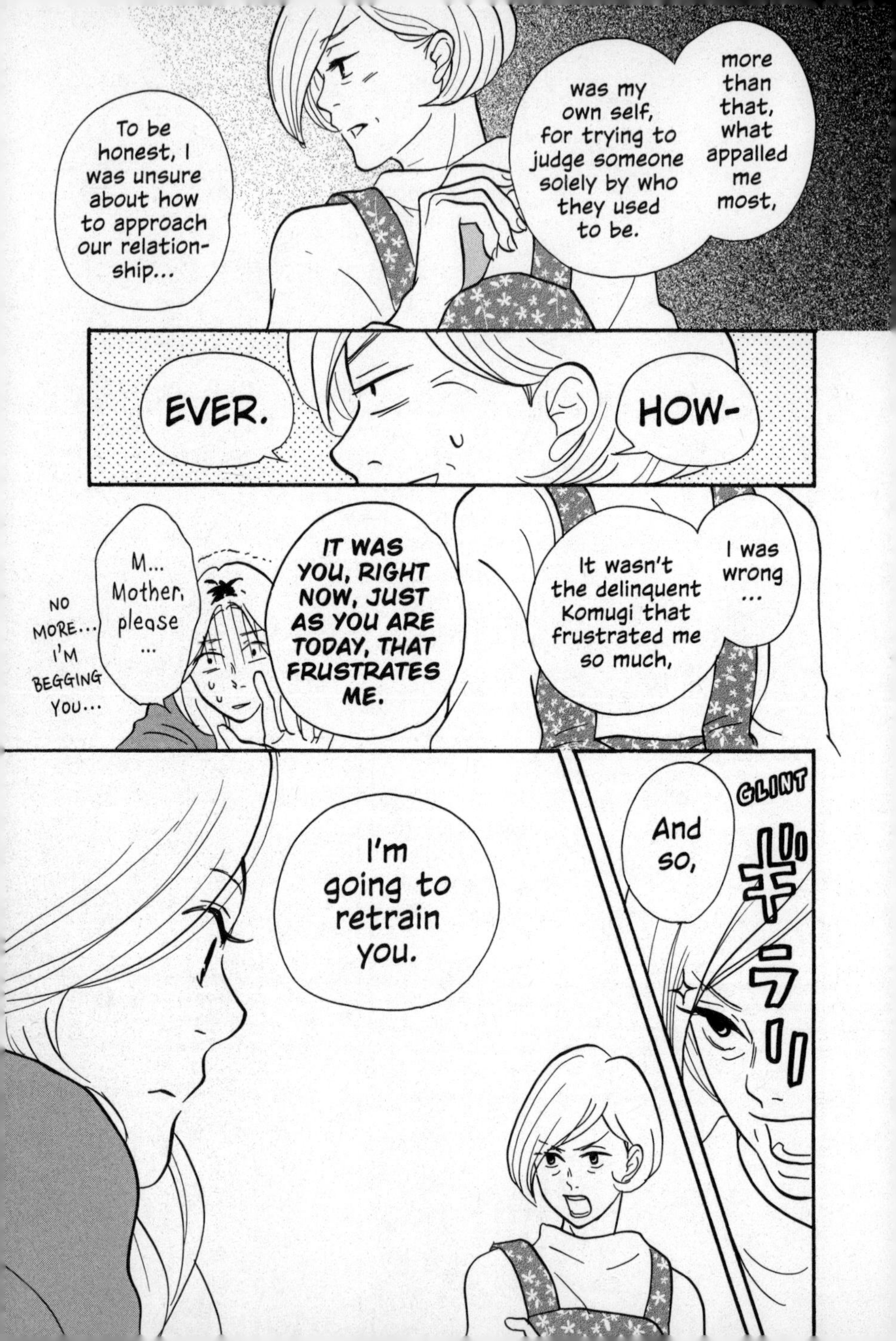

more than that, what appalled me most,
was my own self, for trying to judge someone solely by who they used to be.
To be honest, I was unsure about how to approach our relationship...
HOW-
EVER.
I was wrong...
It wasn't the delinquent Komugi that frustrated me so much,
IT WAS YOU, RIGHT NOW, JUST AS YOU ARE TODAY, THAT FRUSTRATES ME.
M... Mother, please...
NO MORE... I'M BEGGING YOU...
GLINT
ギラリ
And so,
I'm going to retrain you.

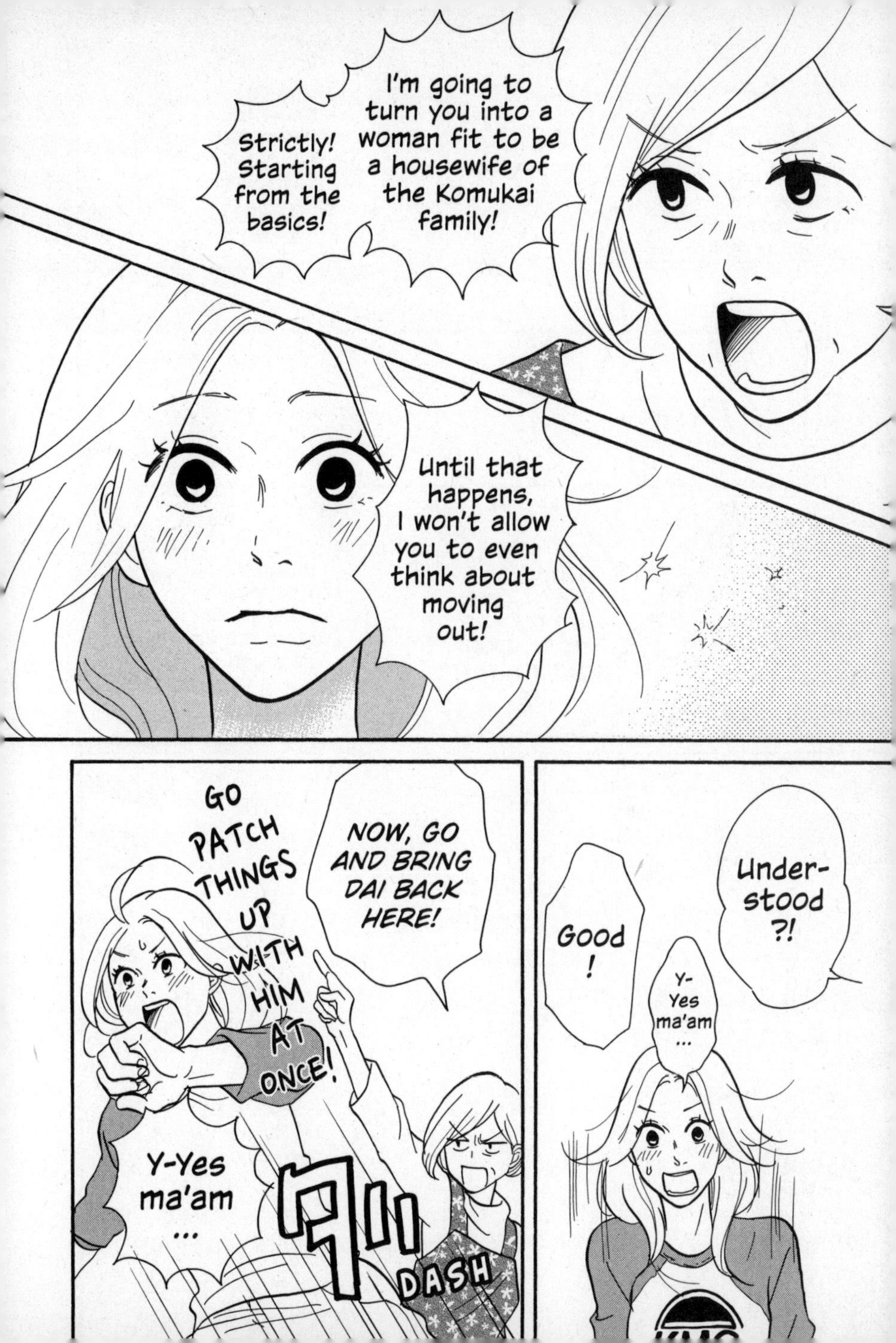
I'm going to turn you into a woman fit to be a housewife of the Komukai family!
Strictly! Starting from the basics!
Until that happens, I won't allow you to even think about moving out!
Under-stood?!
Y-Yes ma'am...
Good!
NOW, GO AND BRING DAI BACK HERE!
GO PATCH THINGS UP WITH HIM AT ONCE!
Y-Yes ma'am...
DASH

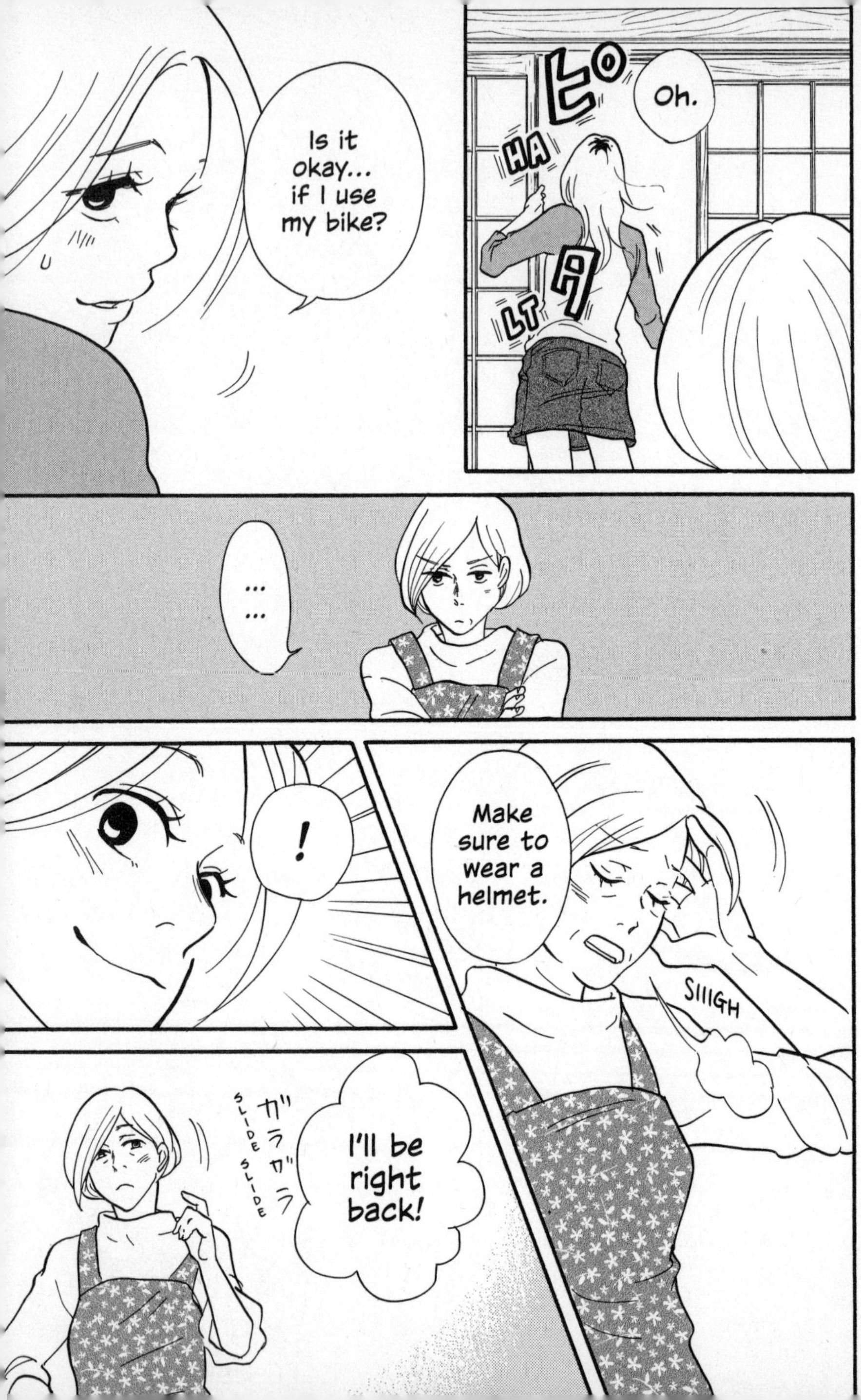
HA
LT
Oh.
Is it okay... if I use my bike?
... ...
Make sure to wear a helmet.
SIIIGH
!
I'll be right back!
ガラガラ
SLIDE SLIDE

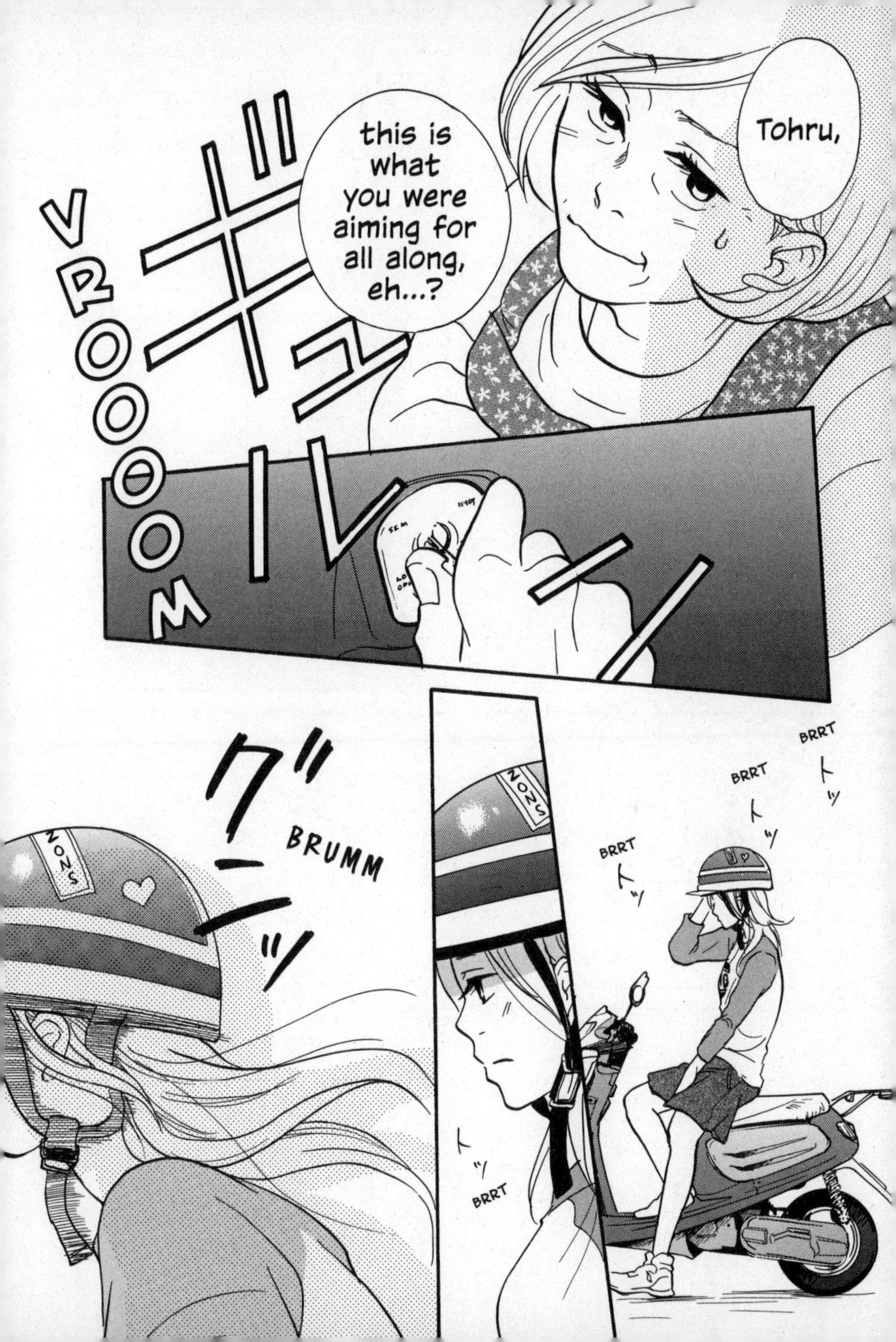
Tohru,
this is what you were aiming for all along, eh...?
VROOOOM
BRRT
BRRT
BRRT
BRRT
BRUMM

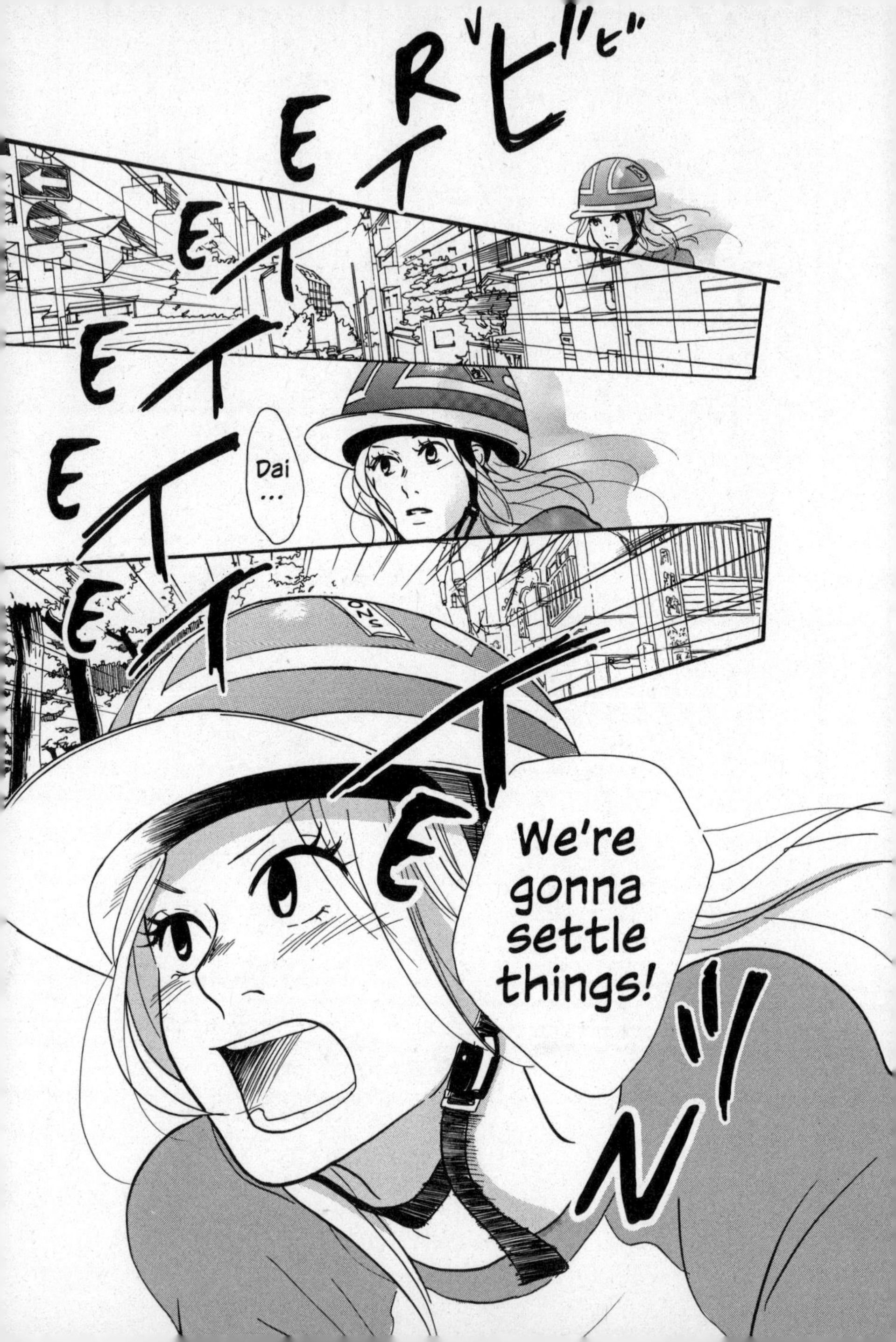
Dai ...
We're gonna settle things!

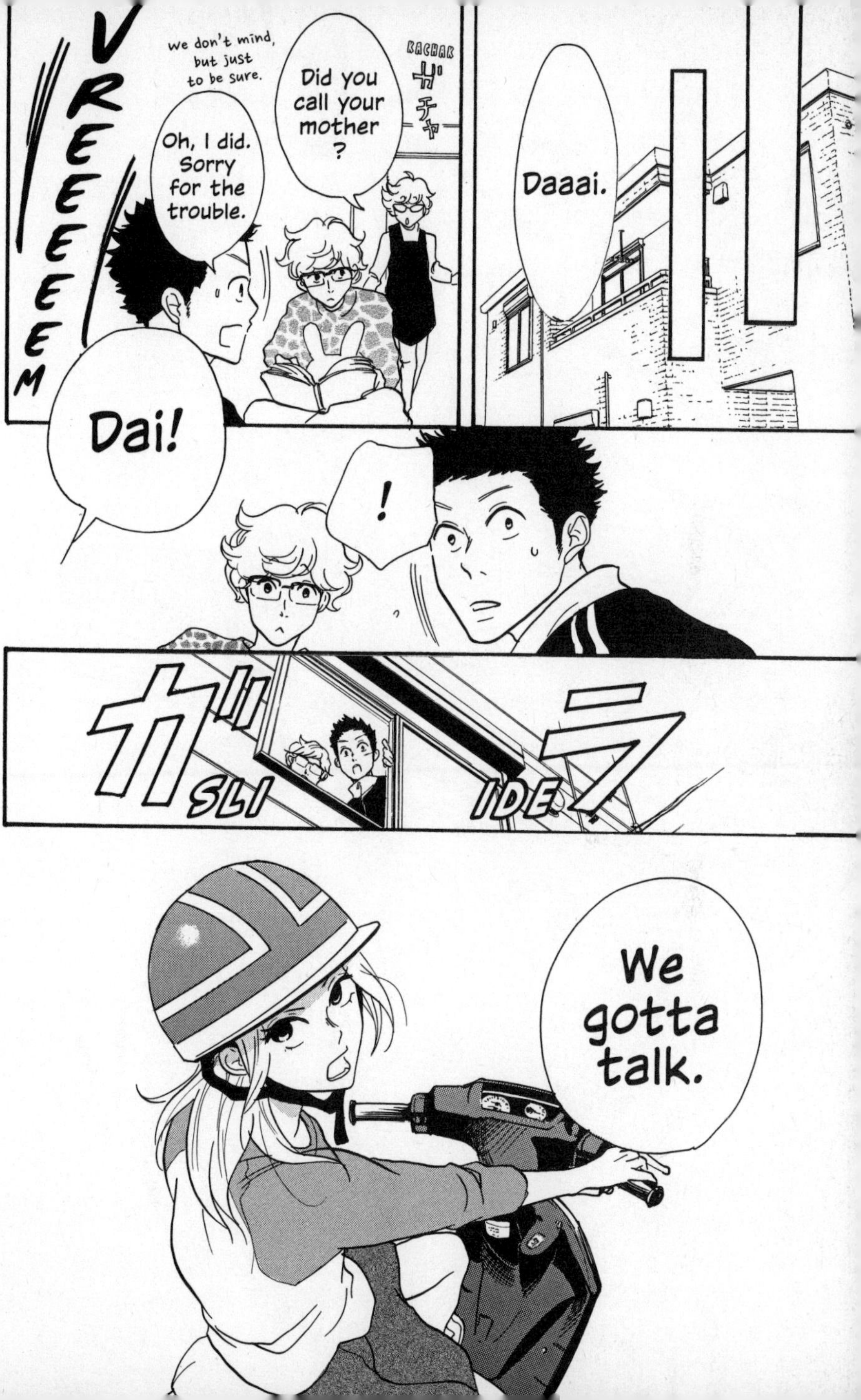
Daaai.
KACHAK
ガチャ
Did you call your mother?
we don't mind, but just to be sure.
Oh, I did. Sorry for the trouble.
VREEEEEEM
Dai!
!
ガラ
SLIDE
We gotta talk.

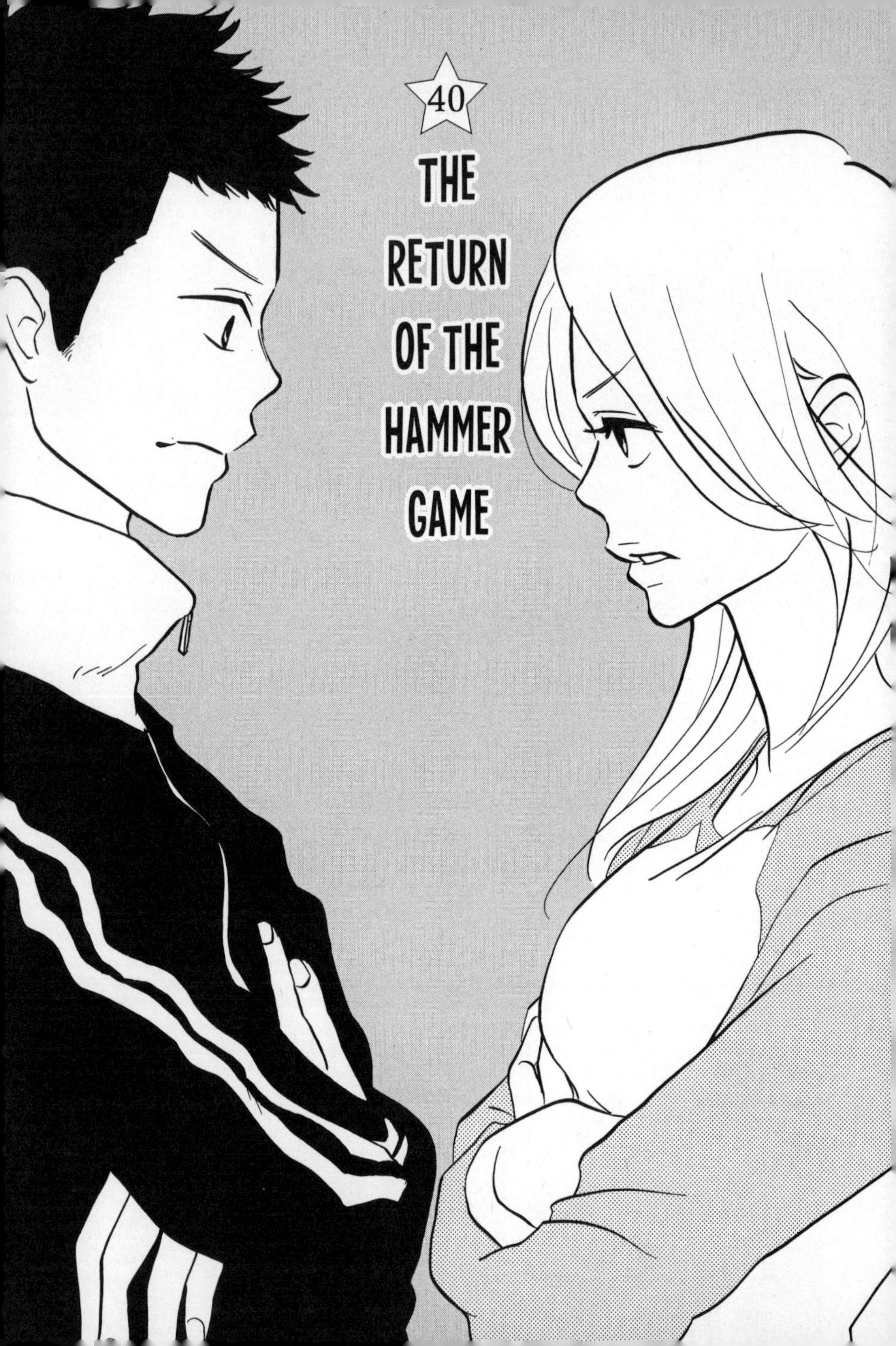
40
THE RETURN OF THE HAMMER GAME

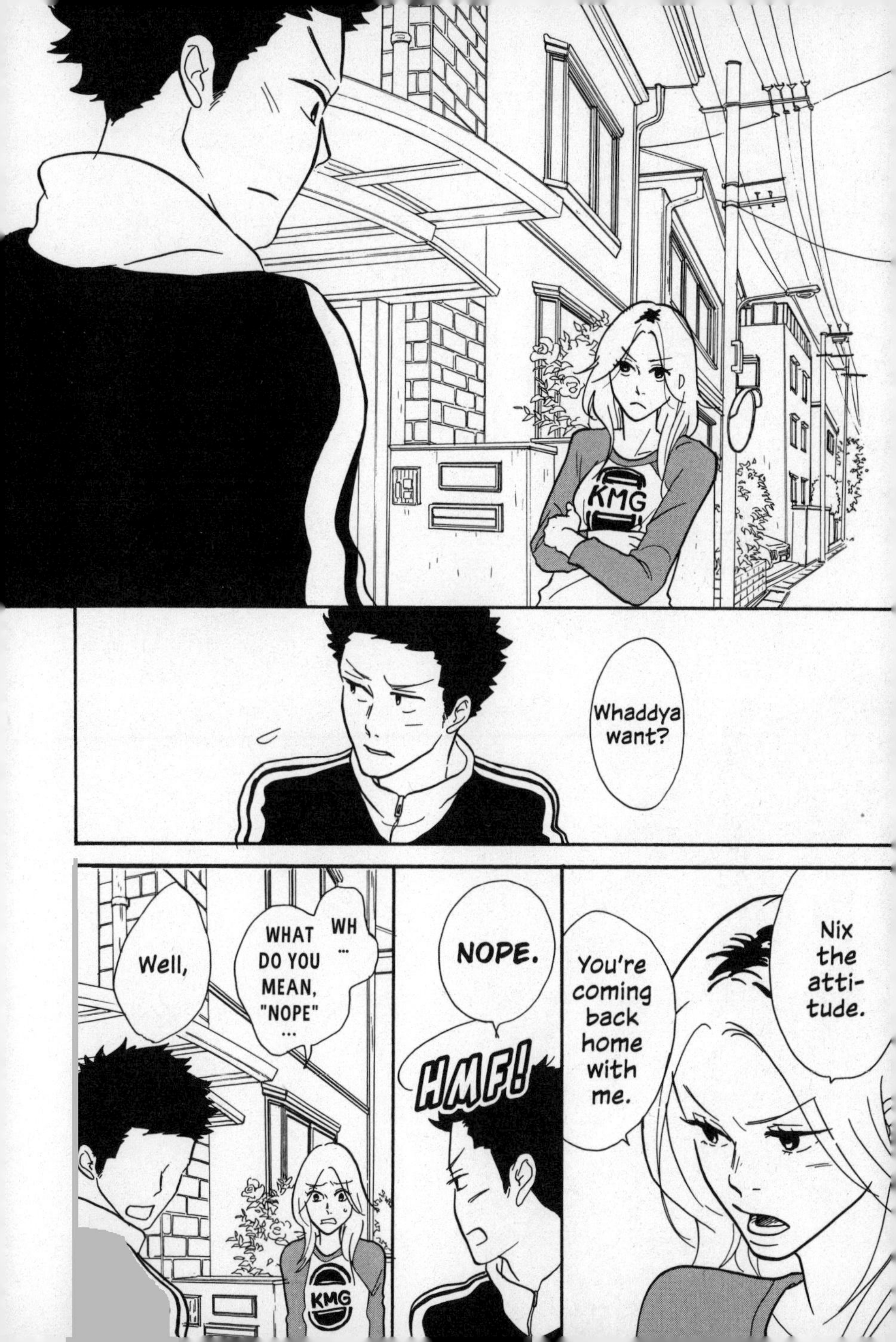
Whaddya want?
Nix the atti- tude.
You're coming back home with me.
NOPE.
HMF!
WH ...
WHAT DO YOU MEAN, "NOPE" ...
Well,

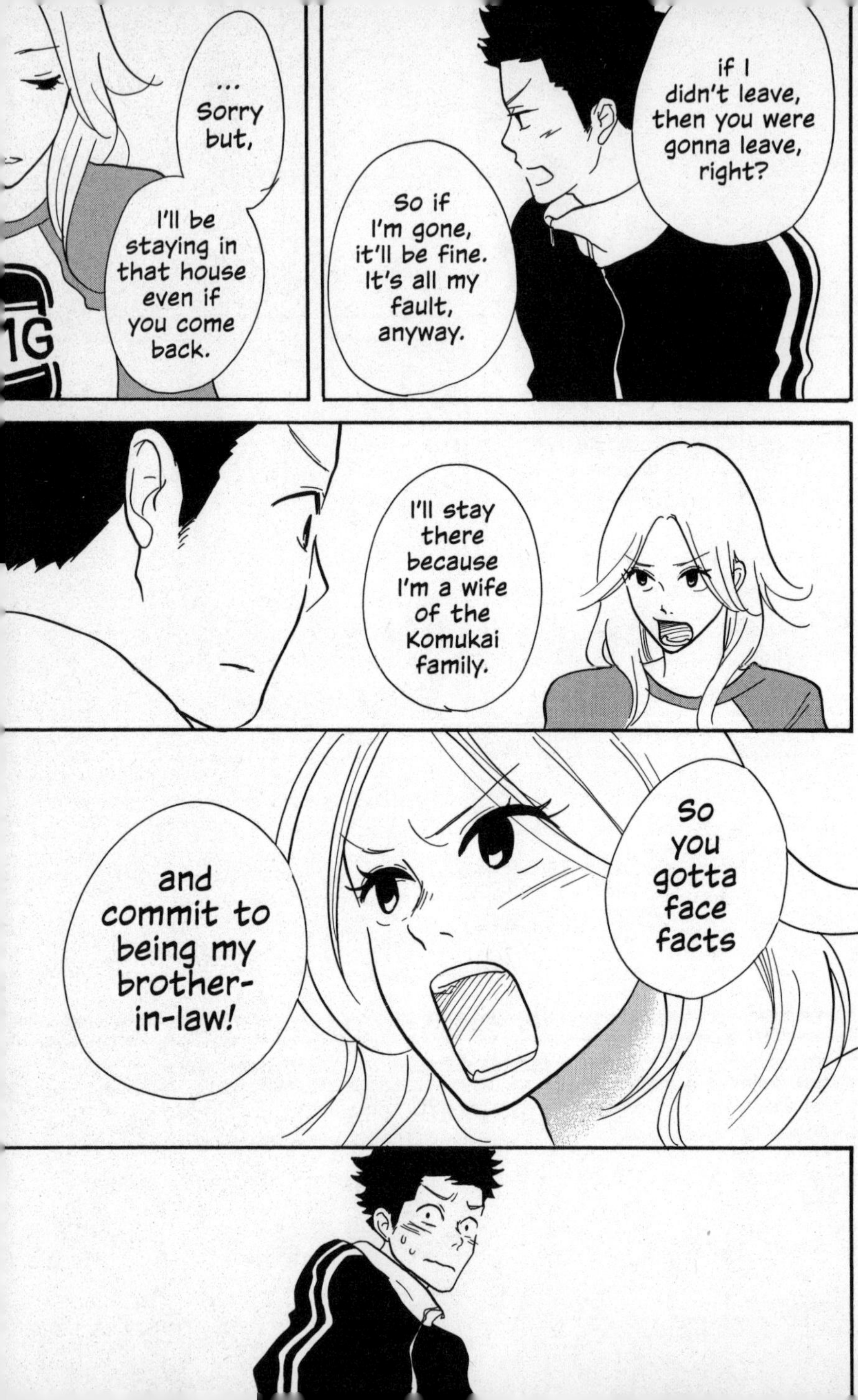
if I didn't leave, then you were gonna leave, right?
So if I'm gone, it'll be fine. It's all my fault, anyway.
... Sorry but,
I'll be staying in that house even if you come back.
I'll stay there because I'm a wife of the Komukai family.
So you gotta face facts
and commit to being my brother-in-law!

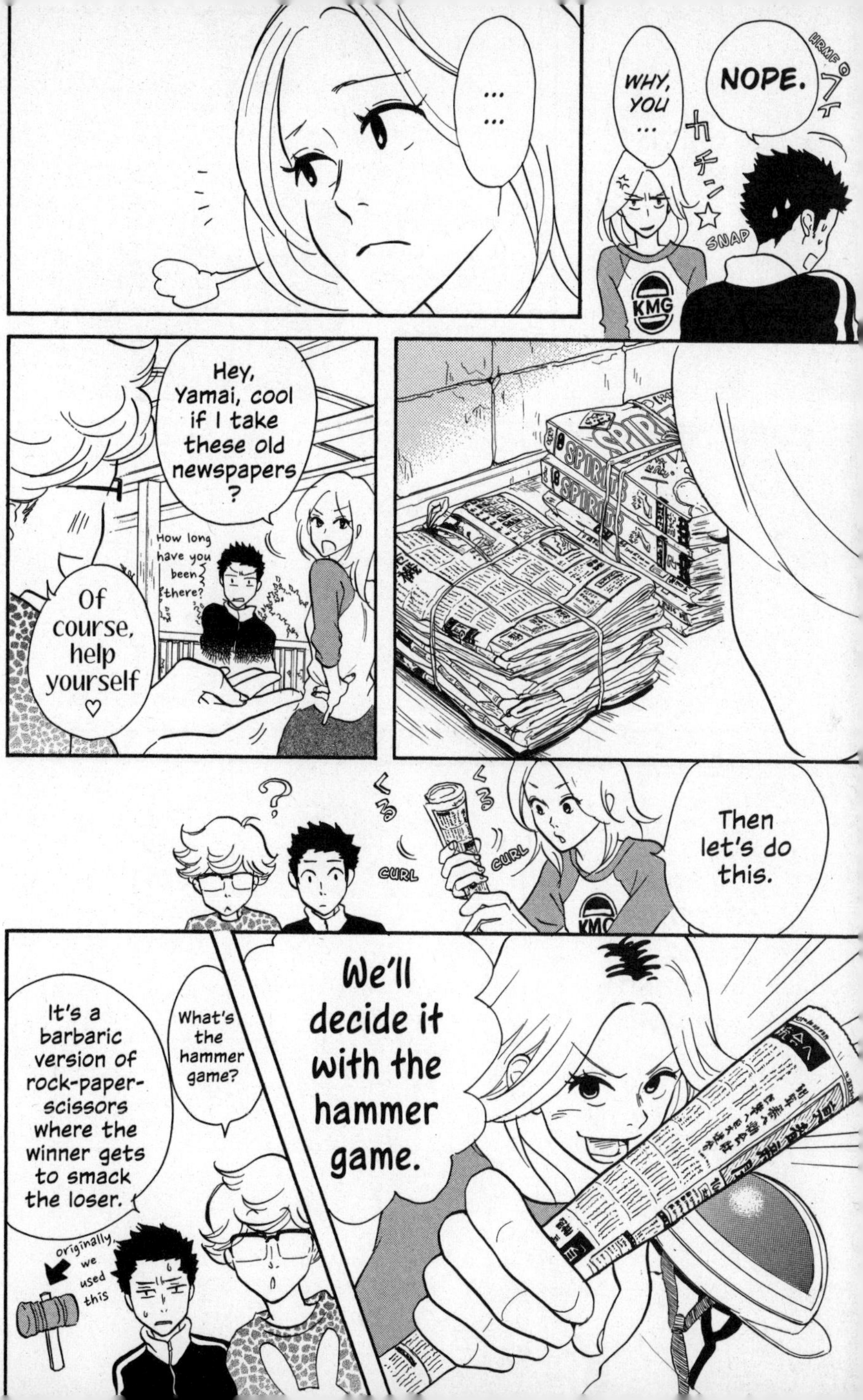
HRMF
NOPE.
WHY, YOU ...
SNAP
... ...
Hey, Yamai, cool if I take these old newspapers ?
How long have you been there?
Of course, help yourself ♡
Then let's do this.
CURL
CURL
?
We'll decide it with the hammer game.
What's the hammer game?
It's a barbaric version of rock-paper-scissors where the winner gets to smack the loser.
originally, we used this

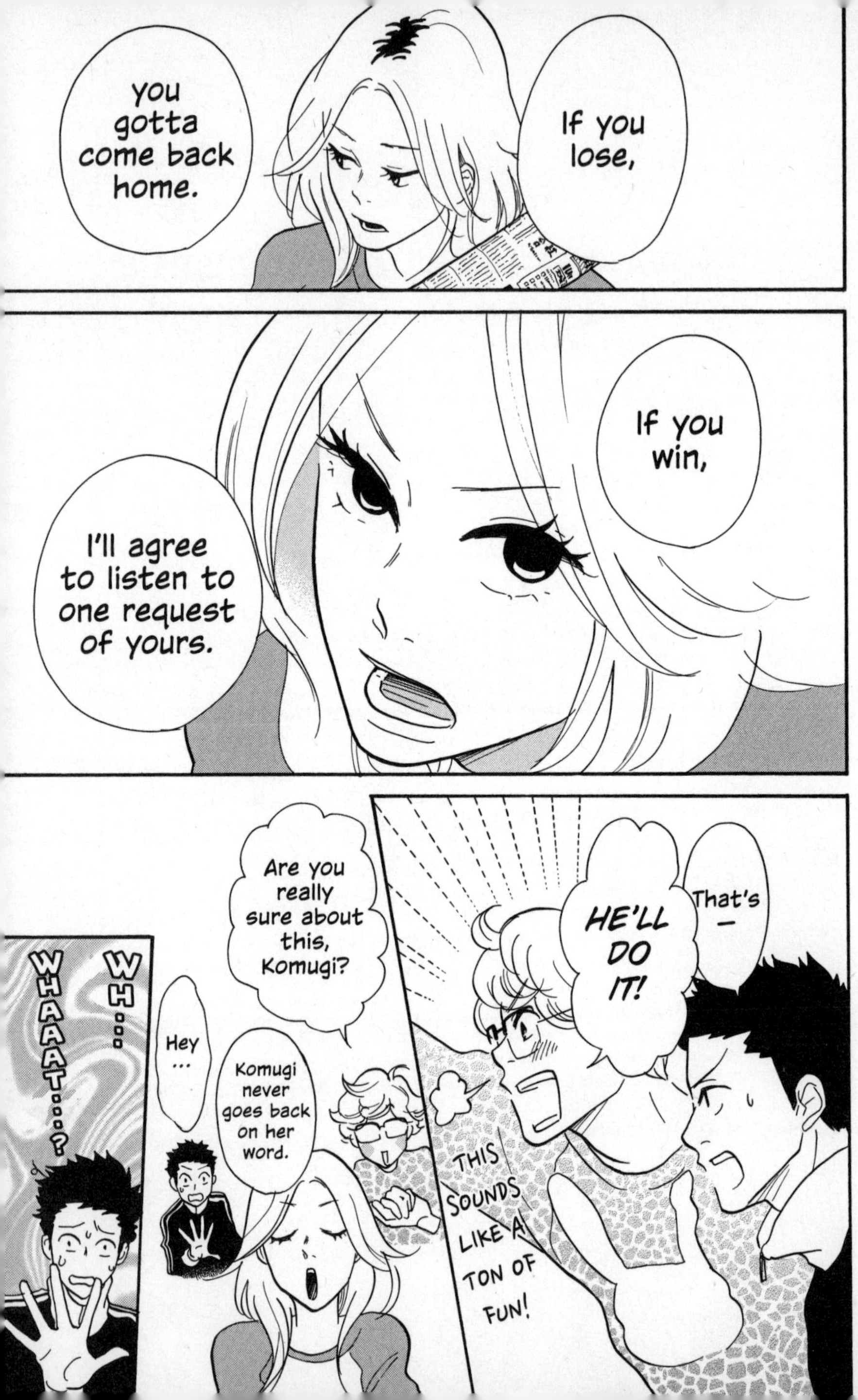
If you lose,
you gotta come back home.
If you win,
I'll agree to listen to one request of yours.
That's —
HE'LL DO IT!
THIS SOUNDS LIKE A TON OF FUN!
Are you really sure about this, Komugi?
Komugi never goes back on her word.
Hey ...
WH...
WHAAAT...?

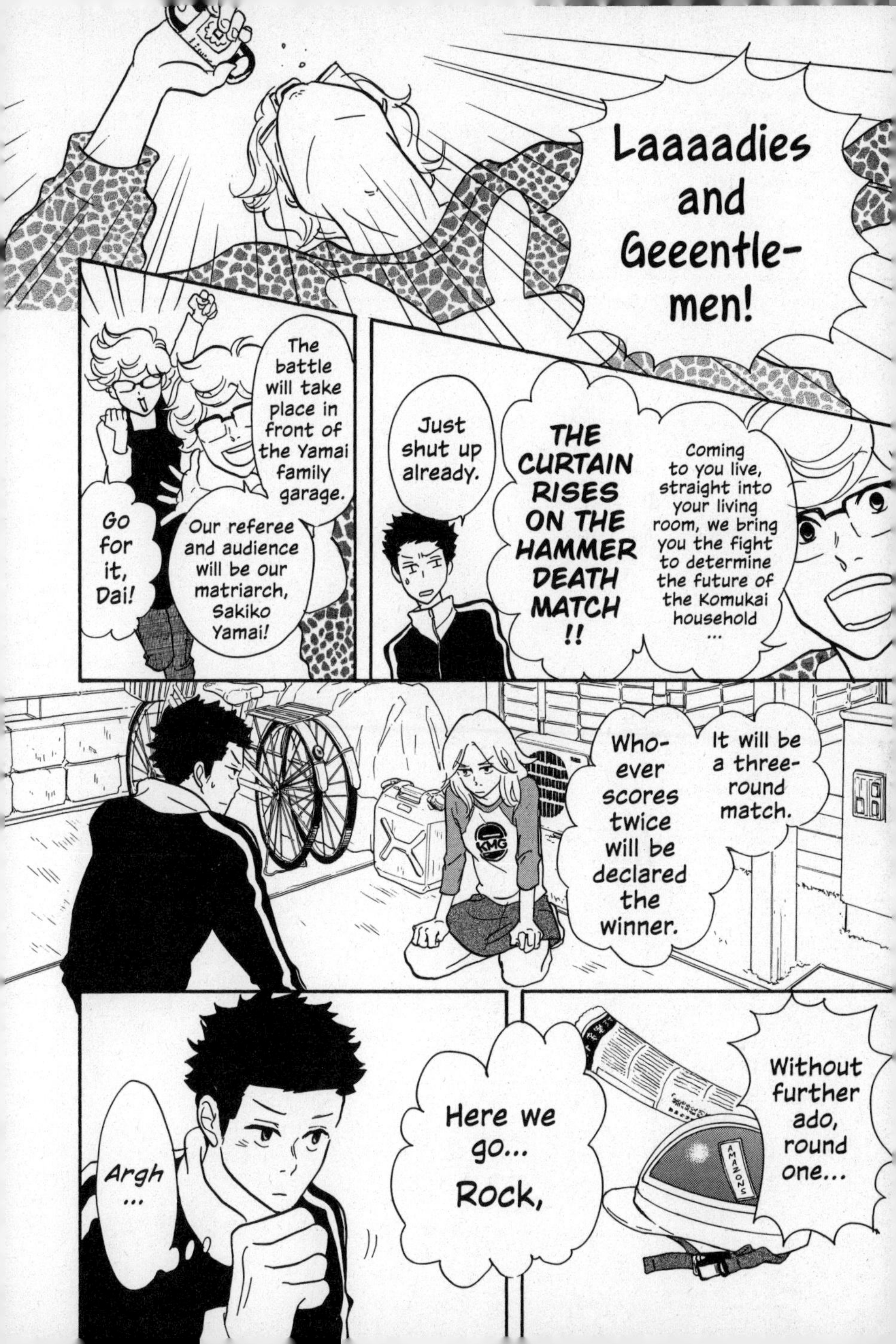
Laaaadies and Geeentle-men!
Coming to you live, straight into your living room, we bring you the fight to determine the future of the Komukai household ...
THE CURTAIN RISES ON THE HAMMER DEATH MATCH !!
Just shut up already.
The battle will take place in front of the Yamai family garage.
Our referee and audience will be our matriarch, Sakiko Yamai!
Go for it, Dai!
It will be a three-round match.
Who-ever scores twice will be declared the winner.
KMG
Without further ado, round one...
AMAZONS
Here we go... Rock,
Argh ...

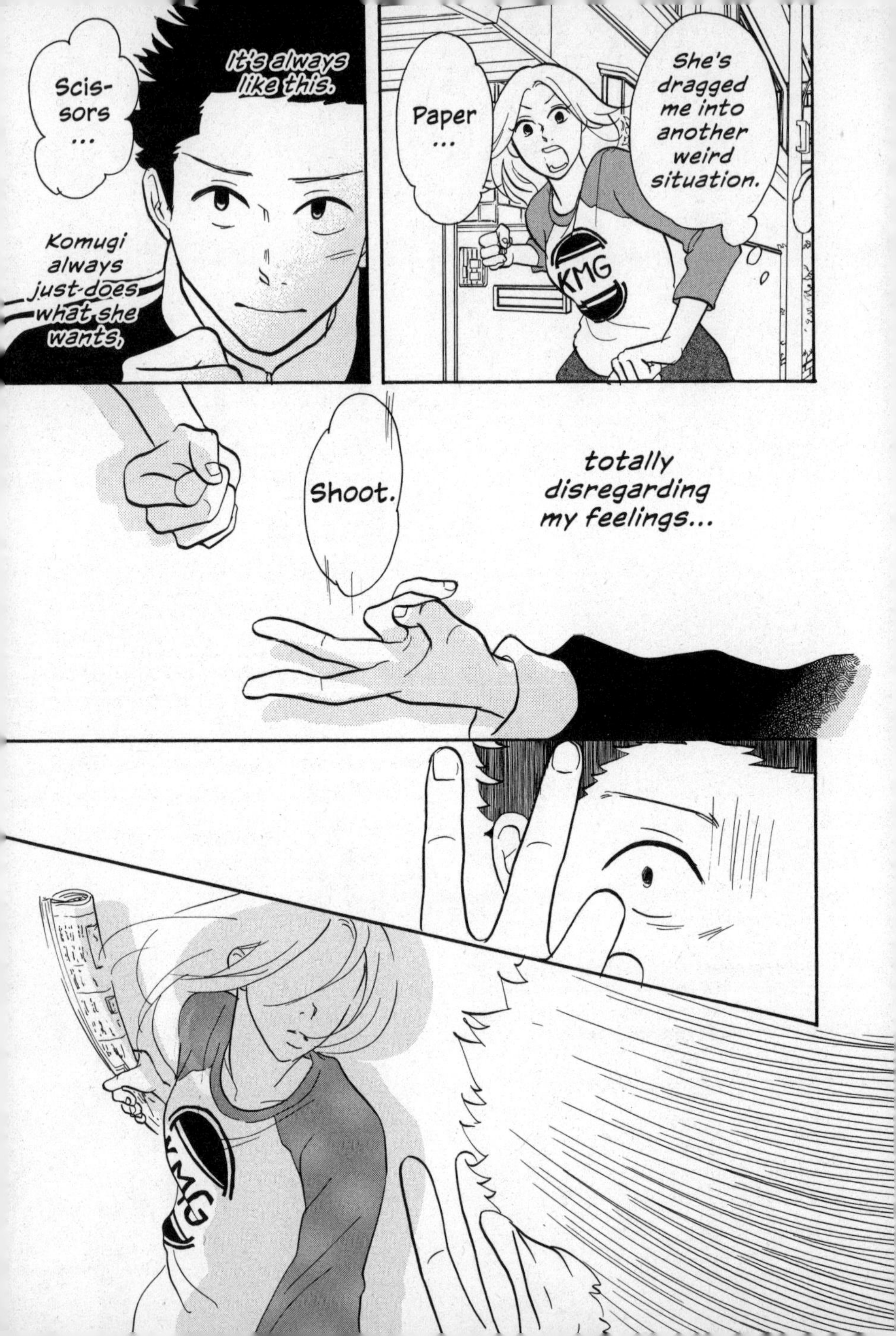
She's dragged me into another weird situation.
Paper ...
It's always like this.
Scis-sors ...
Komugi always just does what she wants,
totally disregarding my feelings...
Shoot.

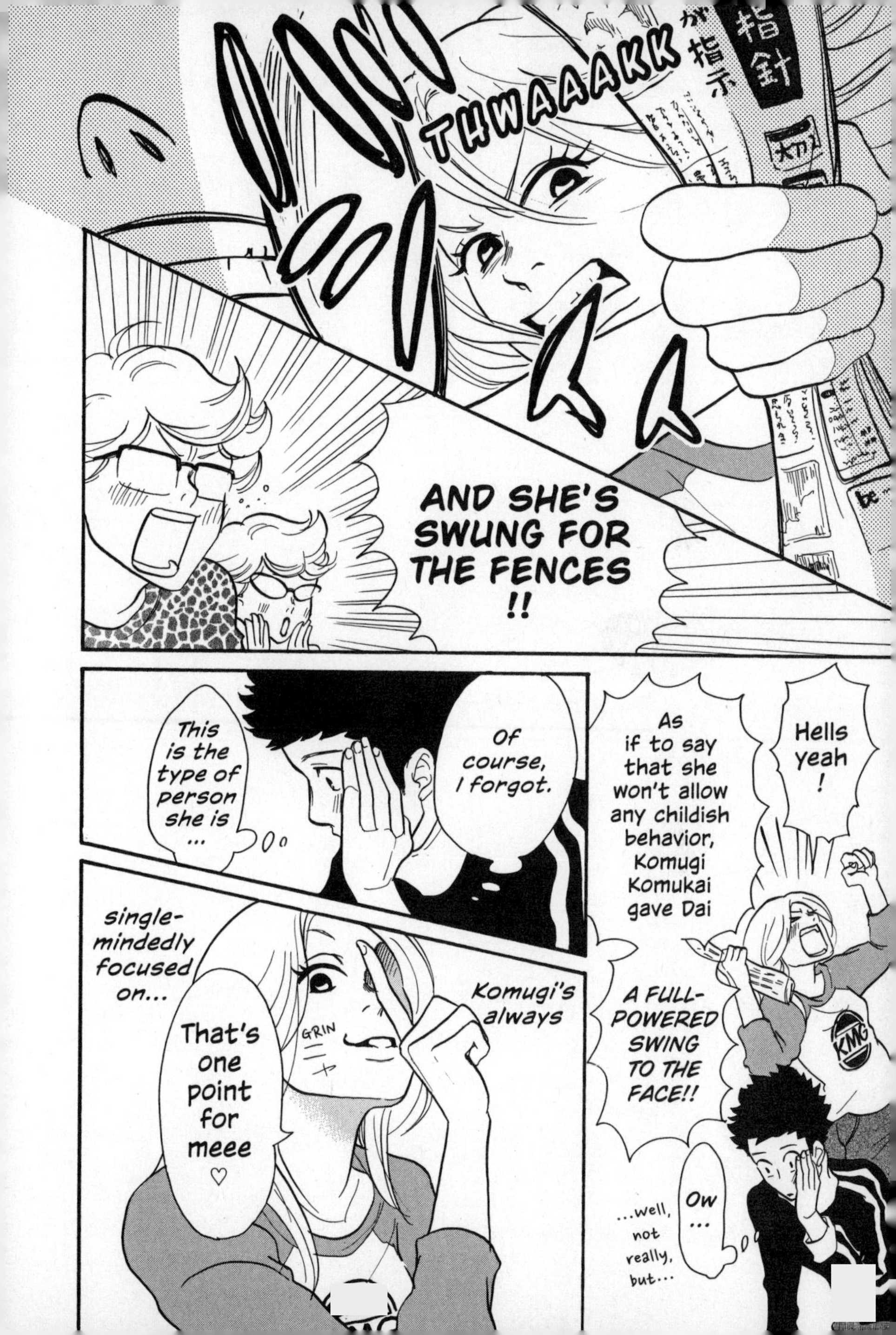
指針
THWAAAKK
が指示
AND SHE'S SWUNG FOR THE FENCES!!
As if to say that she won't allow any childish behavior, Komugi Komukai gave Dai
Hells yeah!
A FULL-POWERED SWING TO THE FACE!!
Ow...
...well, not really, but...
Of course, I forgot.
This is the type of person she is...
Komugi's always
single-mindedly focused on...
GRIN
That's one point for meee ♡

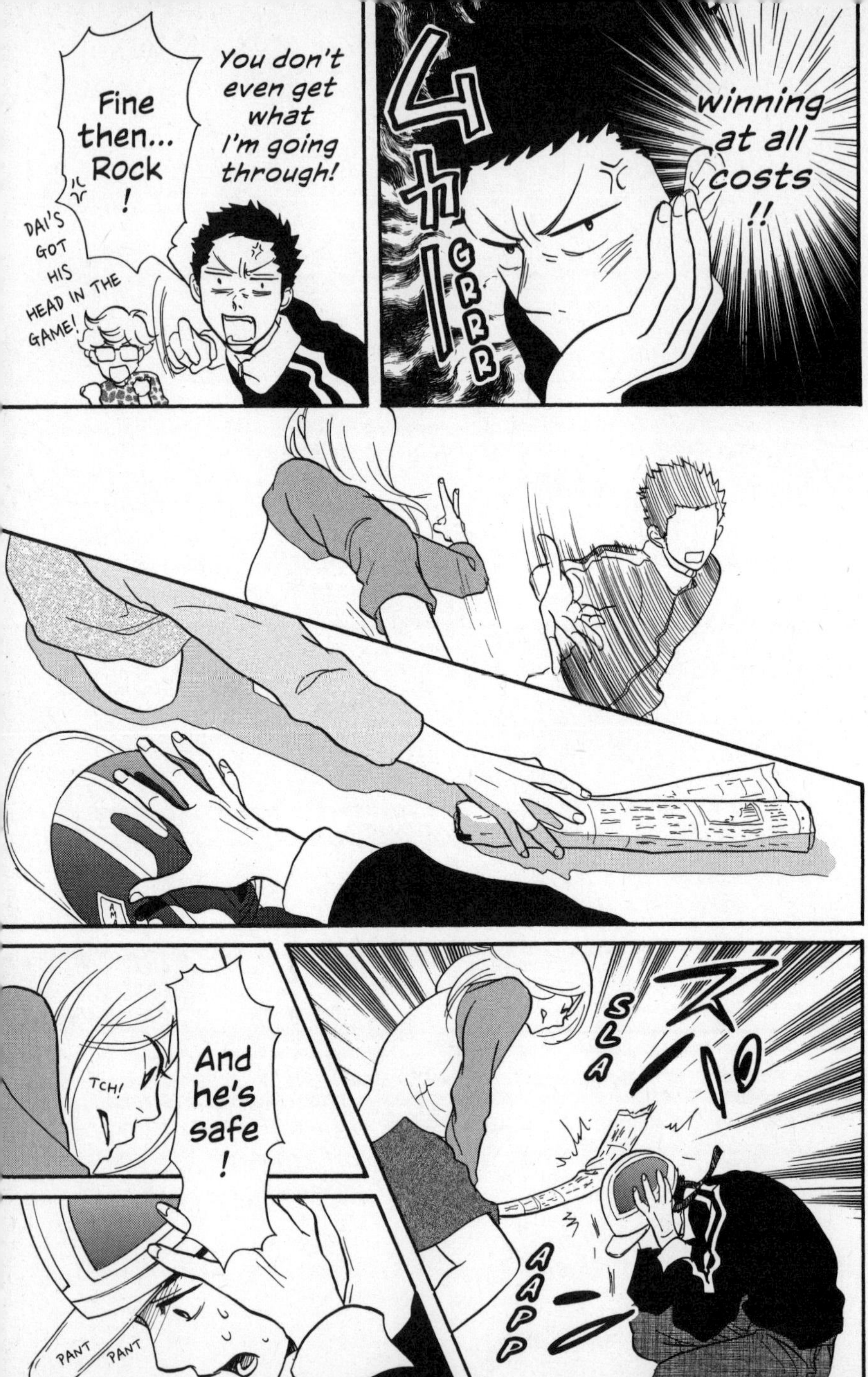

winning at all costs !!
ムカー
GRRR
You don't even get what I'm going through!
Fine then... Rock !
DAI'S GOT HIS HEAD IN THE GAME!
スパー
SLA
AAPP
And he's safe !
TCH!
PANT PANT

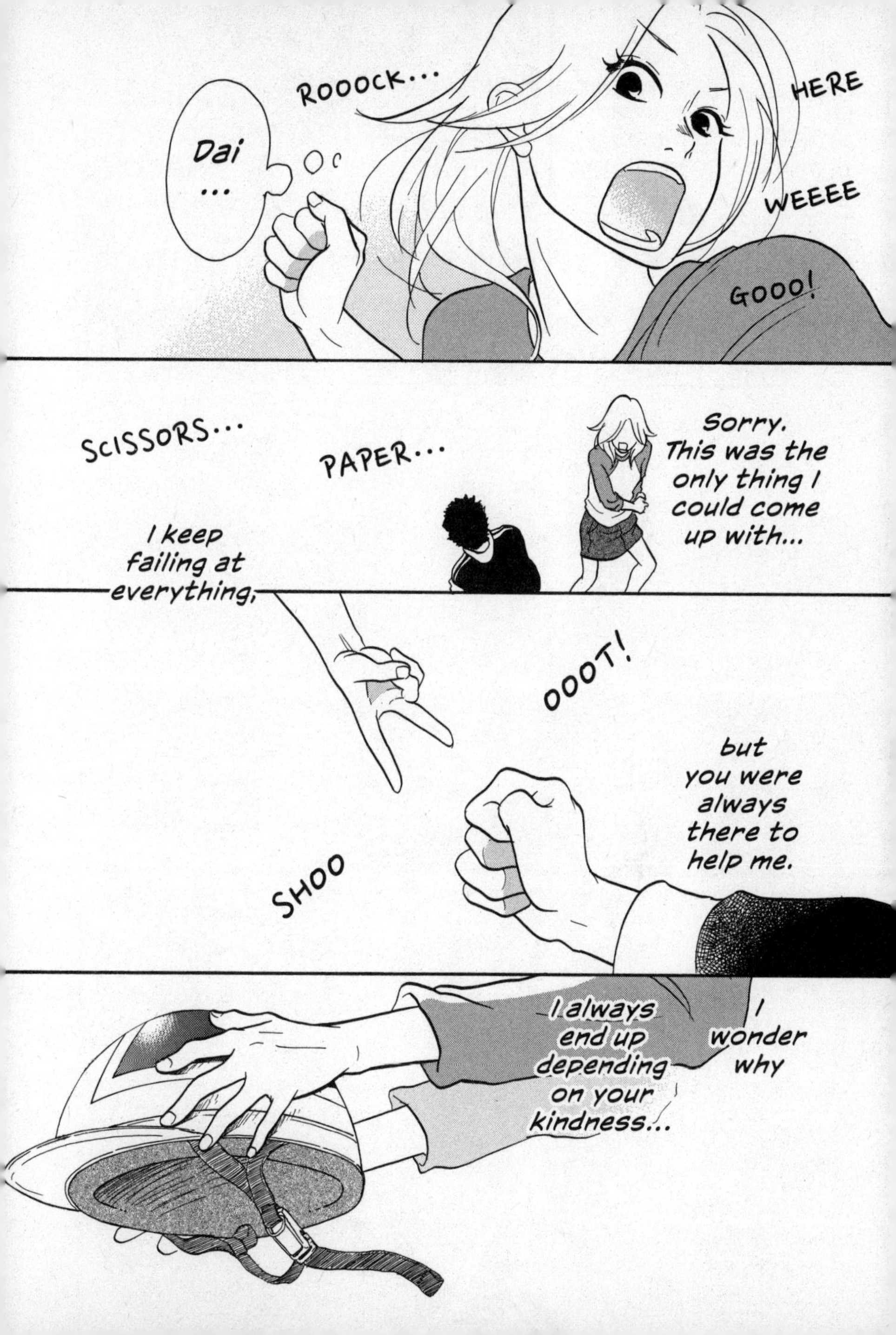
HERE
ROOOCK...
WEEEE
GOOO!
Dai ...
Sorry. This was the only thing I could come up with...
PAPER...
SCISSORS...
I keep failing at everything,
OOOT!
but you were always there to help me.
SHOO
I wonder why
I always end up depending on your kindness...

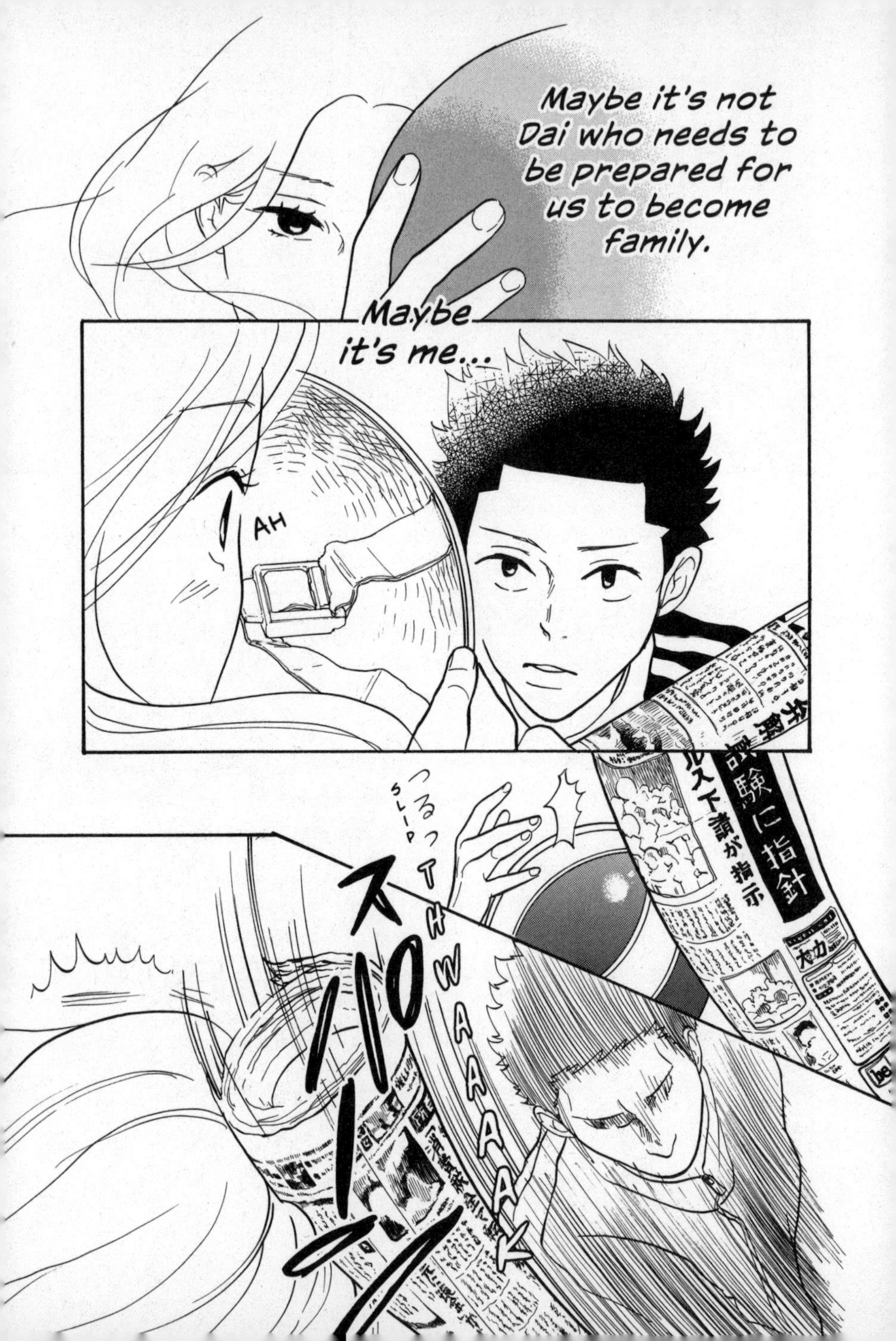
Maybe it's not Dai who needs to be prepared for us to become family.
Maybe it's me...
AH
つるっ
SLIP
スパーン
THWAAAAAK

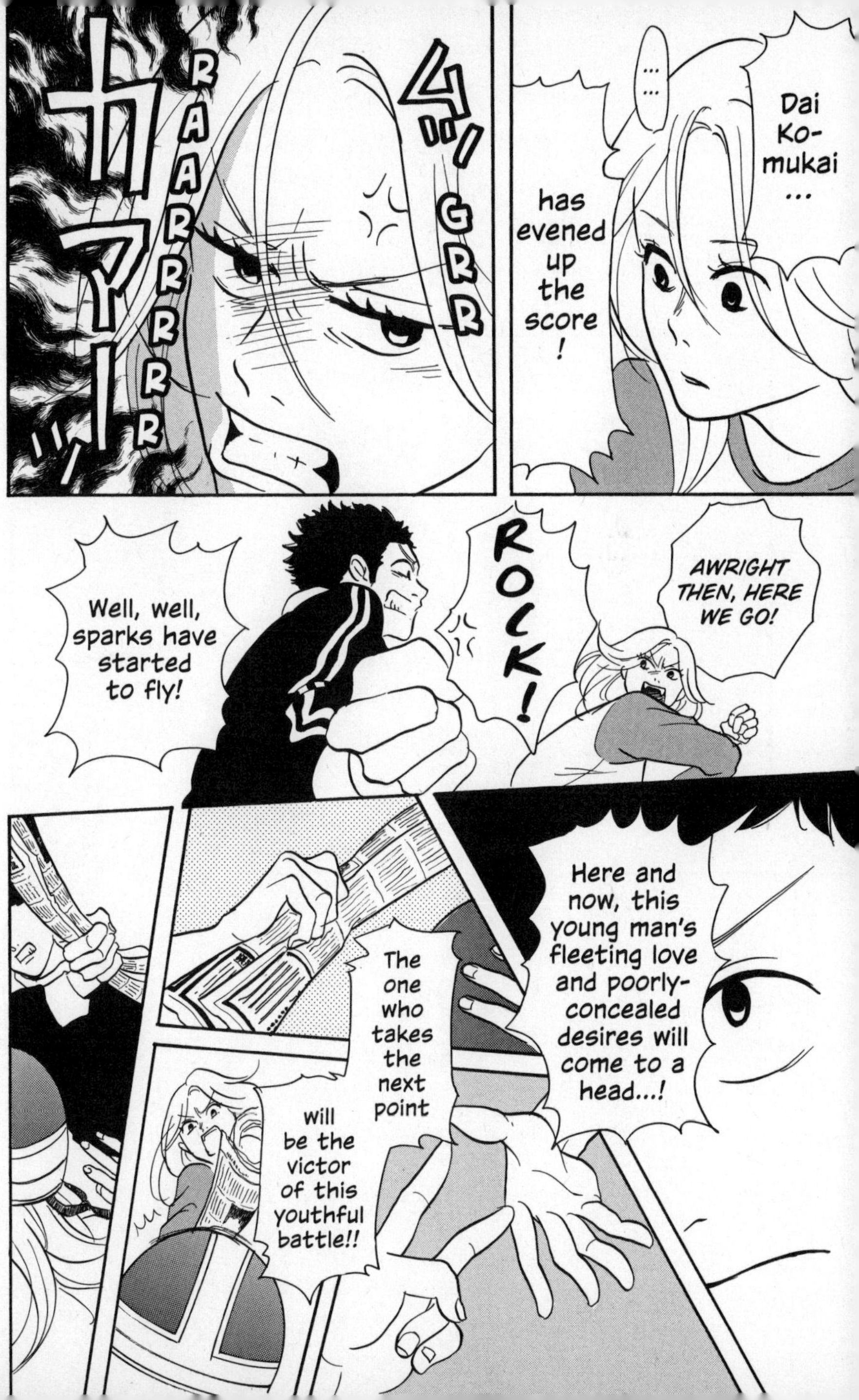
......
Dai Komukai ...
has evened up the score!
GRR
RAARRRRRR
カァーッ
AWRIGHT THEN, HERE WE GO!
ROCK!
Well, well, sparks have started to fly!
Here and now, this young man's fleeting love and poorly-concealed desires will come to a head...!
The one who takes the next point
will be the victor of this youthful battle!!

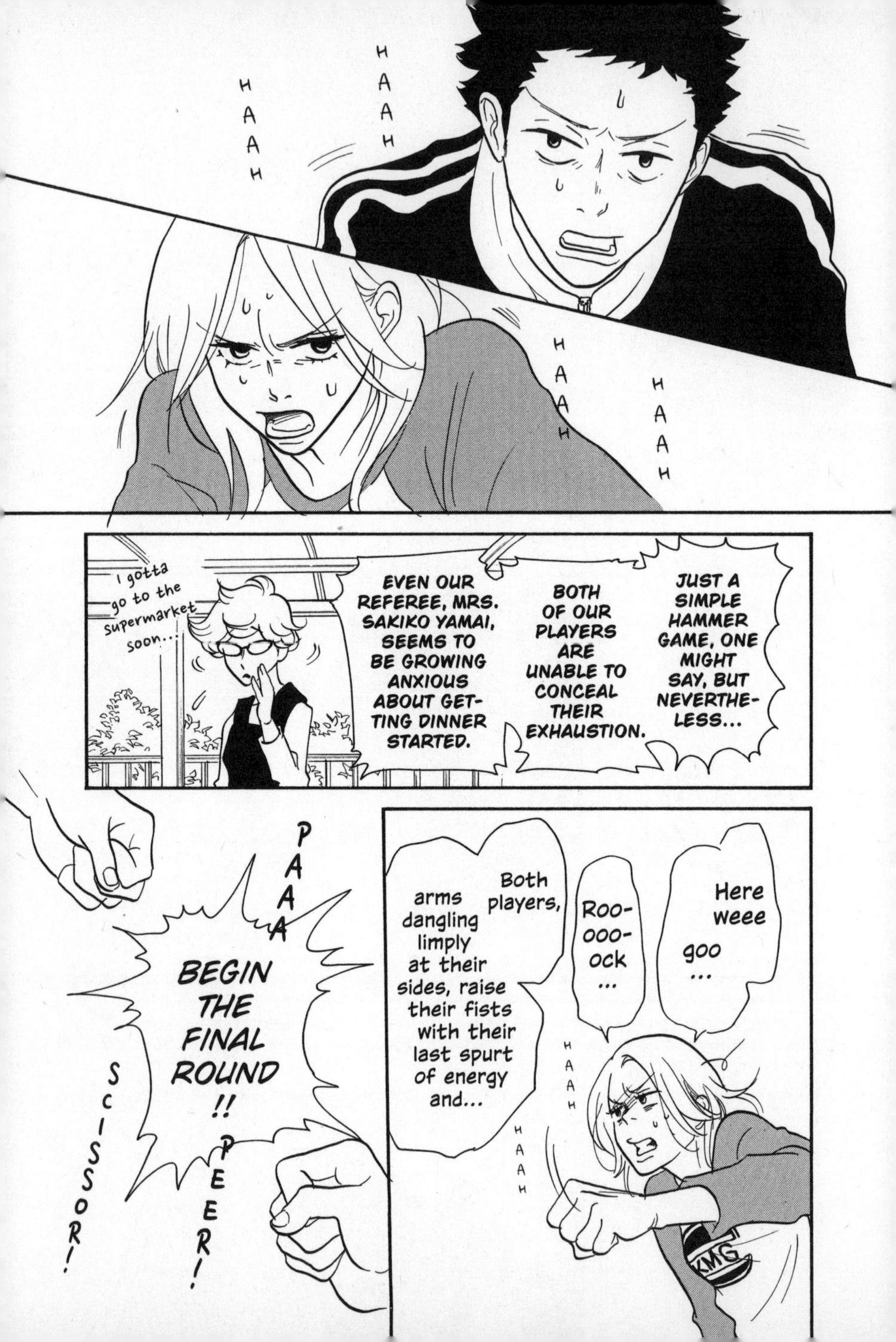
HAAH
HAAH
HAAH
HAAH
JUST A SIMPLE HAMMER GAME, ONE MIGHT SAY, BUT NEVERTHELESS...
BOTH OF OUR PLAYERS ARE UNABLE TO CONCEAL THEIR EXHAUSTION.
EVEN OUR REFEREE, MRS. SAKIKO YAMAI, SEEMS TO BE GROWING ANXIOUS ABOUT GETTING DINNER STARTED.
I gotta go to the supermarket soon...
Here weee goo ...
Roo-ooo-ock ...
Both players, arms dangling limply at their sides, raise their fists with their last spurt of energy and...
HAAH
HAAH
PAAAA
BEGIN THE FINAL ROUND!!
PEER!
SCISSOR!

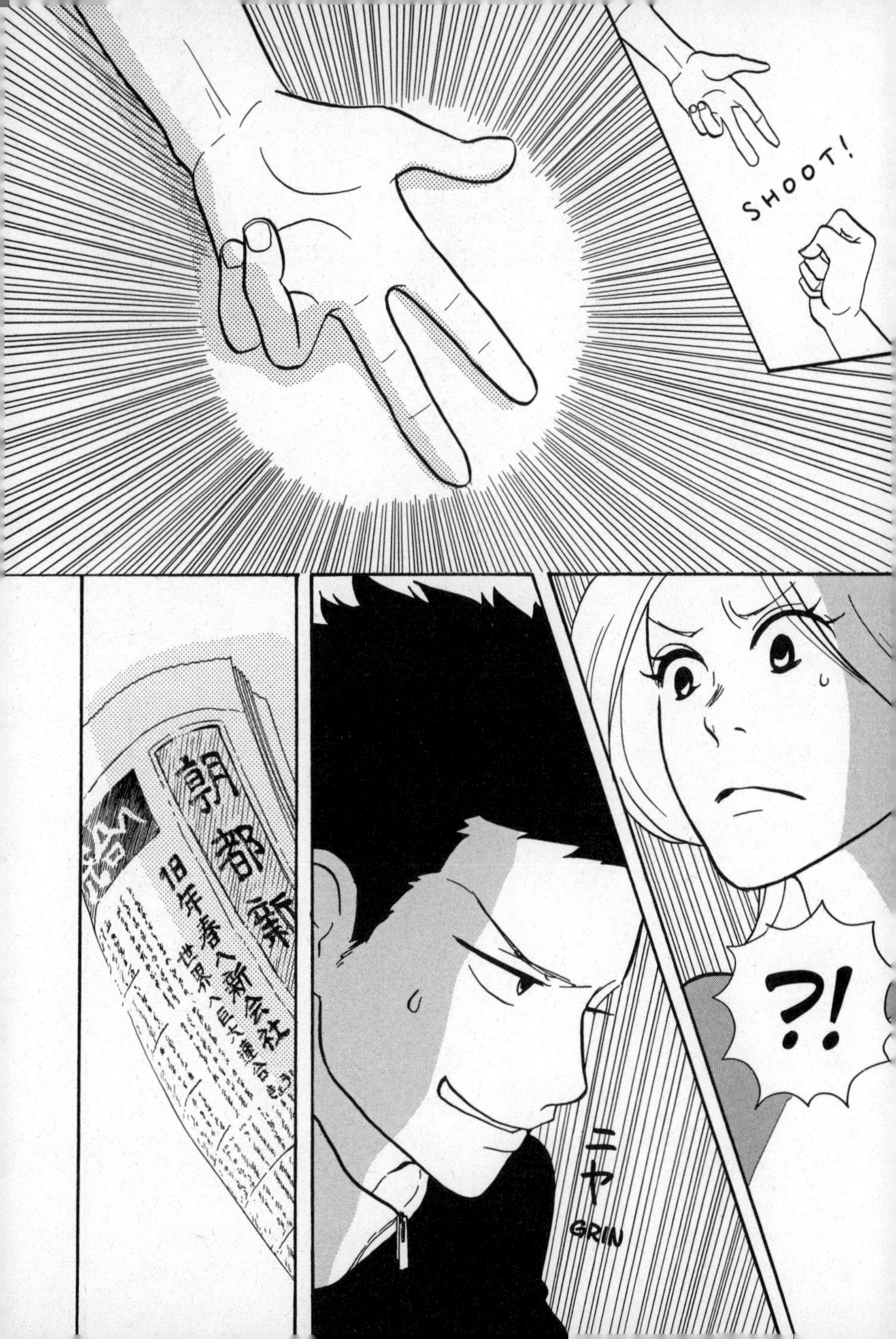
SHOOT!
?!
ニヤ
GRIN
朝都新
18年春入新会社
世界へ巨大連合

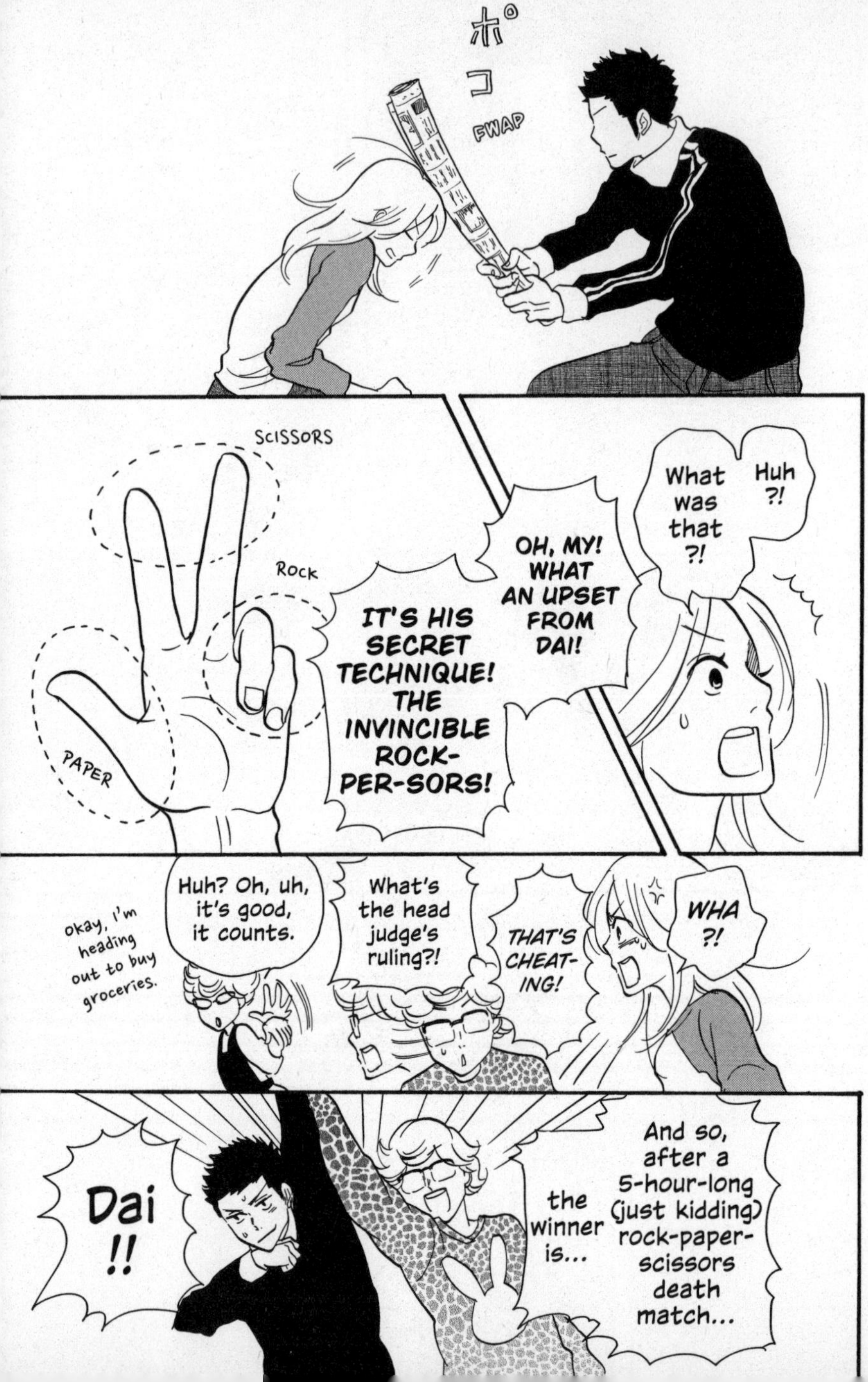
ポコ
FWAP
Huh ?!
What was that ?!
OH, MY! WHAT AN UPSET FROM DAI!
IT'S HIS SECRET TECHNIQUE! THE INVINCIBLE ROCK-PER-SORS!
SCISSORS
ROCK
PAPER
WHA ?!
THAT'S CHEAT-ING!
What's the head judge's ruling?!
Huh? Oh, uh, it's good, it counts.
okay, I'm heading out to buy groceries.
And so, after a 5-hour-long (just kidding) rock-paper-scissors death match...
the winner is...
Dai !!

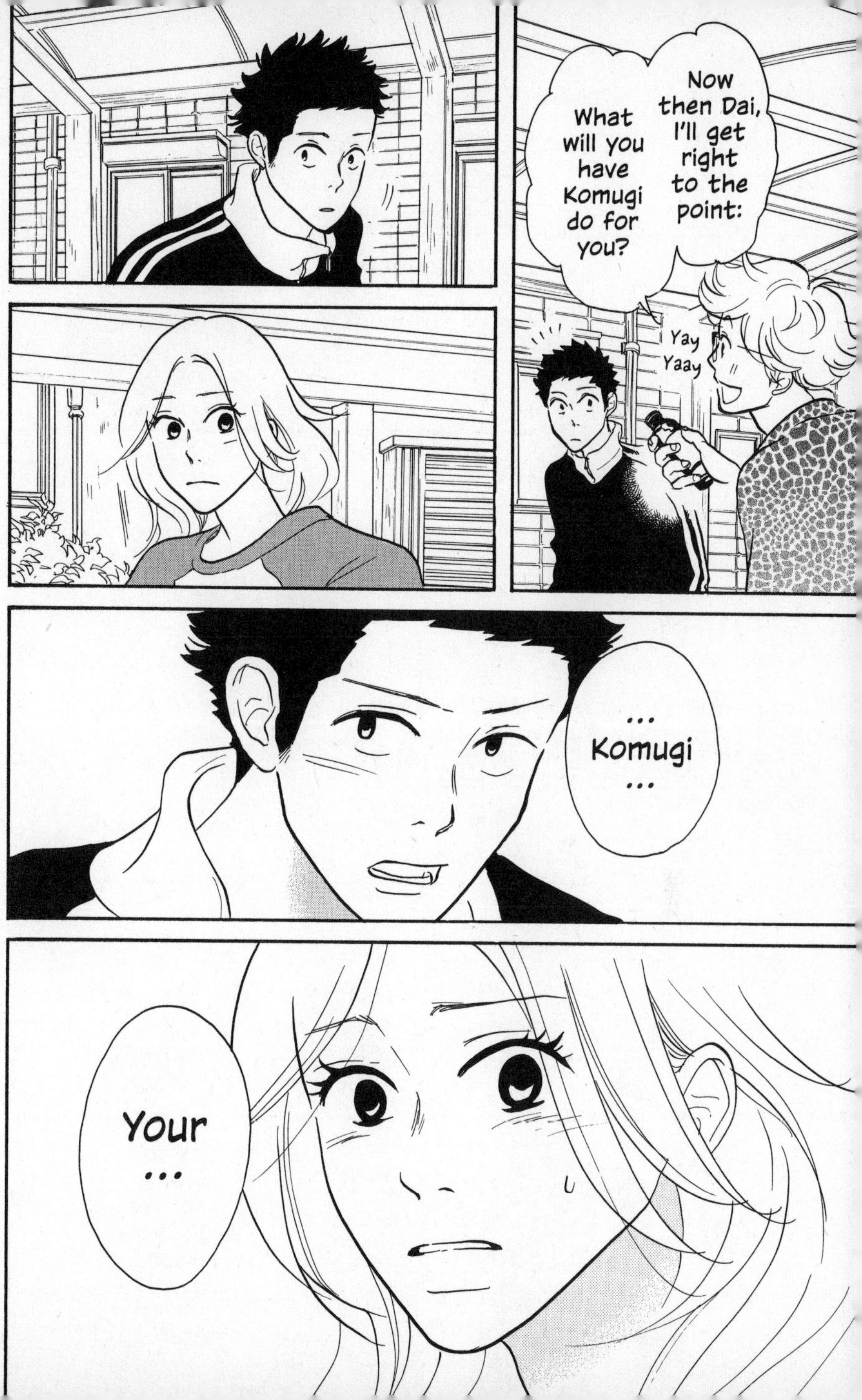
Now then Dai, I'll get right to the point:
What will you have Komugi do for you?
Yay Yaay
... Komugi ...
Your ...

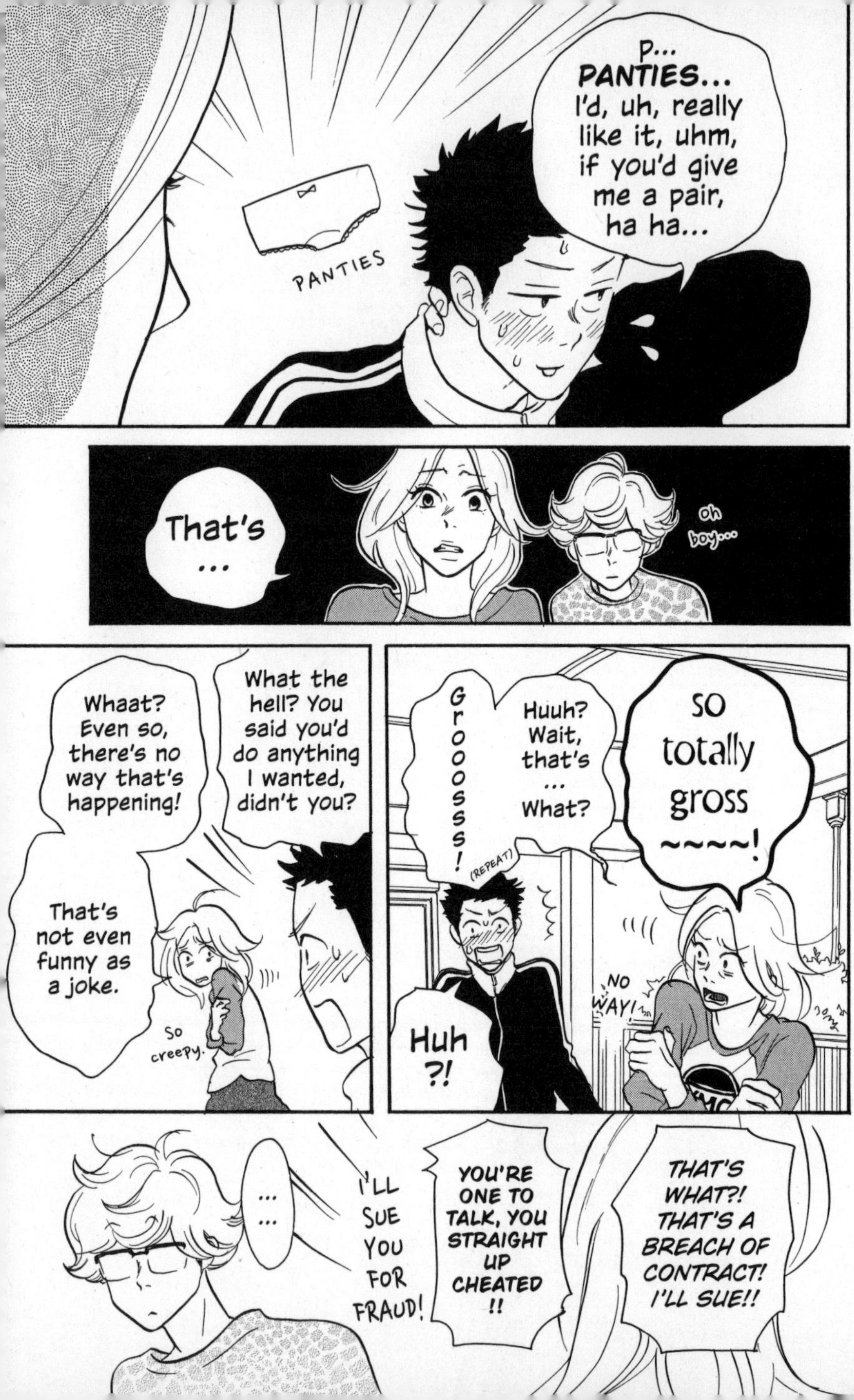
P... PANTIES... I'd, uh, really like it, uhm, if you'd give me a pair, ha ha...
PANTIES
oh boy...
That's ...
SO totally gross ~~~~!
Huuh? Wait, that's ... What?
Groooosss!
(REPEAT)
NO WAY!
Huh ?!
What the hell? You said you'd do anything I wanted, didn't you?
Whaat? Even so, there's no way that's happening!
That's not even funny as a joke.
So creepy.
THAT'S WHAT?! THAT'S A BREACH OF CONTRACT! I'LL SUE!!
YOU'RE ONE TO TALK, YOU STRAIGHT UP CHEATED !!
I'LL SUE YOU FOR FRAUD!
... ...

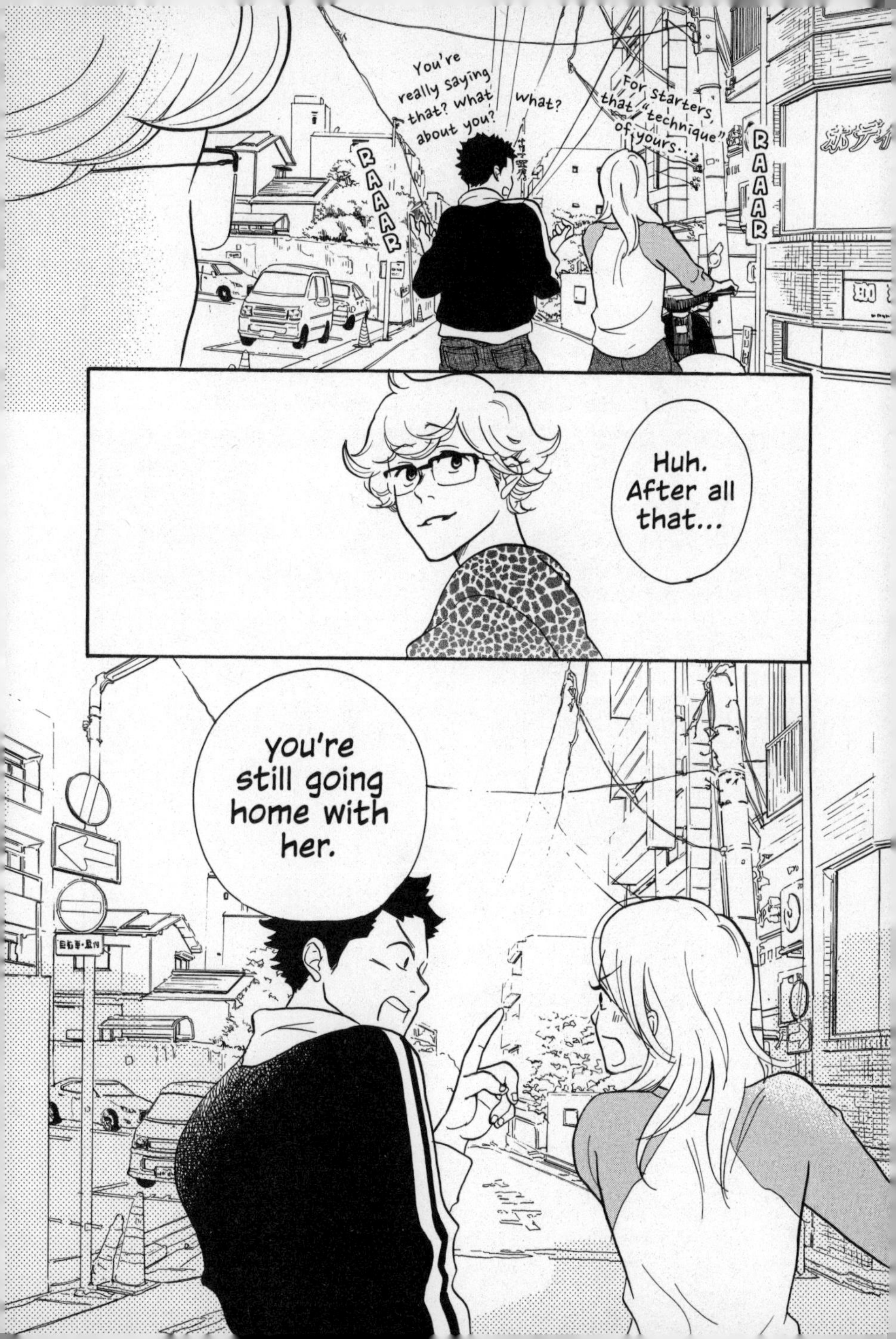
For starters, that "technique" of yours...
RAAAR
what?
You're really saying that? what about you?
RAAAR
Huh. After all that...
you're still going home with her.

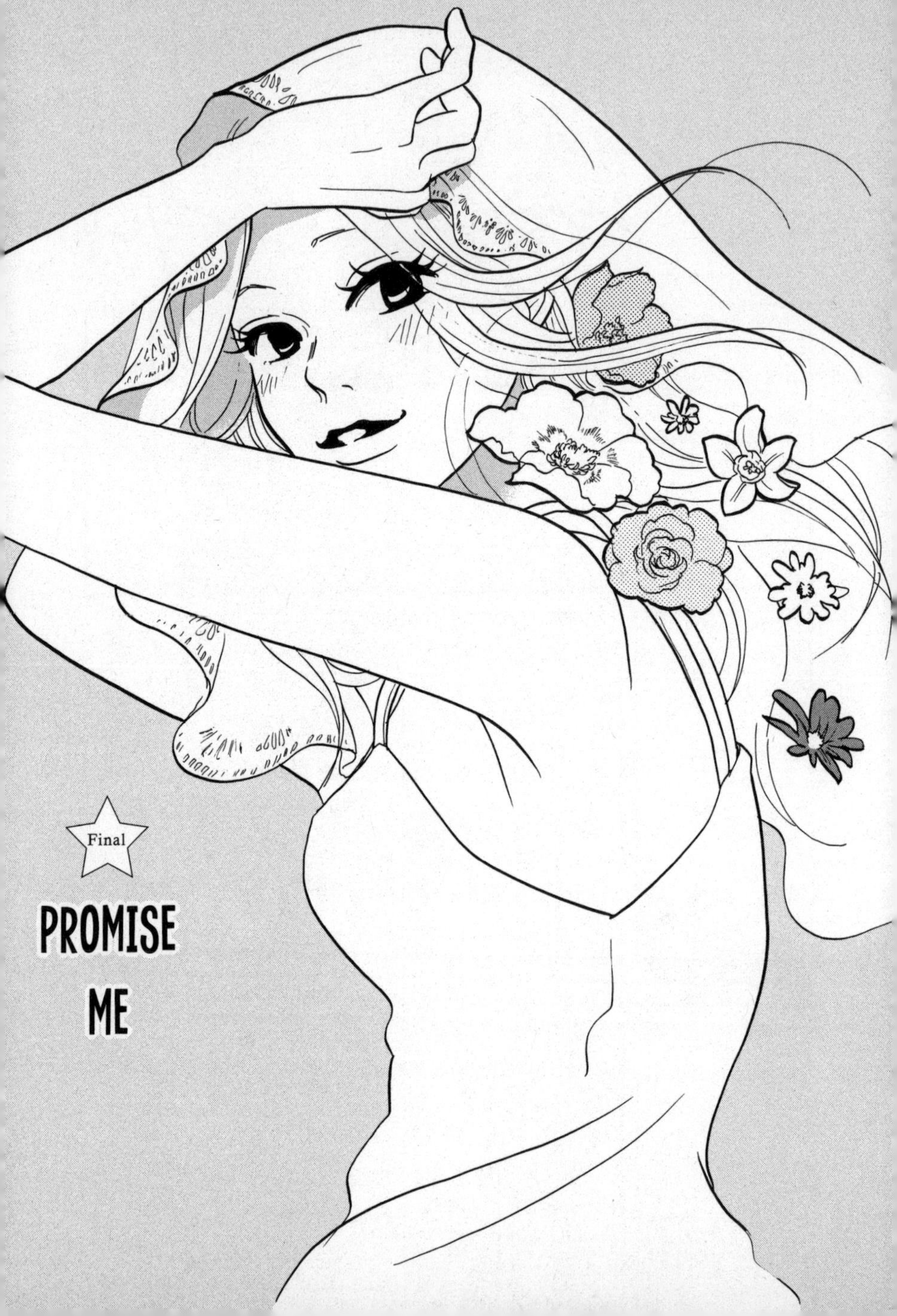
Final
PROMISE ME

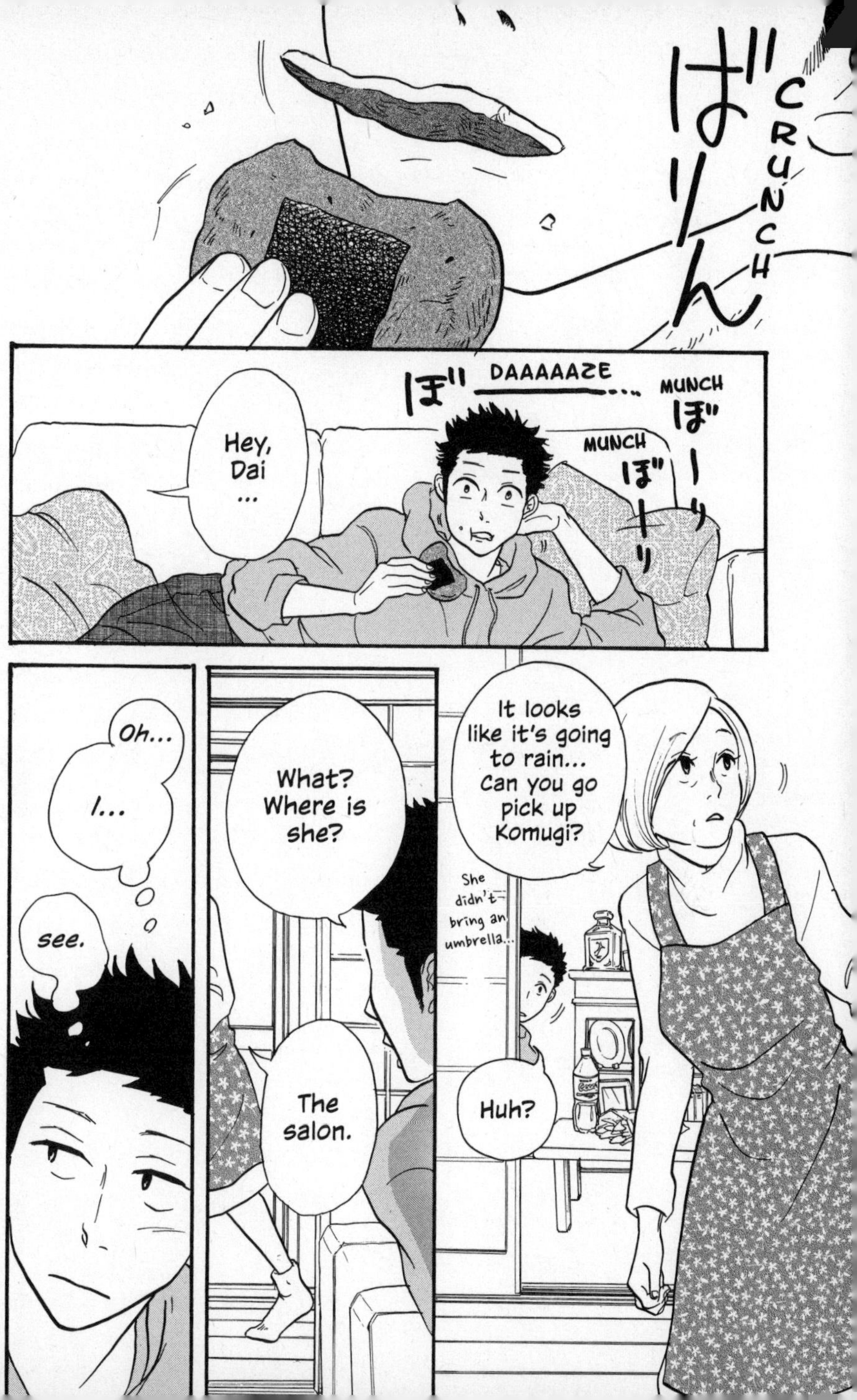

ばりん
CRUNCH
ぼー
DAAAAAZE...
MUNCH
ぼーり
MUNCH
ぼーり
Hey, Dai...
It looks like it's going to rain... Can you go pick up Komugi?
She didn't bring an umbrella...
Huh?
What? Where is she?
The salon.
Oh...
I...
see.

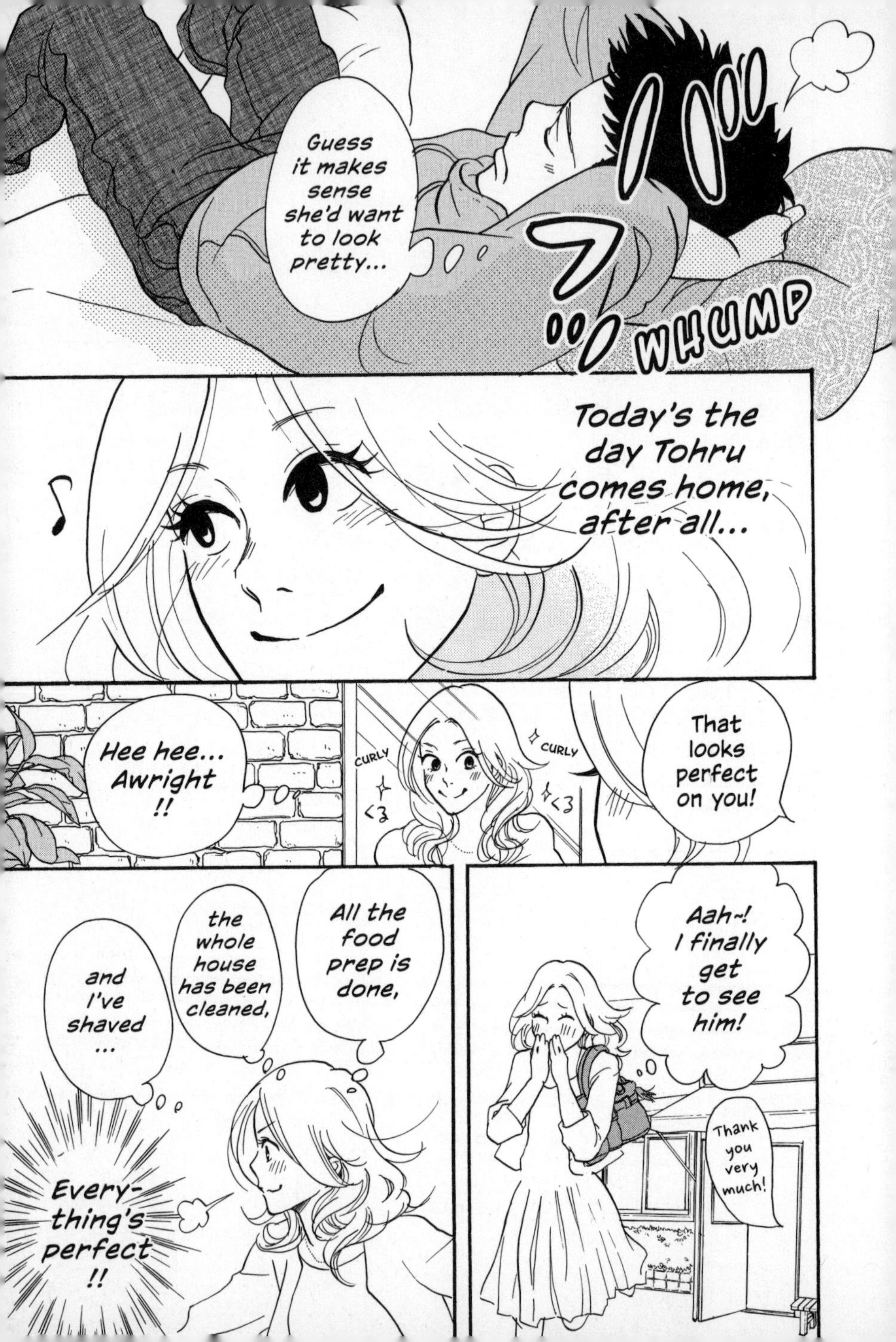
WHUMP
Guess it makes sense she'd want to look pretty...
Today's the day Tohru comes home, after all...
That looks perfect on you!
CURLY
CURLY
<3
<3
Hee hee... Awright !!
Aah~! I finally get to see him!
Thank you very much!
All the food prep is done,
the whole house has been cleaned,
and I've shaved ...
Every-thing's perfect !!

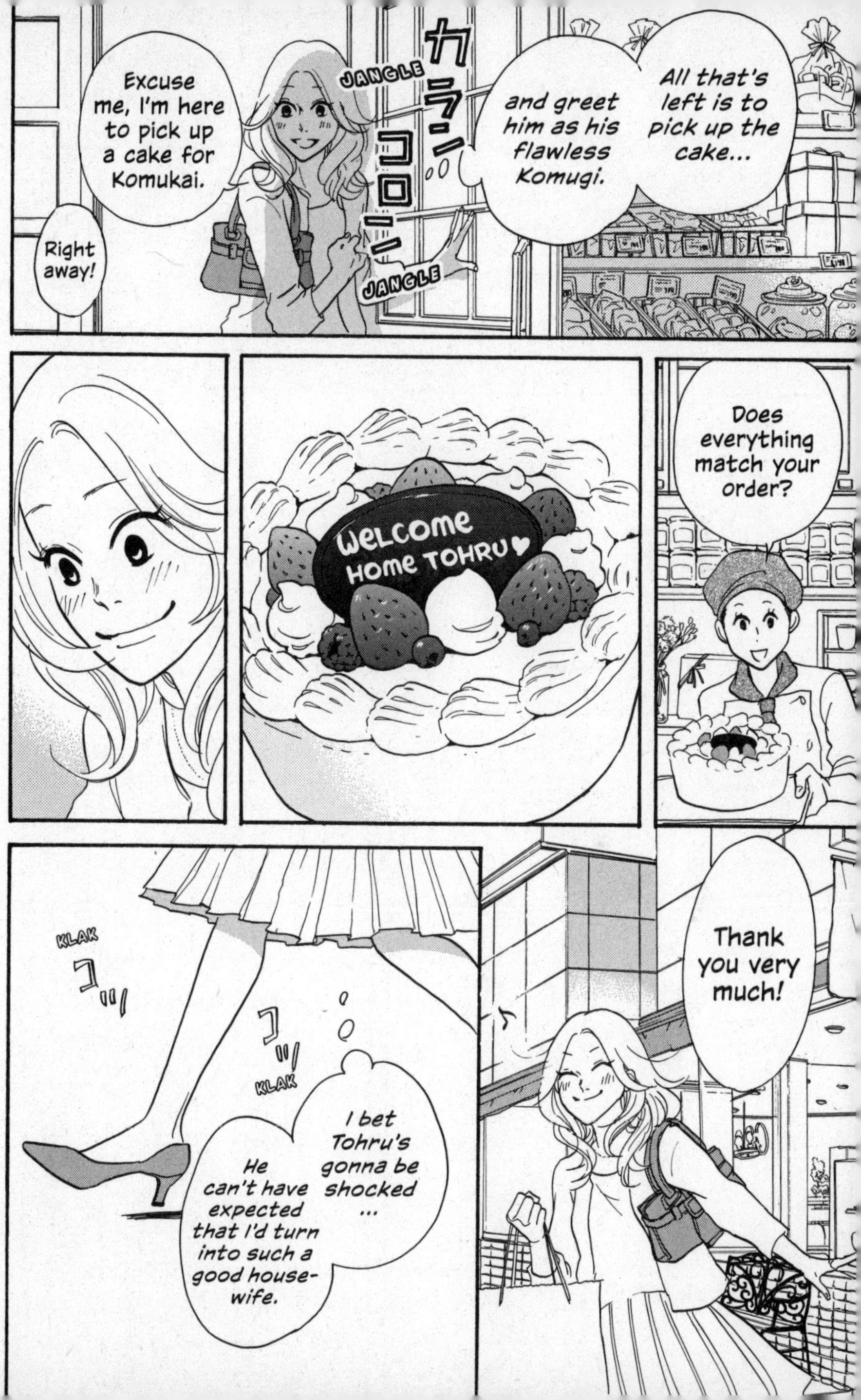
All that's left is to pick up the cake...
and greet him as his flawless Komugi.
JANGLE
JANGLE
Excuse me, I'm here to pick up a cake for Komukai.
Right away!
Does everything match your order?
WELCOME HOME TOHRU♥
Thank you very much!
KLAK
KLAK
I bet Tohru's gonna be shocked ...
He can't have expected that I'd turn into such a good house-wife.

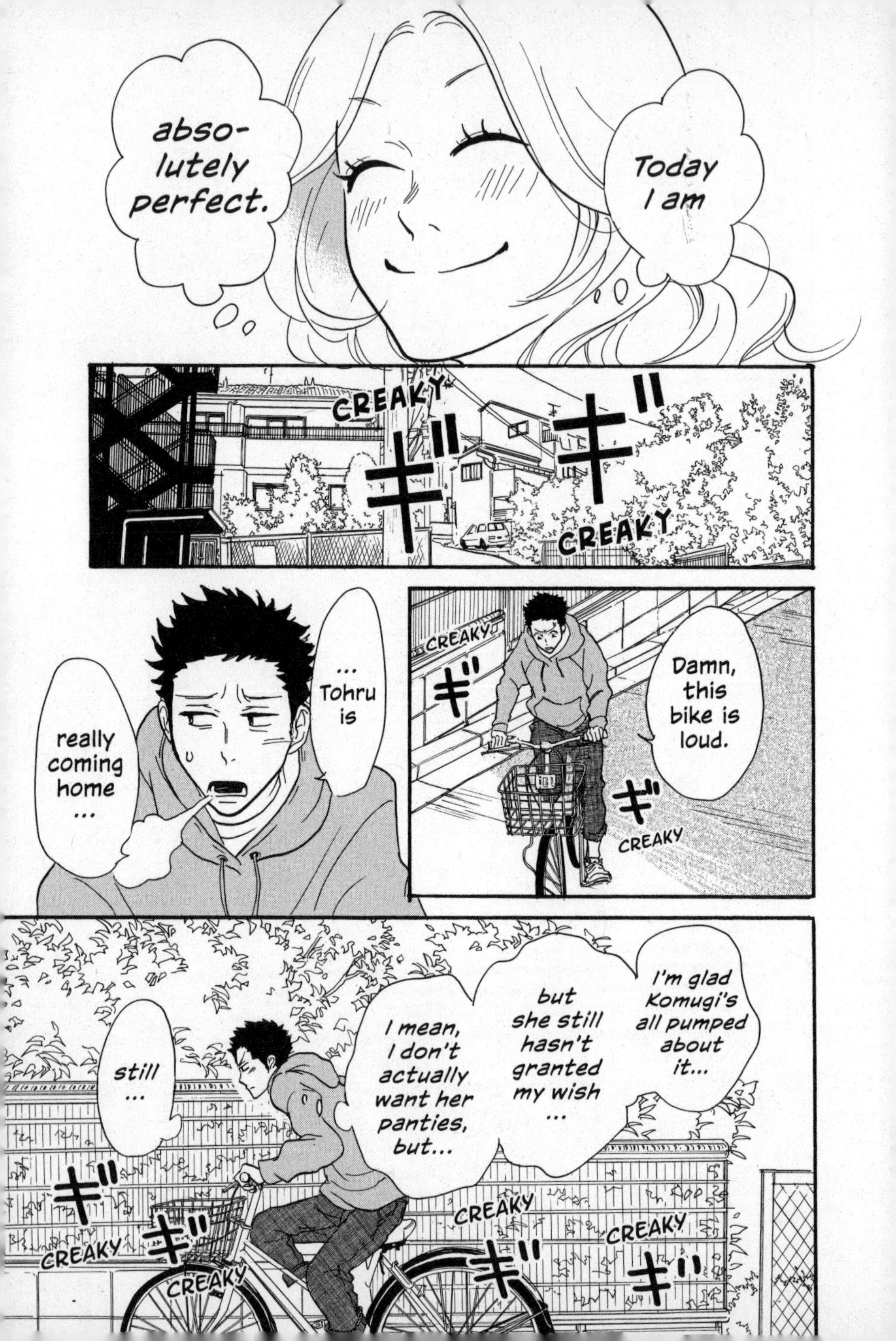
Today I am
abso-lutely perfect.
ギー
CREAKY
ギー
CREAKY
ギ
CREAKY
Damn, this bike is loud.
ギ
CREAKY
... Tohru is
really coming home ...
I'm glad Komugi's all pumped about it...
but she still hasn't granted my wish ...
I mean, I don't actually want her panties, but...
still ...
ギ
CREAKY
ギ
CREAKY
ギ
CREAKY
ギ
CREAKY
ギ
CREAKY

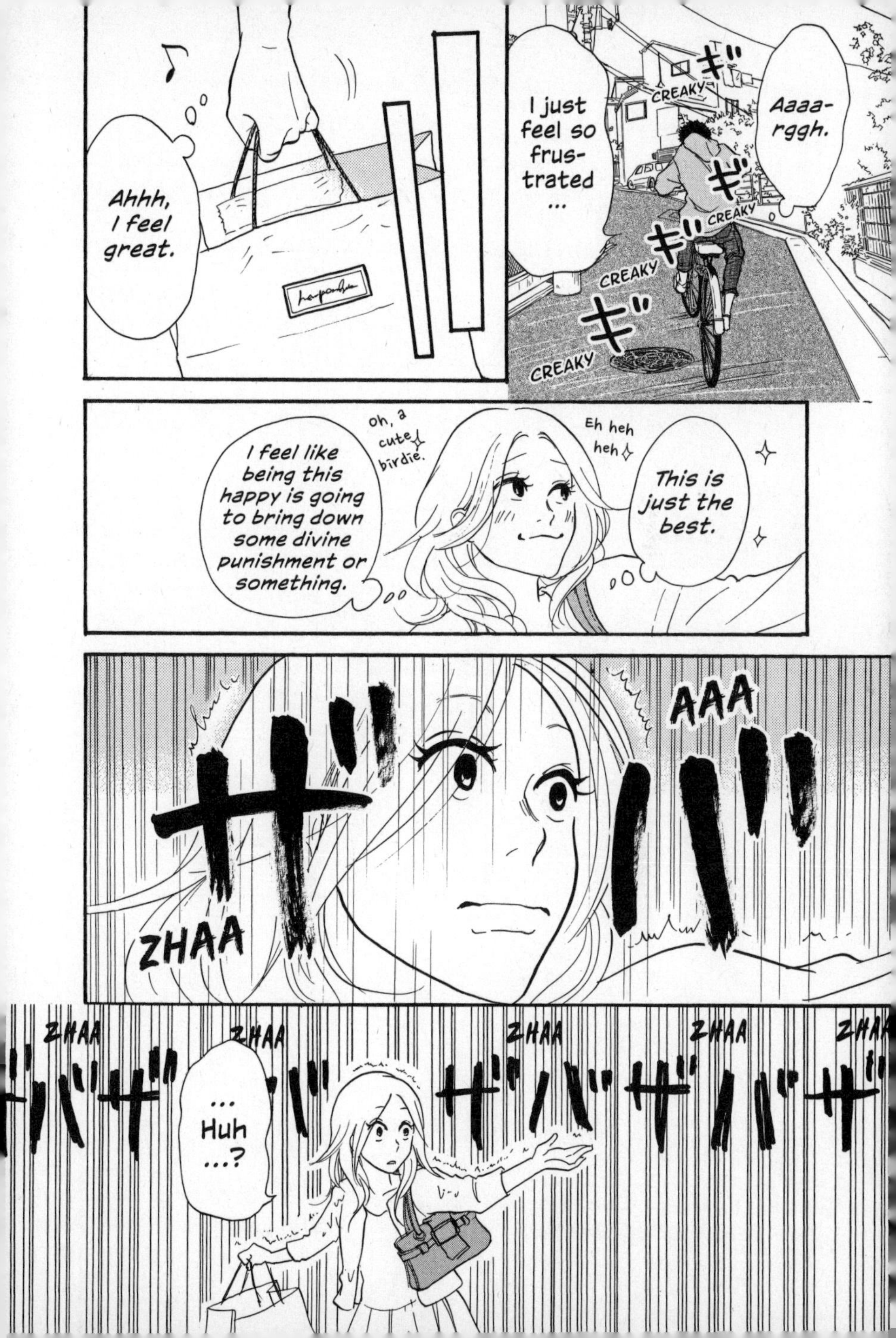

Aaaa-rggh.
ギ
CREAKY
ギ
CREAKY
ギ
CREAKY
ギ
CREAKY
I just feel so frus-trated ...
Ahhh, I feel great.
This is just the best.
Eh heh heh
Oh, a cute birdie.
I feel like being this happy is going to bring down some divine punishment or something.
AAA
ZHAA
ZHAA
ZHAA
ZHAA
ZHAA
ZHAA
... Huh ...?

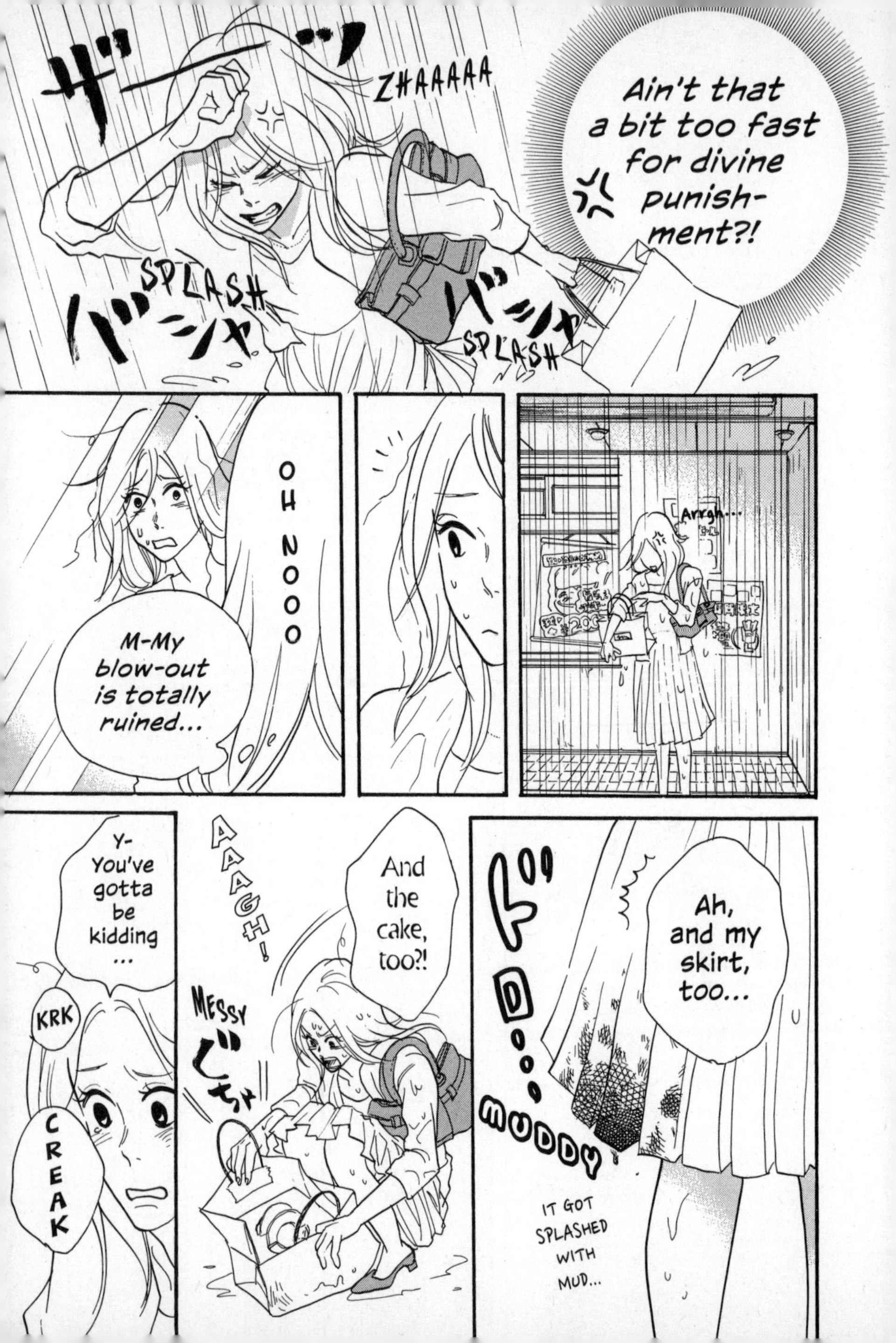
ザーッ
ZHAAAAA
Ain't that a bit too fast for divine punish-ment?!
バシャ
SPLASH
バッシャ
SPLASH
Arrgh...
OH NOOO
M-My blow-out is totally ruined...
Ah, and my skirt, too...
ドロッ
MUDDY
IT GOT SPLASHED WITH MUD...
And the cake, too?!
AAAGH!
ぐちゃ
MESSY
Y-You've gotta be kidding ...
KRK
CREAK

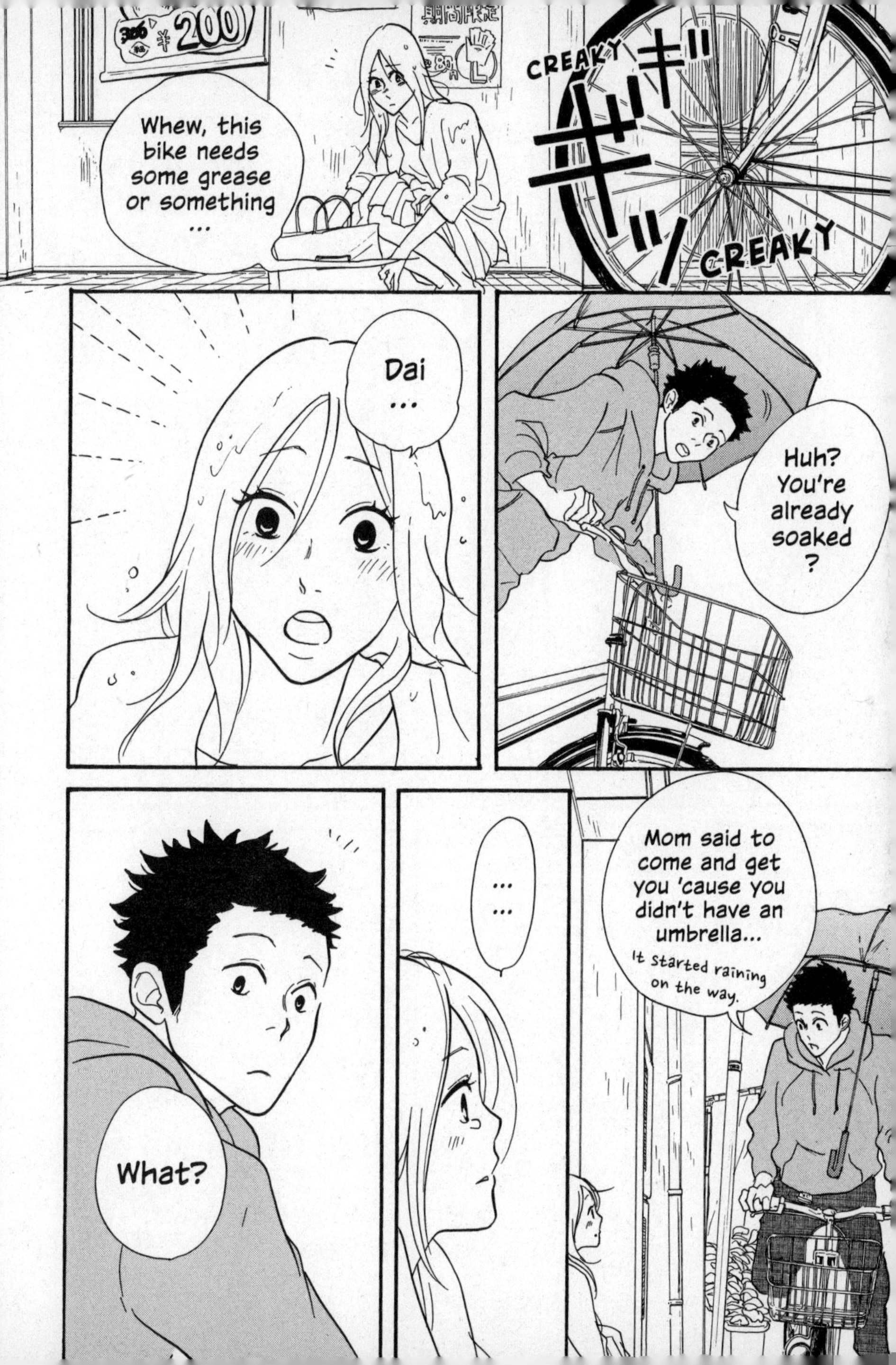
CREAKY
ギッギッ
CREAKY
Whew, this bike needs some grease or something ...
Huh? You're already soaked ?
Dai ...
Mom said to come and get you 'cause you didn't have an umbrella...
It started raining on the way.
... ...
What?

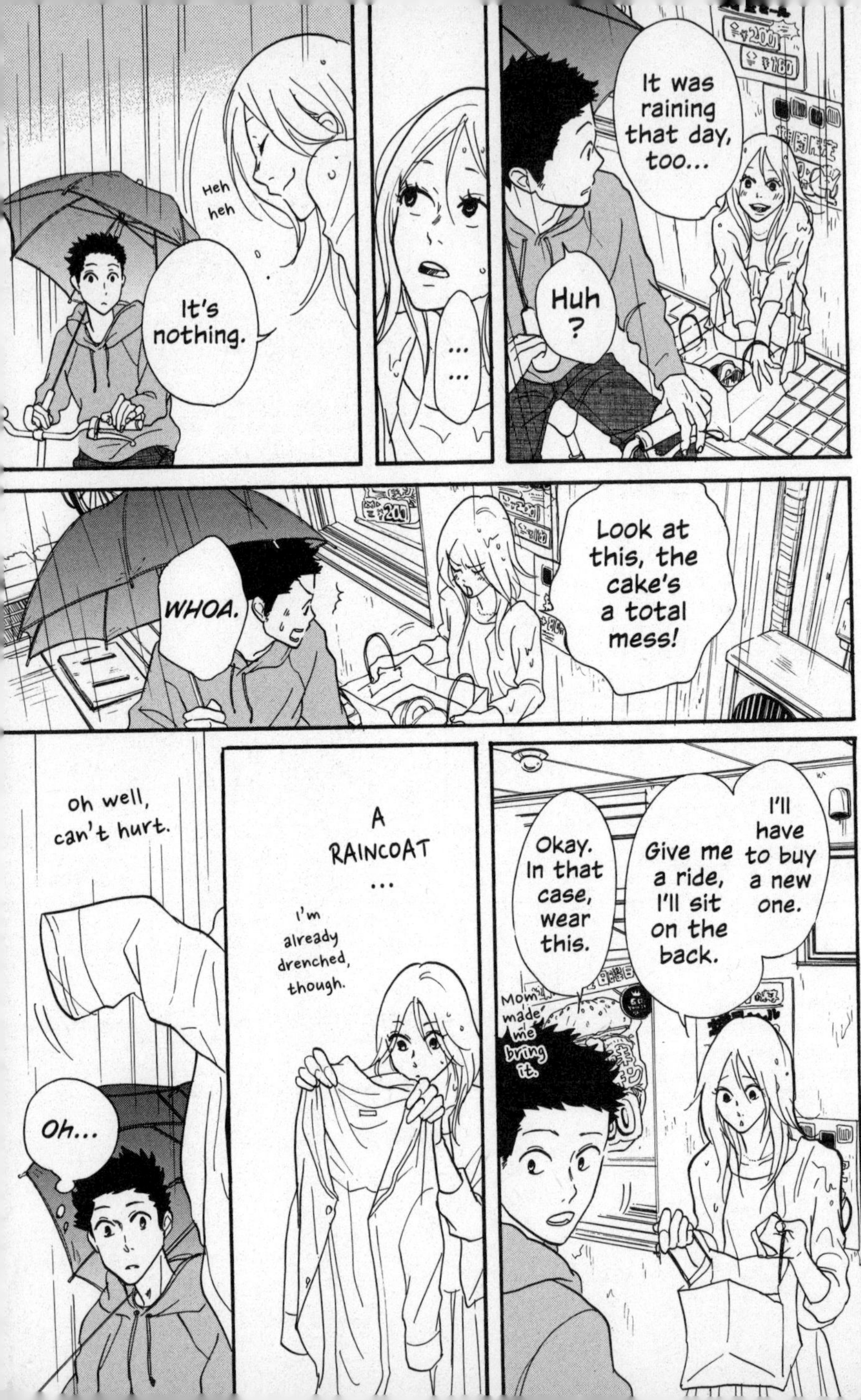
It was raining that day, too...
Huh?
......
Heh heh
It's nothing.
Look at this, the cake's a total mess!
WHOA.
I'll have to buy a new one.
Give me a ride, I'll sit on the back.
Okay. In that case, wear this.
Mom made me bring it.
A RAINCOAT ...
I'm already drenched, though.
Oh well, can't hurt.
Oh...

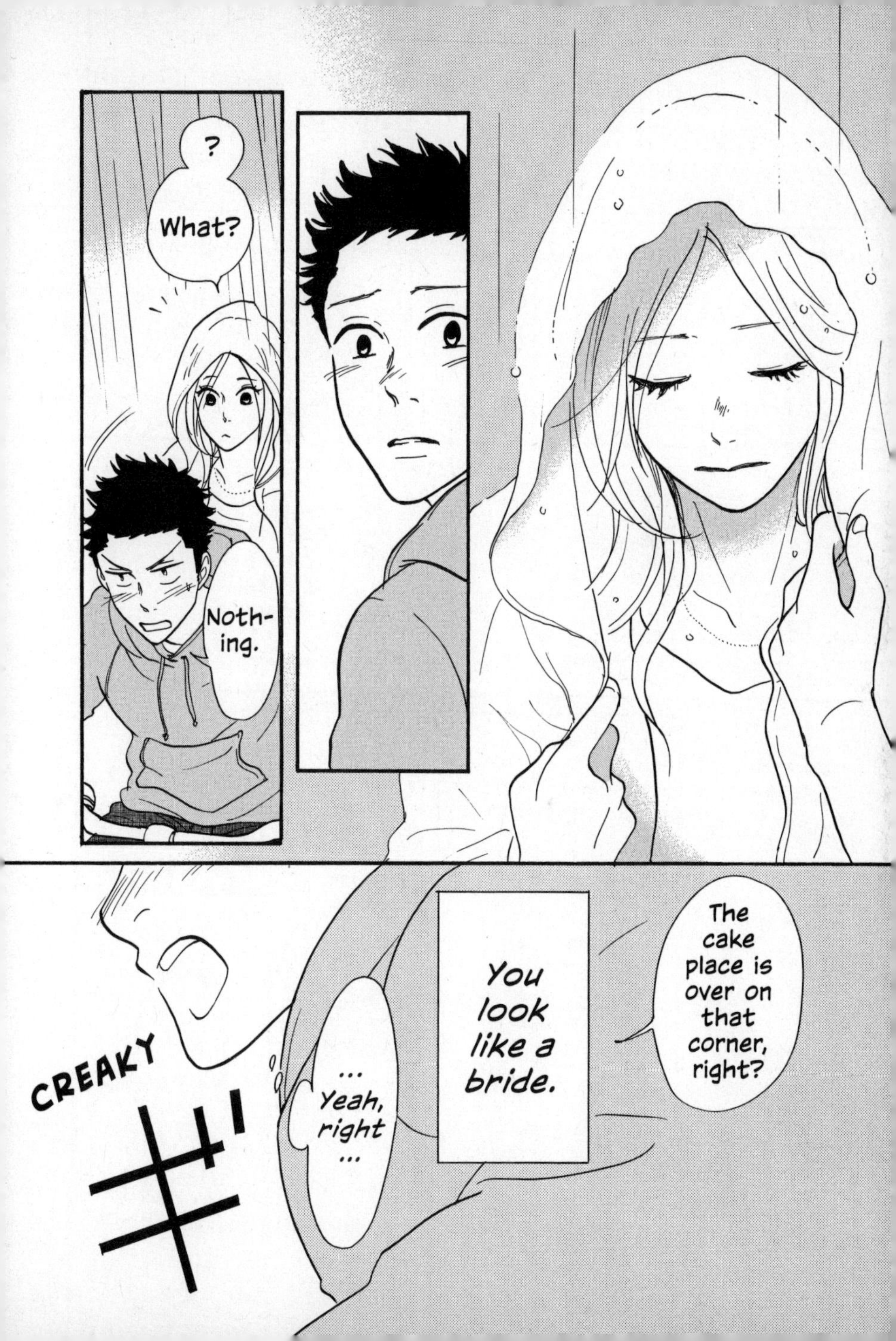
?
What?
Noth-ing.
The cake place is over on that corner, right?
You look like a bride.
... Yeah, right ...
CREAKY

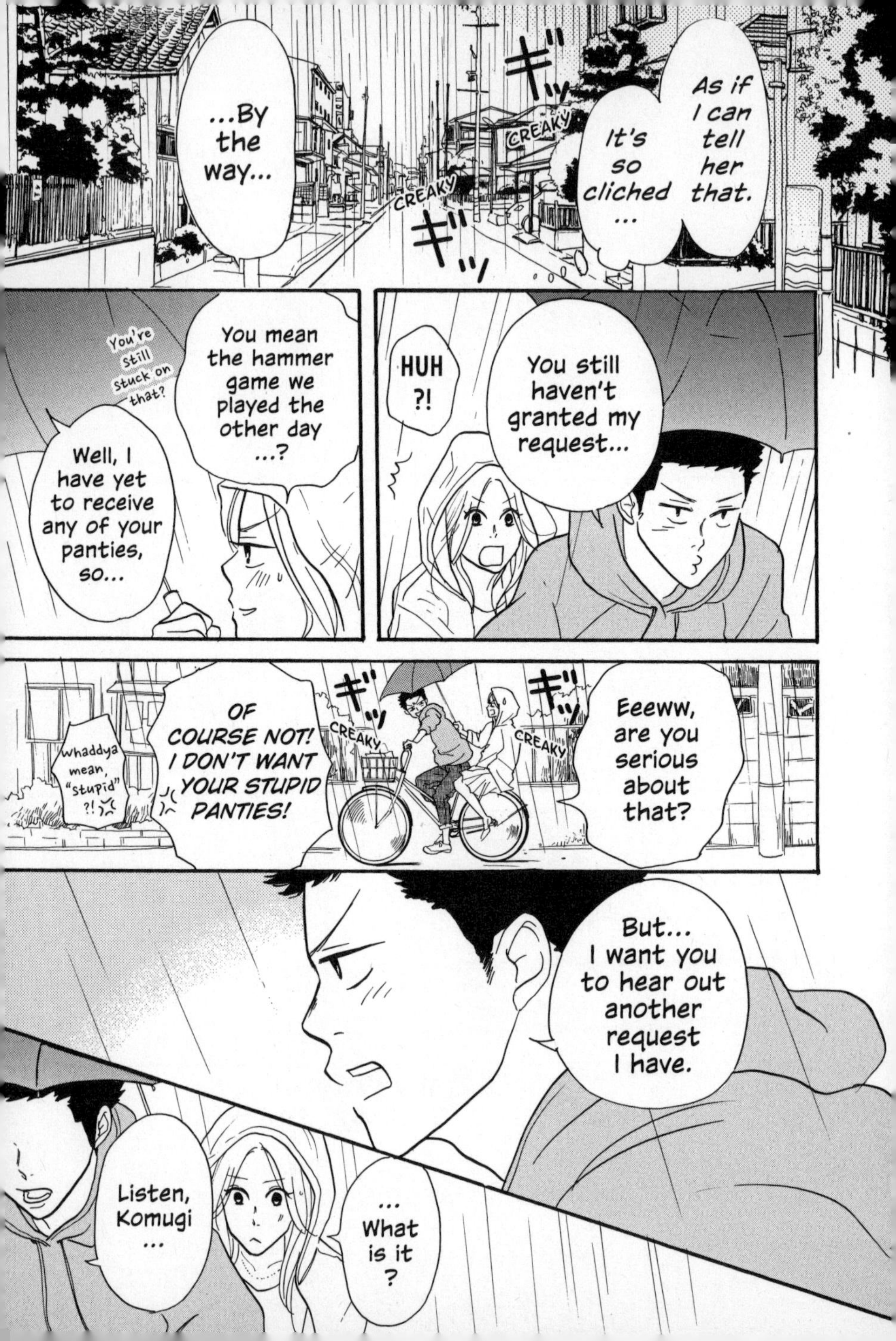
As if I can tell her that.
It's so cliched ...
CREAKY
CREAKY
...By the way...
You still haven't granted my request...
HUH ?!
You mean the hammer game we played the other day ...?
You're still stuck on that?
Well, I have yet to receive any of your panties, so...
Eeeww, are you serious about that?
CREAKY
CREAKY
OF COURSE NOT! I DON'T WANT YOUR STUPID PANTIES!
Whaddya mean, "stupid" ?!
But... I want you to hear out another request I have.
... What is it ?
Listen, Komugi ...

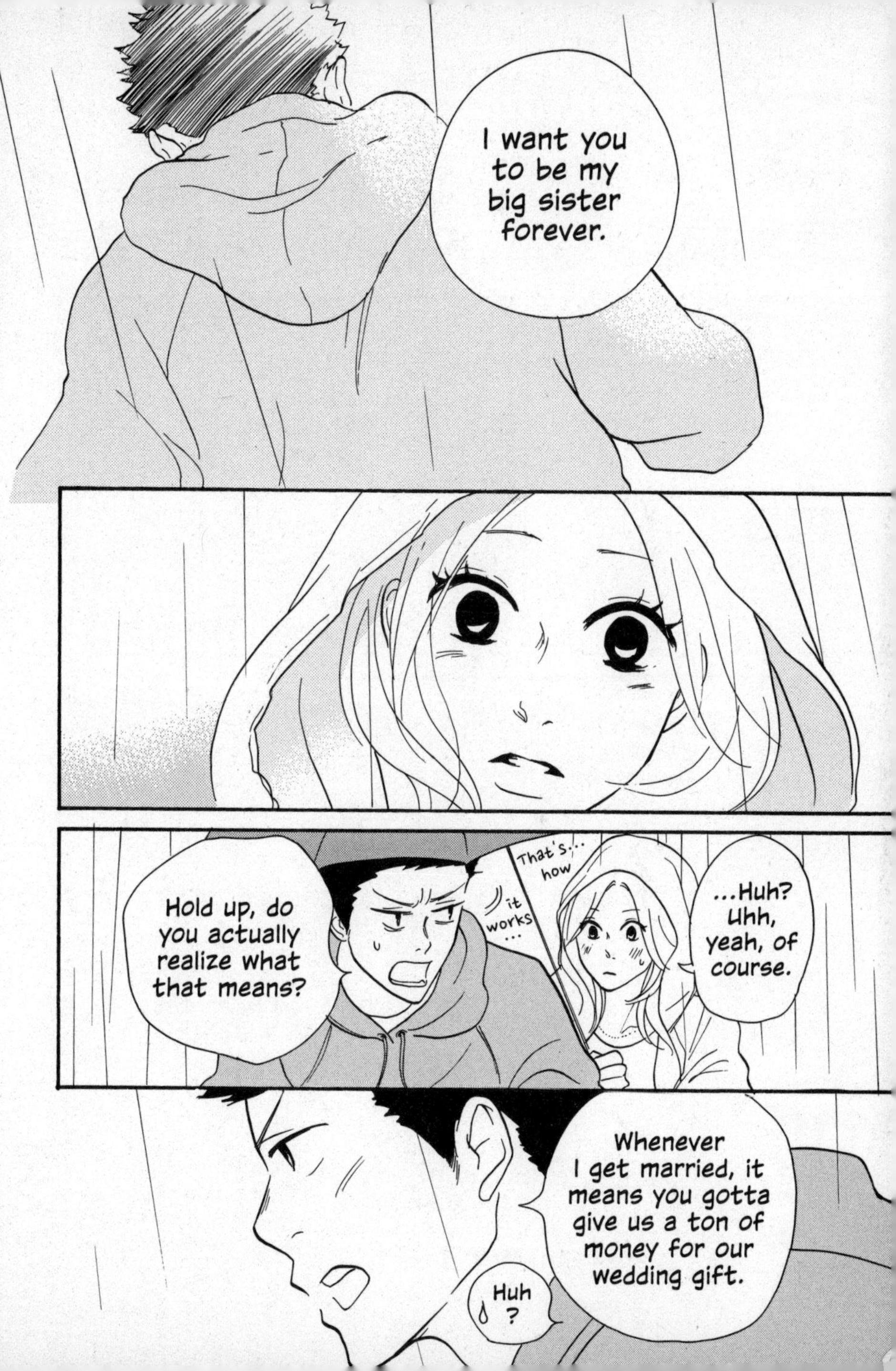
I want you to be my big sister forever.
...Huh? Uhh, yeah, of course.
That's... how it works...
Hold up, do you actually realize what that means?
Whenever I get married, it means you gotta give us a ton of money for our wedding gift.
Huh?

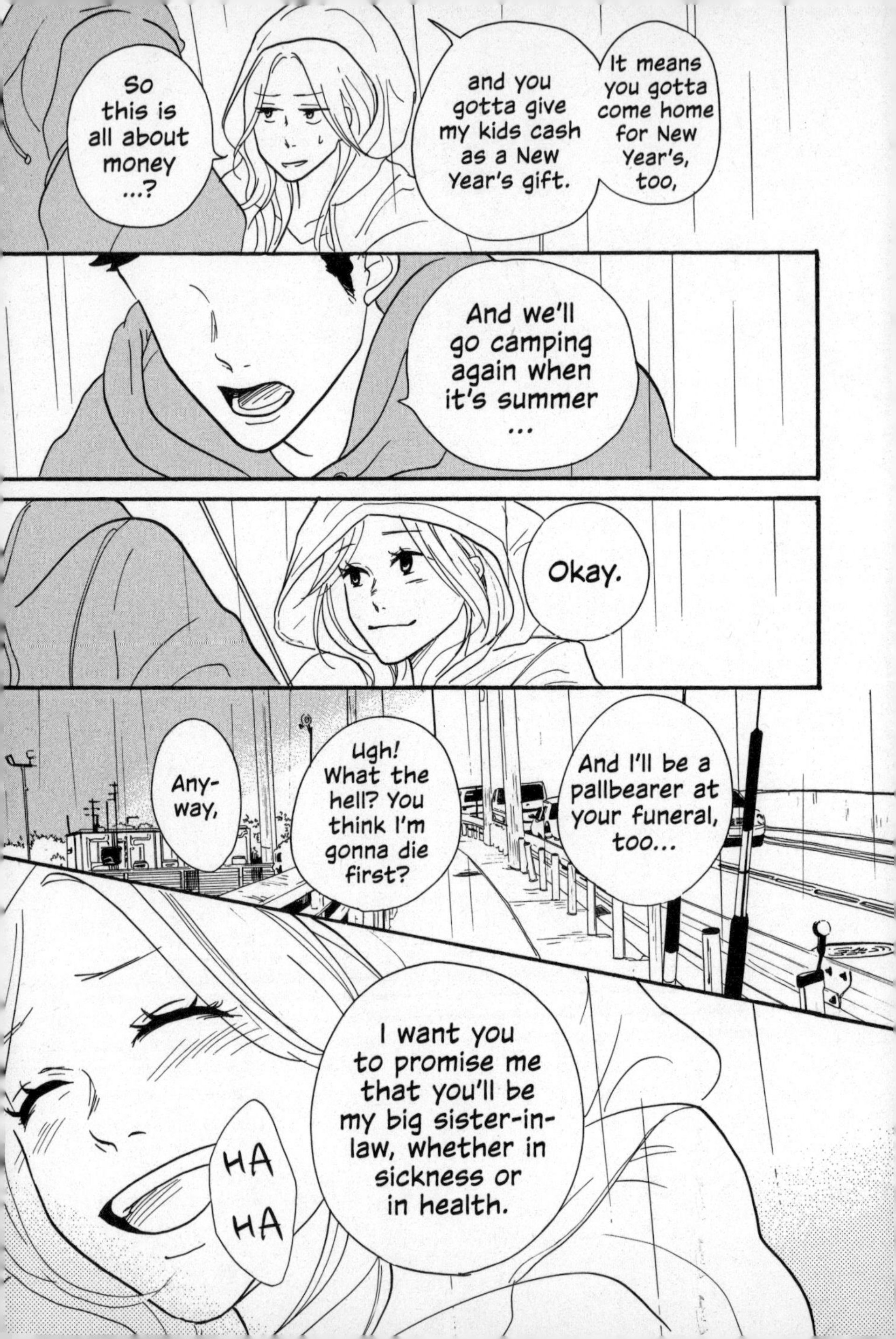
It means you gotta come home for New Year's, too,
and you gotta give my kids cash as a New Year's gift.
So this is all about money ...?
And we'll go camping again when it's summer ...
Okay.
And I'll be a pallbearer at your funeral, too...
Ugh! What the hell? You think I'm gonna die first?
Any-way,
I want you to promise me that you'll be my big sister-in-law, whether in sickness or in health.
HA HA

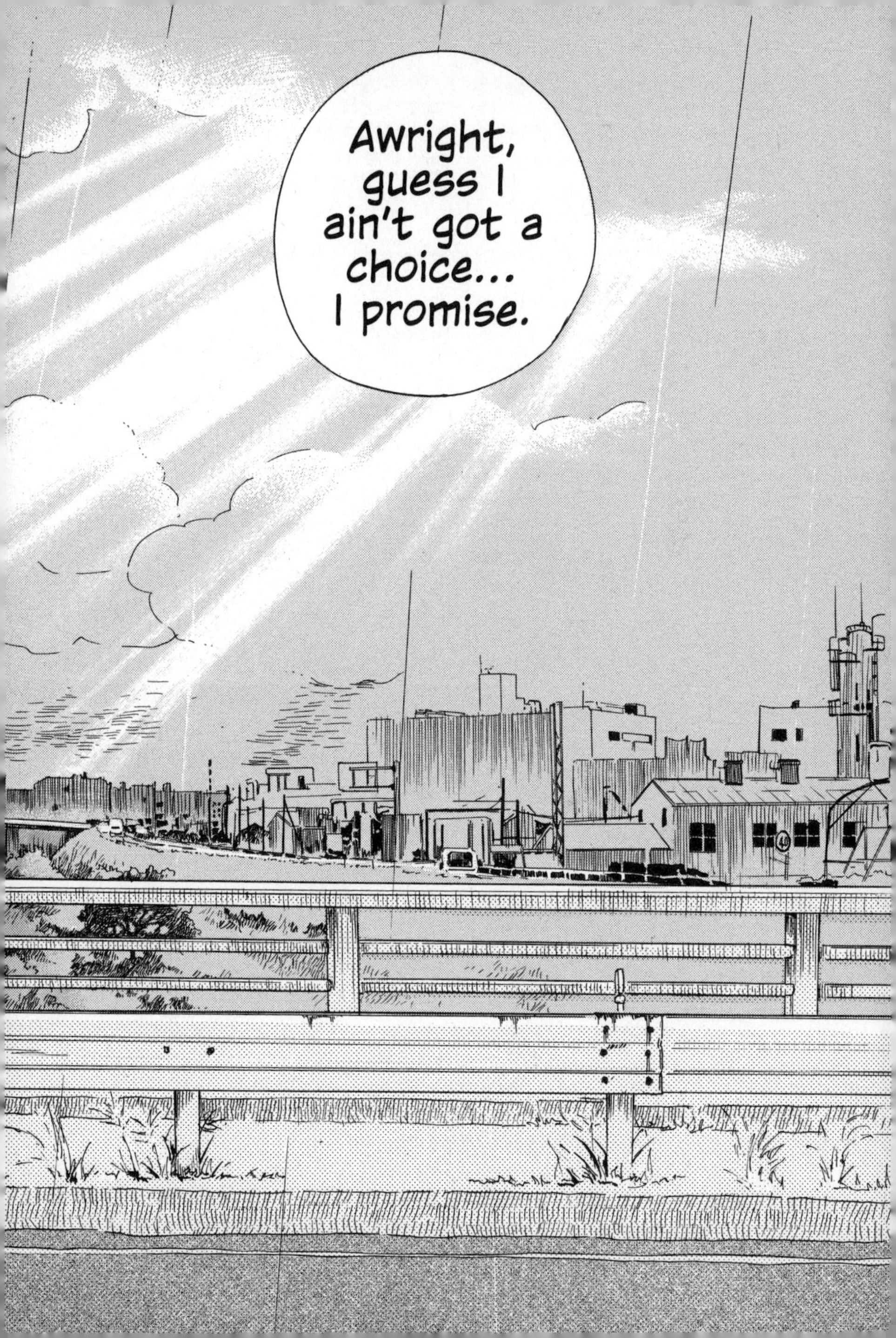
Awright, guess I ain't got a choice... I promise.

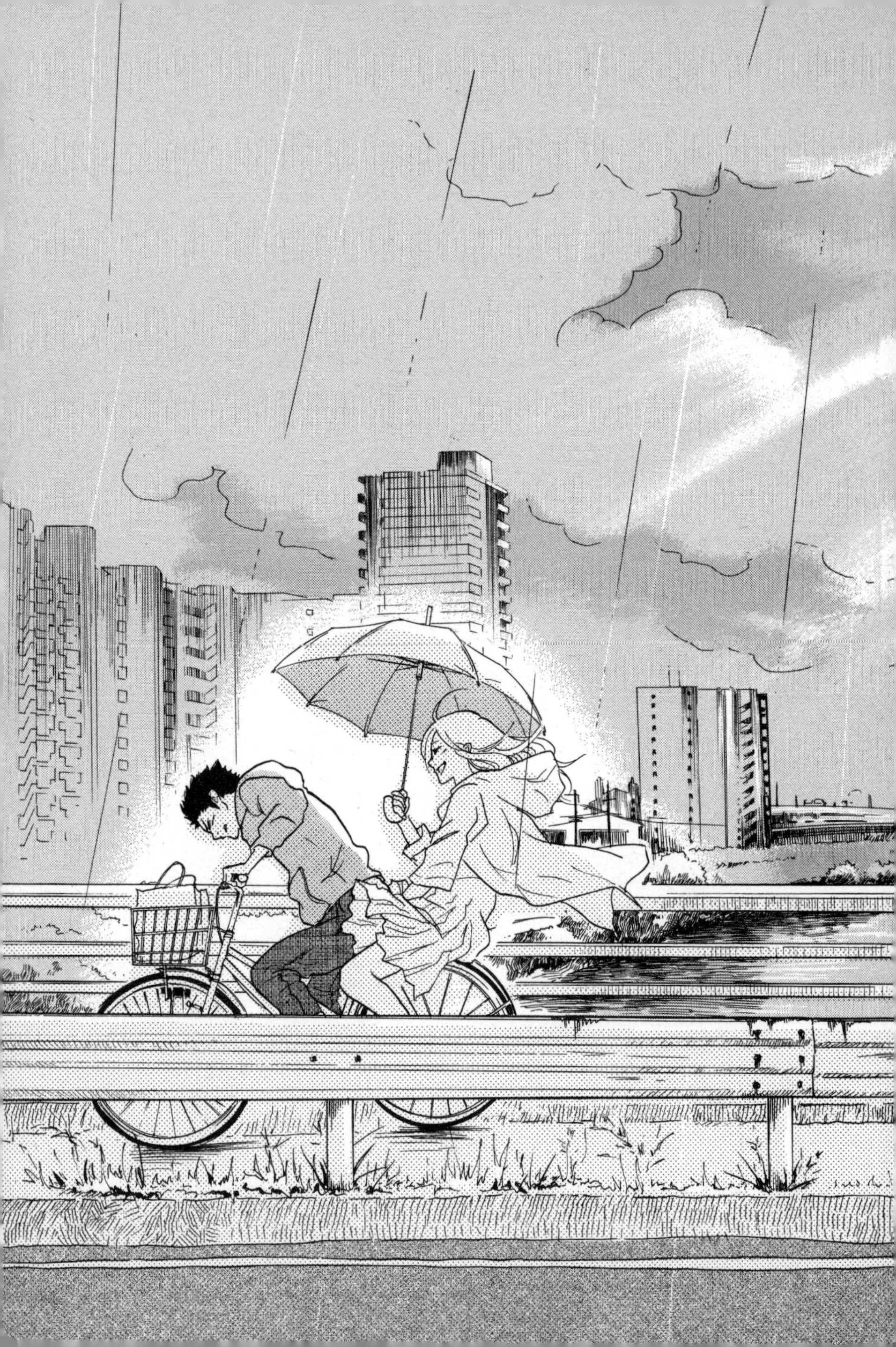

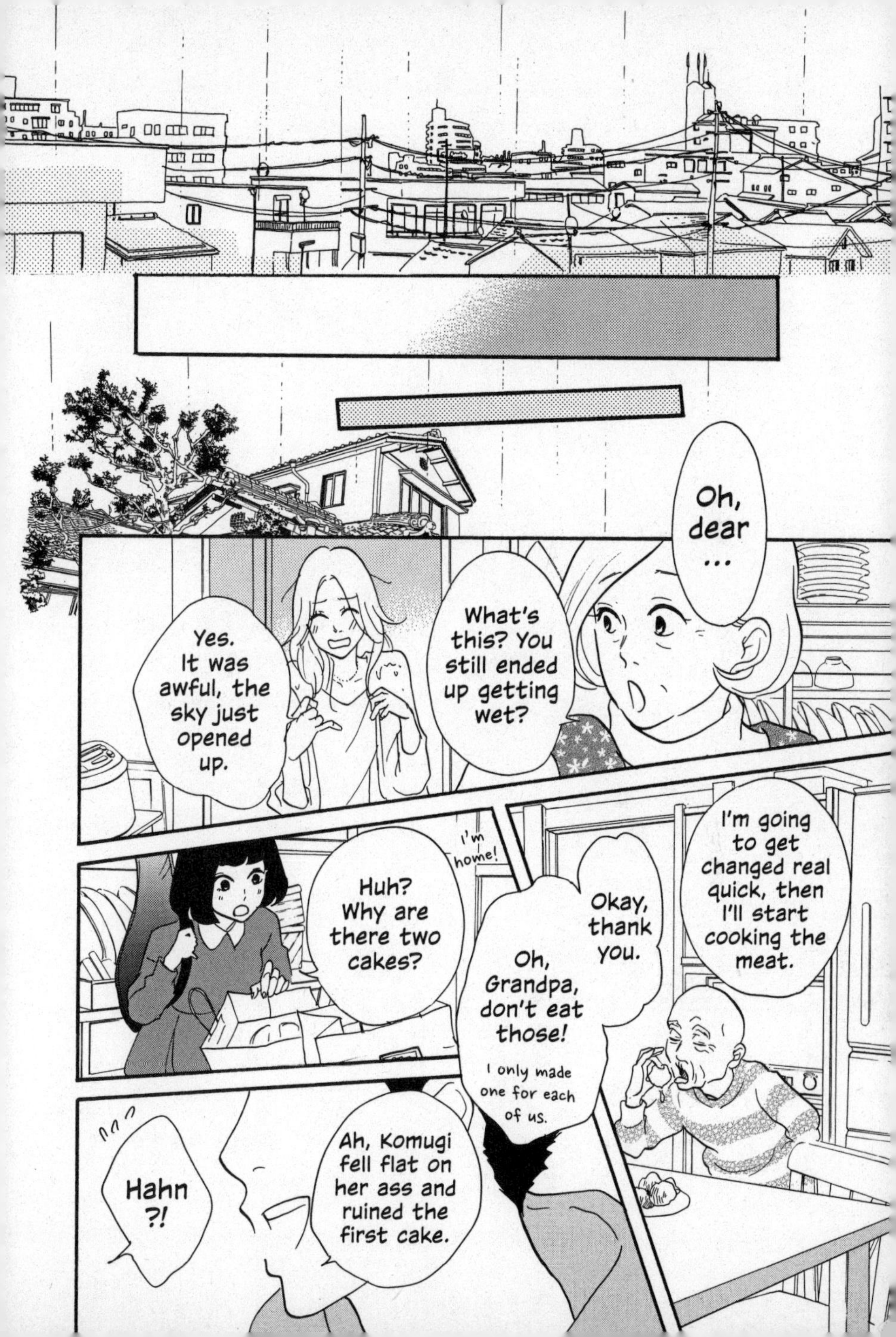
Oh, dear ...
What's this? You still ended up getting wet?
Yes. It was awful, the sky just opened up.
I'm going to get changed real quick, then I'll start cooking the meat.
Okay, thank you.
Oh, Grandpa, don't eat those!
I only made one for each of us.
I'm home!
Huh? Why are there two cakes?
Ah, Komugi fell flat on her ass and ruined the first cake.
Hahn ?!

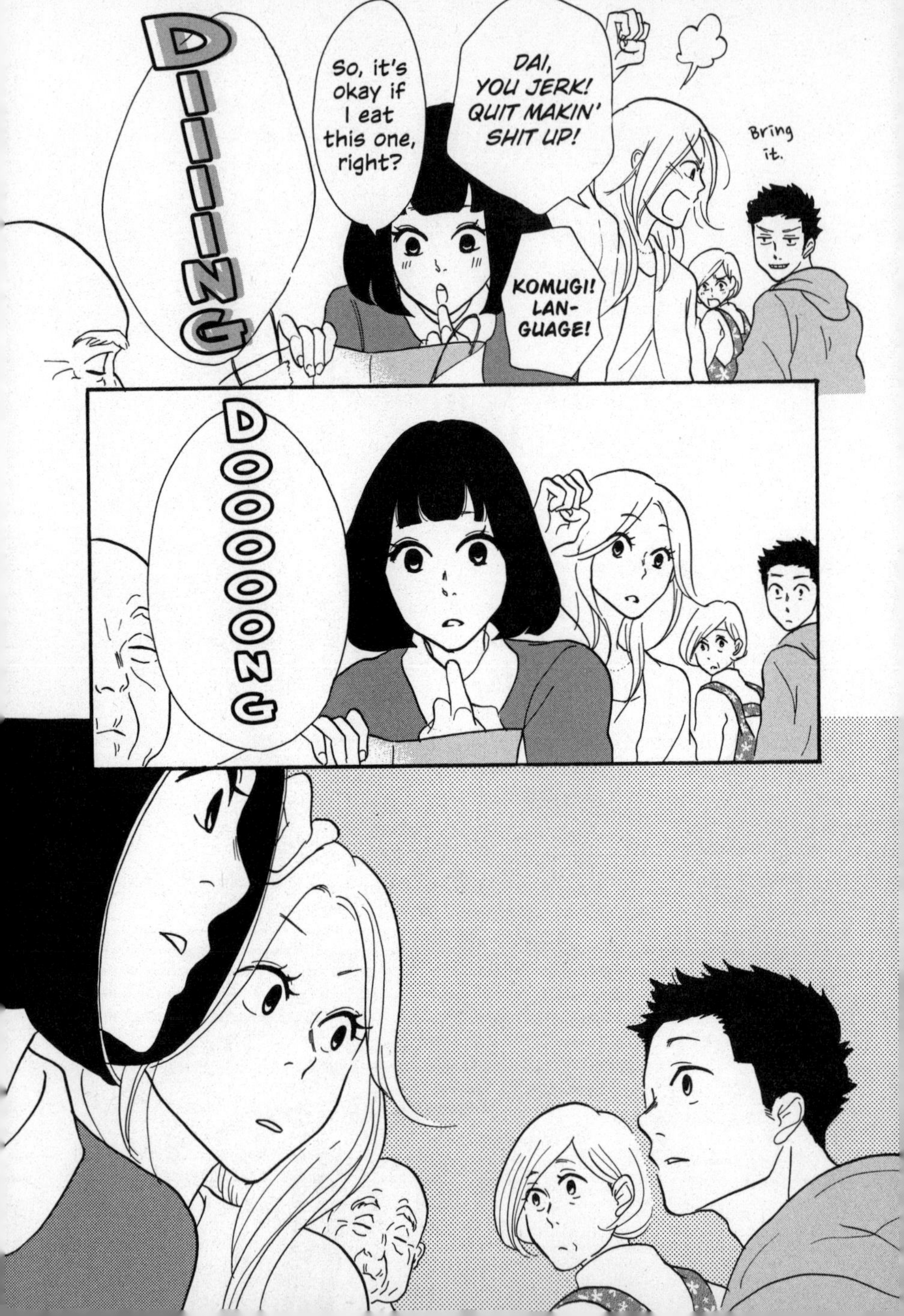
Bring it.
DAI, YOU JERK! QUIT MAKIN' SHIT UP!
So, it's okay if I eat this one, right?
KOMUGI! LAN-GUAGE!
DIIIING
DOOOOOONG

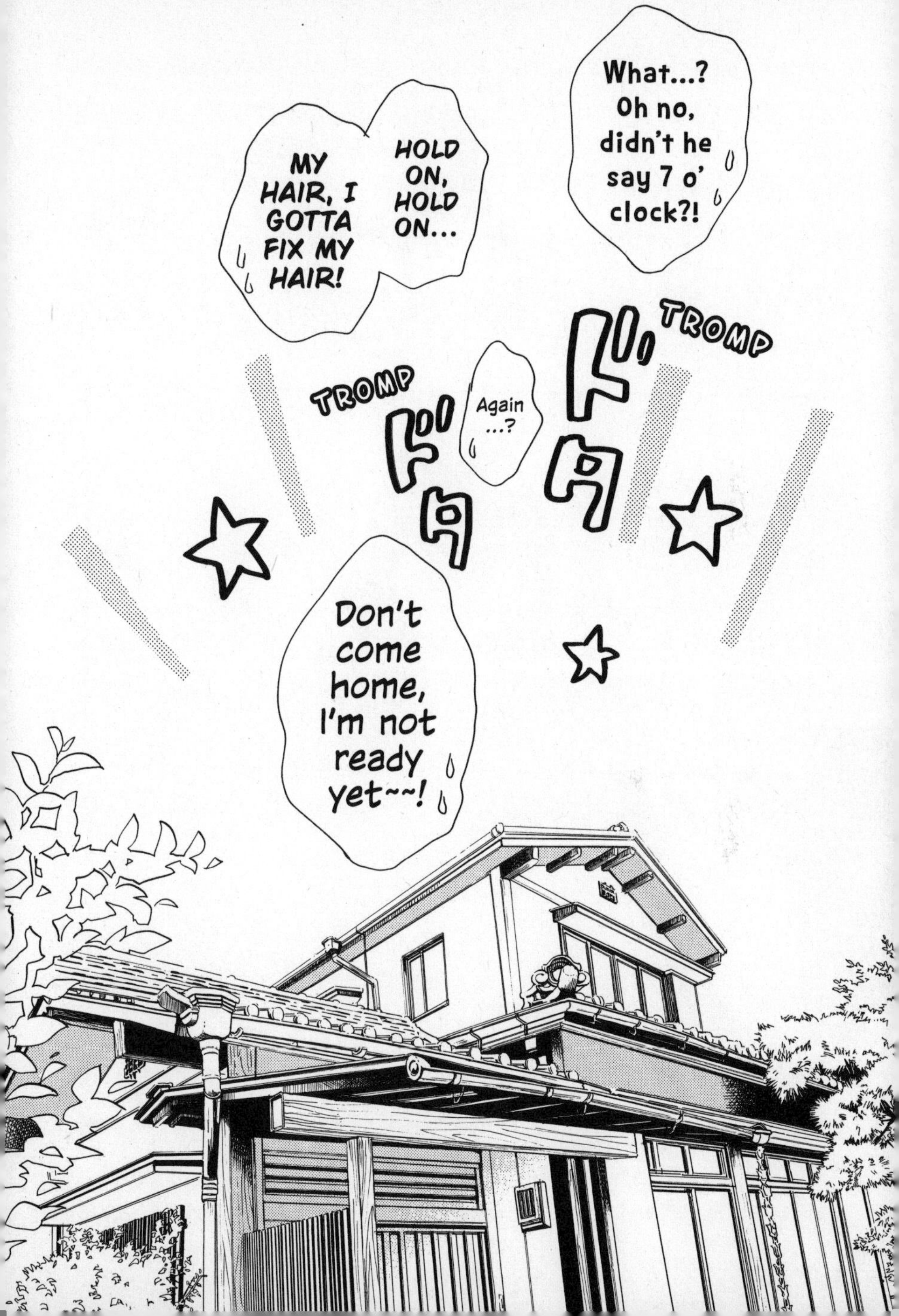
What...? Oh no, didn't he say 7 o' clock?!
HOLD ON, HOLD ON...
MY HAIR, I GOTTA FIX MY HAIR!
TROMP
ドタ
Again ...?
TROMP
ドタ
Don't come home, I'm not ready yet~~!

The End ♡

This is the 4th and final volume of The Delinquent Housewife!

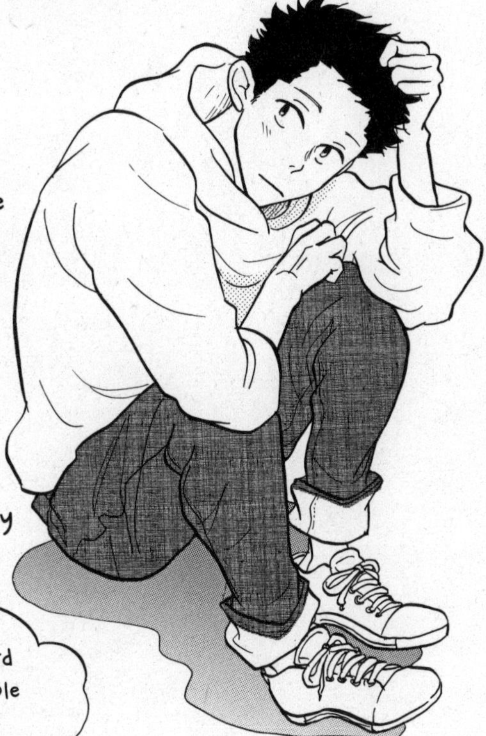

I'm happy for all the love you've shown Komugi, Dai, and the rest of the story's characters.

Thank you all for all the support you've given me and this story throughout its run!

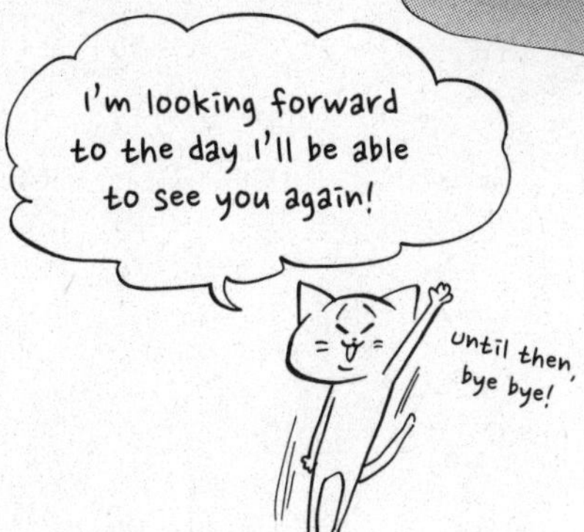
I'm looking forward to the day I'll be able to see you again!
Until then, bye bye!

Jan. 2017
Nemu Yoko

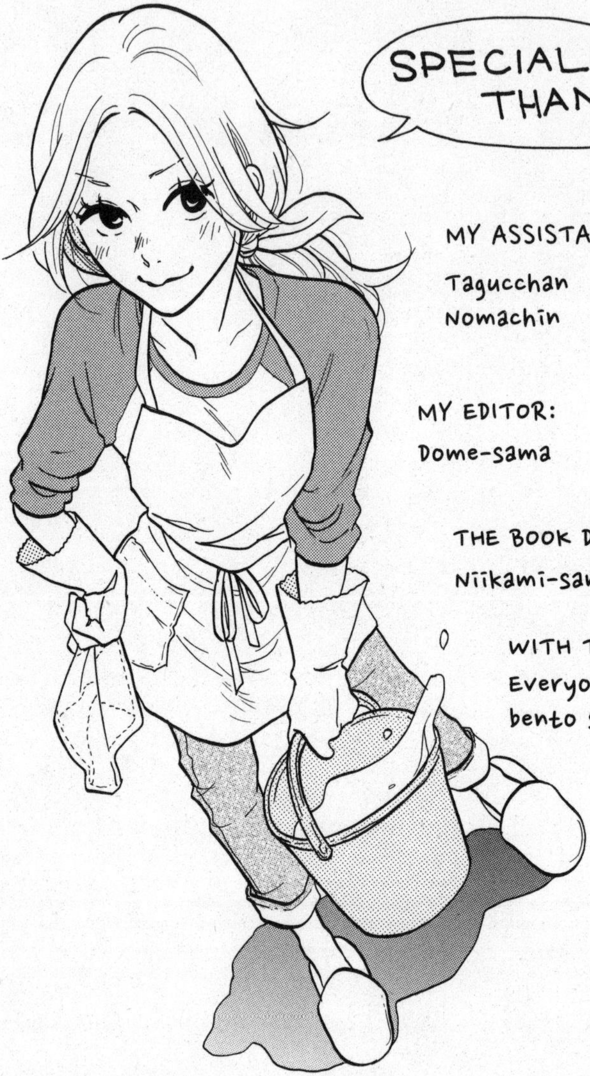

SPECIAL
THANKS

MY ASSISTANTS:
Tagucchan   Tsune-chan
Nomachin   Yuchika-chan

MY EDITOR:
Dome-sama

THE BOOK DESIGNER:
Niikami-sama

WITH THE SUPPORT OF:
Everyone at the
bento shop

The Delinquent HOUSEWIFE!

The Delinquent Housewife! 4

Translation: David Musto
Production: Risa Cho
          Eve Grandt

FUTSUTSUKA NA YOME DESUGA! Vol. 4
by Nemu Yoko

Original Japanese edition published by SHOGAKUKAN.
English translation rights in the United States of America and Canada
arranged with SHOGAKUKAN through Tuttle-Mori Agency, Inc.

Translation provided by Vertical Comics, 2019
Published by Vertical Comics, an imprint of Vertical, Inc., New York

Originally published in Japanese as *Futsutsuka Na Yome Desuga!* 4 by Shogakukan, 2017
Futsutsuka Na Yome Desuga! serialized in *Shuukan Biggu Komikku Supirittsu*,
Shogakukan, 2016

This is a work of fiction.

ISBN: 978-1-947194-51-9

Manufactured in the United States of America

First Edition

Vertical, Inc.
451 Park Avenue South
7th Floor
New York, NY 10016
www.vertical-comics.com

Vertical books are distributed through Penguin-Random House Publisher Services.